Roanoke County Public Library
Hollins Branch Library
9624 Peters Creek Road
Roanoke, VA 24019

Serial Publication

第6巻

STORY BY

大川七瀬
AGEHA OHKAWA

RG VEDA

聖伝

牙狼争覇篇

新書館

COMIC BY

もこなあぱぱ
MOKONA

WINGS COMICS

WINGS

PLANNING

CLAMP

SIX STARS WILL FALL TO THIS PLANE, THE DARK STARS THAT WILL DEFY THE HEAVENS.
AND YOU SHALL UNDERTAKE A JOURNEY, ONE THAT BEGINS WHEN YOU FIND THE CHILD OF A VANISHED RACE.
I CANNOT DISCERN THE CHILD'S ALIGNMENT... I ONLY KNOW THAT IT IS HE ALONE WHO CAN TURN THE WHEEL OF TENKAI'S DESTINY.
FOR IT IS BY HEAVENLY MANDATE THAT THROUGH THIS CHILD, THE SIX STARS SHALL BEGIN TO GATHER.
AND THEN SOMEONE SHALL APPEAR FROM THE SHADOWS. EVEN MY POWERS CANNOT CLEARLY MAKE OUT HIS FIGURE, BUT HE KNOWS THE FUTURE AND CAN MANIPULATE BOTH EVIL AND HEAVENLY STARS.
A ROARING FLAME WILL RAZE THE WICKED.
SIX STARS WILL OVERPOWER ALL OTHERS...
AND INEVITABLY...THEY WILL BE THE SCHISM THAT SPLITS THE HEAVENS.

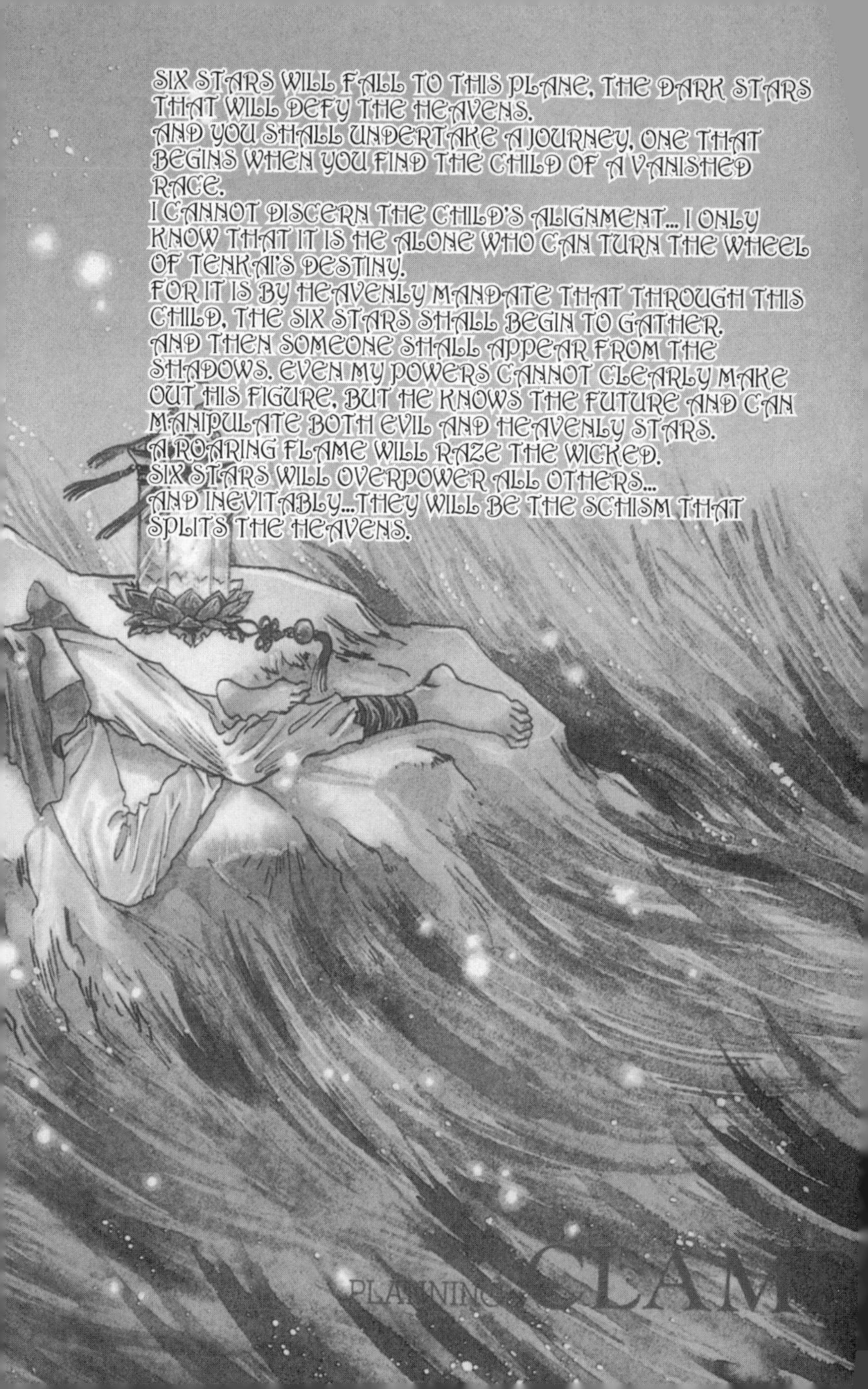
PLANNING CLAM

# RG VEDA 聖伝



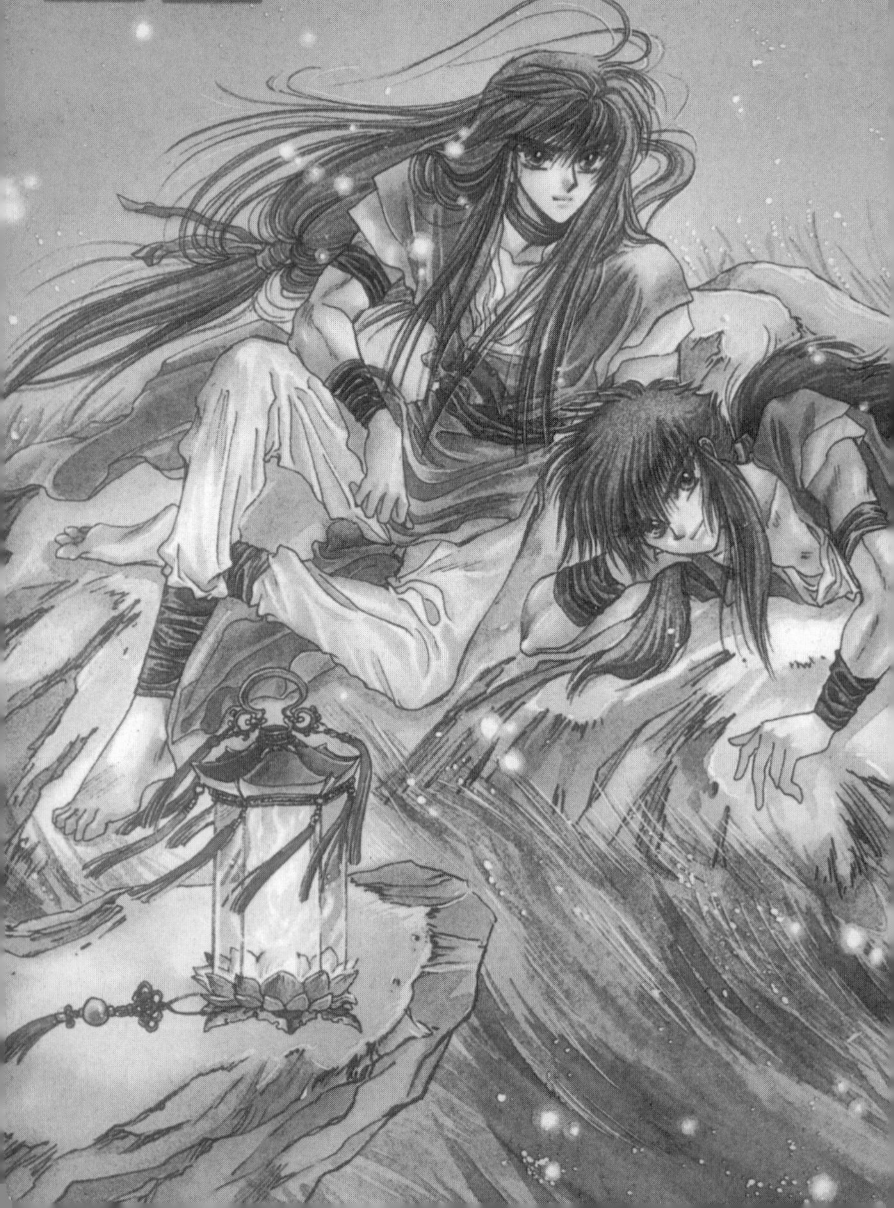

H O S H I G A · N A G A R E R U

**Book Designer**

大川七瀬
AGEHA OHKAWA

**Director**

もこなあぱぱ
MOKONA

**Short Comic**

猫井みっく
TSUBAKI NEKOI

**Art Assistants**

猫井みっく
TSUBAKI NEKOI

五十嵐さつき
SATSUKI IGARASHI

CLAMP MEMBERS

YOU WILL BE THE SCHISM THAT SPLITS HEAVEN.

**Main**

CLAMP MEMBERS

STORY
大川七瀬
AGEHA OHKAWA

COMIC
もこなあぱぱ
MOKONA

PLANNING & PRESENTED by

CLAMP

# RG 聖 VEDA 伝

## VOLUME 6

## BY CLAMP

HAMBURG // LONDON // LOS ANGELES // TOKYO

## *RG Veda Vol. 6*
### created by CLAMP

Translation - Haruko Furukawa
English Adaptation - Christine Schilling
Copy Editor - Peter Ahlstrom
Retouch and Lettering - Jihye "Sophia" Hong
Production Artist - Camellia Cox
Cover Design - Jorge Negrete

Editor - Troy Lewter
Digital Imaging Manager - Chris Buford
Production Manager - Elisabeth Brizzi
Editor-in-Chief - Rob Tokar
VP of Production - Ron Klamert
Publisher - Mike Kiley
President and C.O.O. - John Parker
Chief Creative Officer and C.E.O. - Stuart Levy

A TOKYOPOP Manga

TOKYOPOP Inc.
5900 Wilshire Blvd. Suite 2000
Los Angeles, CA 90036

E-mail: info@TOKYOPOP.com
Come visit us online at www.TOKYOPOP.com

© 1992 CLAMP. All Rights Reserved. First published in Japan in 1992 by Shinshokan Publishing Co., Ltd., Tokyo, Japan. English publication rights arranged through Shinshokan Publishing Co., Ltd.

English text copyright © 2006 TOKYOPOP Inc.

All rights reserved. No portion of this book may be reproduced or transmitted in any form or by any means without written permission from the copyright holders. This manga is a work of fiction. Any resemblance to actual events or locales or persons, living or dead, is entirely coincidental.

ISBN: 1-59532-489-5

First TOKYOPOP printing: July 2006

10  9  8  7  6  5  4  3  2  1

Printed in the USA

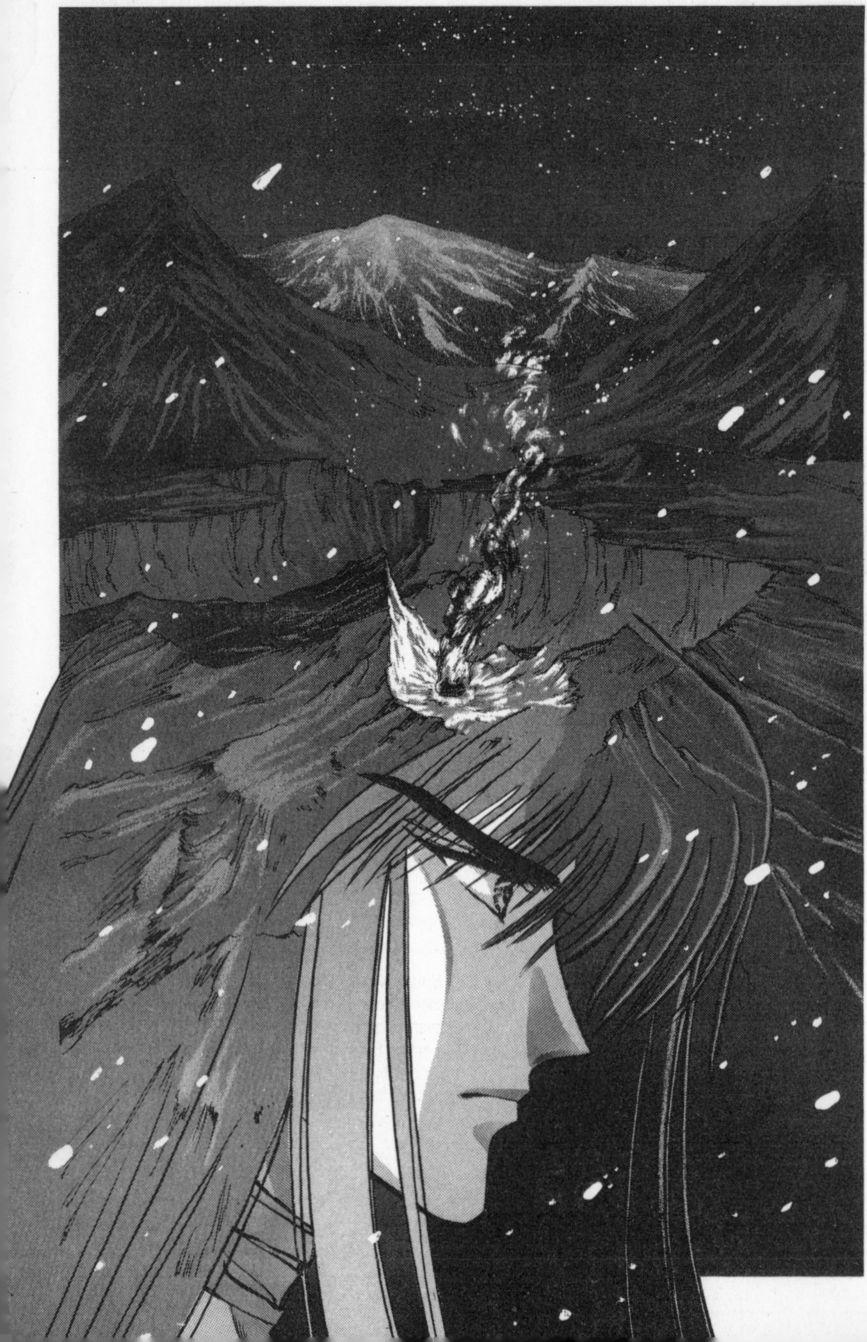

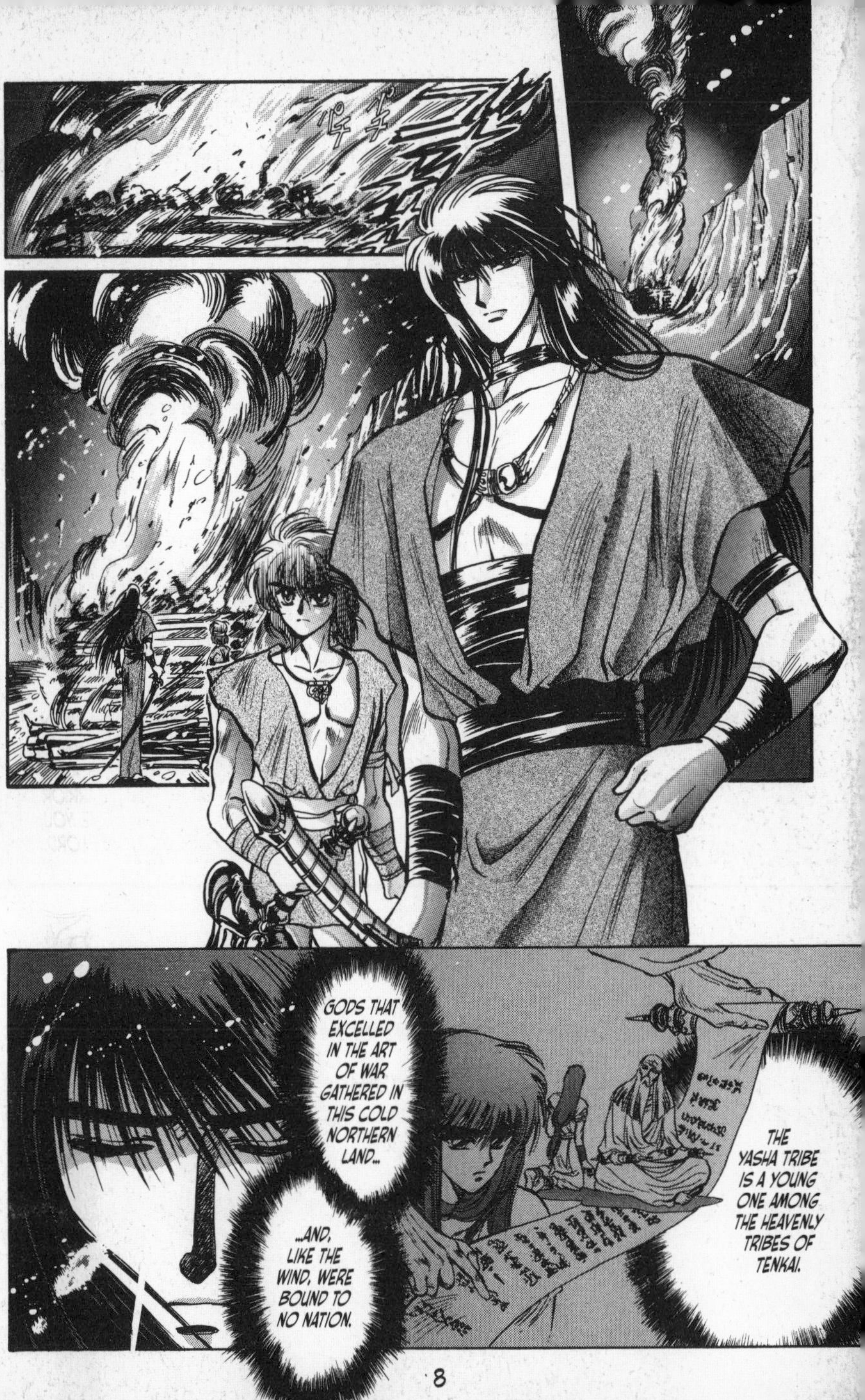
THE YASHA TRIBE IS A YOUNG ONE AMONG THE HEAVENLY TRIBES OF TENKAI.
GODS THAT EXCELLED IN THE ART OF WAR GATHERED IN THIS COLD NORTHERN LAND...
...AND, LIKE THE WIND, WERE BOUND TO NO NATION.

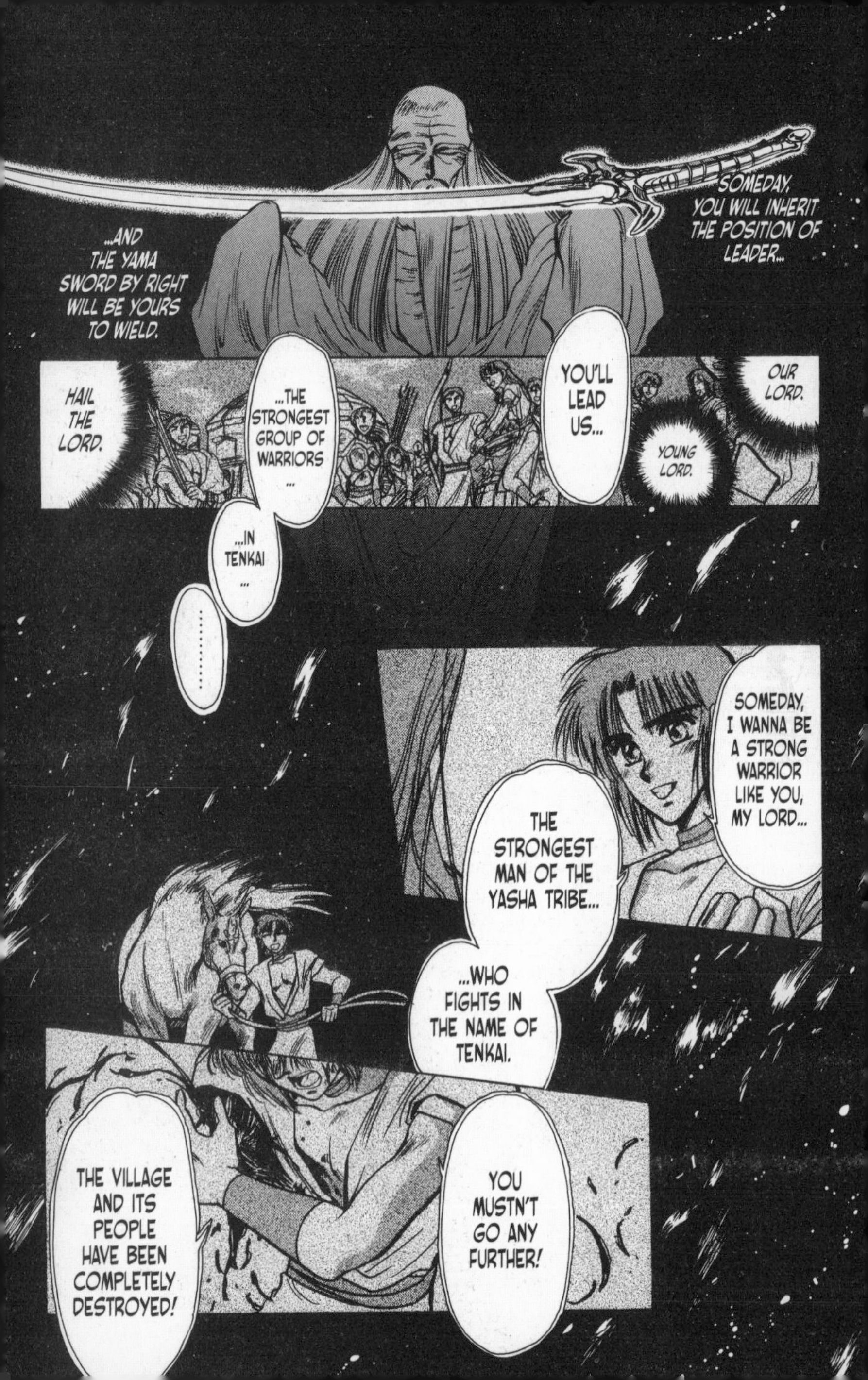
SOMEDAY, YOU WILL INHERIT THE POSITION OF LEADER...
...AND THE YAMA SWORD BY RIGHT WILL BE YOURS TO WIELD.
OUR LORD.
YOU'LL LEAD US...
YOUNG LORD.
...THE STRONGEST GROUP OF WARRIORS ...
HAIL THE LORD.
...IN TENKAI ...
......
SOMEDAY, I WANNA BE A STRONG WARRIOR LIKE YOU, MY LORD...
THE STRONGEST MAN OF THE YASHA TRIBE...
...WHO FIGHTS IN THE NAME OF TENKAI.
YOU MUSTN'T GO ANY FURTHER!
THE VILLAGE AND ITS PEOPLE HAVE BEEN COMPLETELY DESTROYED!

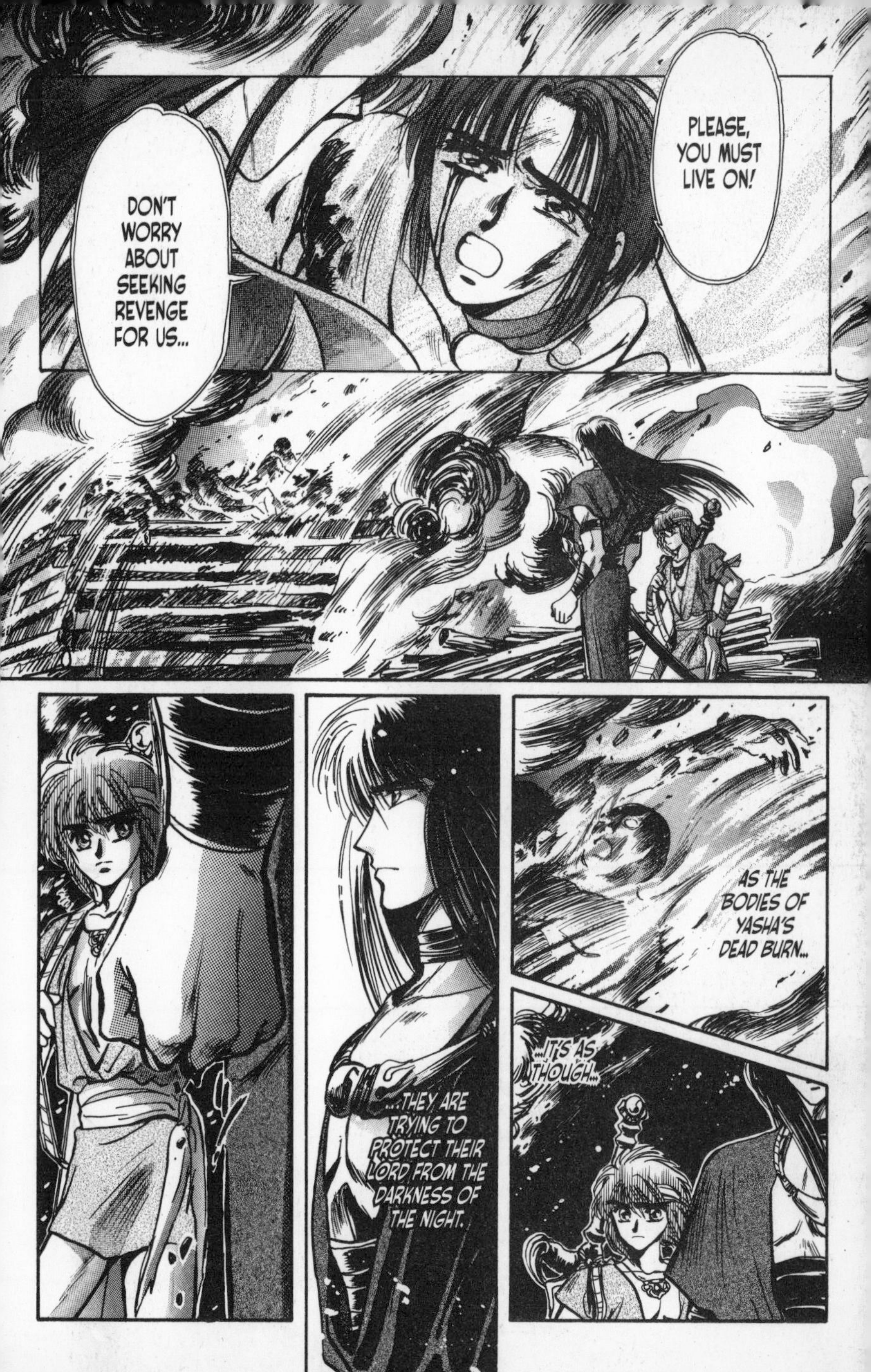
PLEASE, YOU MUST LIVE ON!
DON'T WORRY ABOUT SEEKING REVENGE FOR US...
AS THE BODIES OF YASHA'S DEAD BURN...
...IT'S AS THOUGH...
...THEY ARE TRYING TO PROTECT THEIR LORD FROM THE DARKNESS OF THE NIGHT.

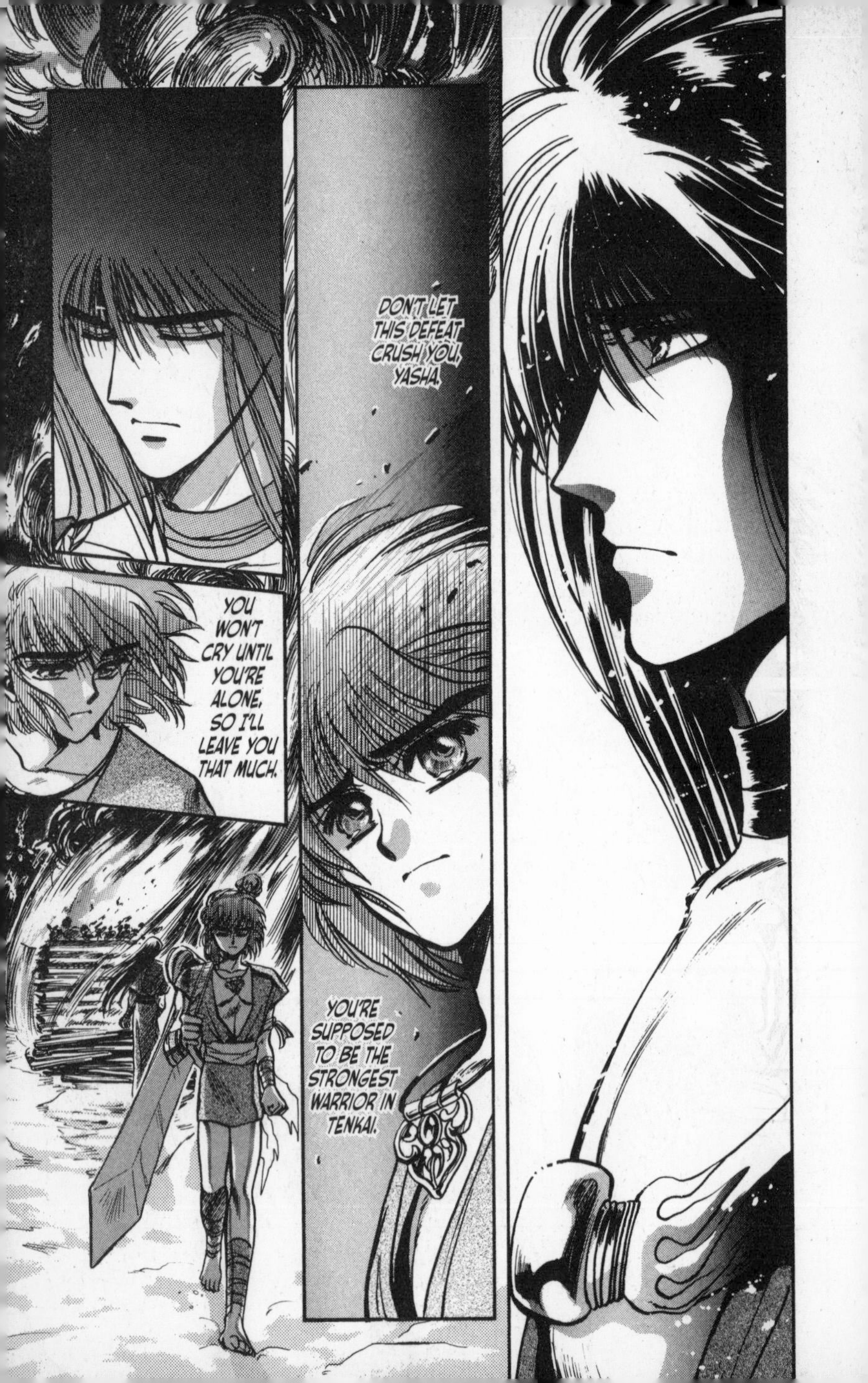
DON'T LET THIS DEFEAT CRUSH YOU, YASHA.
YOU'RE SUPPOSED TO BE THE STRONGEST WARRIOR IN TENKAI.
YOU WON'T CRY UNTIL YOU'RE ALONE, SO I'LL LEAVE YOU THAT MUCH.

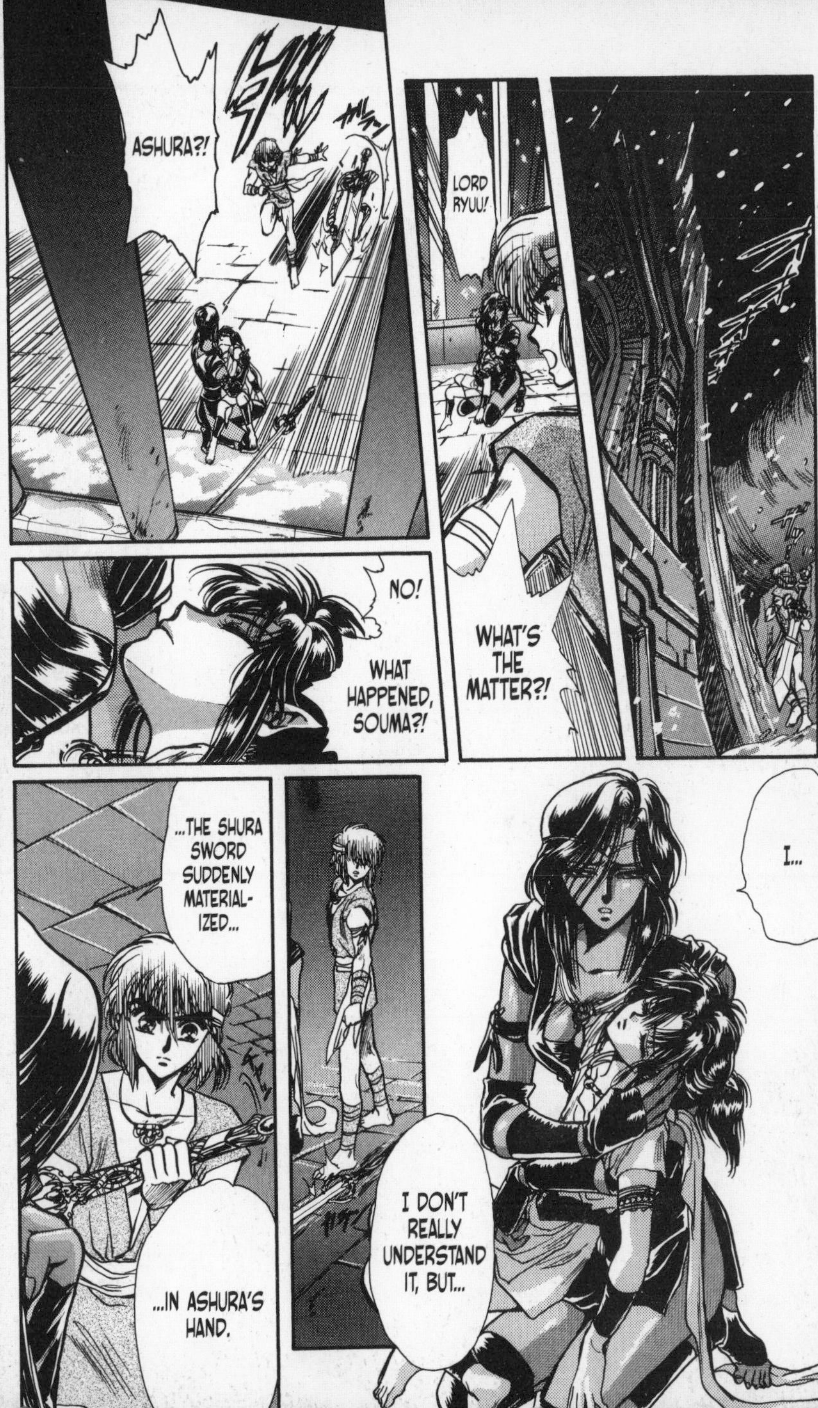
LORD RYUU!
WHAT'S THE MATTER?!
ASHURA?!
NO!
WHAT HAPPENED, SOUMA?!
I...
I DON'T REALLY UNDERSTAND IT, BUT...
...THE SHURA SWORD SUDDENLY MATERIALIZED...
...IN ASHURA'S HAND.

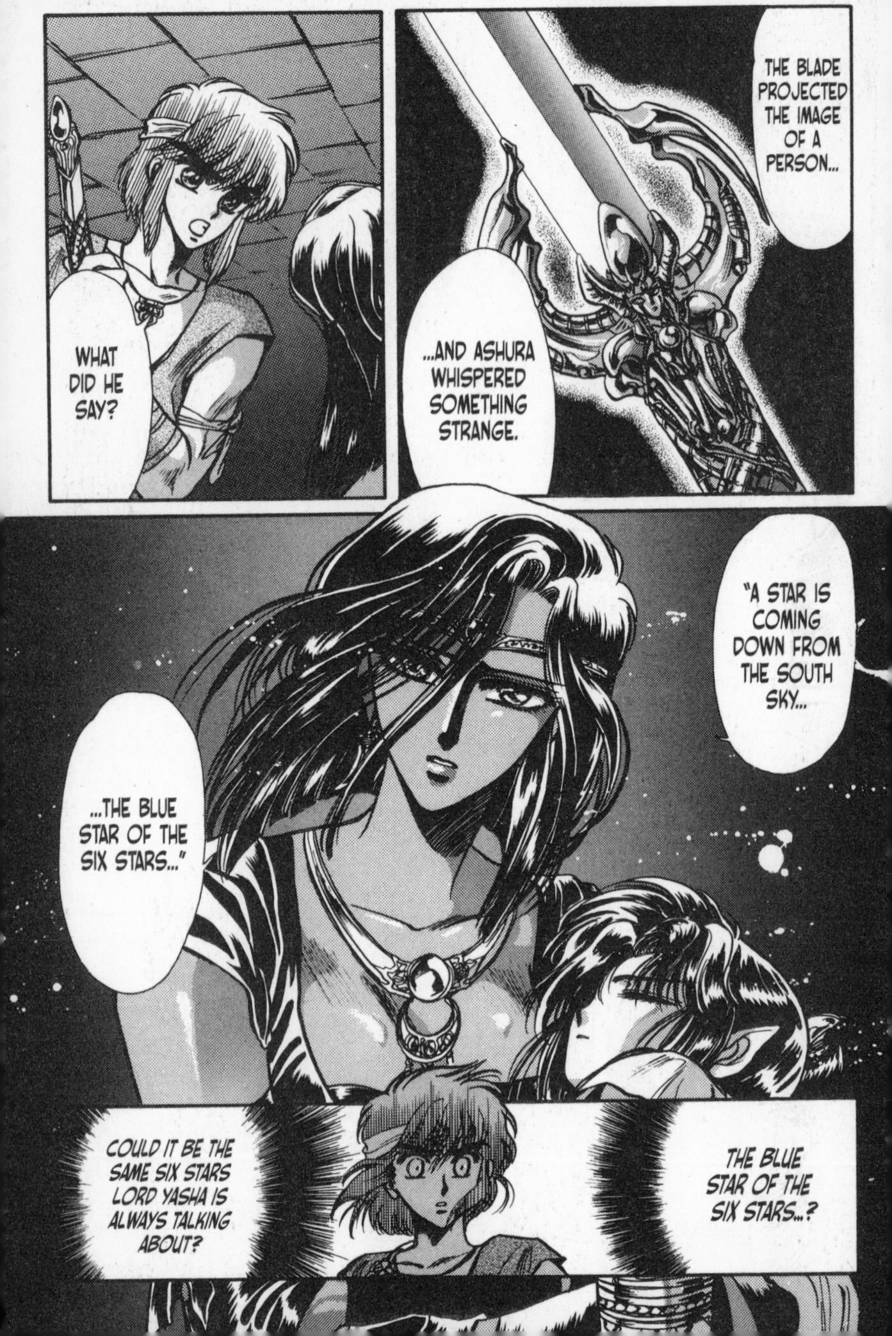
THE BLADE PROJECTED THE IMAGE OF A PERSON...
...AND ASHURA WHISPERED SOMETHING STRANGE.
WHAT DID HE SAY?
"A STAR IS COMING DOWN FROM THE SOUTH SKY...
...THE BLUE STAR OF THE SIX STARS..."
THE BLUE STAR OF THE SIX STARS...?
COULD IT BE THE SAME SIX STARS LORD YASHA IS ALWAYS TALKING ABOUT?

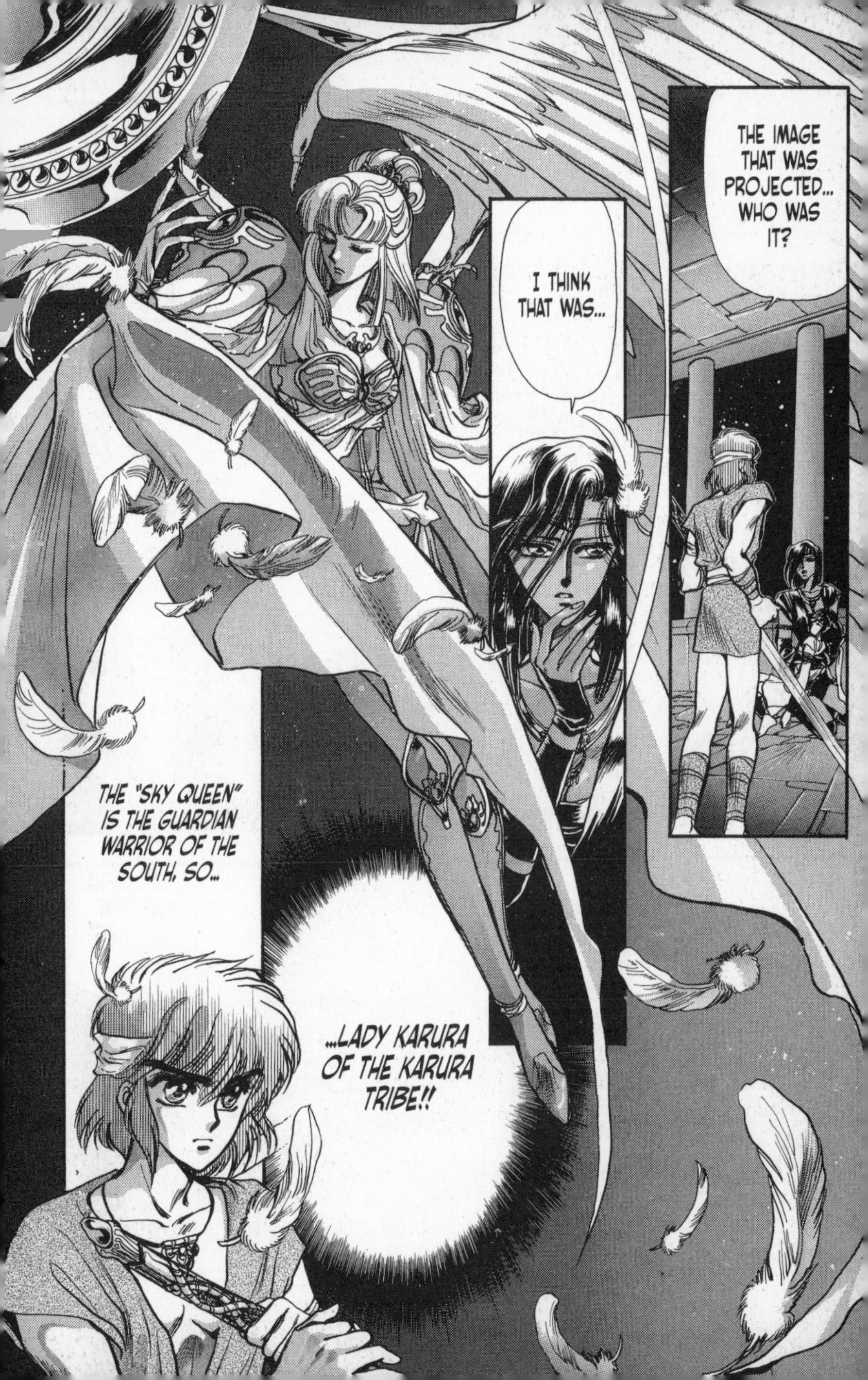
THE IMAGE THAT WAS PROJECTED... WHO WAS IT?
I THINK THAT WAS...
THE "SKY QUEEN" IS THE GUARDIAN WARRIOR OF THE SOUTH, SO...
...LADY KARURA OF THE KARURA TRIBE!!

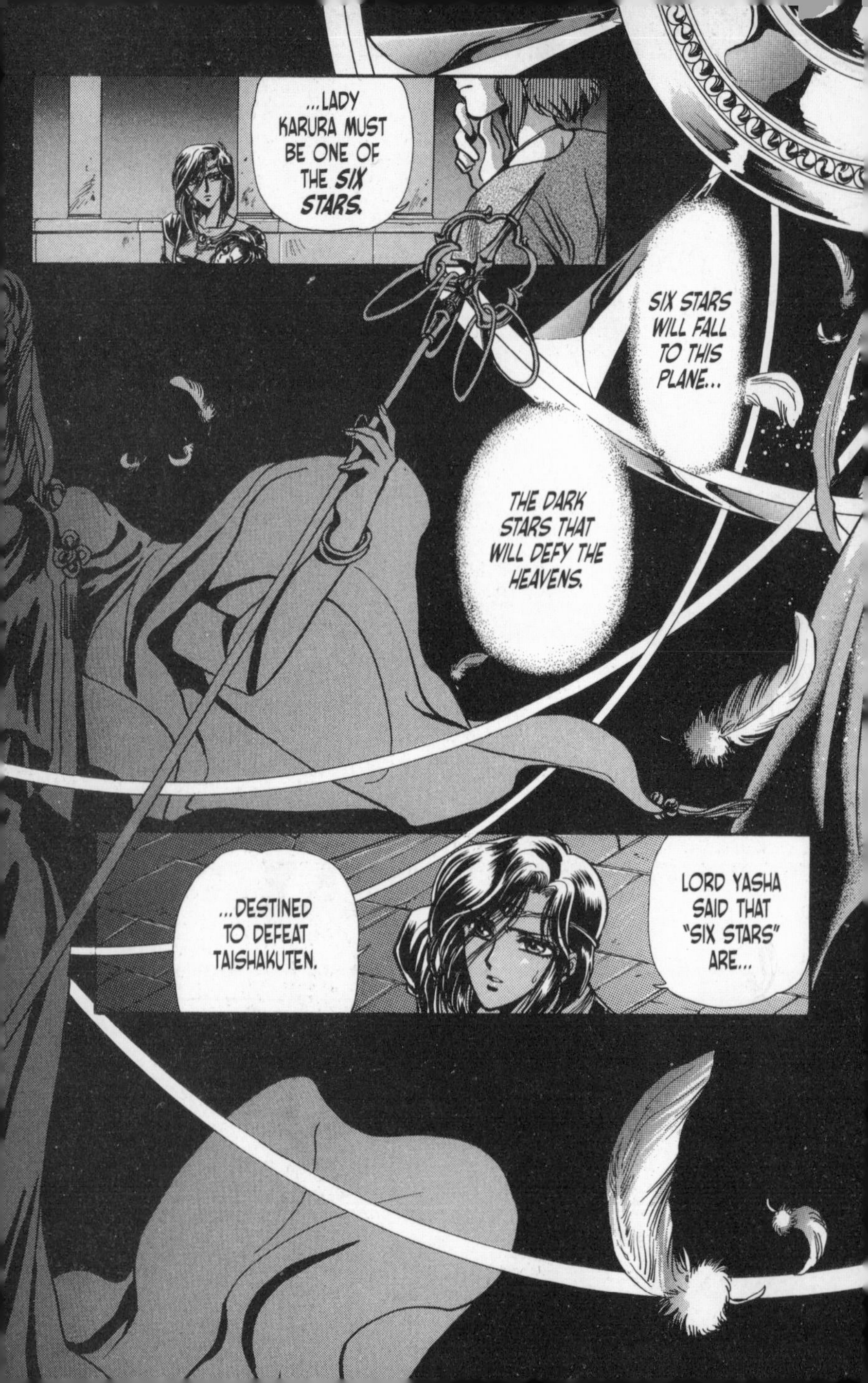
...LADY KARURA MUST BE ONE OF THE SIX STARS.
SIX STARS WILL FALL TO THIS PLANE...
THE DARK STARS THAT WILL DEFY THE HEAVENS.
LORD YASHA SAID THAT "SIX STARS" ARE...
...DESTINED TO DEFEAT TAISHAKUTEN.

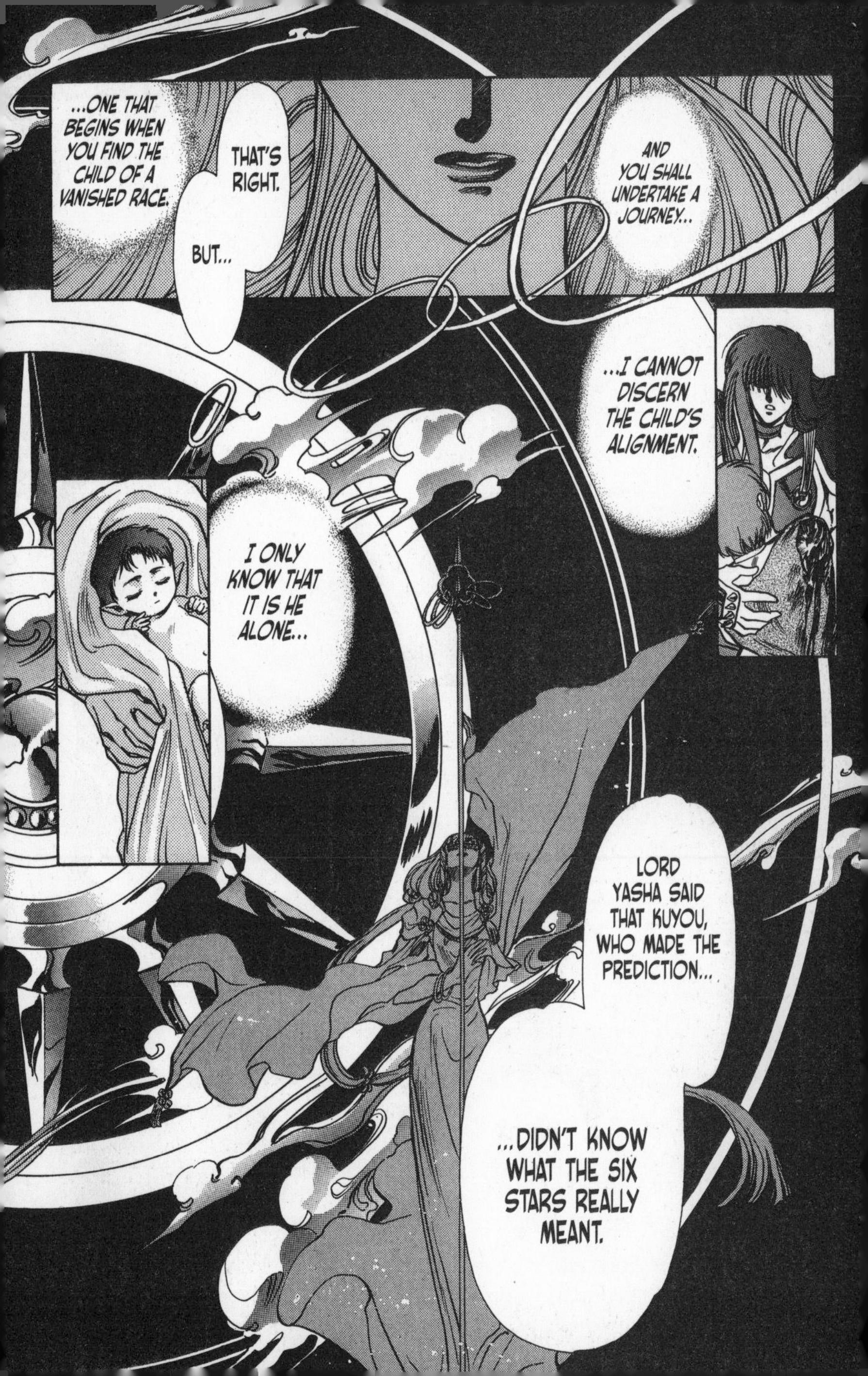
AND YOU SHALL UNDERTAKE A JOURNEY...
...ONE THAT BEGINS WHEN YOU FIND THE CHILD OF A VANISHED RACE.
THAT'S RIGHT.
BUT...
...I CANNOT DISCERN THE CHILD'S ALIGNMENT.
I ONLY KNOW THAT IT IS HE ALONE...
LORD YASHA SAID THAT KUYOU, WHO MADE THE PREDICTION...
...DIDN'T KNOW WHAT THE SIX STARS REALLY MEANT.

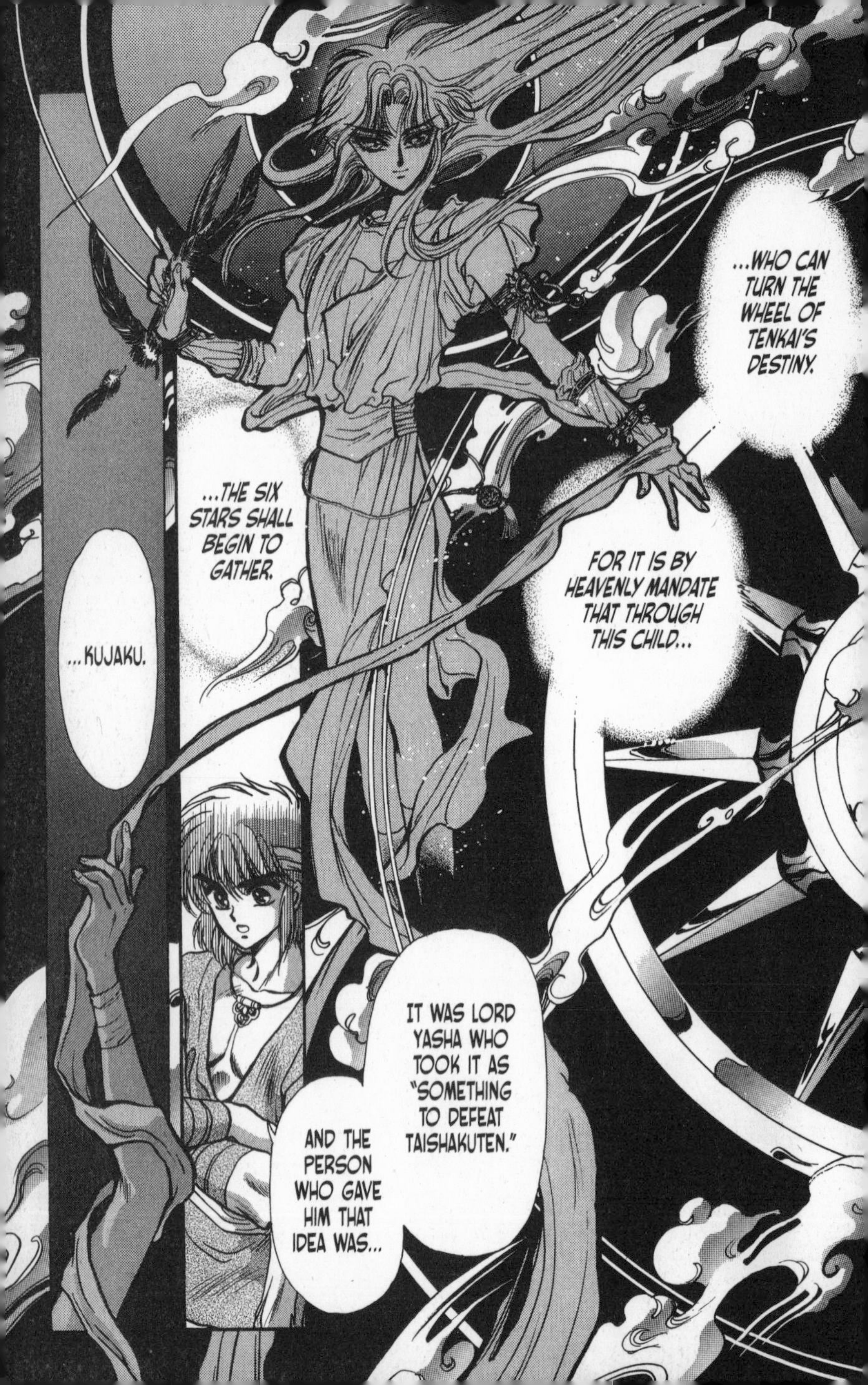
...WHO CAN TURN THE WHEEL OF TENKAI'S DESTINY.
FOR IT IS BY HEAVENLY MANDATE THAT THROUGH THIS CHILD...
...THE SIX STARS SHALL BEGIN TO GATHER.
IT WAS LORD YASHA WHO TOOK IT AS "SOMETHING TO DEFEAT TAISHAKUTEN."
AND THE PERSON WHO GAVE HIM THAT IDEA WAS...
...KUJAKU.

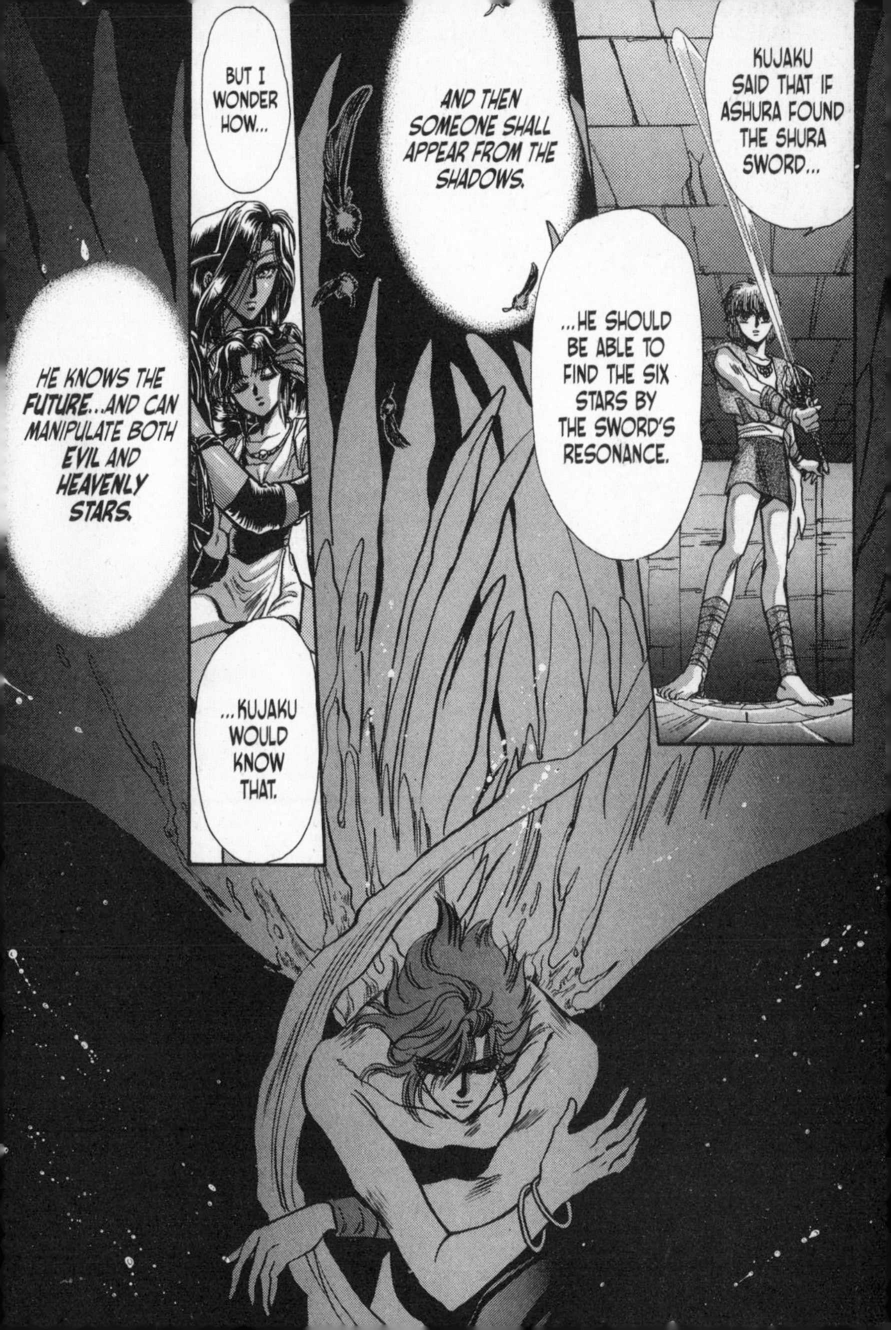
KUJAKU SAID THAT IF ASHURA FOUND THE SHURA SWORD...
...HE SHOULD BE ABLE TO FIND THE SIX STARS BY THE SWORD'S RESONANCE.
AND THEN SOMEONE SHALL APPEAR FROM THE SHADOWS.
BUT I WONDER HOW...
...KUJAKU WOULD KNOW THAT.
HE KNOWS THE FUTURE...AND CAN MANIPULATE BOTH EVIL AND HEAVENLY STARS.

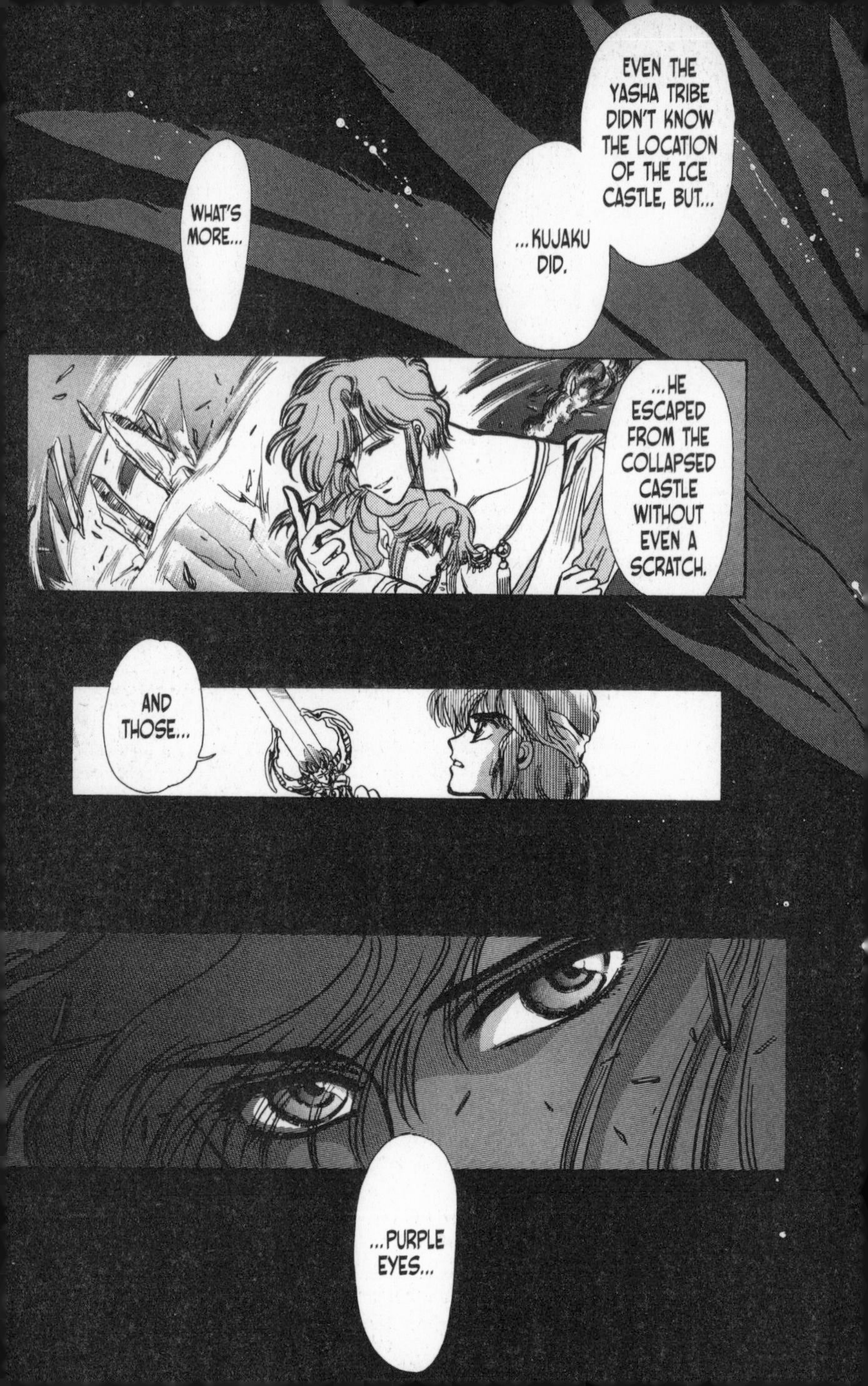
EVEN THE YASHA TRIBE DIDN'T KNOW THE LOCATION OF THE ICE CASTLE, BUT...
...KUJAKU DID.
WHAT'S MORE...
...HE ESCAPED FROM THE COLLAPSED CASTLE WITHOUT EVEN A SCRATCH.
AND THOSE...
...PURPLE EYES...

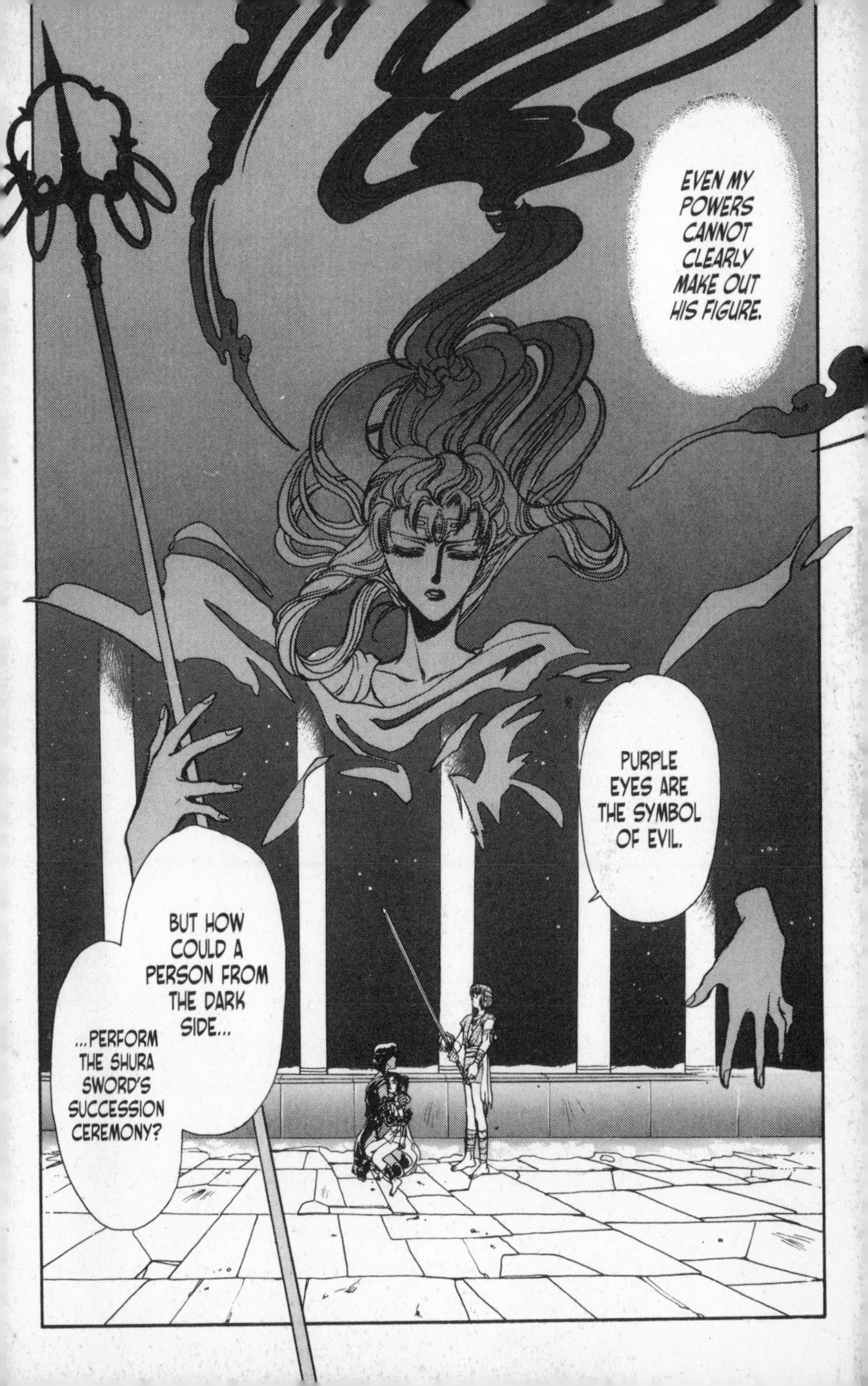
EVEN MY POWERS CANNOT CLEARLY MAKE OUT HIS FIGURE.
PURPLE EYES ARE THE SYMBOL OF EVIL.
BUT HOW COULD A PERSON FROM THE DARK SIDE...
...PERFORM THE SHURA SWORD'S SUCCESSION CEREMONY?

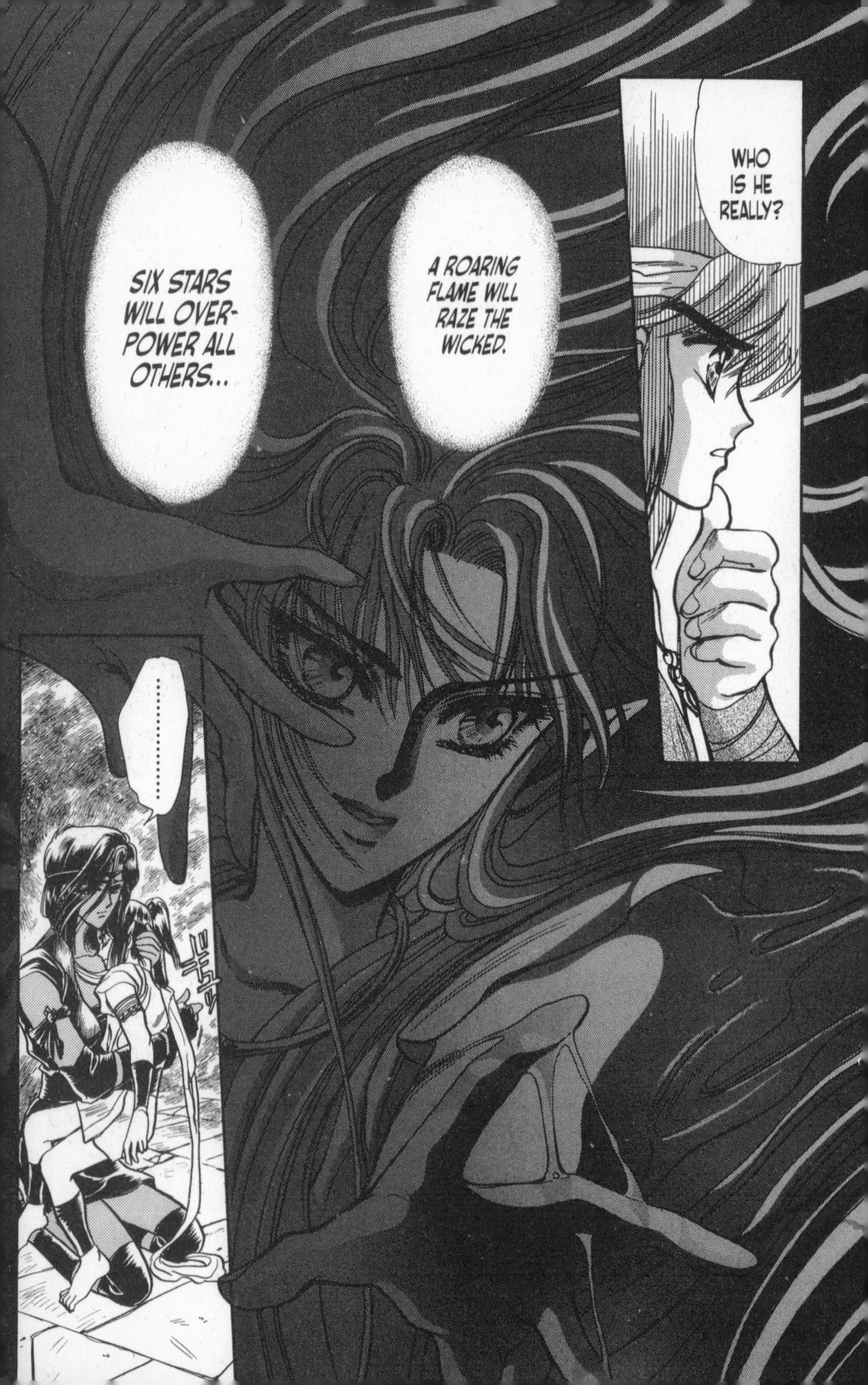

WHO IS HE REALLY?
A ROARING FLAME WILL RAZE THE WICKED.
SIX STARS WILL OVER-POWER ALL OTHERS...
......

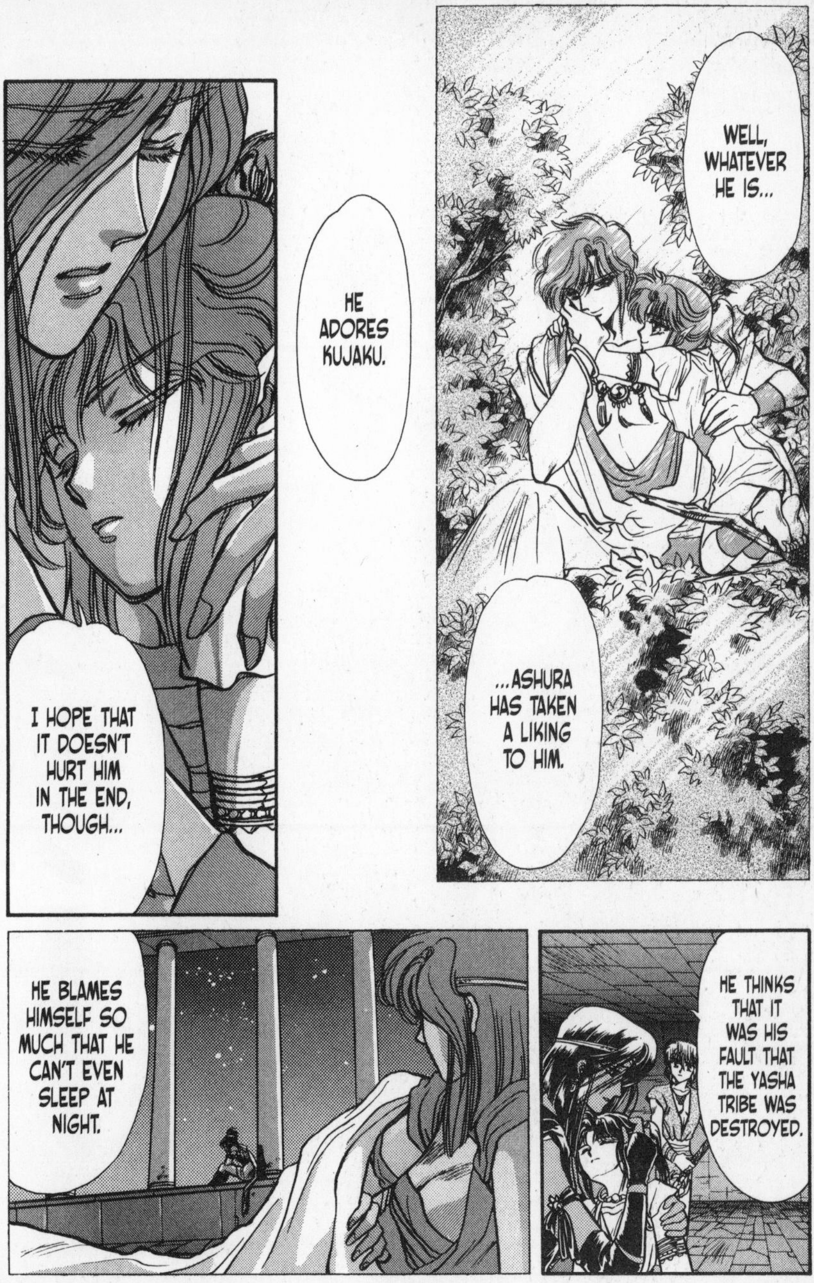
WELL, WHATEVER HE IS...
...ASHURA HAS TAKEN A LIKING TO HIM.
HE ADORES KUJAKU.
I HOPE THAT IT DOESN'T HURT HIM IN THE END, THOUGH...
HE THINKS THAT IT WAS HIS FAULT THAT THE YASHA TRIBE WAS DESTROYED.
HE BLAMES HIMSELF SO MUCH THAT HE CAN'T EVEN SLEEP AT NIGHT.

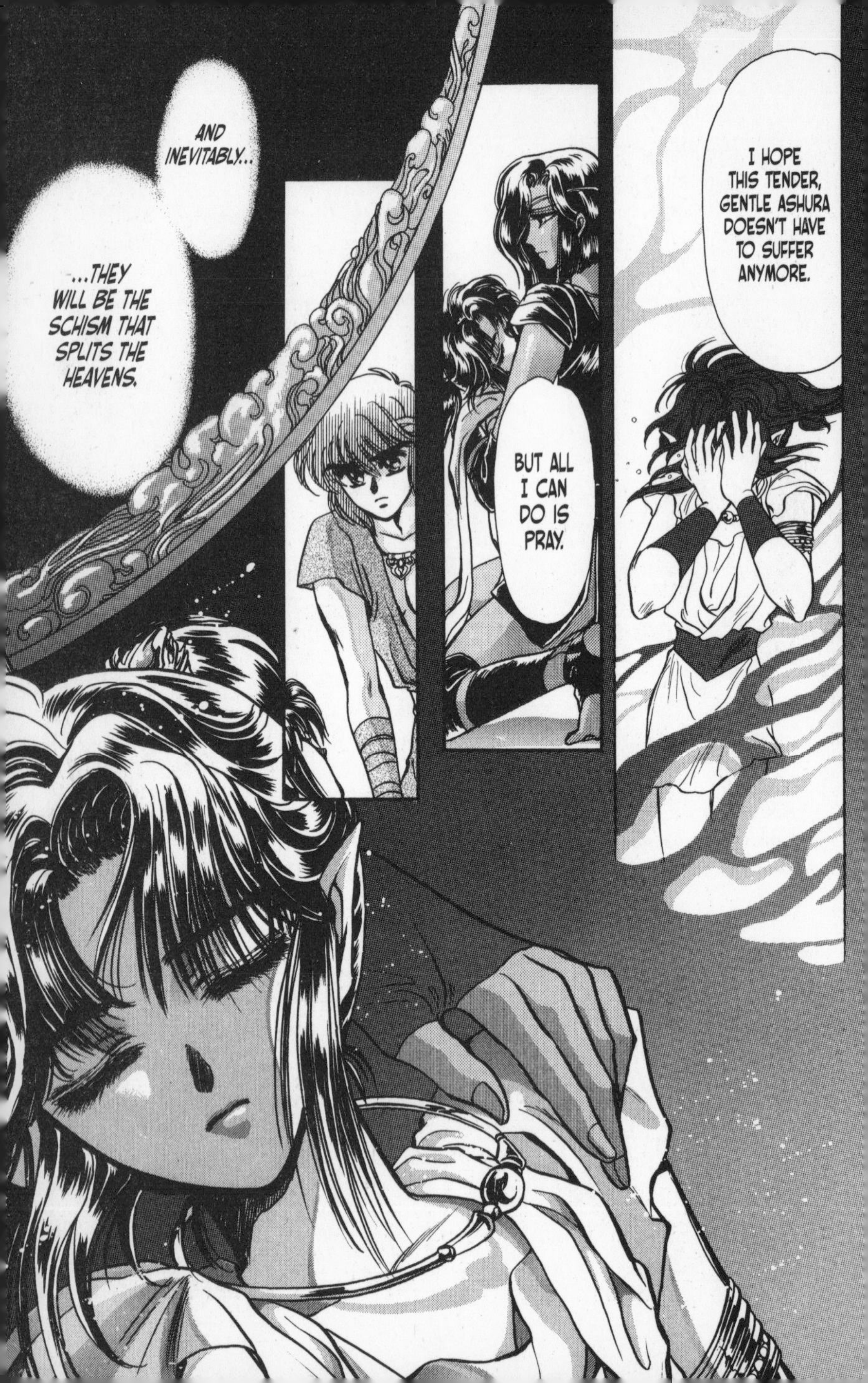
I HOPE THIS TENDER, GENTLE ASHURA DOESN'T HAVE TO SUFFER ANYMORE.
BUT ALL I CAN DO IS PRAY.
AND INEVITABLY...
...THEY WILL BE THE SCHISM THAT SPLITS THE HEAVENS.

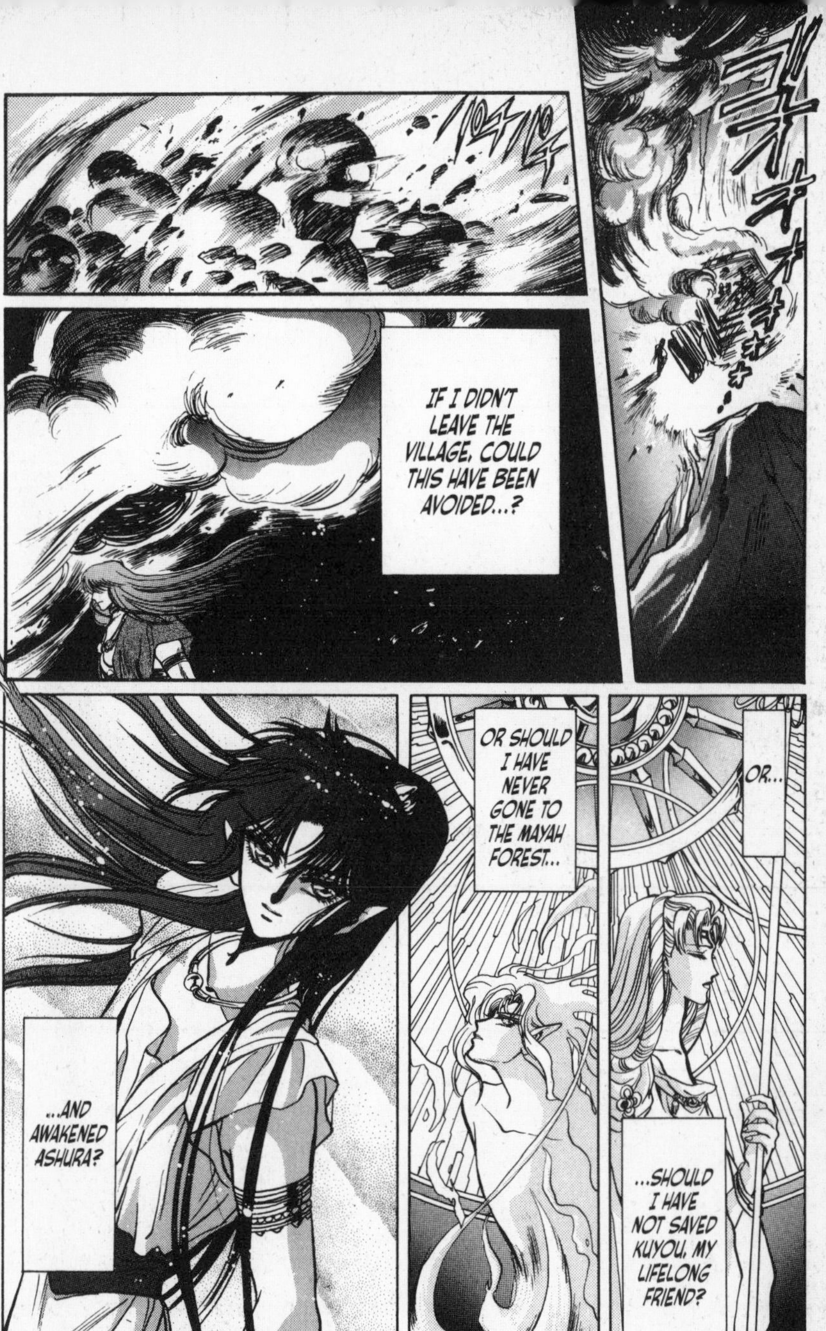
IF I DIDN'T LEAVE THE VILLAGE, COULD THIS HAVE BEEN AVOIDED...?
OR...
...SHOULD I HAVE NOT SAVED KUYOU, MY LIFELONG FRIEND?
OR SHOULD I HAVE NEVER GONE TO THE MAYAH FOREST...
...AND AWAKENED ASHURA?

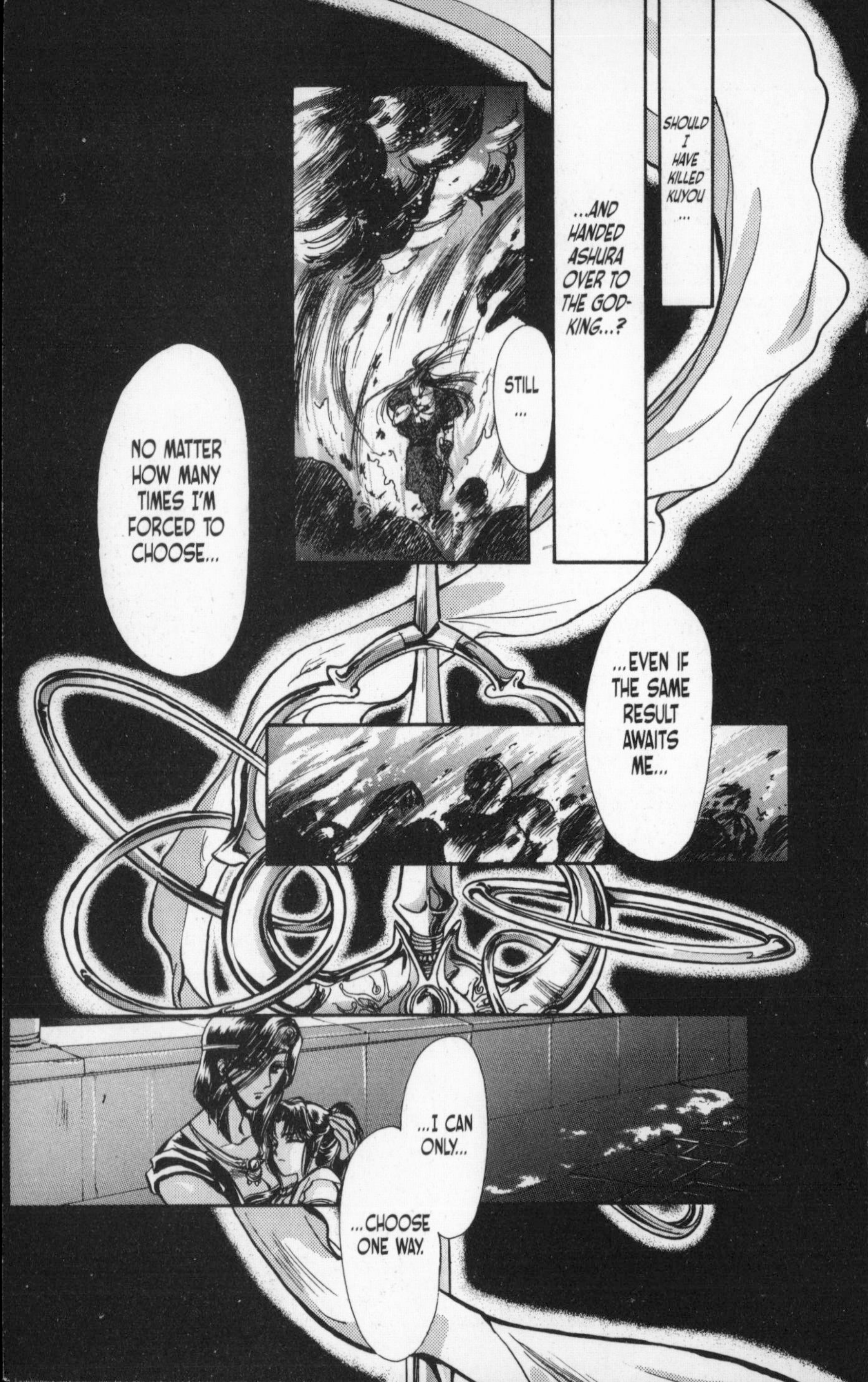
SHOULD I HAVE KILLED KUYOU...
...AND HANDED ASHURA OVER TO THE GOD-KING...?
STILL...
NO MATTER HOW MANY TIMES I'M FORCED TO CHOOSE...
...EVEN IF THE SAME RESULT AWAITS ME...
...I CAN ONLY...
...CHOOSE ONE WAY.

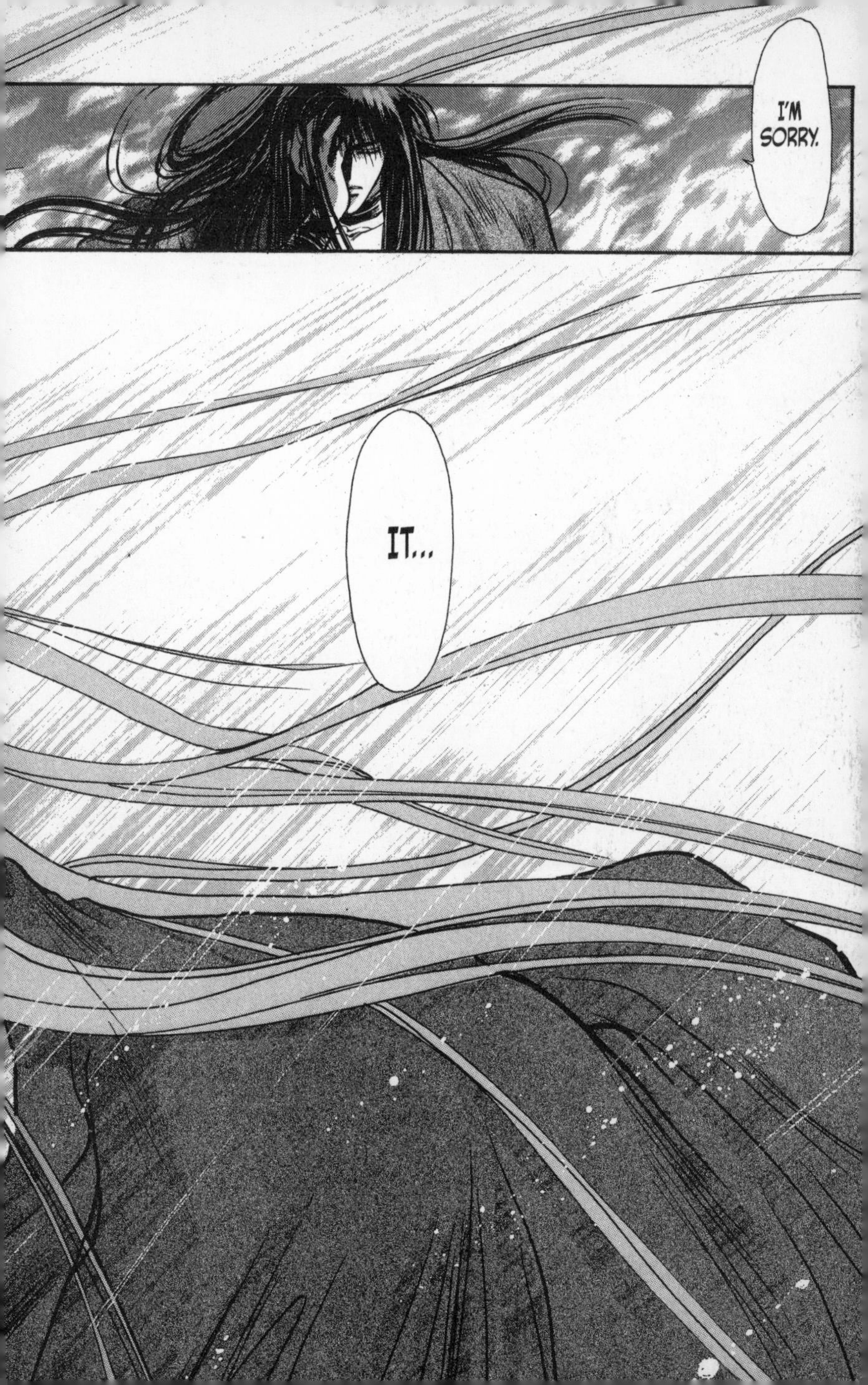
I'M SORRY.
IT...

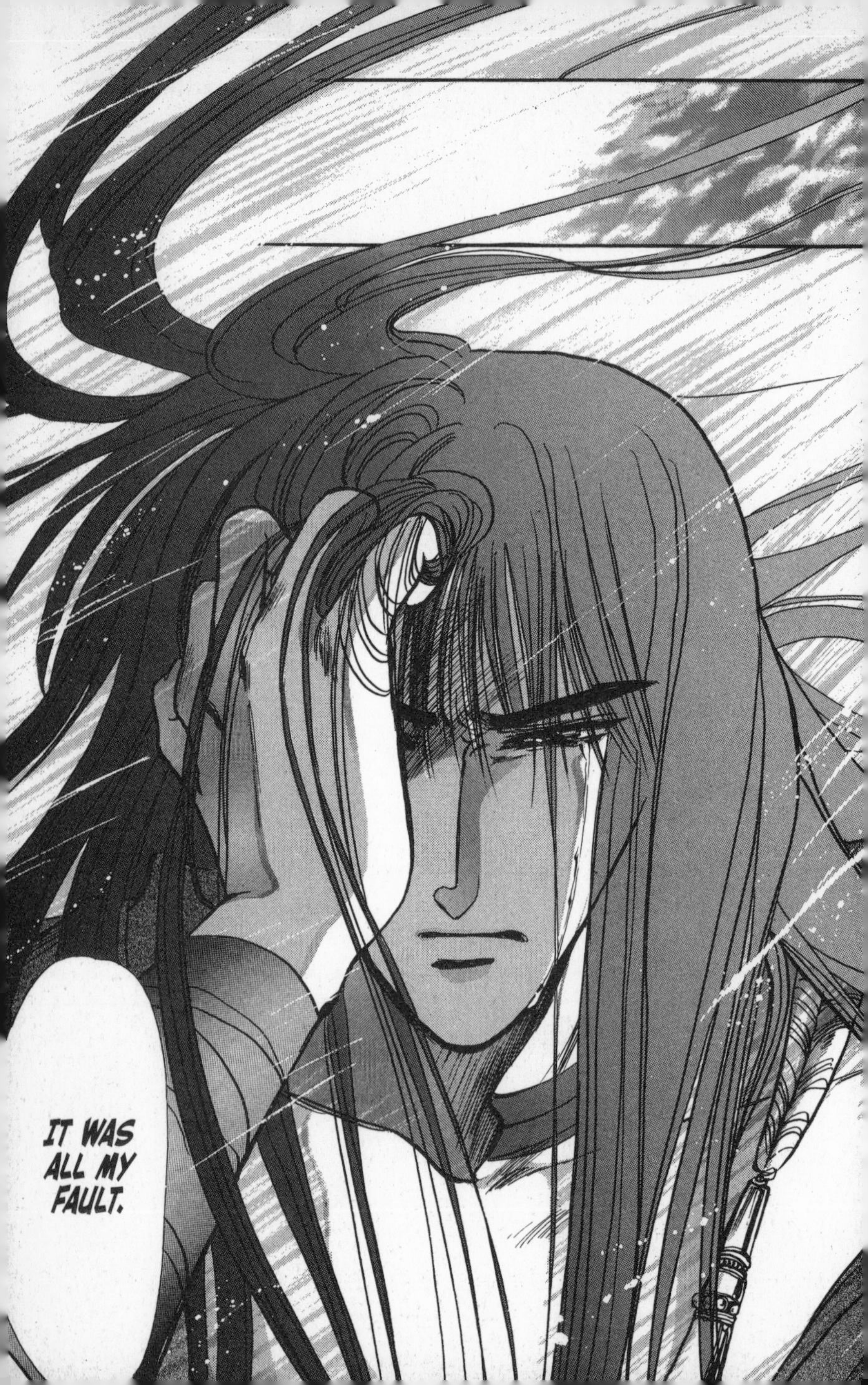
IT WAS ALL MY FAULT.

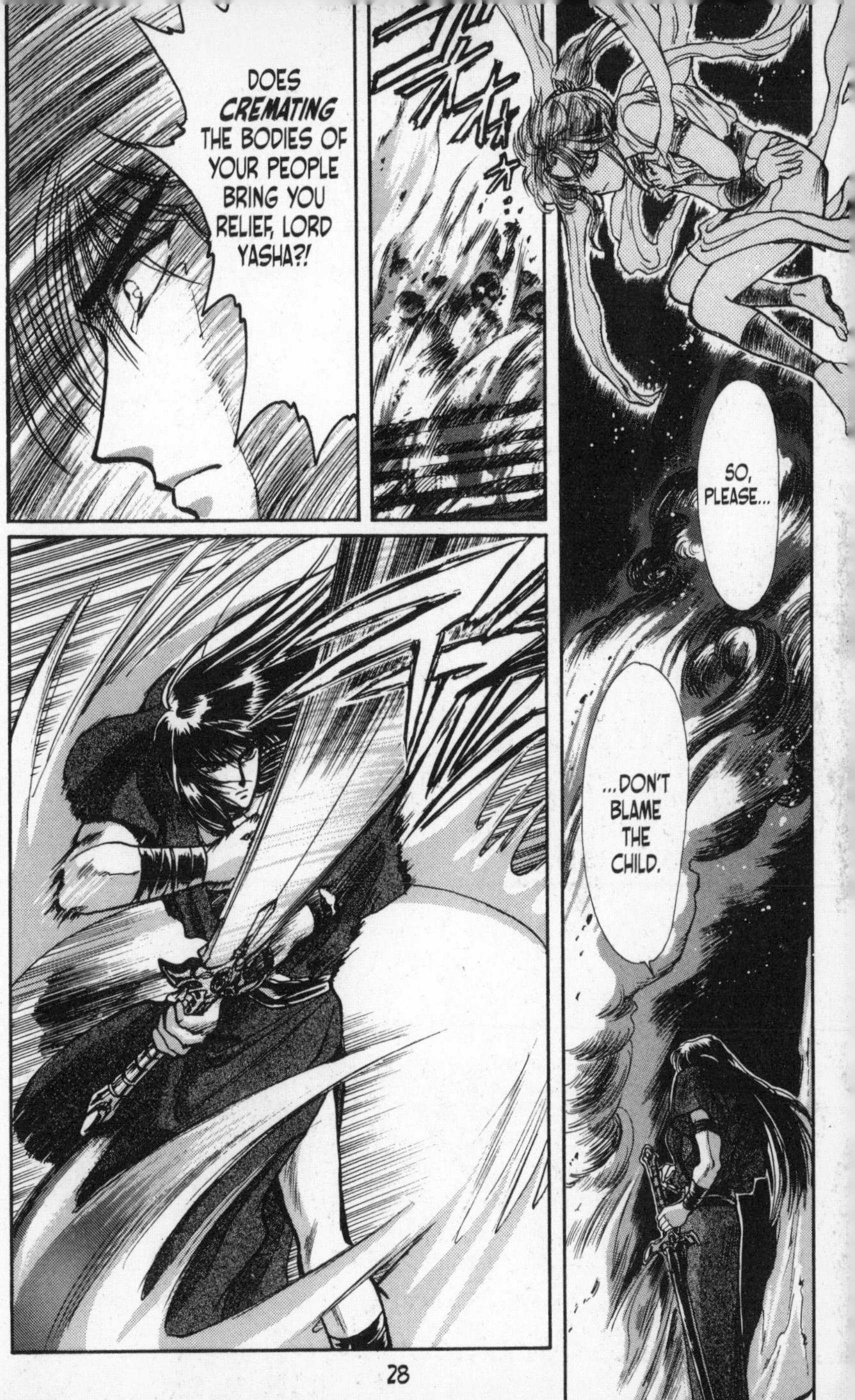
SO, PLEASE...
...DON'T BLAME THE CHILD.
DOES *CREMATING* THE BODIES OF YOUR PEOPLE BRING YOU RELIEF, LORD YASHA?!

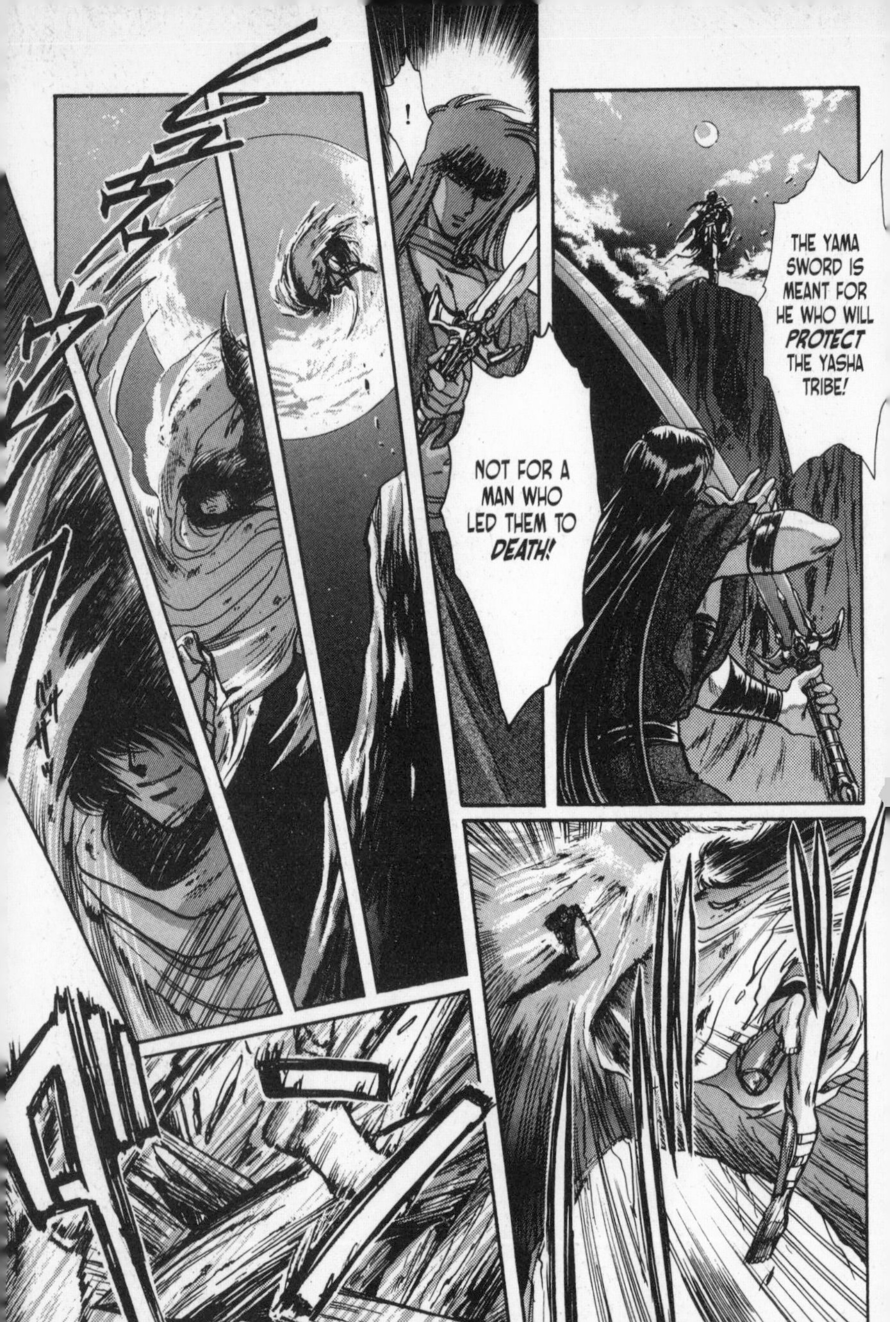
THE YAMA SWORD IS MEANT FOR HE WHO WILL *PROTECT* THE YASHA TRIBE!
NOT FOR A MAN WHO LED THEM TO *DEATH!*
!

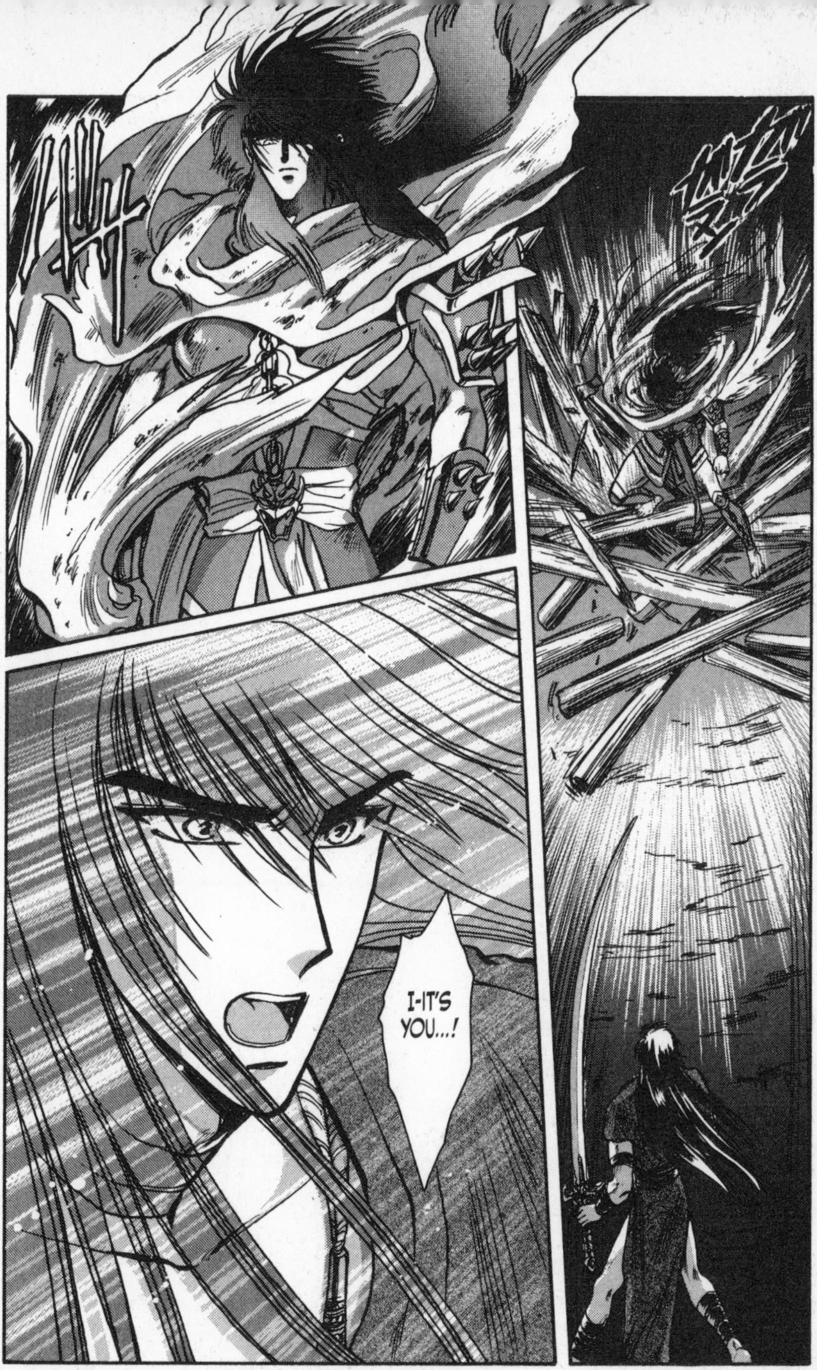
I-IT'S YOU...!

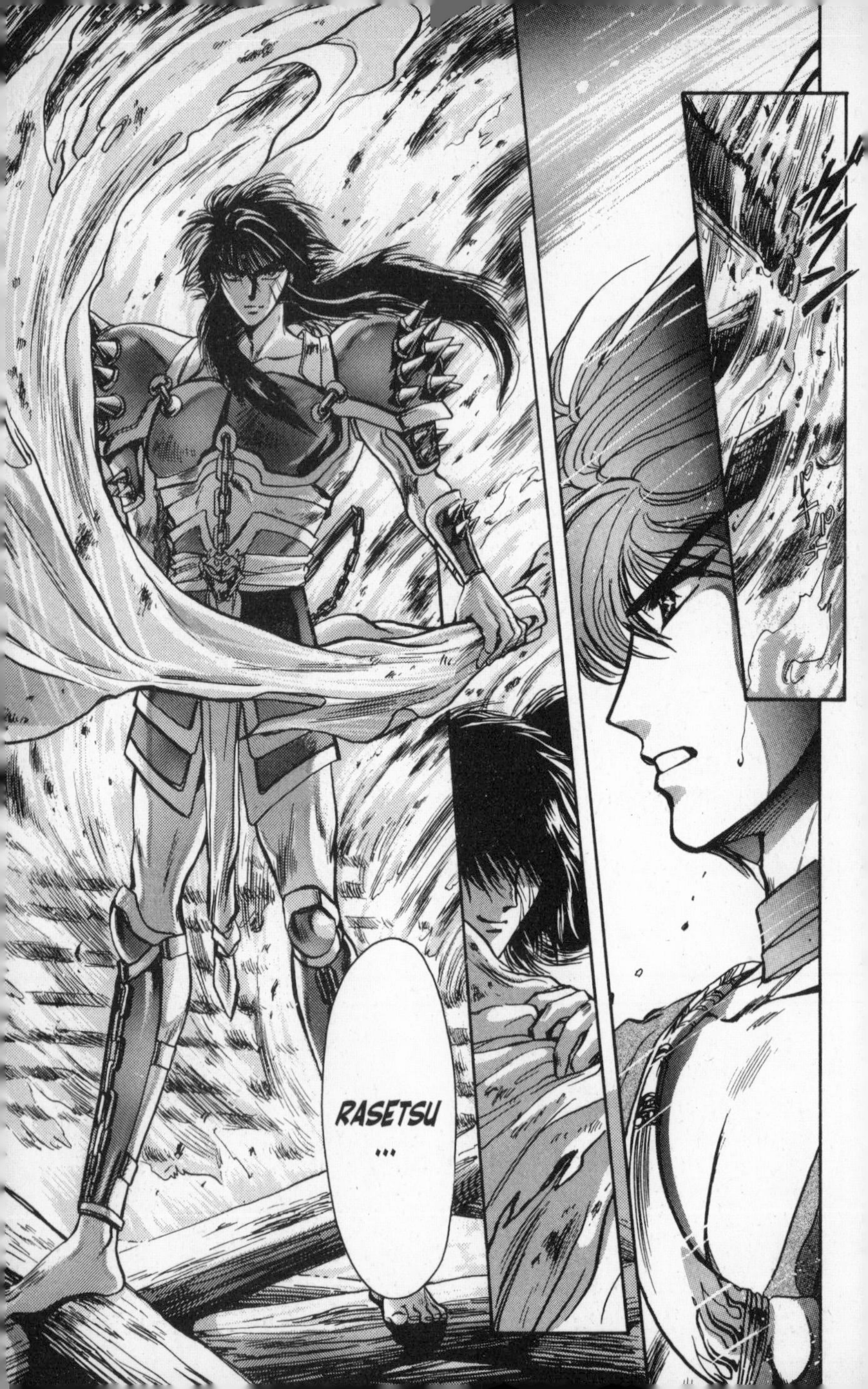
RASETSU
...

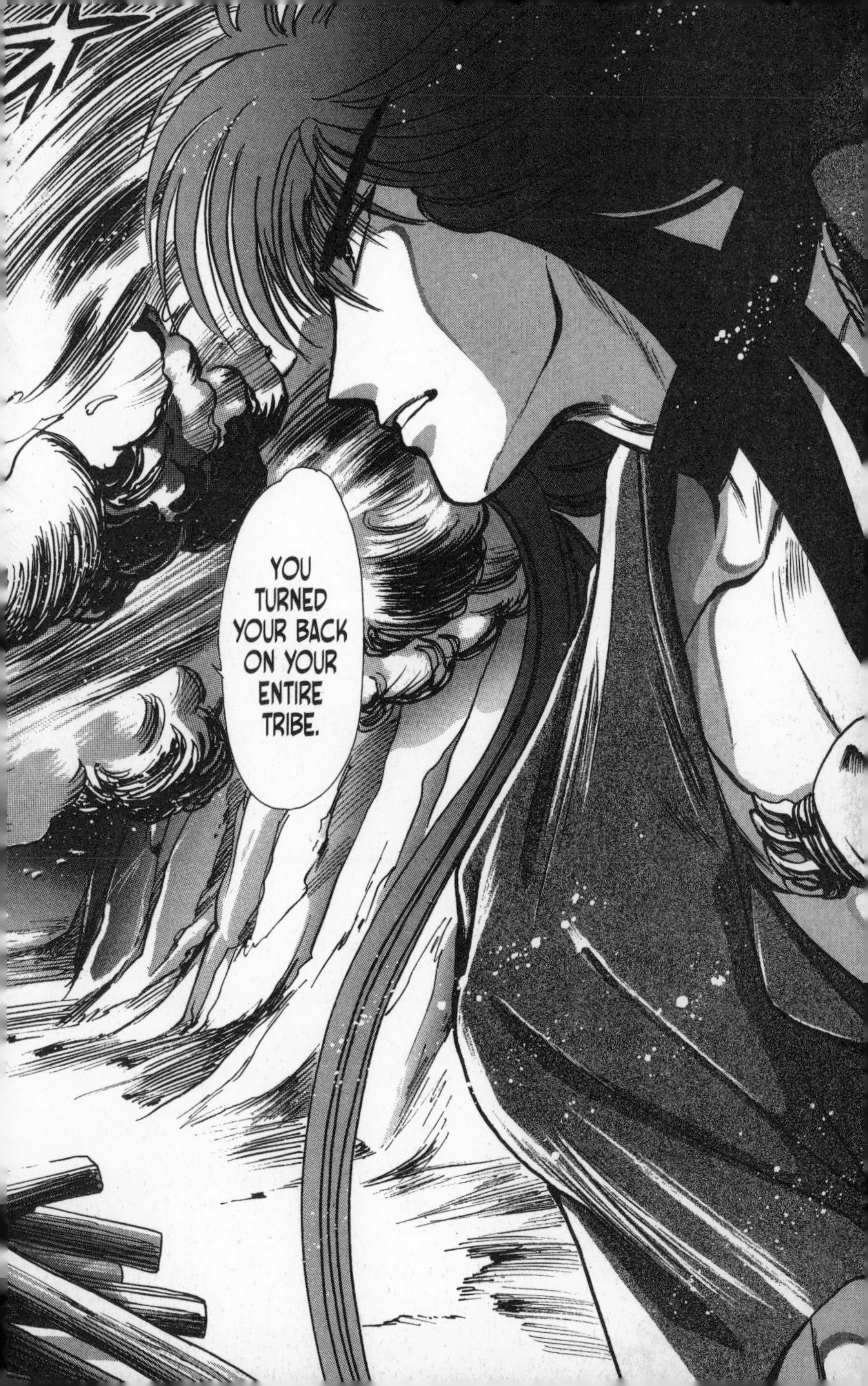
YOU TURNED YOUR BACK ON YOUR ENTIRE TRIBE.

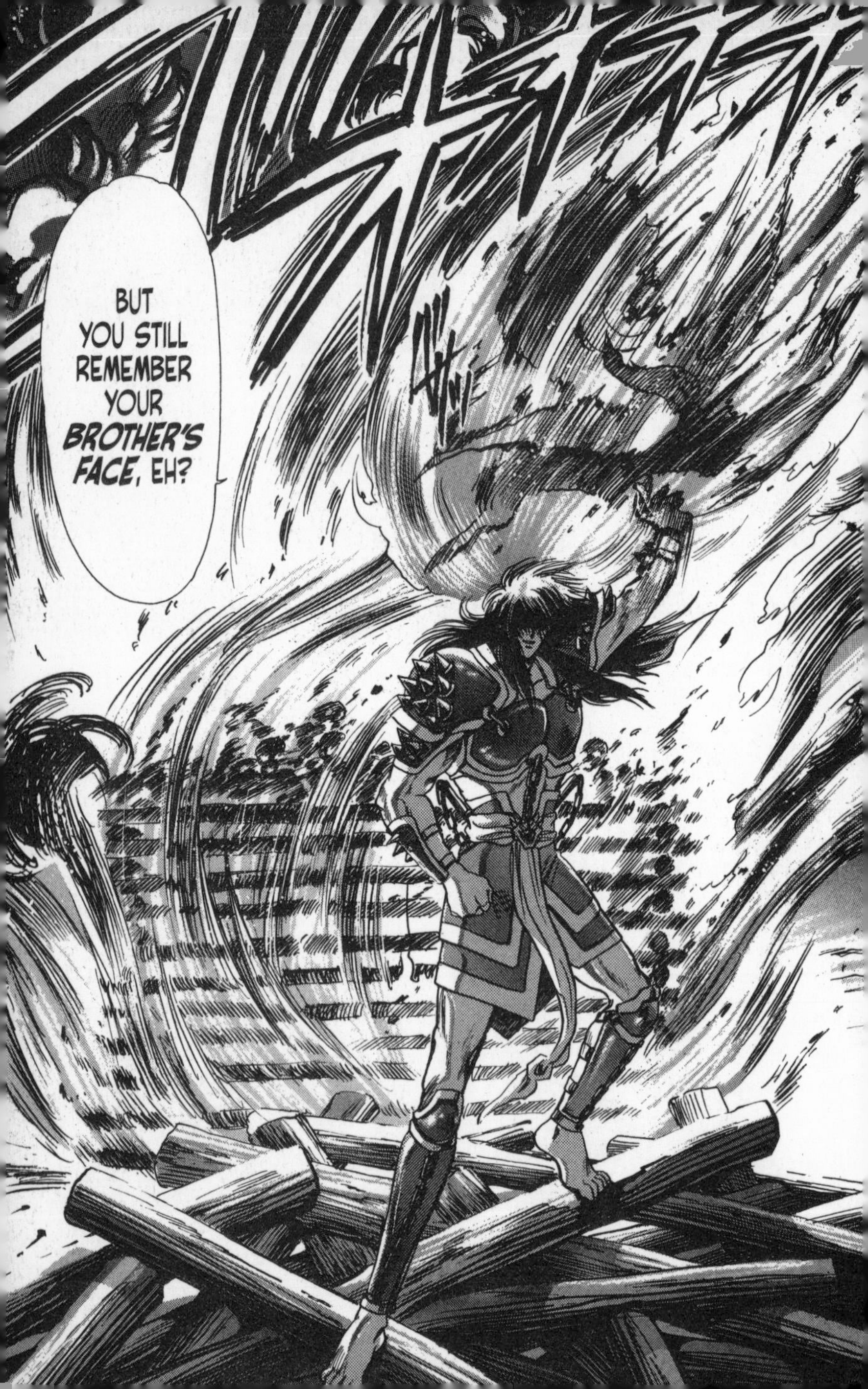
BUT YOU STILL REMEMBER YOUR BROTHER'S FACE, EH?

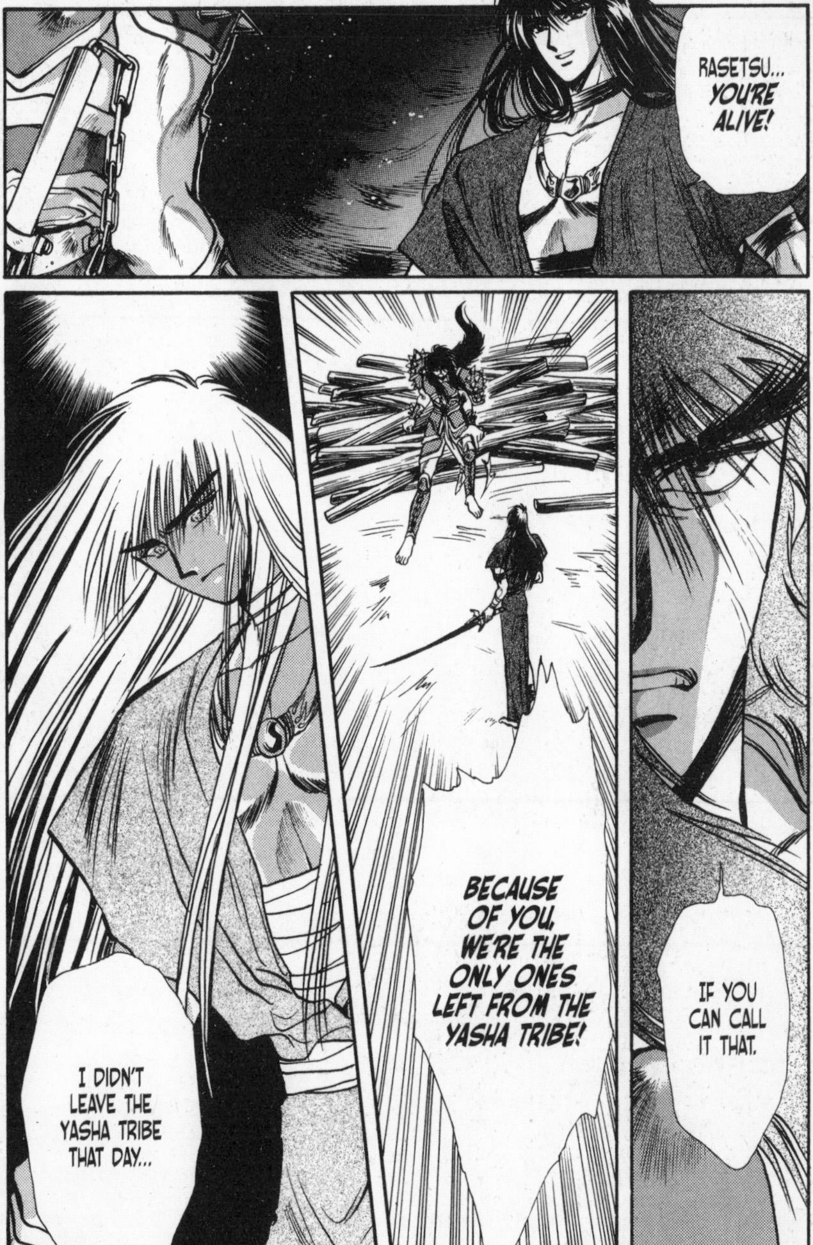
RASETSU... YOU'RE ALIVE!
IF YOU CAN CALL IT THAT.
BECAUSE OF YOU, WE'RE THE ONLY ONES LEFT FROM THE YASHA TRIBE!
I DIDN'T LEAVE THE YASHA TRIBE THAT DAY...

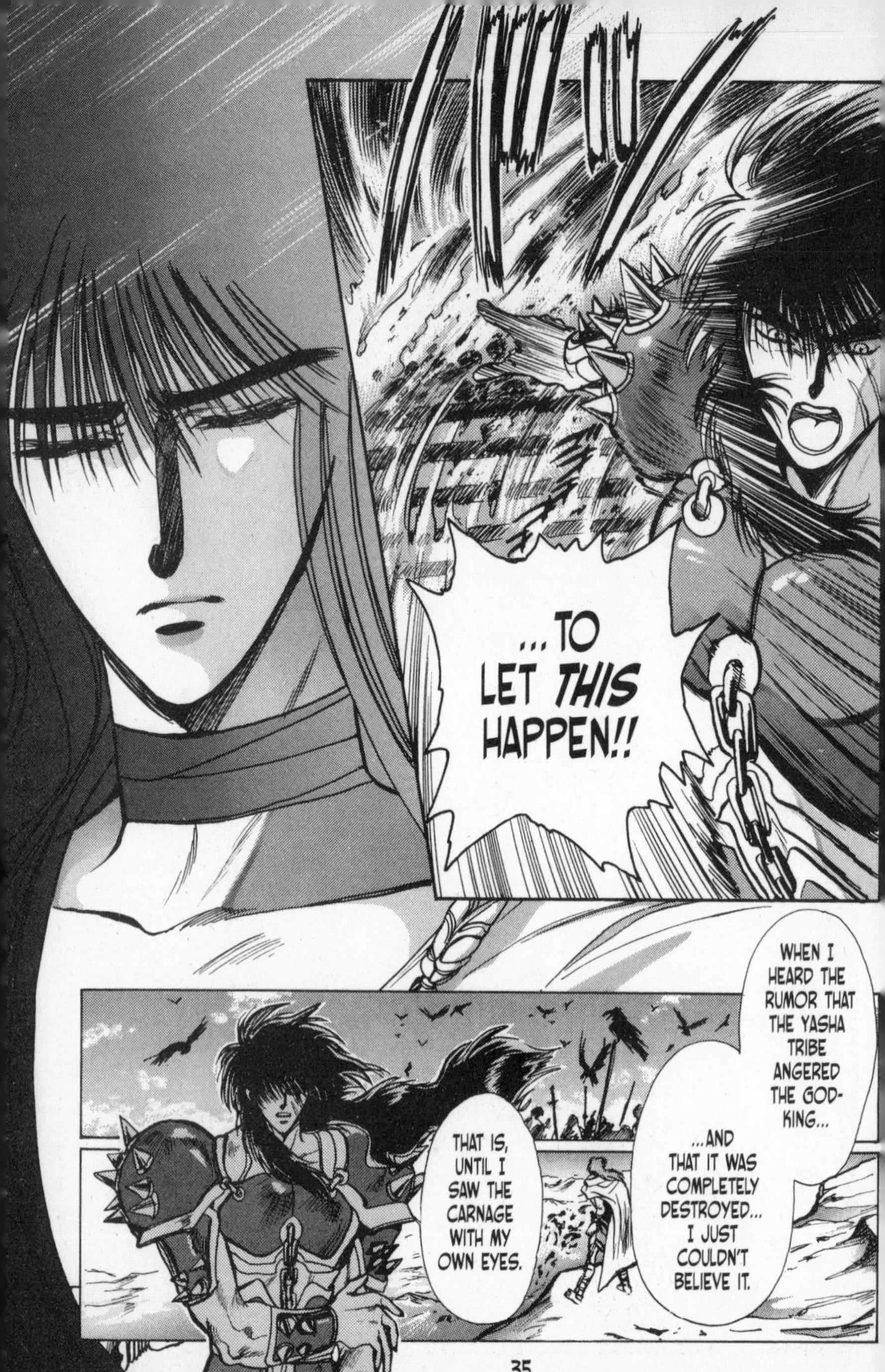
...TO LET THIS HAPPEN!!
WHEN I HEARD THE RUMOR THAT THE YASHA TRIBE ANGERED THE GOD-KING...
...AND THAT IT WAS COMPLETELY DESTROYED... I JUST COULDN'T BELIEVE IT.
THAT IS, UNTIL I SAW THE CARNAGE WITH MY OWN EYES.

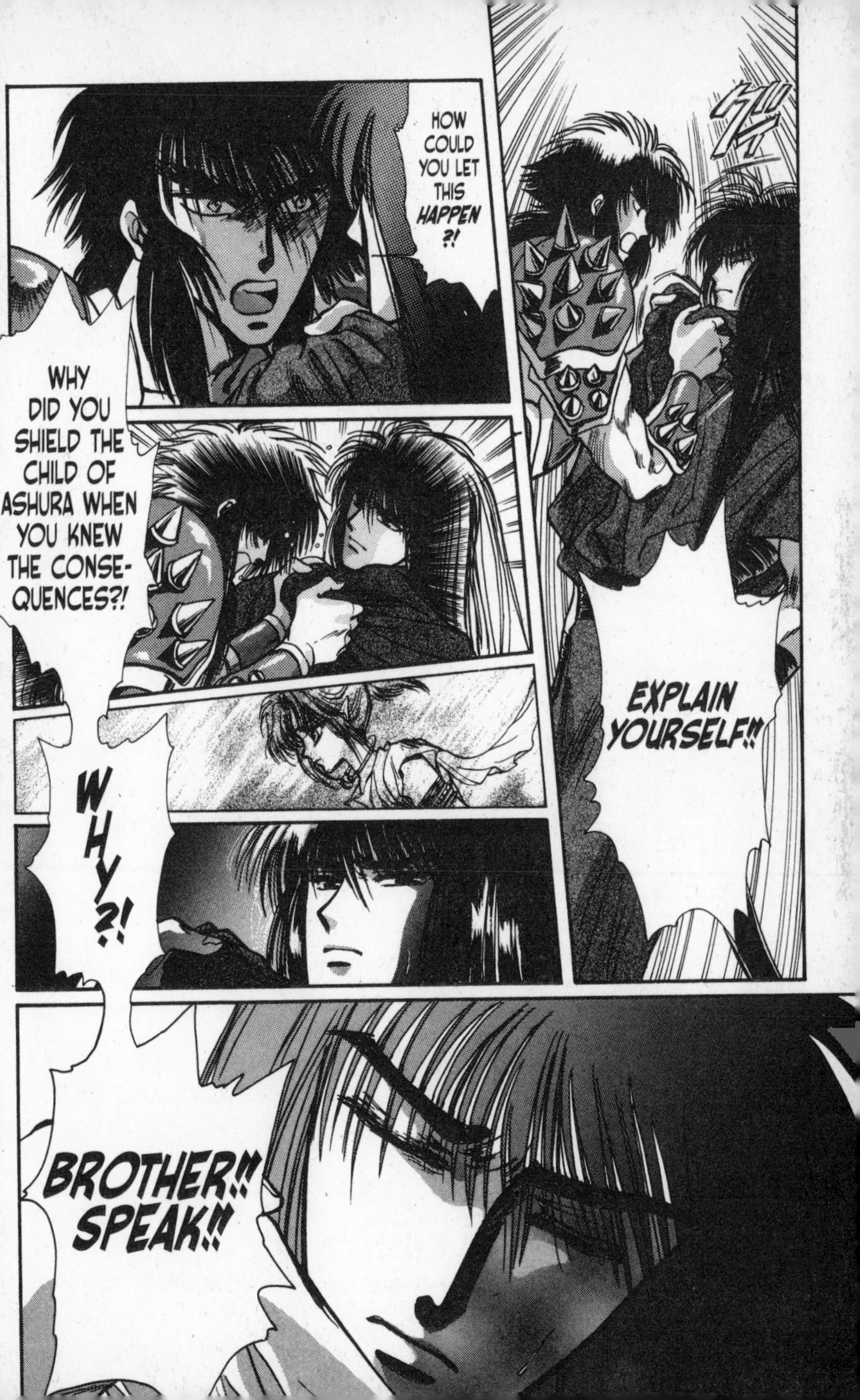
EXPLAIN YOURSELF!!
HOW COULD YOU LET THIS HAPPEN ?!
WHY DID YOU SHIELD THE CHILD OF ASHURA WHEN YOU KNEW THE CONSE-QUENCES?!
WHY?!
BROTHER!! SPEAK!!

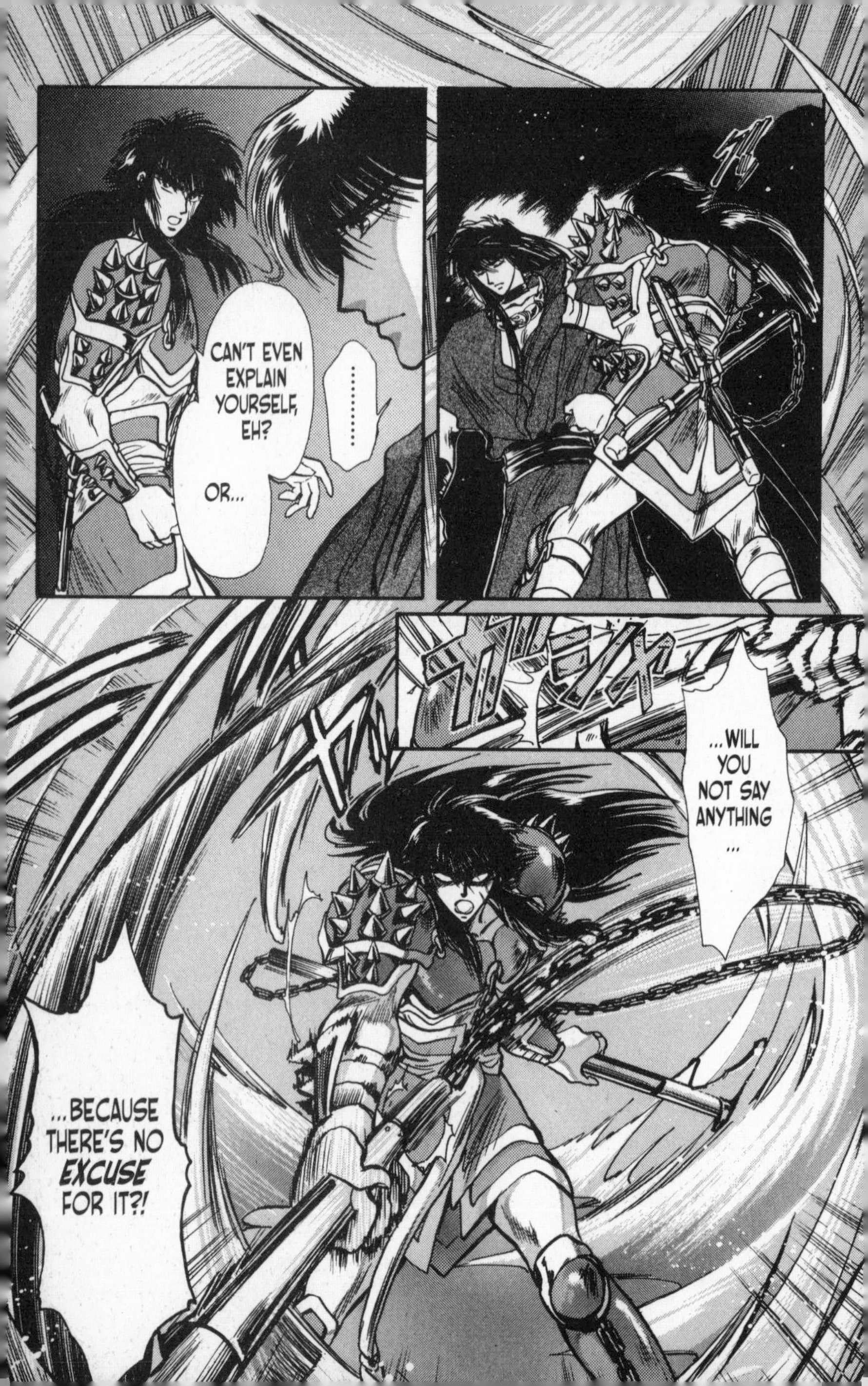
CAN'T EVEN EXPLAIN YOURSELF, EH?
OR...
......
...WILL YOU NOT SAY ANYTHING ...
...BECAUSE THERE'S NO *EXCUSE* FOR IT?!

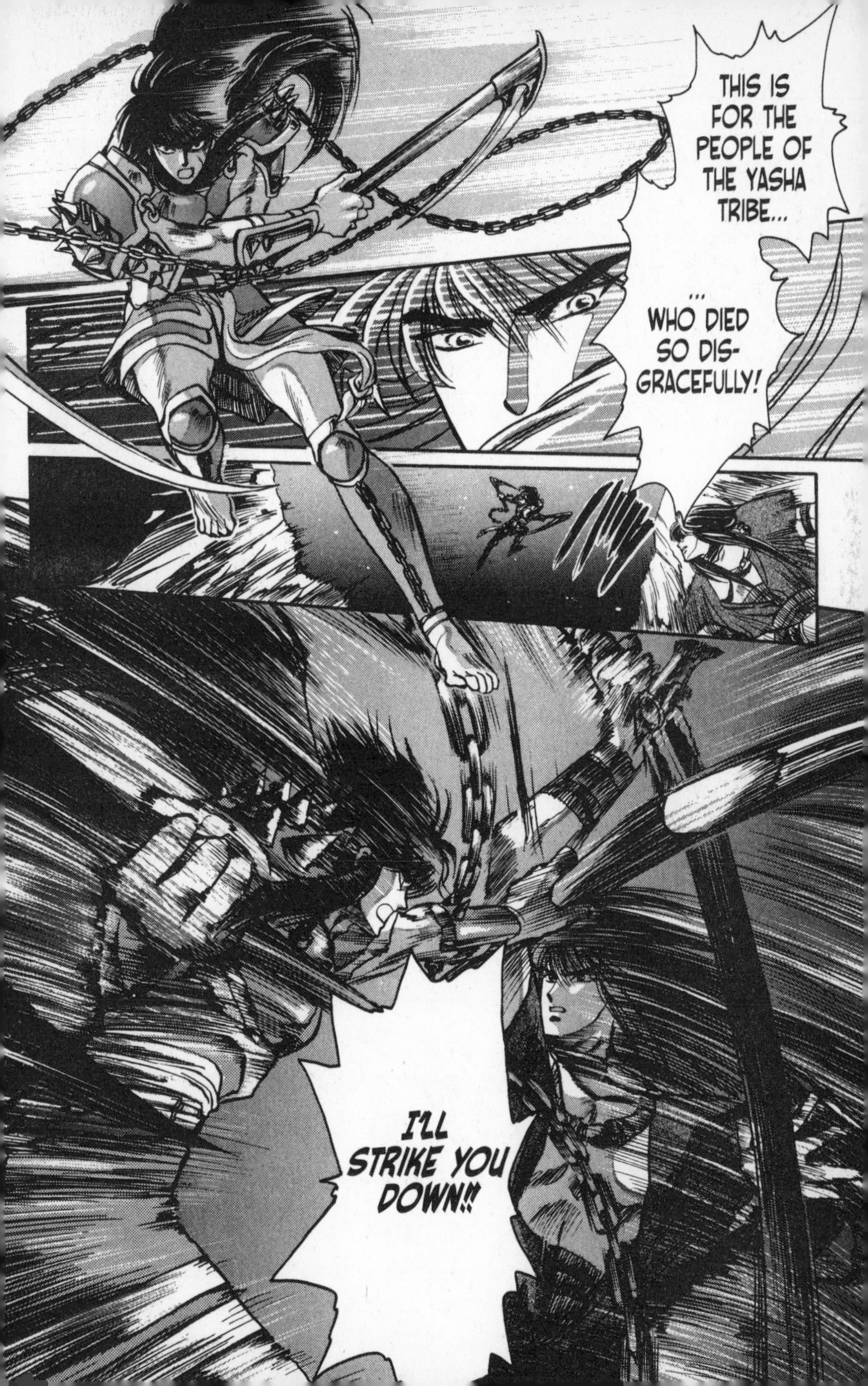
THIS IS FOR THE PEOPLE OF THE YASHA TRIBE...
...WHO DIED SO DIS-GRACEFULLY!
I'LL STRIKE YOU DOWN!!

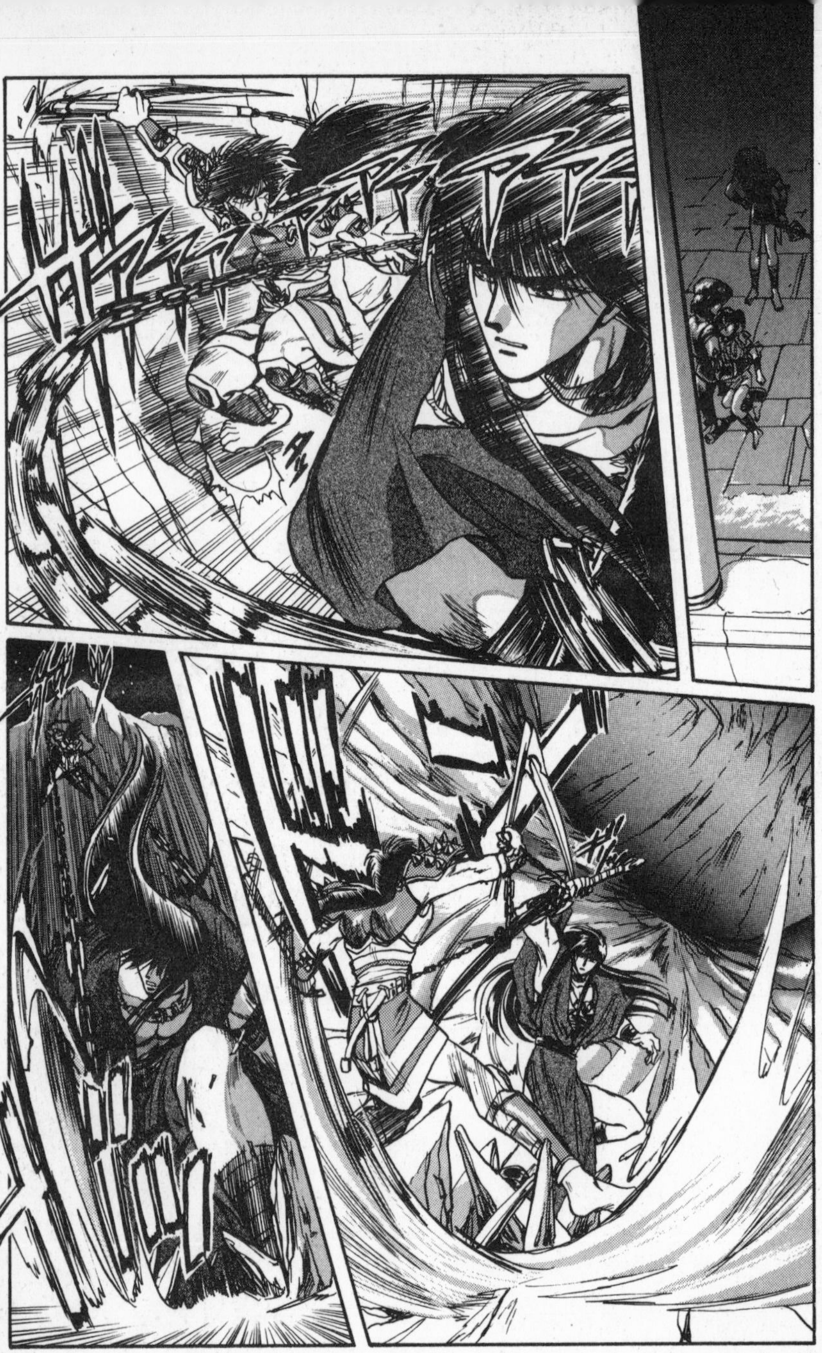

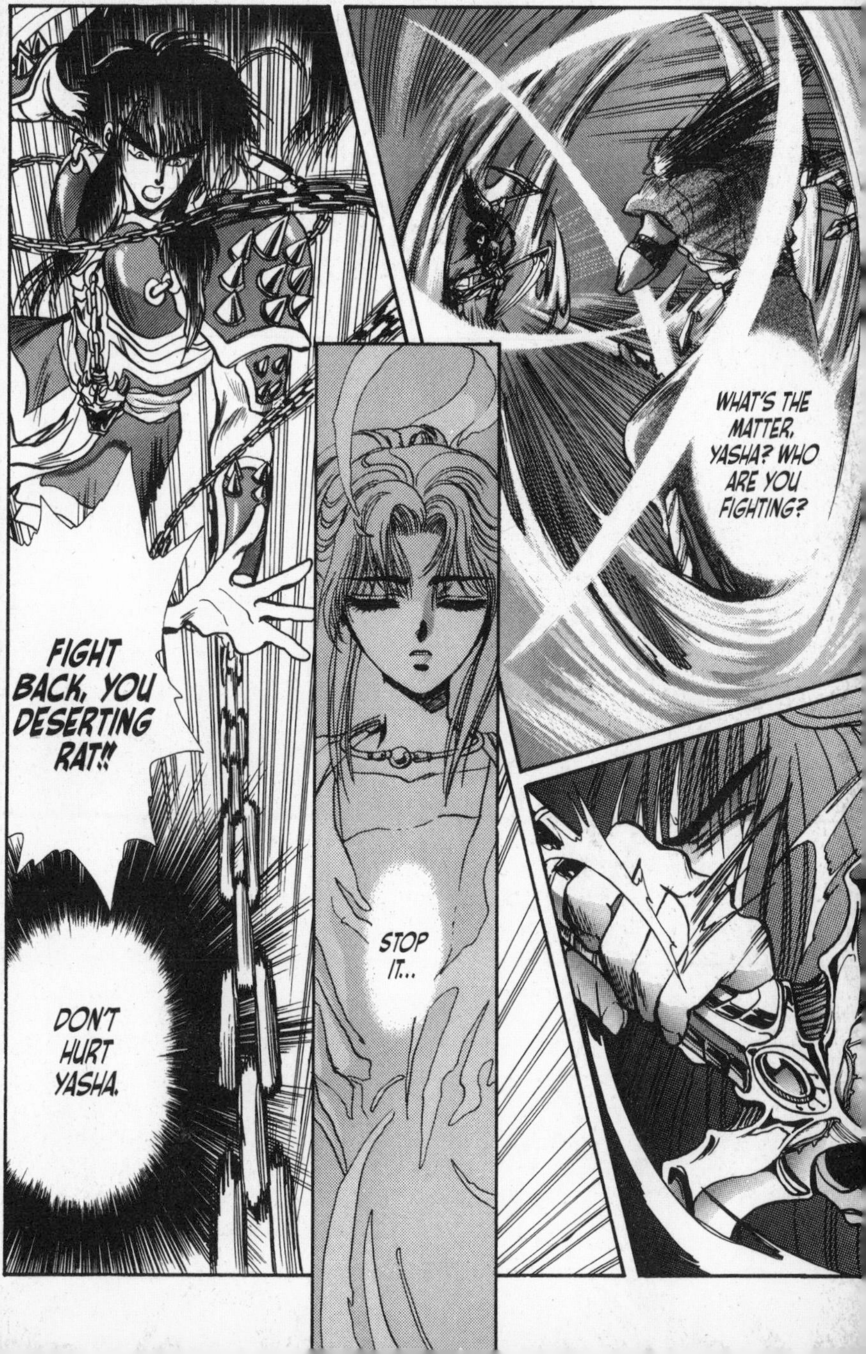
WHAT'S THE MATTER, YASHA? WHO ARE YOU FIGHTING?
FIGHT BACK, YOU DESERTING RAT!!
STOP IT...
DON'T HURT YASHA.

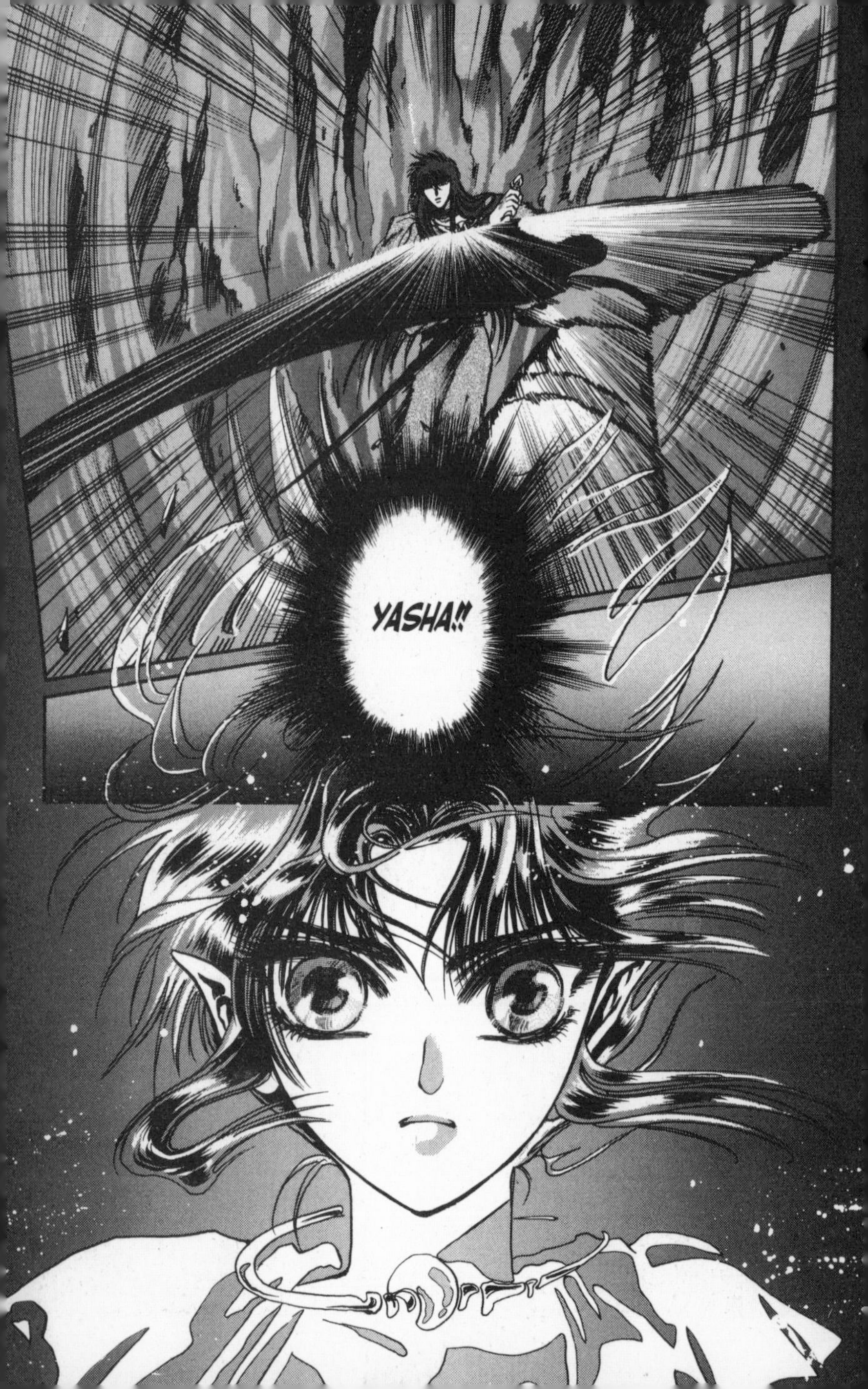
YASHA!!

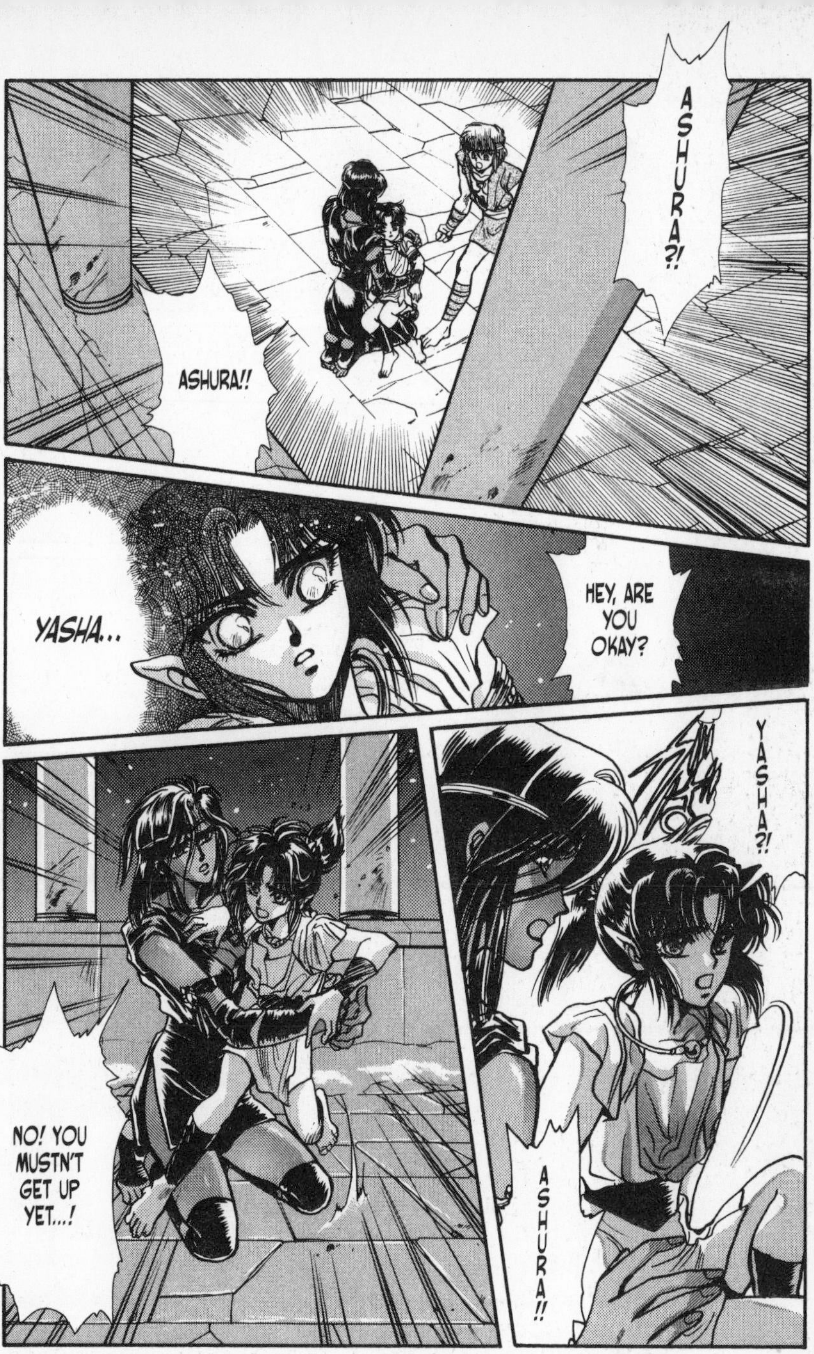
ASHURA?!
ASHURA!!
HEY, ARE YOU OKAY?
YASHA...
YASHA?!
ASHURA!!
NO! YOU MUSTN'T GET UP YET...!

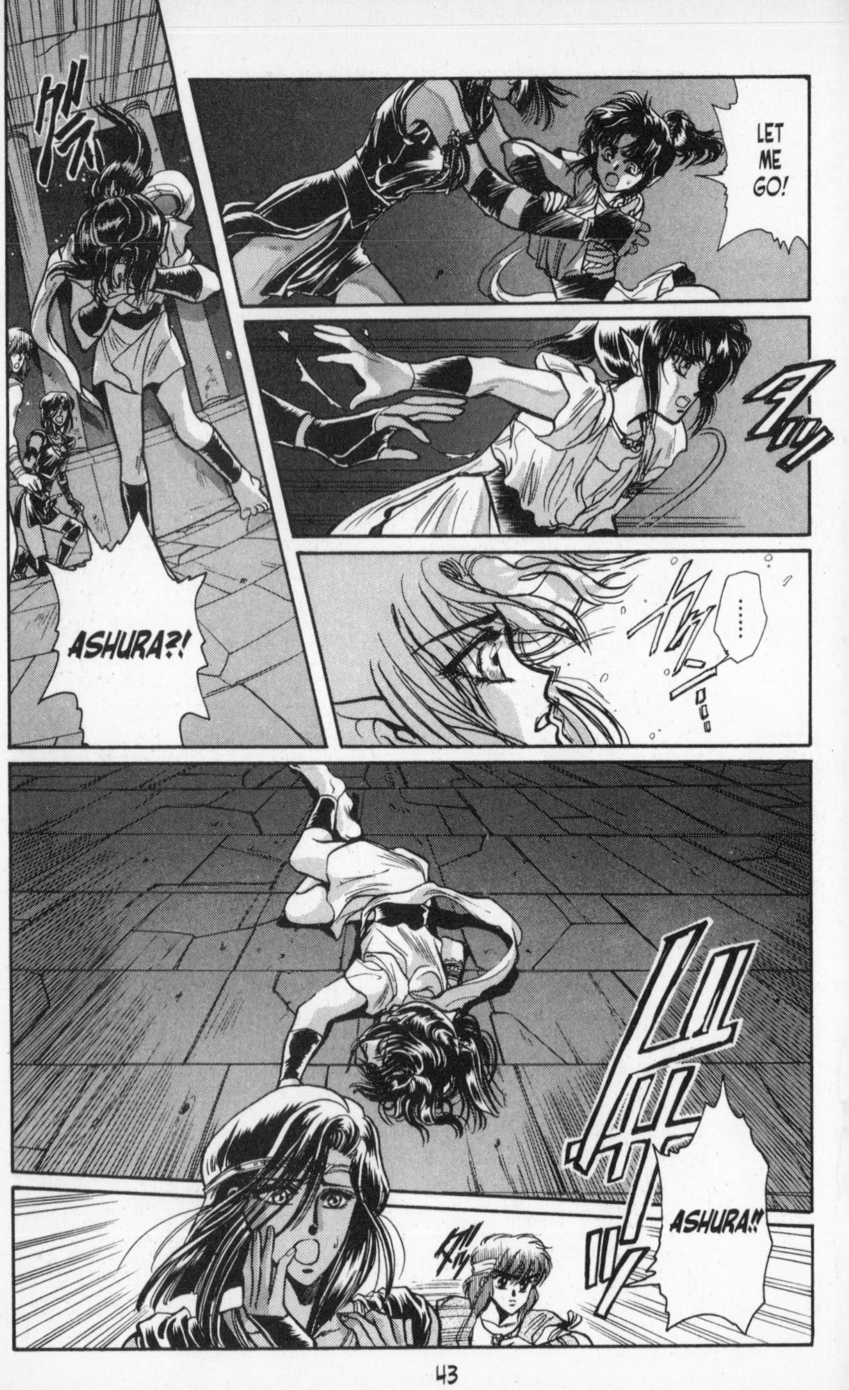
LET ME GO!
......
ASHURA?!
ASHURA!!

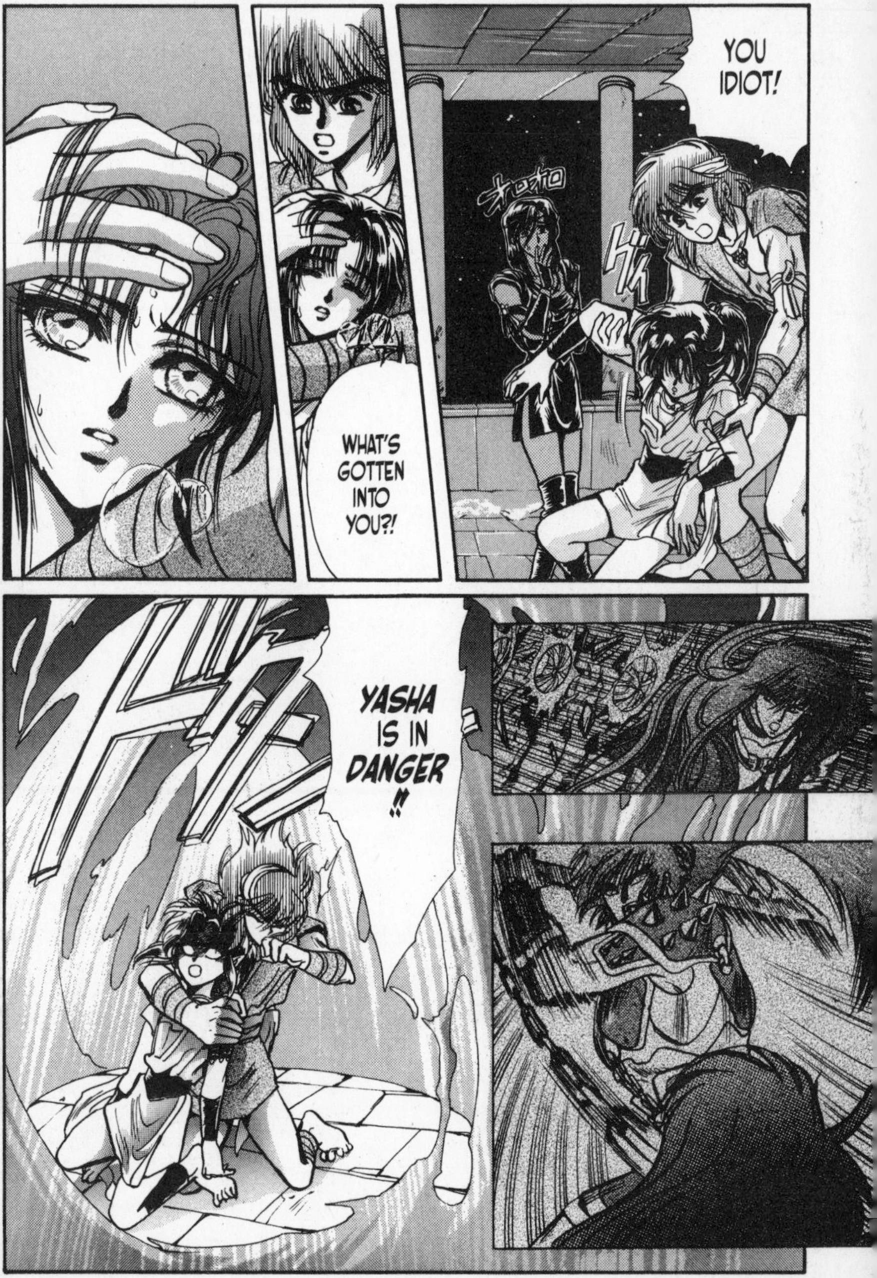
YOU IDIOT!
WHAT'S GOTTEN INTO YOU?!
YASHA IS IN DANGER!!

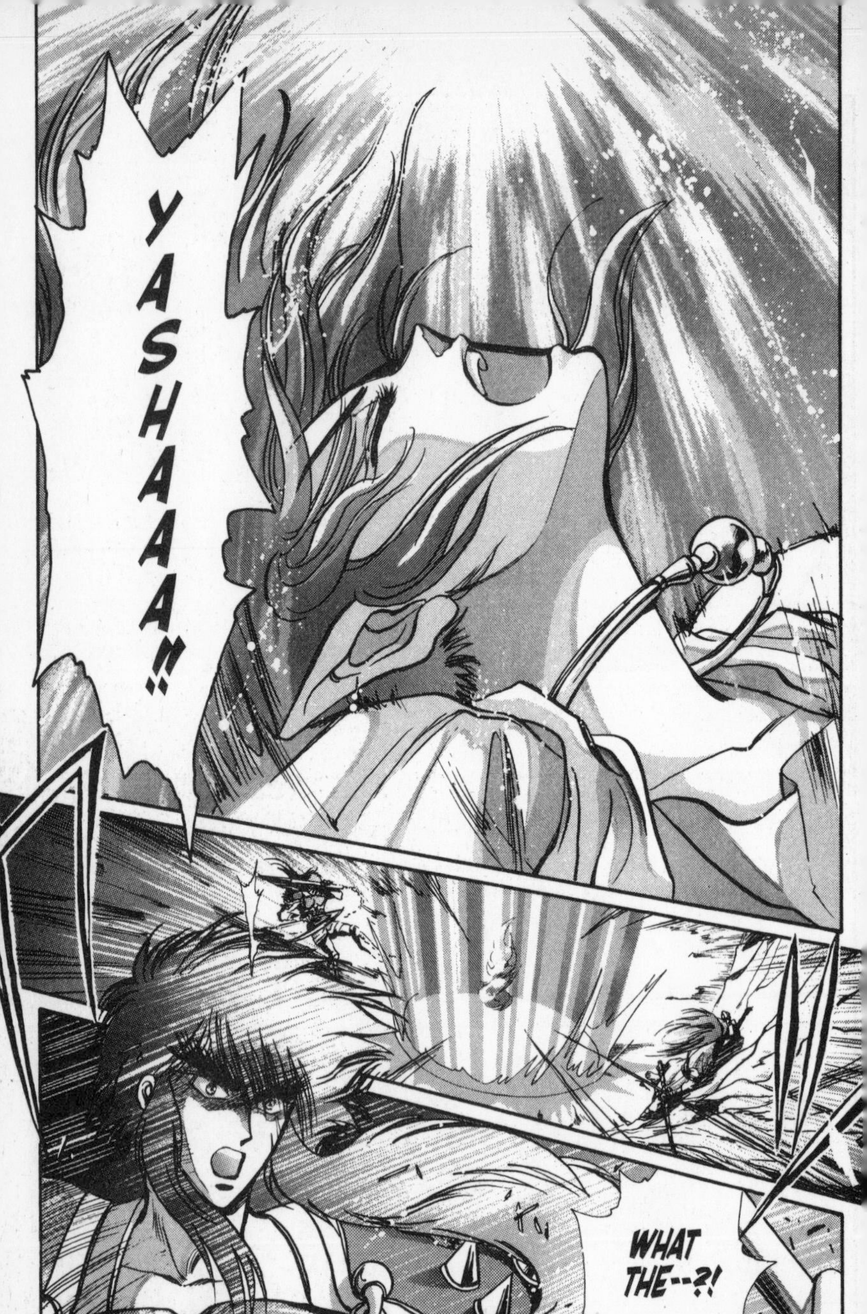
YASHAAAAA!!
WHAT THE--?!

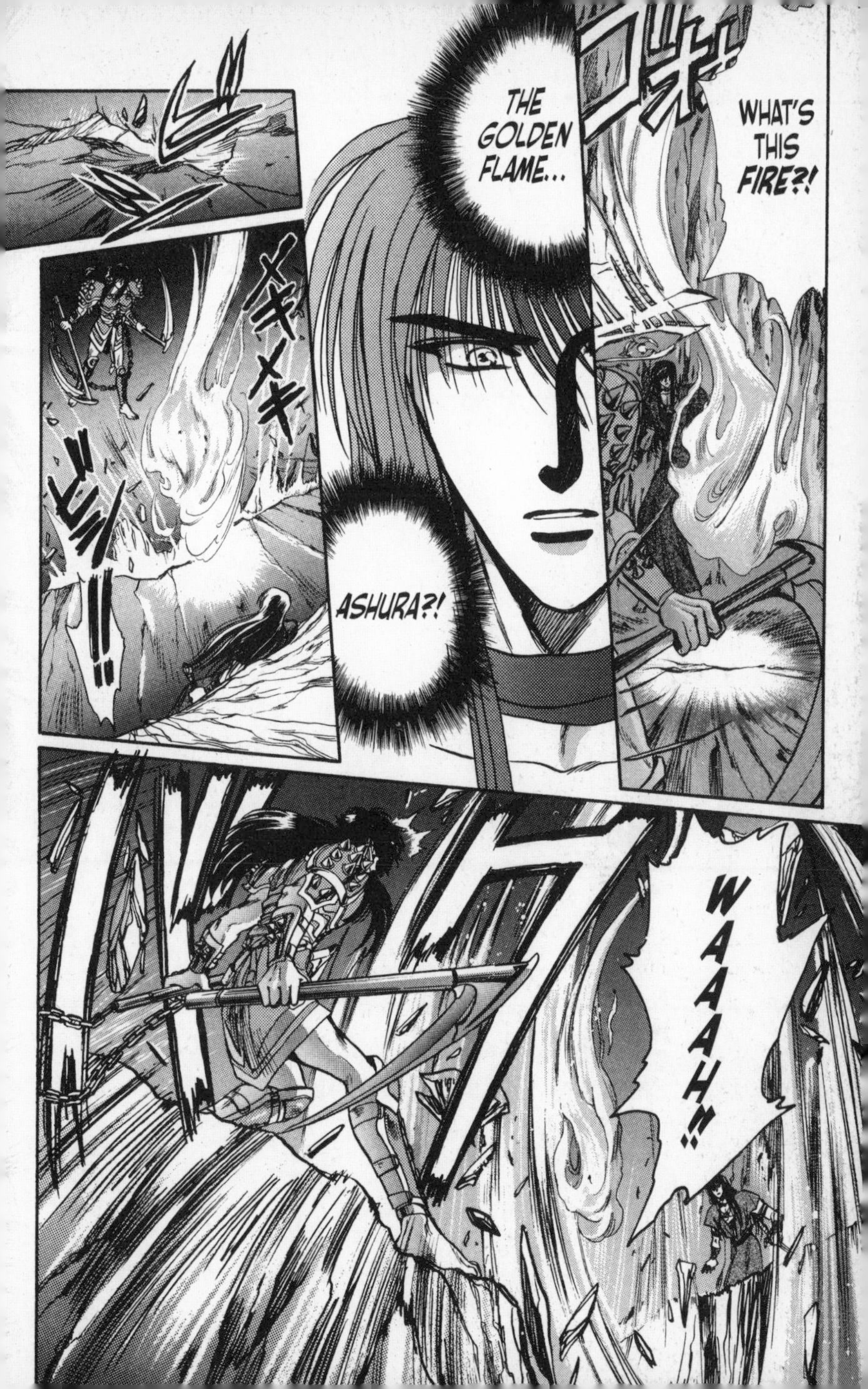
WHAT'S THIS FIRE?!
THE GOLDEN FLAME...
ASHURA?!
WAAAAH!!

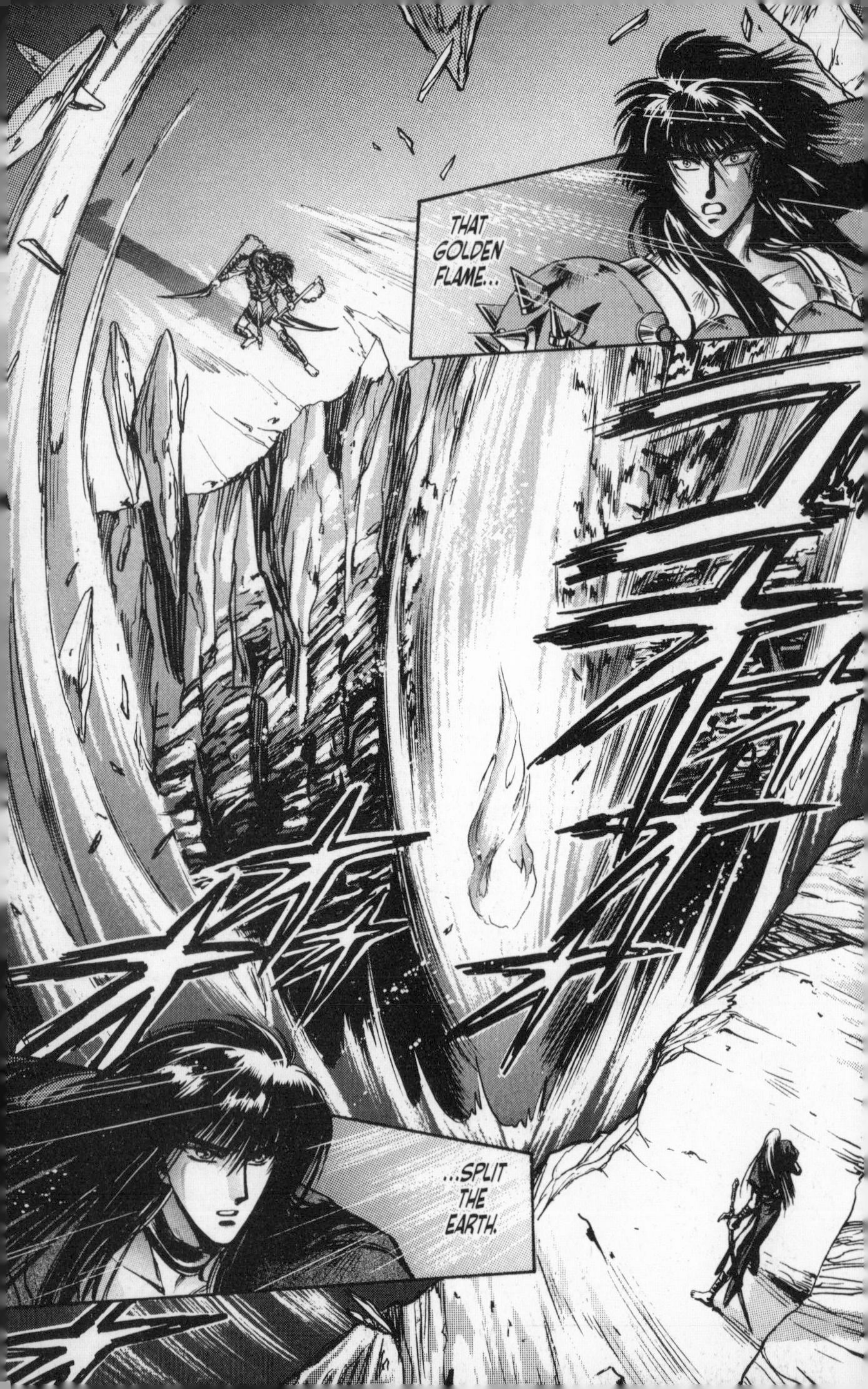
THAT GOLDEN FLAME...
...SPLIT THE EARTH.

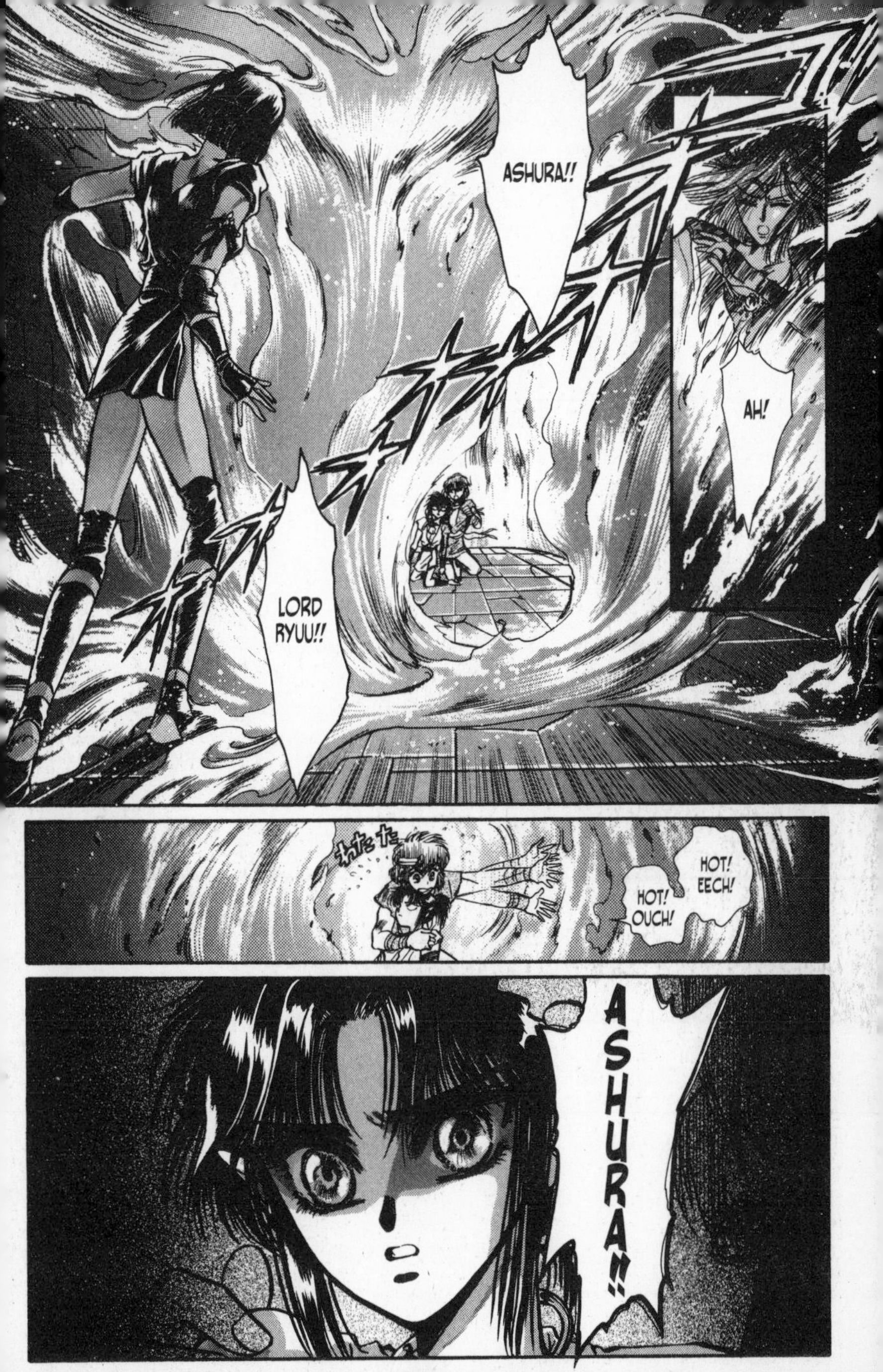
ASHURA!!
AH!
LORD RYUU!!
HOT! EECH!
HOT! OUCH!
ASHURA!!

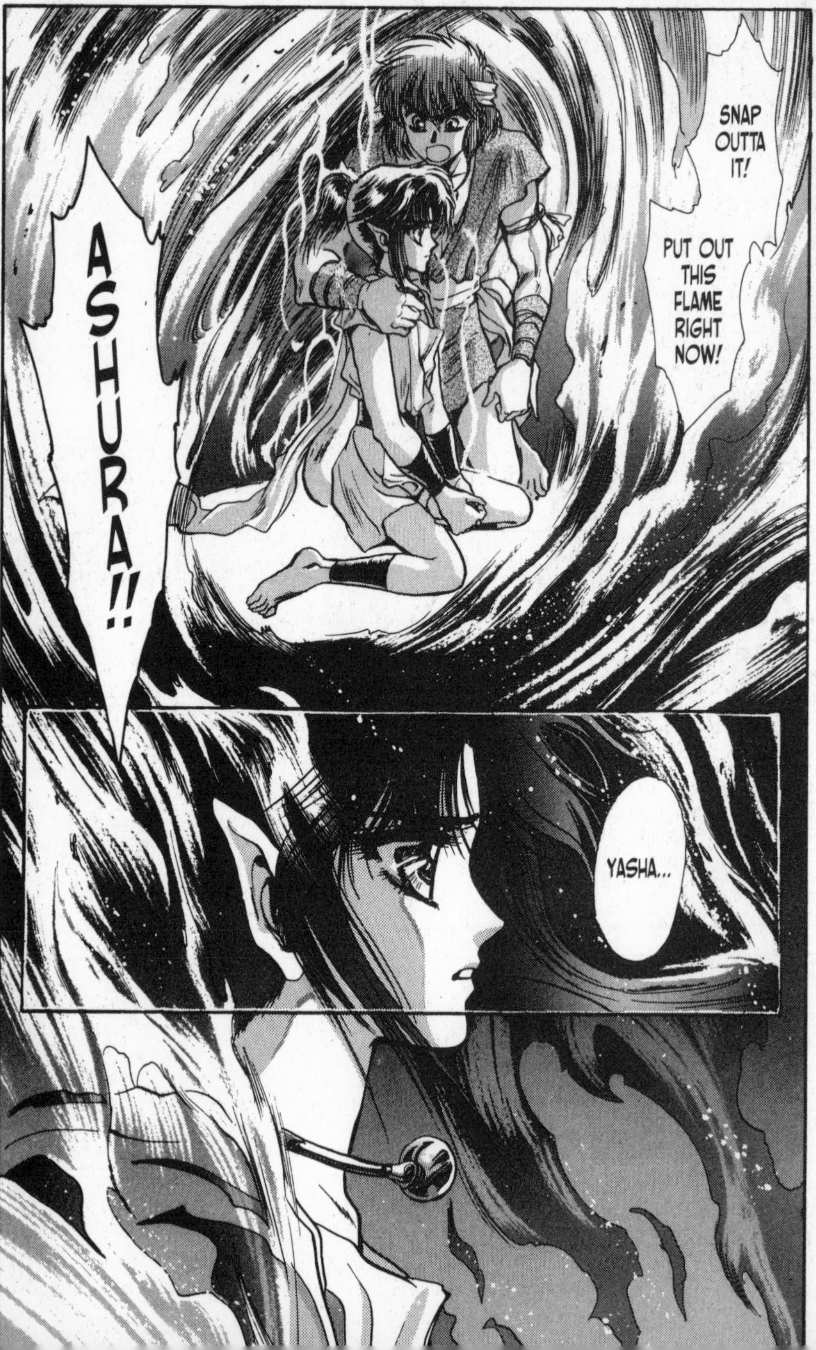
SNAP OUTTA IT!
PUT OUT THIS FLAME RIGHT NOW!
ASHURA!!
YASHA...

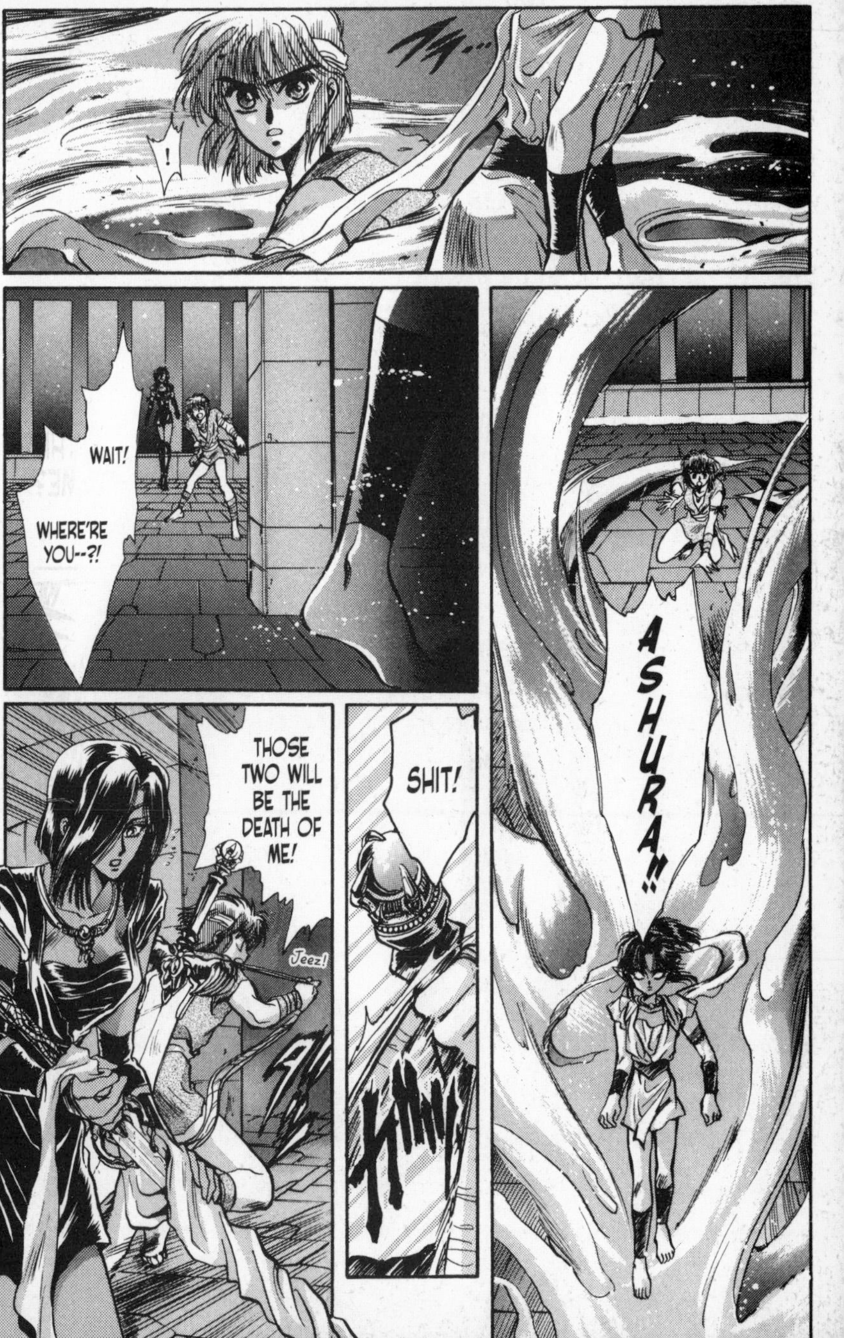
!
ASHURA!!
WAIT!
WHERE'RE YOU--?!
SHIT!
THOSE TWO WILL BE THE DEATH OF ME!
Jeez!

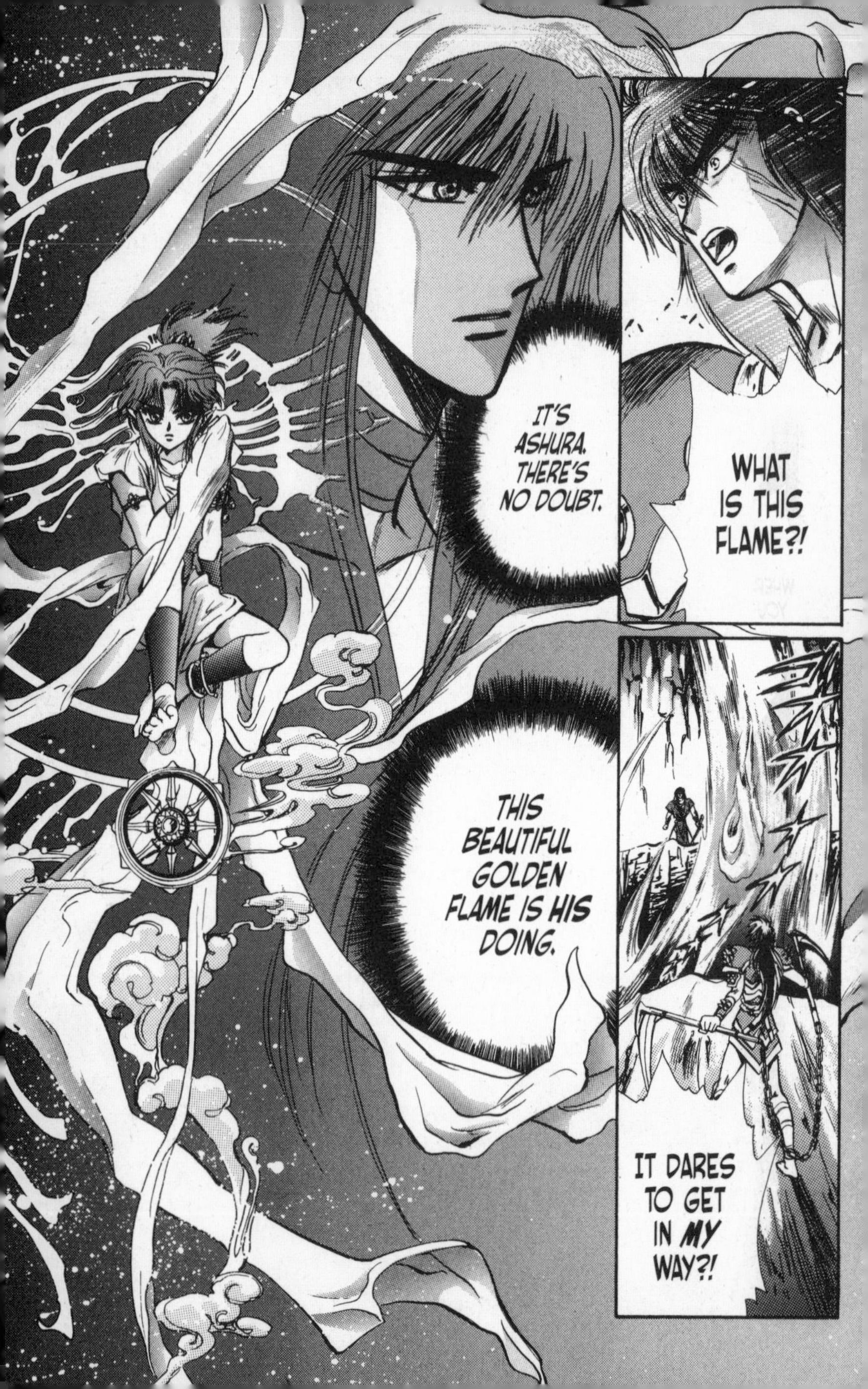
WHAT IS THIS FLAME?!
IT DARES TO GET IN *MY* WAY?!
IT'S ASHURA. THERE'S NO DOUBT.
THIS BEAUTIFUL GOLDEN FLAME IS **HIS** DOING.

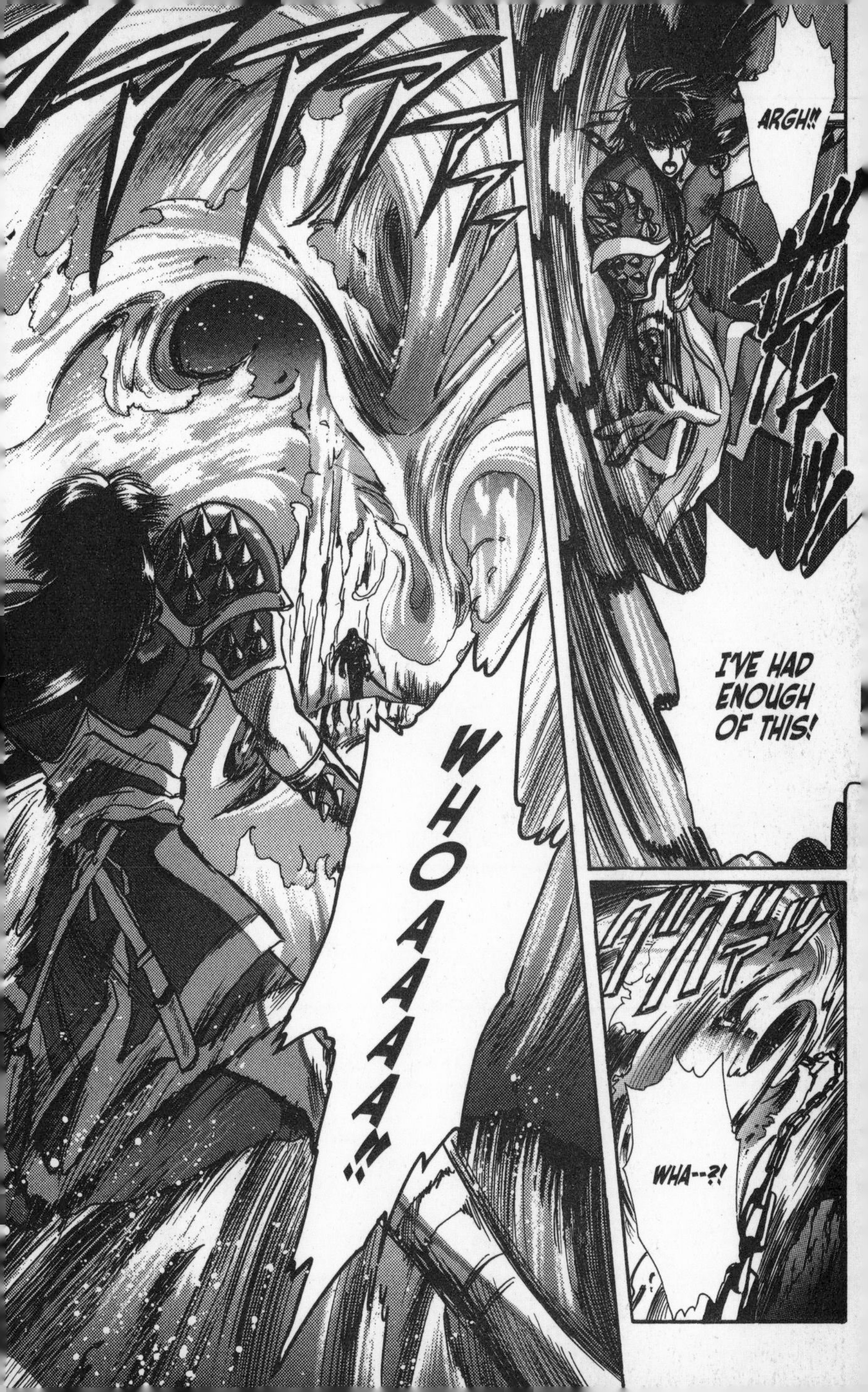
ARGH!!
I'VE HAD ENOUGH OF THIS!
WHA--?!
WHOAAAAM!!

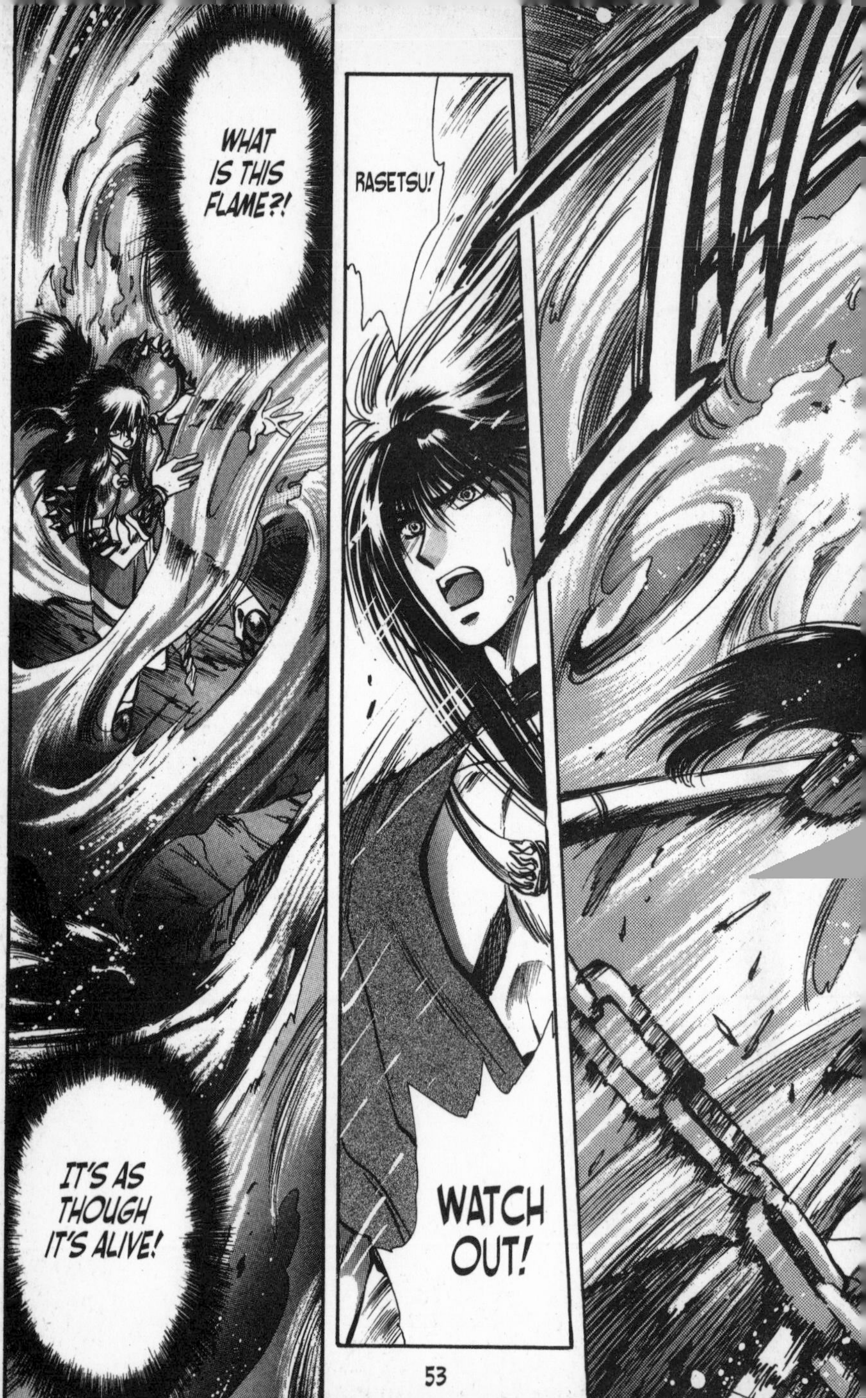
RASETSU!
WATCH OUT!
WHAT IS THIS FLAME?!
IT'S AS THOUGH IT'S ALIVE!

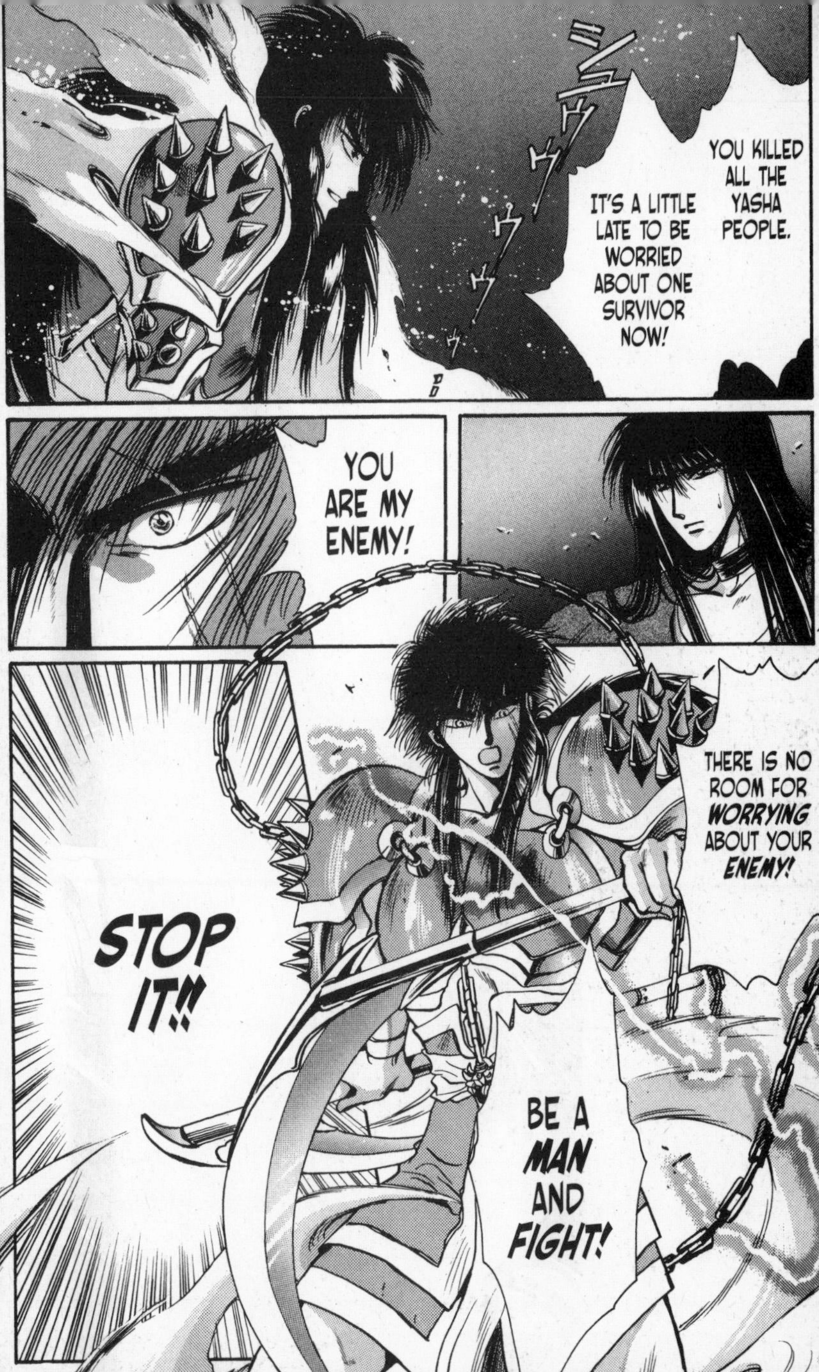
YOU KILLED ALL THE YASHA PEOPLE.
IT'S A LITTLE LATE TO BE WORRIED ABOUT ONE SURVIVOR NOW!
YOU ARE MY ENEMY!
THERE IS NO ROOM FOR *WORRYING* ABOUT YOUR *ENEMY!*
BE A *MAN* AND *FIGHT!*
STOP IT!!

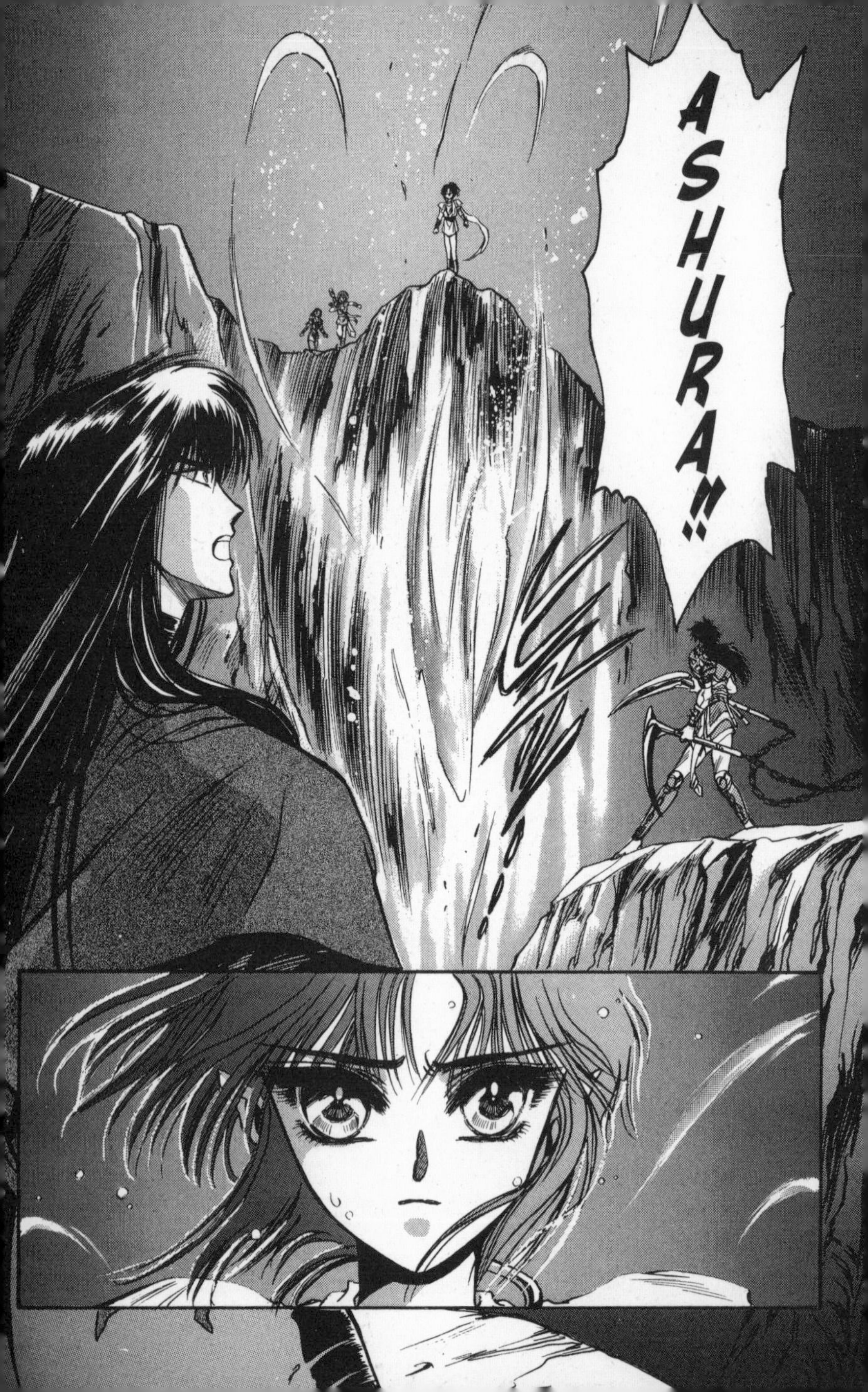
ASHURA!!

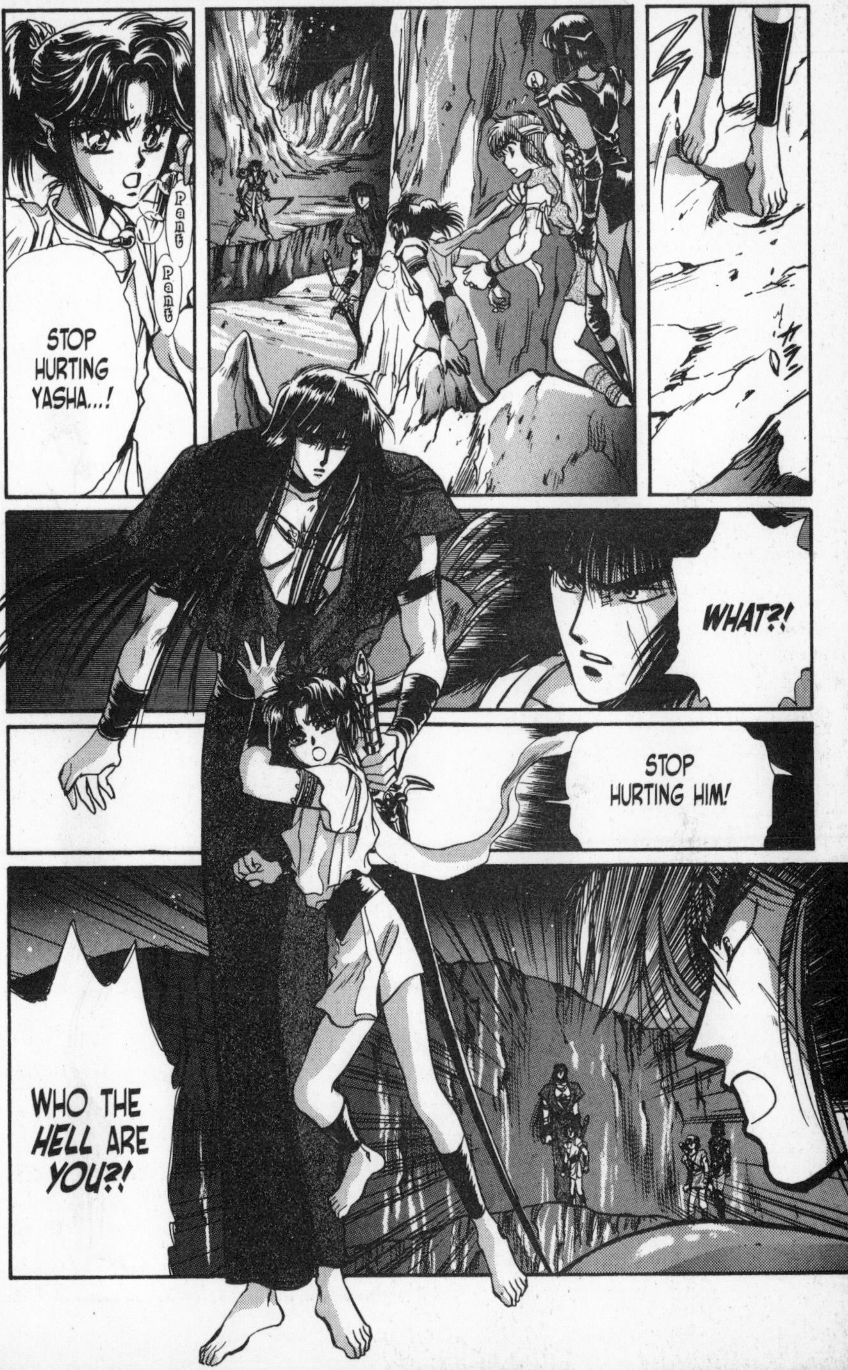
Pant
Pant
STOP HURTING YASHA...!
WHAT?!
STOP HURTING HIM!
WHO THE HELL ARE YOU?!

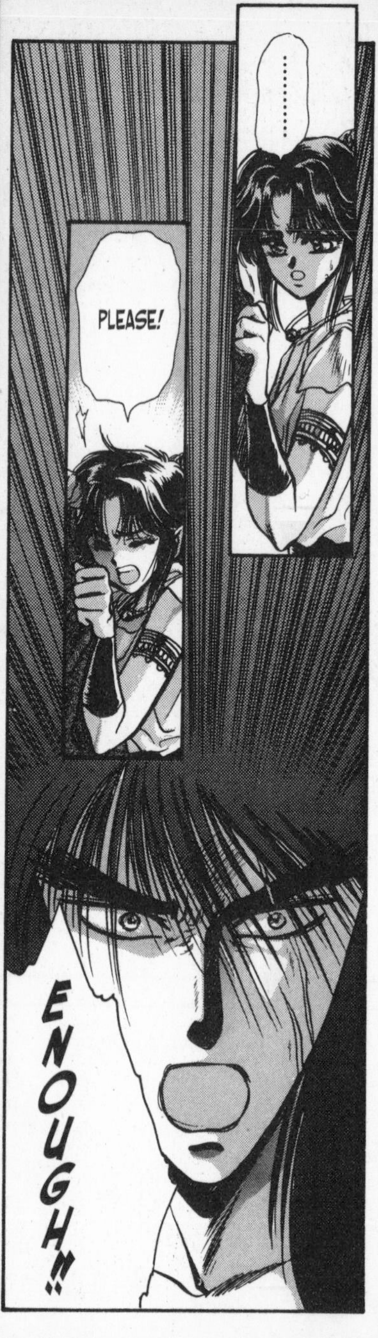
......
PLEASE!
ENOUGH!!
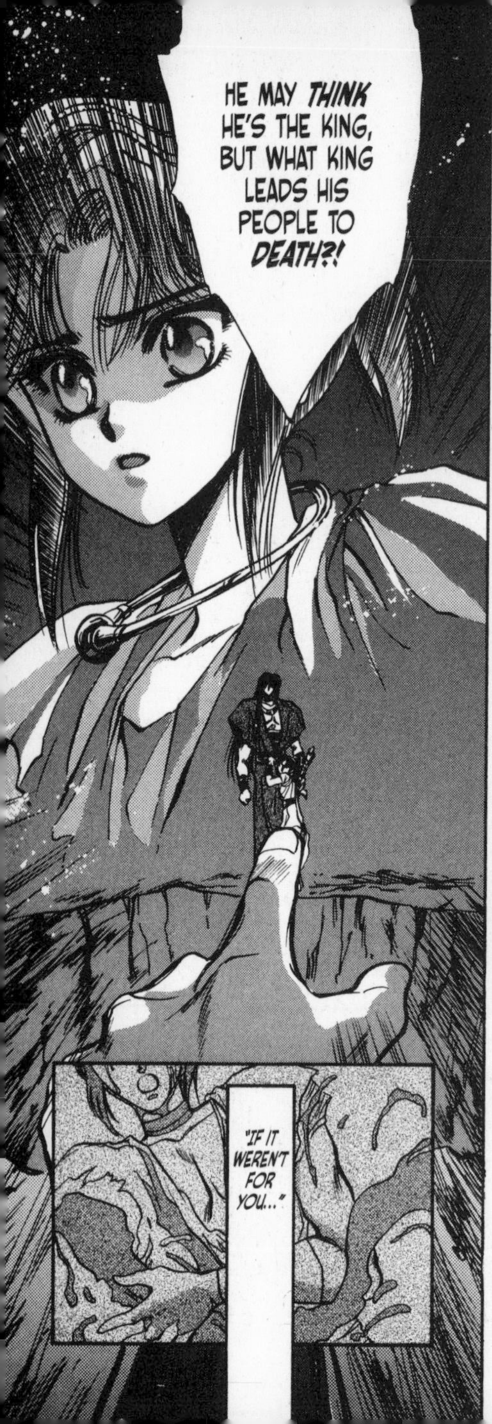
HE MAY THINK HE'S THE KING, BUT WHAT KING LEADS HIS PEOPLE TO DEATH?!
"IF IT WEREN'T FOR YOU..."

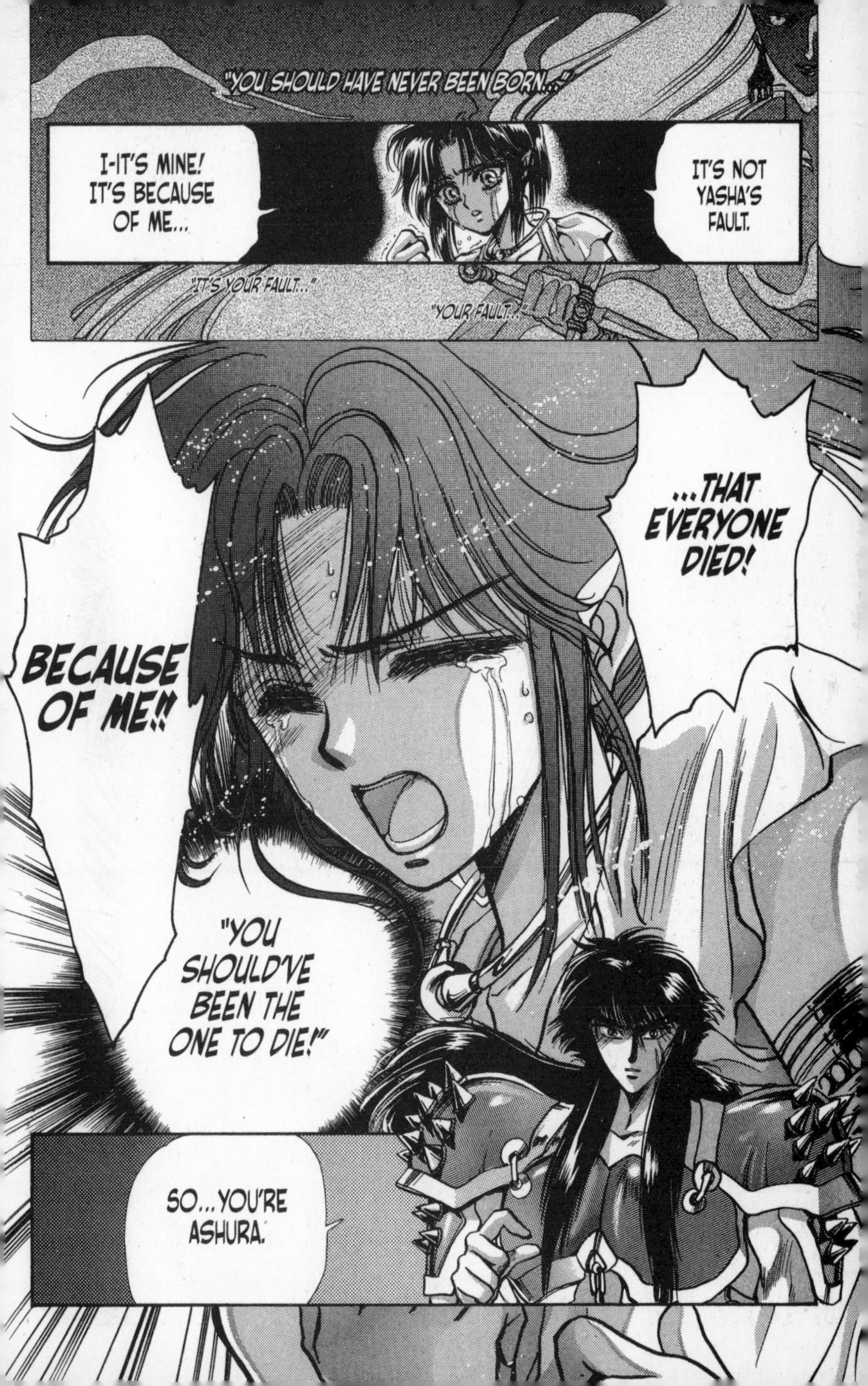
"YOU SHOULD HAVE NEVER BEEN BORN..."
IT'S NOT YASHA'S FAULT.
I-IT'S MINE! IT'S BECAUSE OF ME...
"IT'S YOUR FAULT..."
"YOUR FAULT..."
...THAT EVERYONE DIED!
BECAUSE OF ME!!
"YOU SHOULD'VE BEEN THE ONE TO DIE!"
SO...YOU'RE ASHURA.

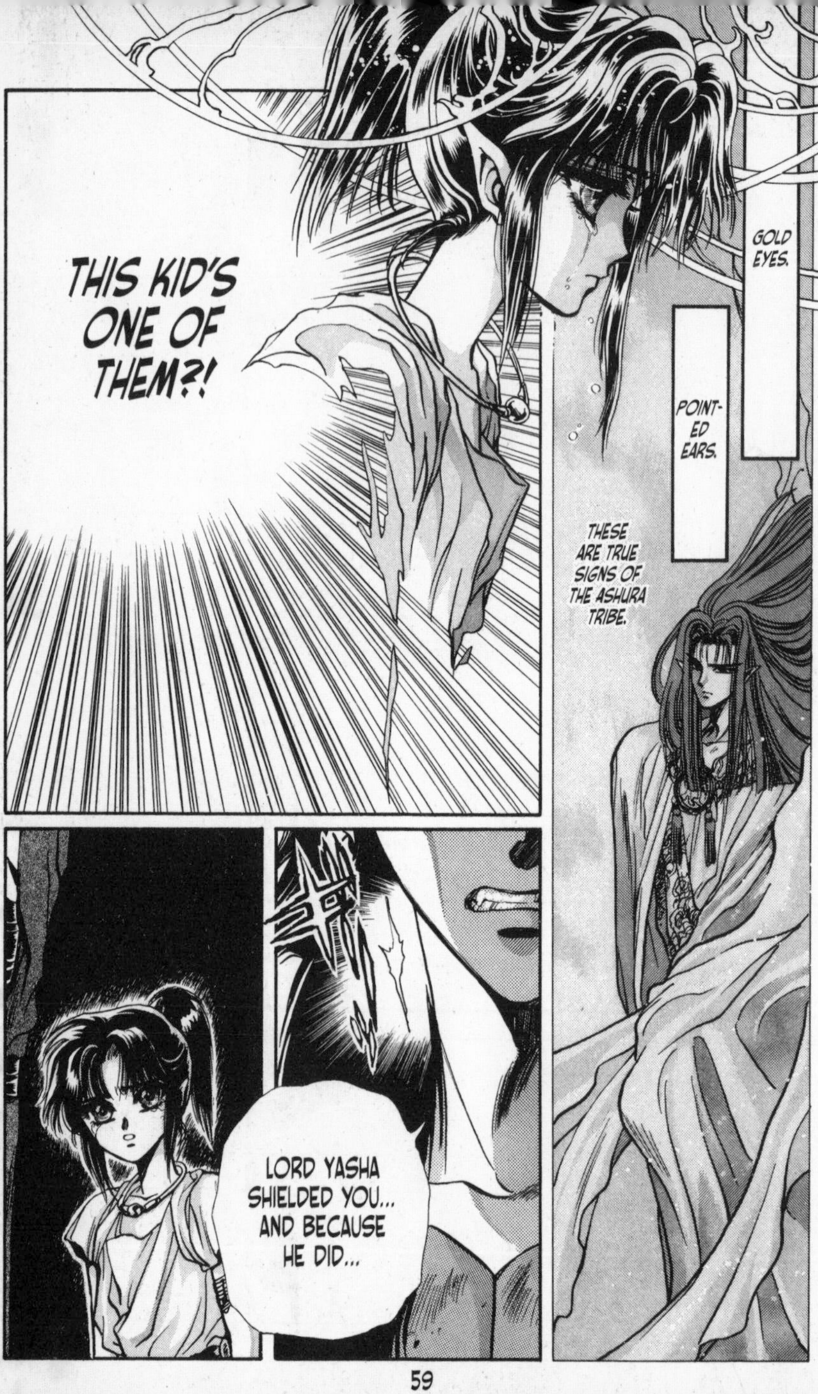
GOLD EYES.
POINT-ED EARS.
THESE ARE TRUE SIGNS OF THE ASHURA TRIBE.
THIS KID'S ONE OF THEM?!
LORD YASHA SHIELDED YOU... AND BECAUSE HE DID...

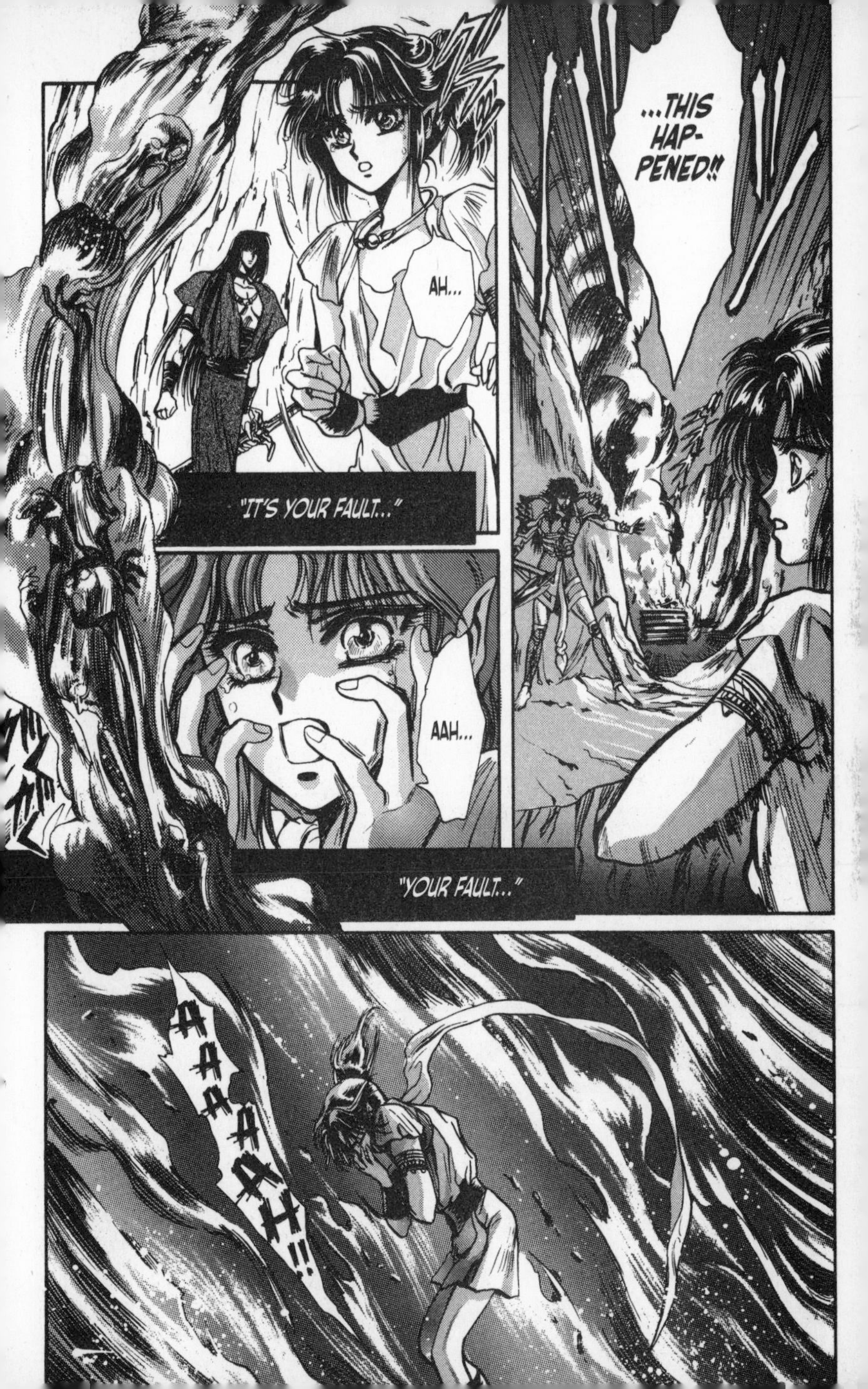
...THIS HAP-PENED!!
AH...
"IT'S YOUR FAULT..."
AAH...
"YOUR FAULT..."
AAAAAH!!

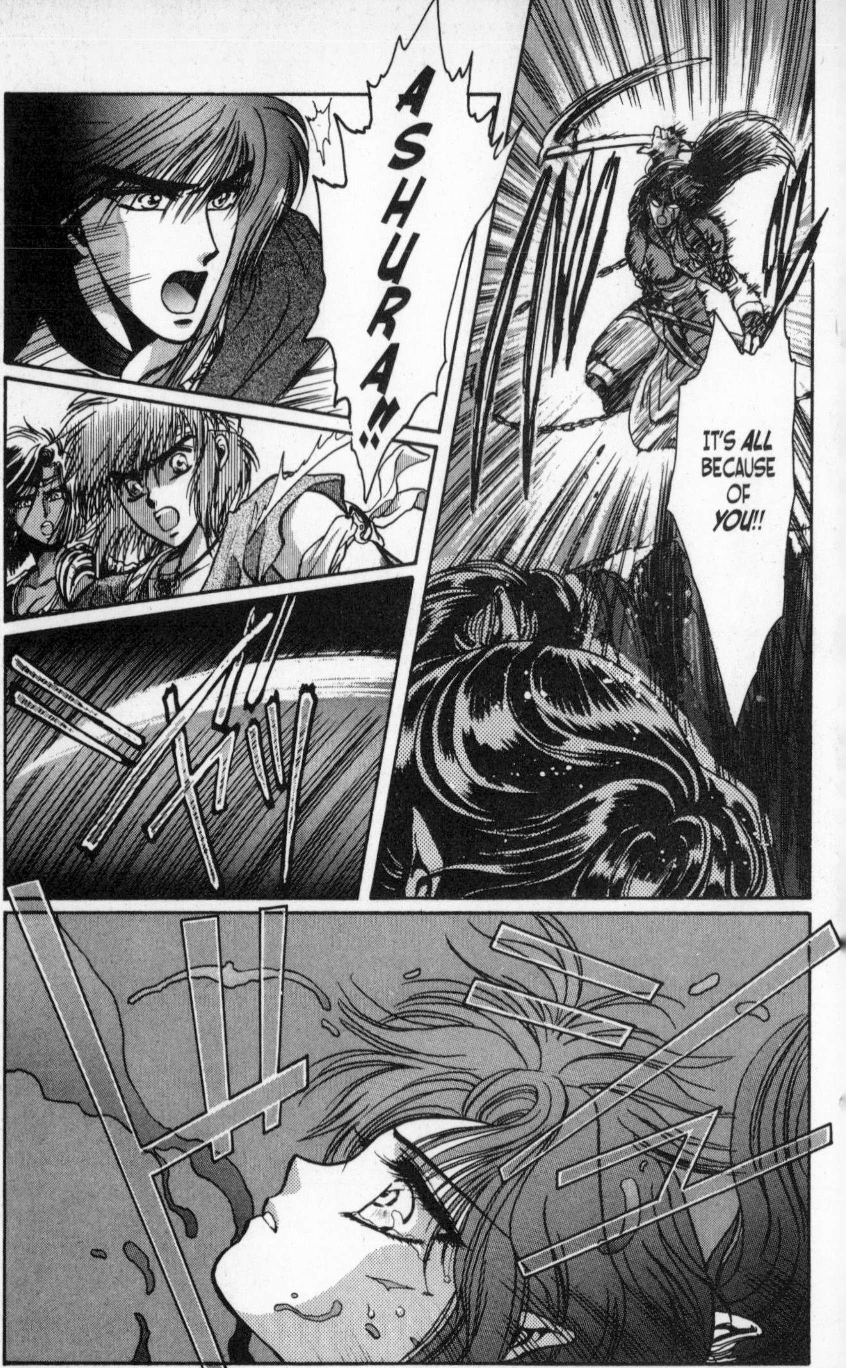
IT'S ALL BECAUSE OF YOU!!
ASHURA!!

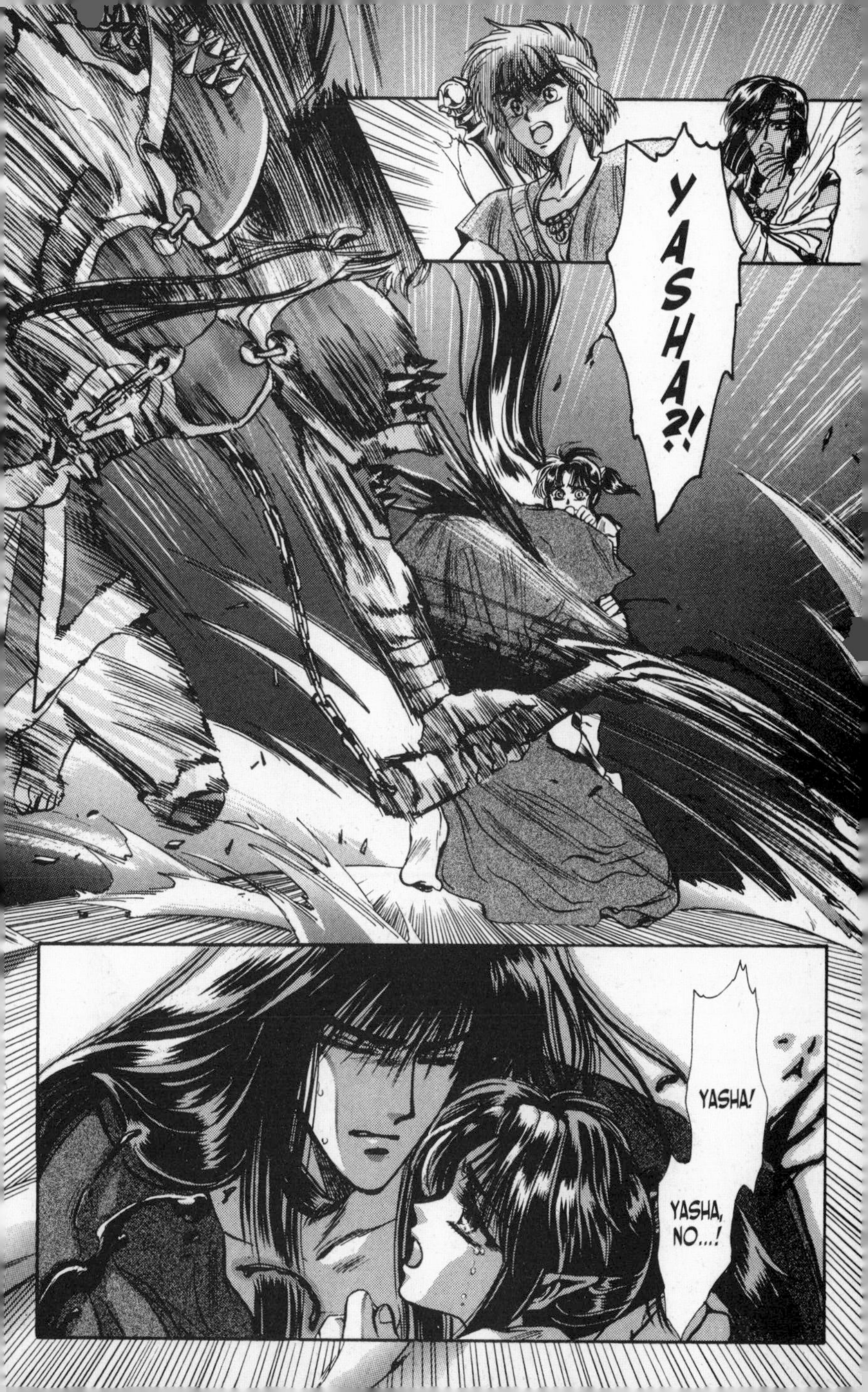
YASHA?!
YASHA!
YASHA, NO...!

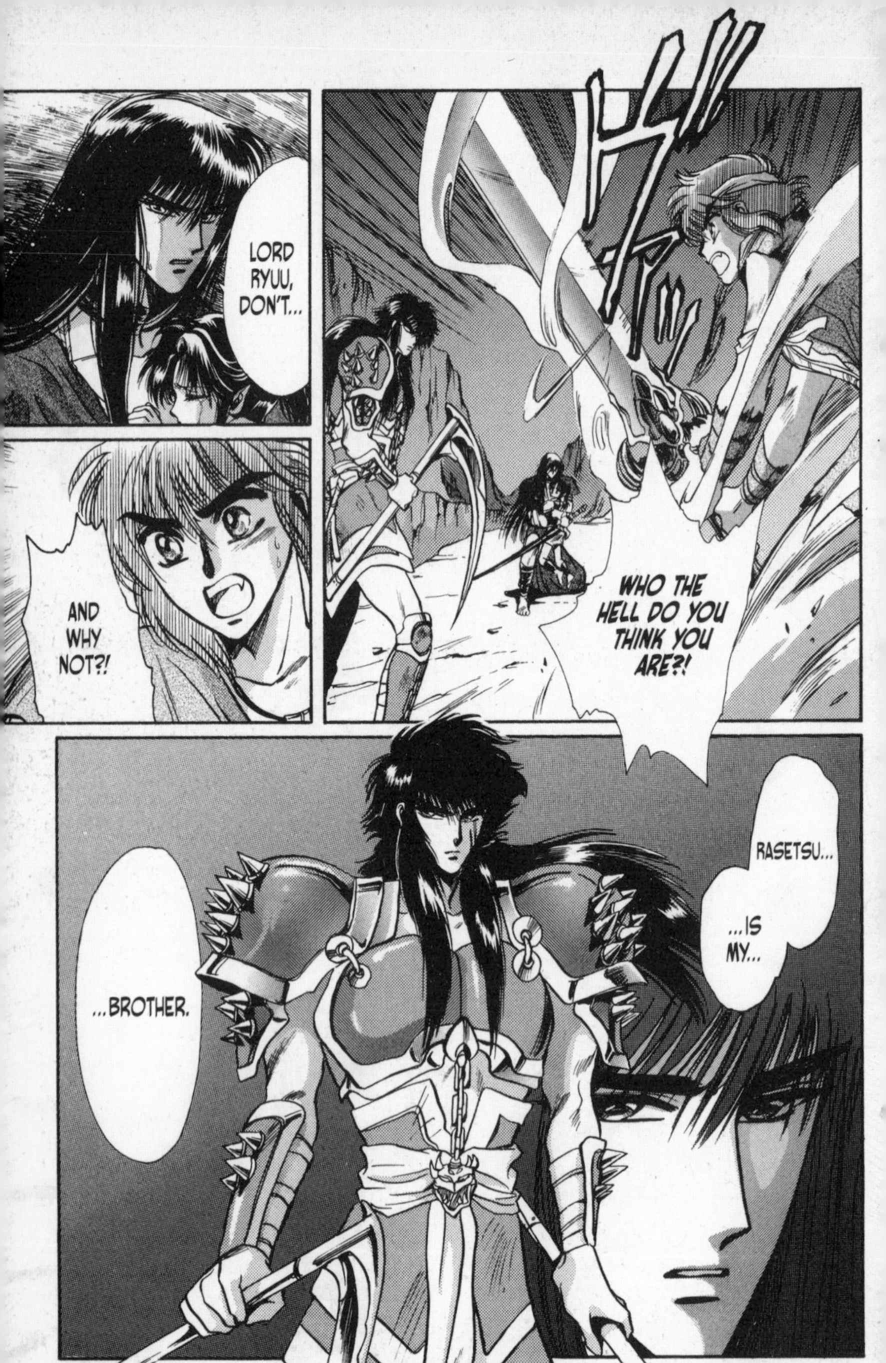
WHO THE HELL DO YOU THINK YOU ARE?!
LORD RYUU, DON'T...
AND WHY NOT?!
RASETSU...
...IS MY...
...BROTHER.

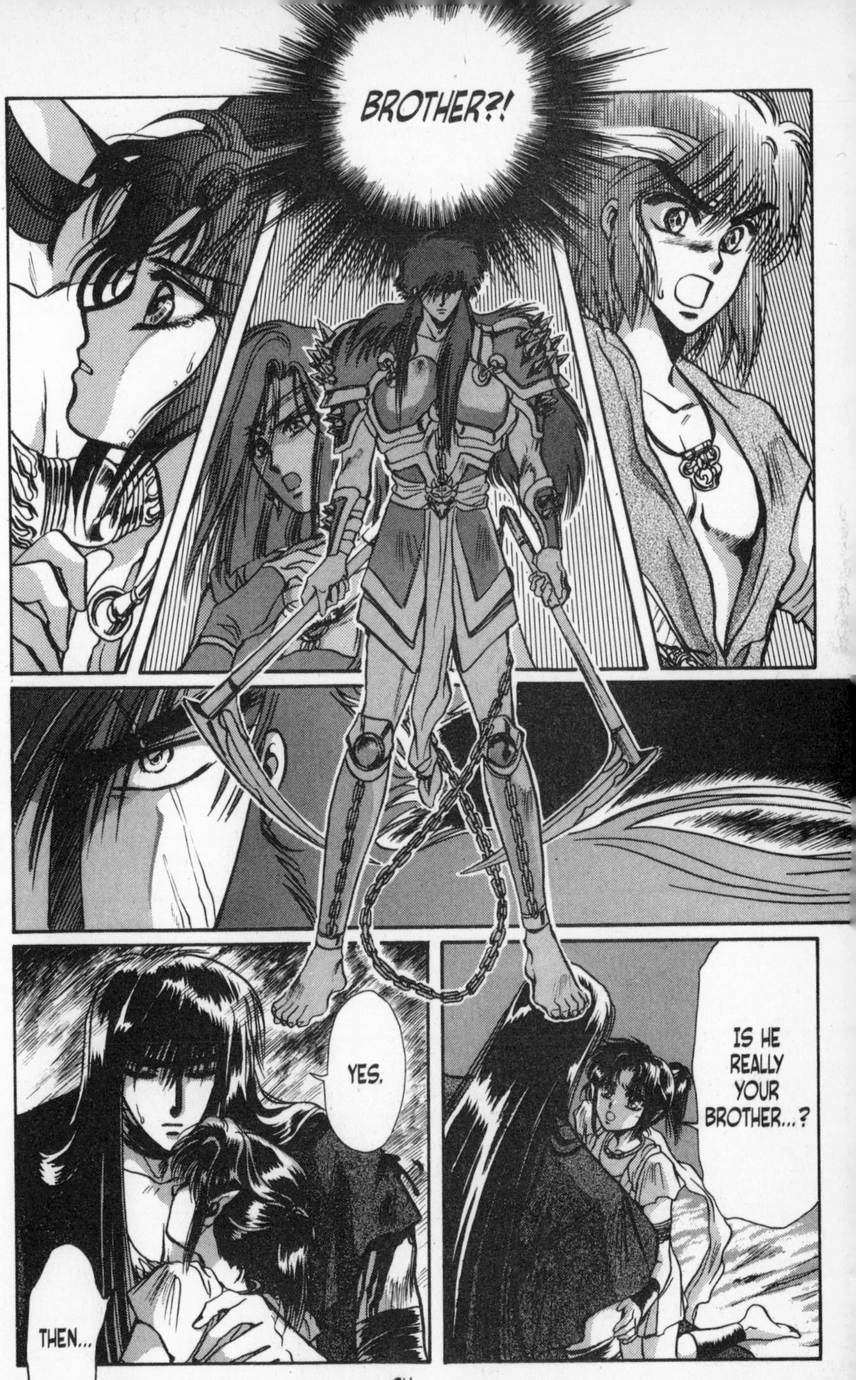
BROTHER?!
IS HE REALLY YOUR BROTHER...?
YES.
THEN...

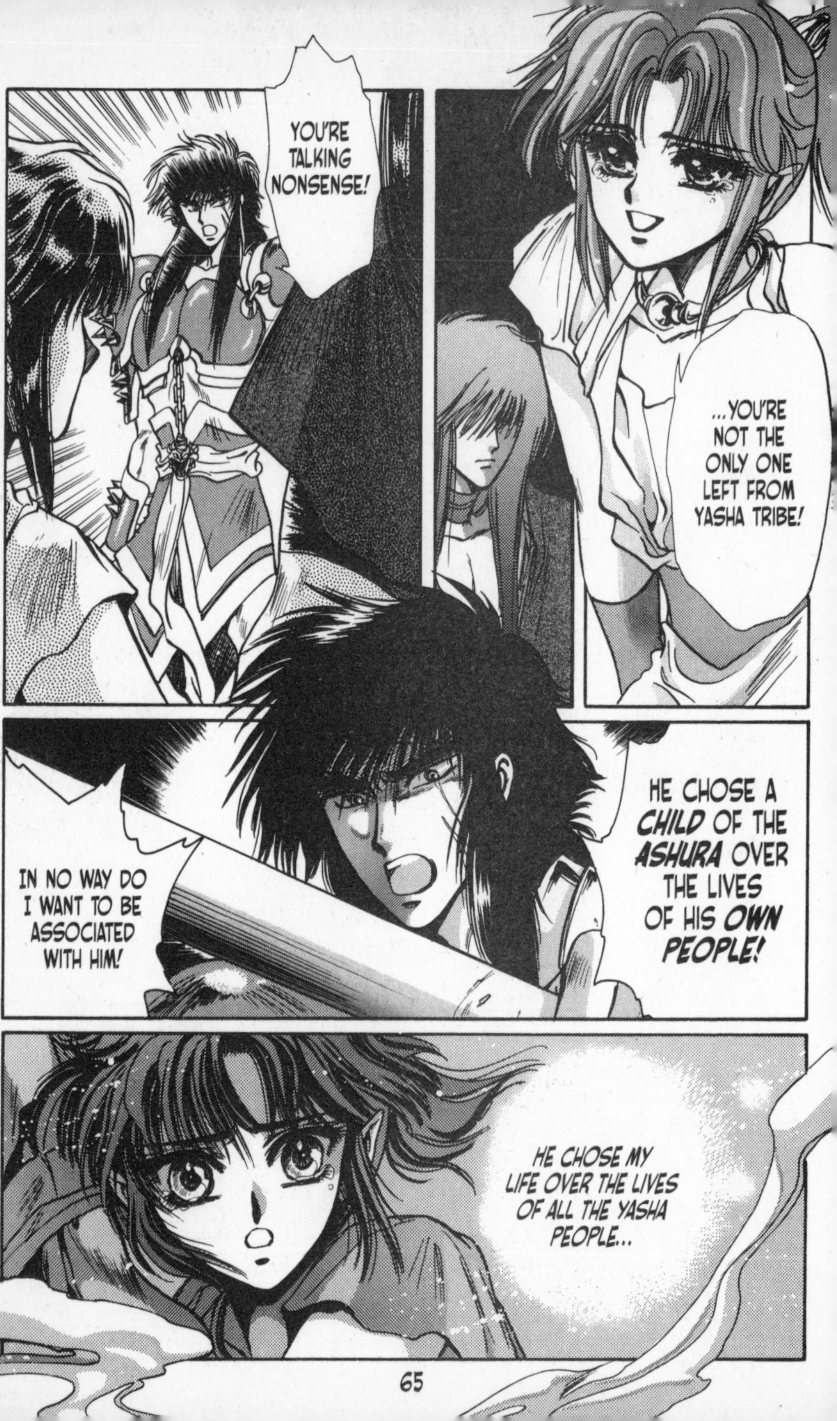
...YOU'RE NOT THE ONLY ONE LEFT FROM YASHA TRIBE!
YOU'RE TALKING NONSENSE!
HE CHOSE A *CHILD* OF THE *ASHURA* OVER THE LIVES OF HIS *OWN PEOPLE!*
IN NO WAY DO I WANT TO BE ASSOCIATED WITH HIM!
*HE CHOSE MY LIFE OVER THE LIVES OF ALL THE YASHA PEOPLE...*

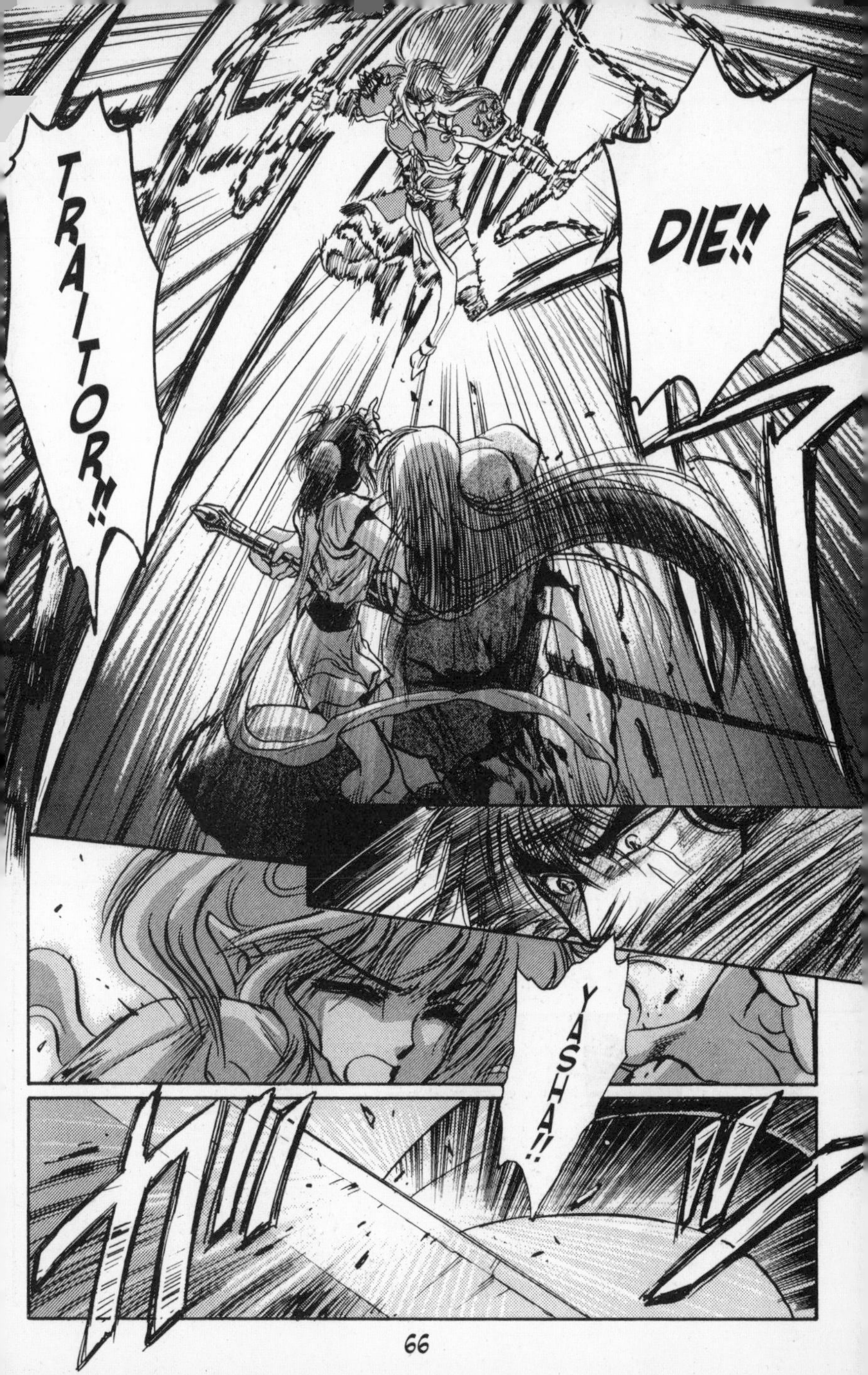
DIE!!
TRAITOR!!
YASHA!!

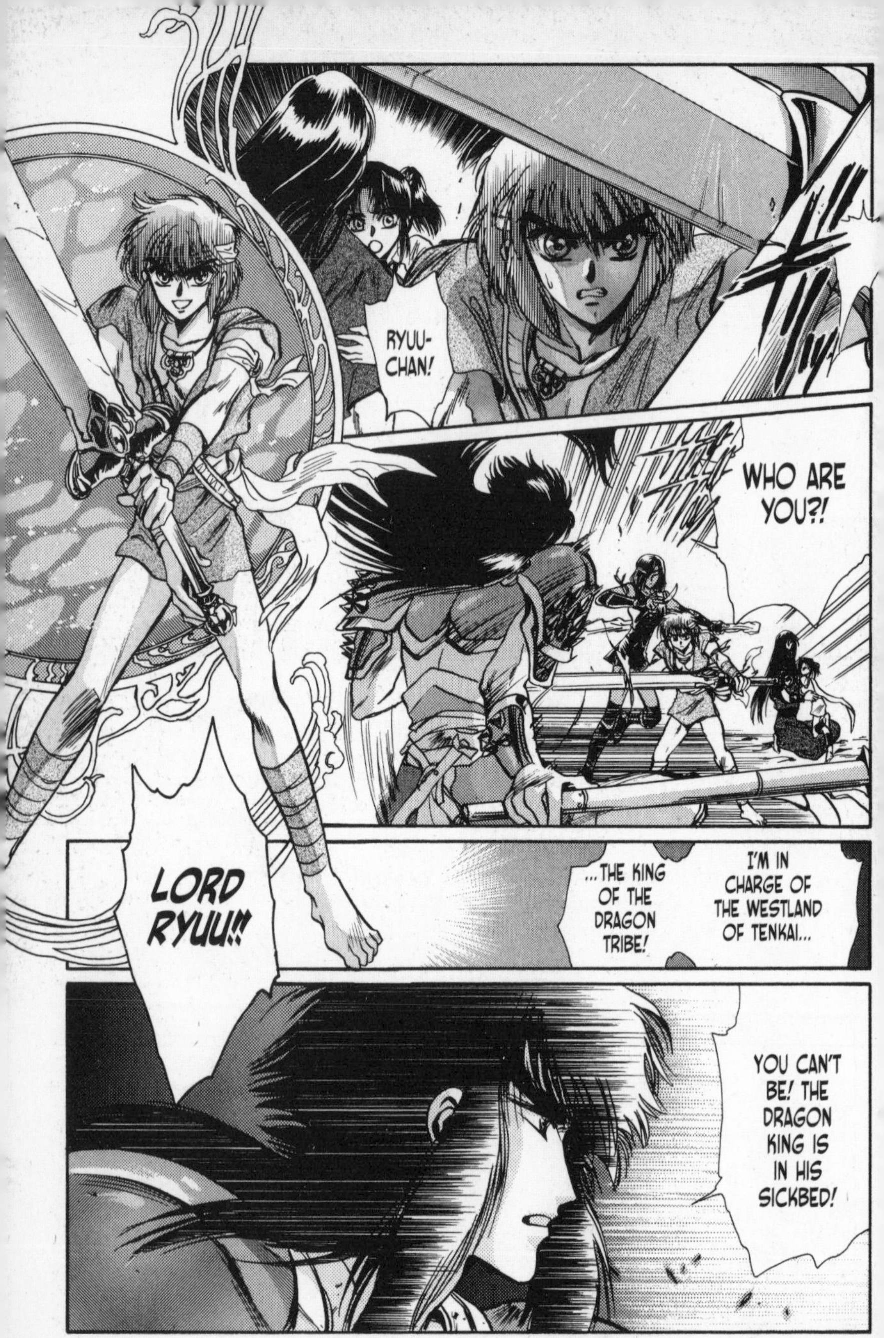
RYUU-CHAN!
WHO ARE YOU?!
I'M IN CHARGE OF THE WESTLAND OF TENKAI...
...THE KING OF THE DRAGON TRIBE!
LORD RYUU!!
YOU CAN'T BE! THE DRAGON KING IS IN HIS SICKBED!

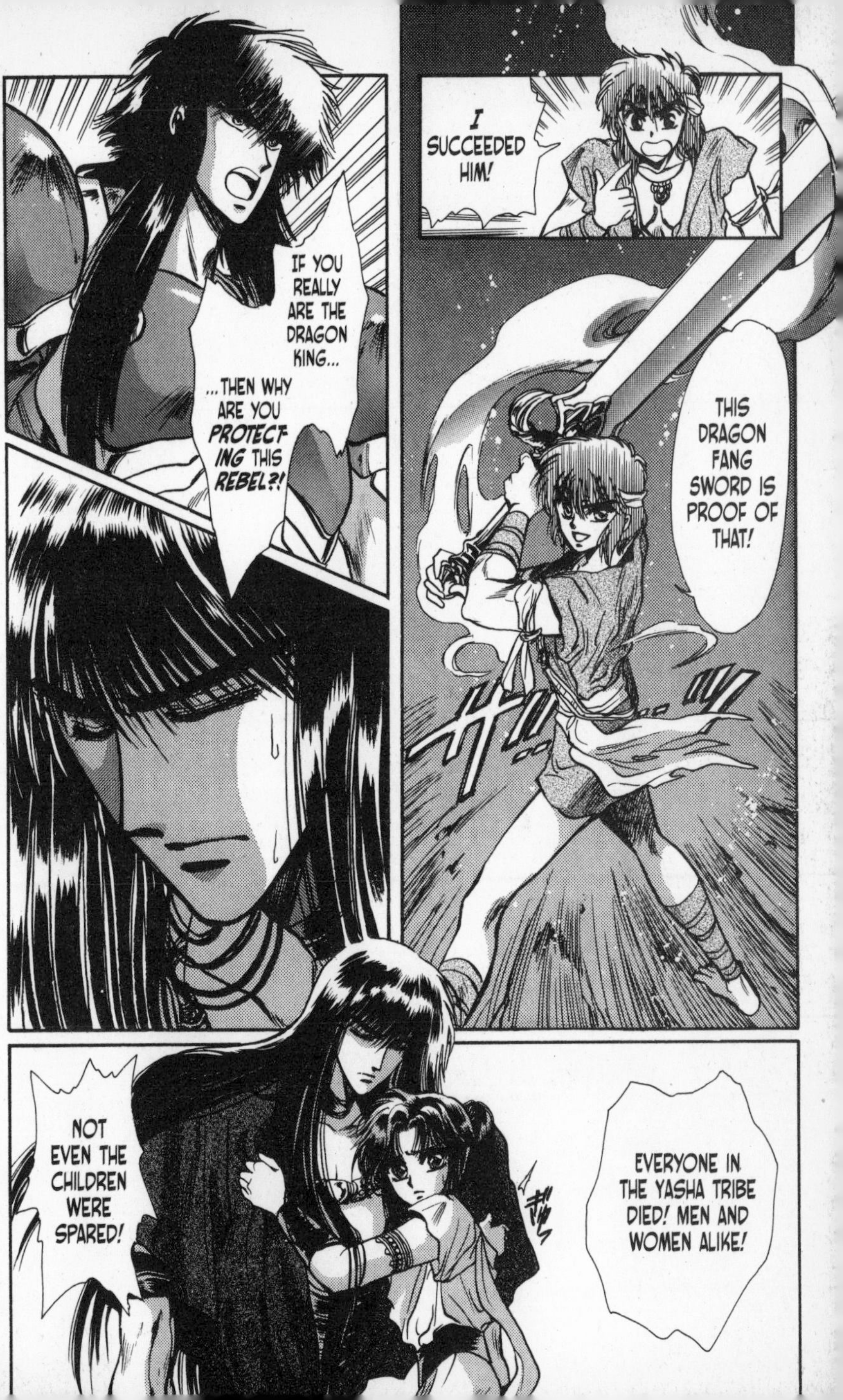
I SUCCEEDED HIM!
THIS DRAGON FANG SWORD IS PROOF OF THAT!
IF YOU REALLY ARE THE DRAGON KING...
...THEN WHY ARE YOU PROTECTING THIS REBEL?!
EVERYONE IN THE YASHA TRIBE DIED! MEN AND WOMEN ALIKE!
NOT EVEN THE CHILDREN WERE SPARED!

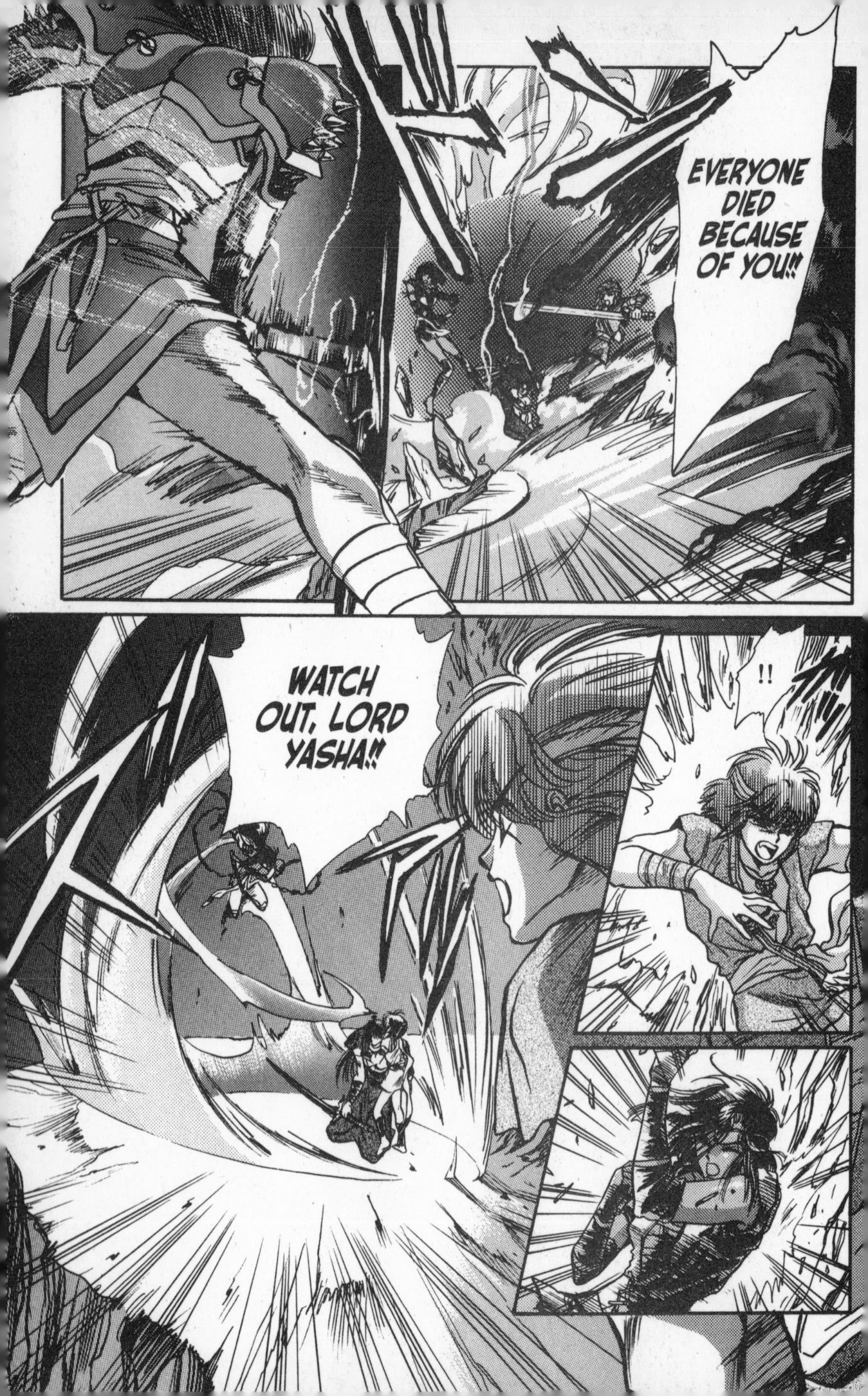
EVERYONE DIED BECAUSE OF YOU!!
!!
WATCH OUT, LORD YASHA!!

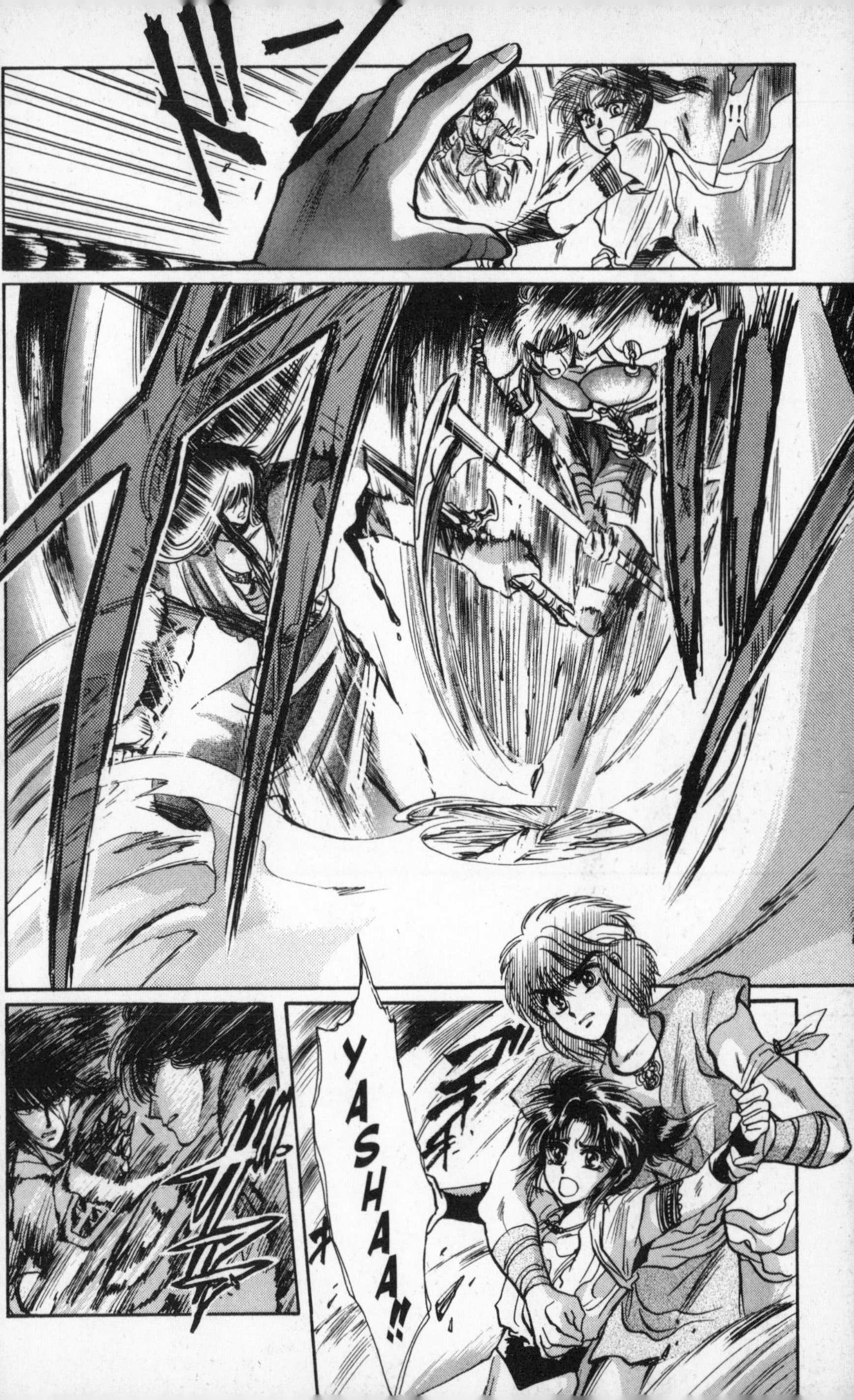

!!
YASHAAA!!

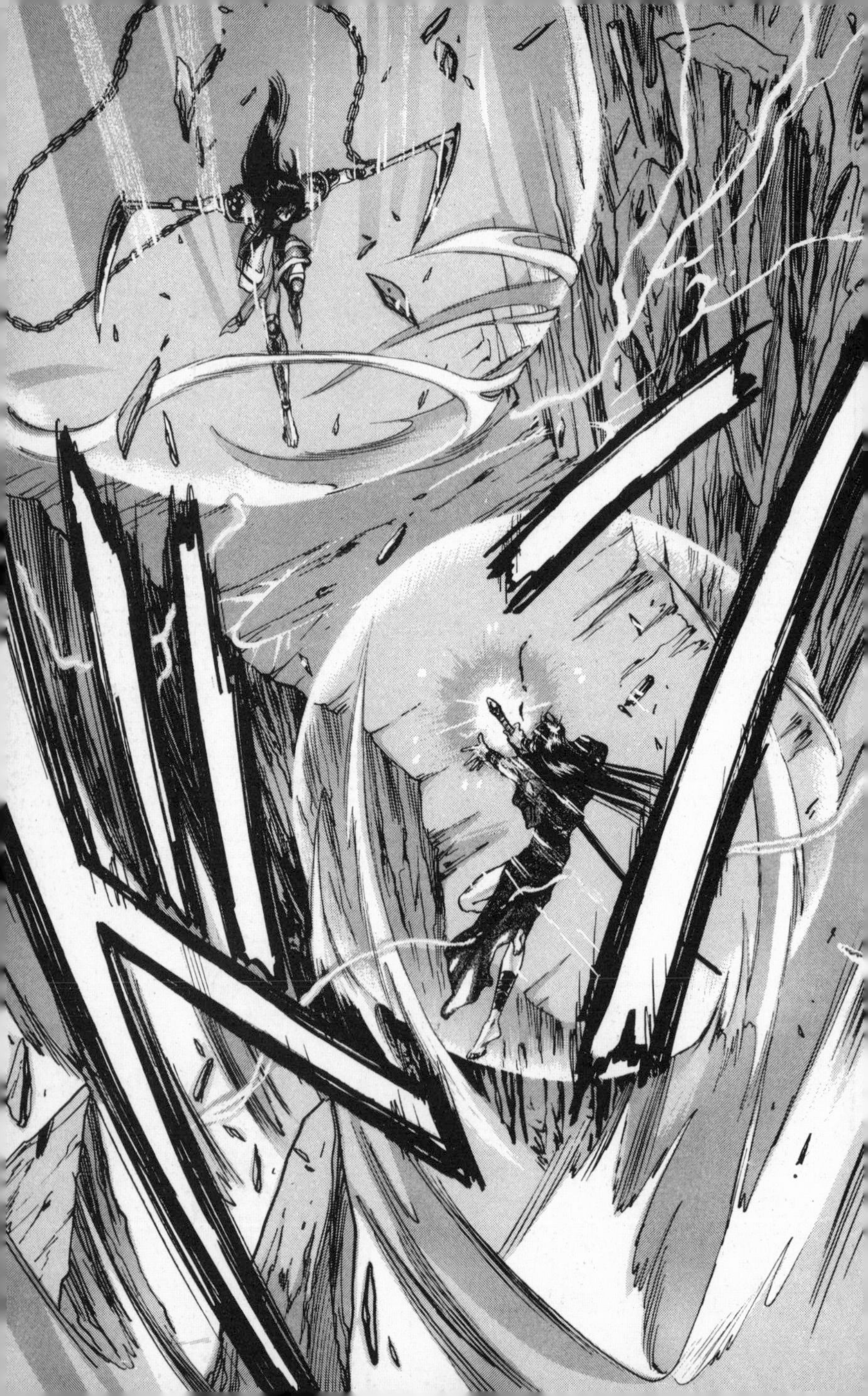

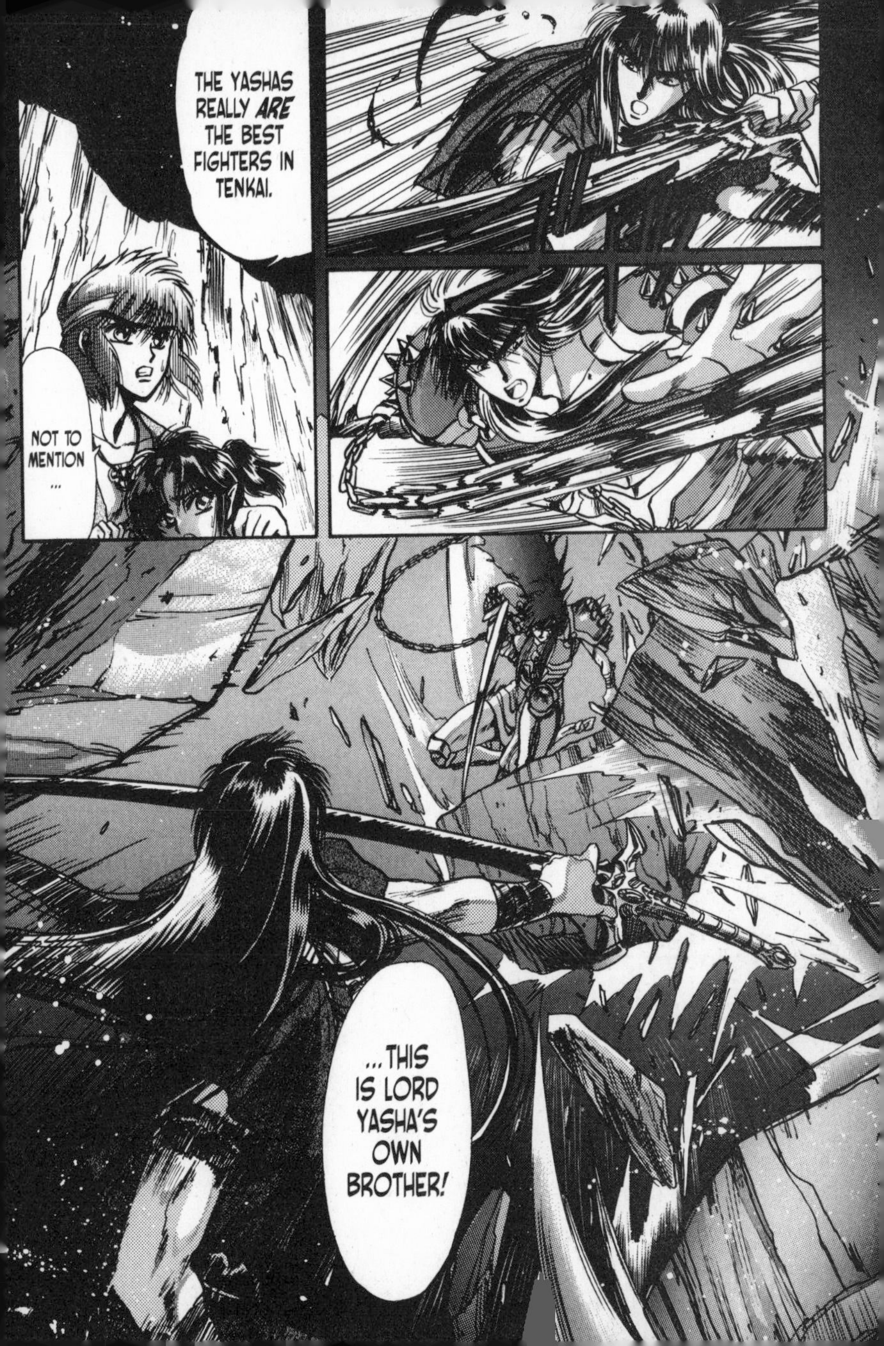
THE YASHAS REALLY *ARE* THE BEST FIGHTERS IN TENKAI.
NOT TO MENTION ...
...THIS IS LORD YASHA'S OWN BROTHER!

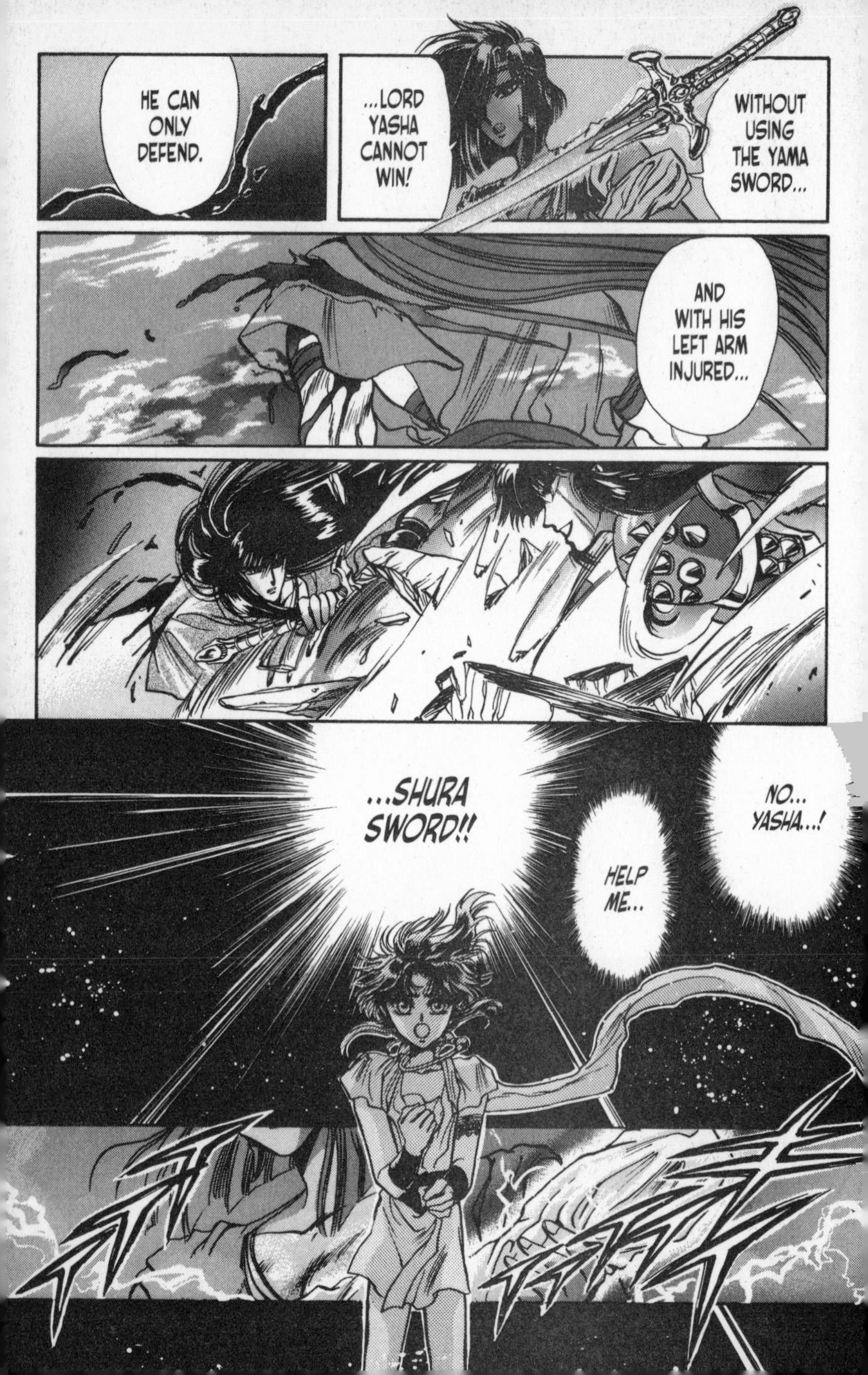
WITHOUT USING THE YAMA SWORD...
...LORD YASHA CANNOT WIN!
HE CAN ONLY DEFEND.
AND WITH HIS LEFT ARM INJURED...
NO... YASHA...!
HELP ME...
...SHURA SWORD!!

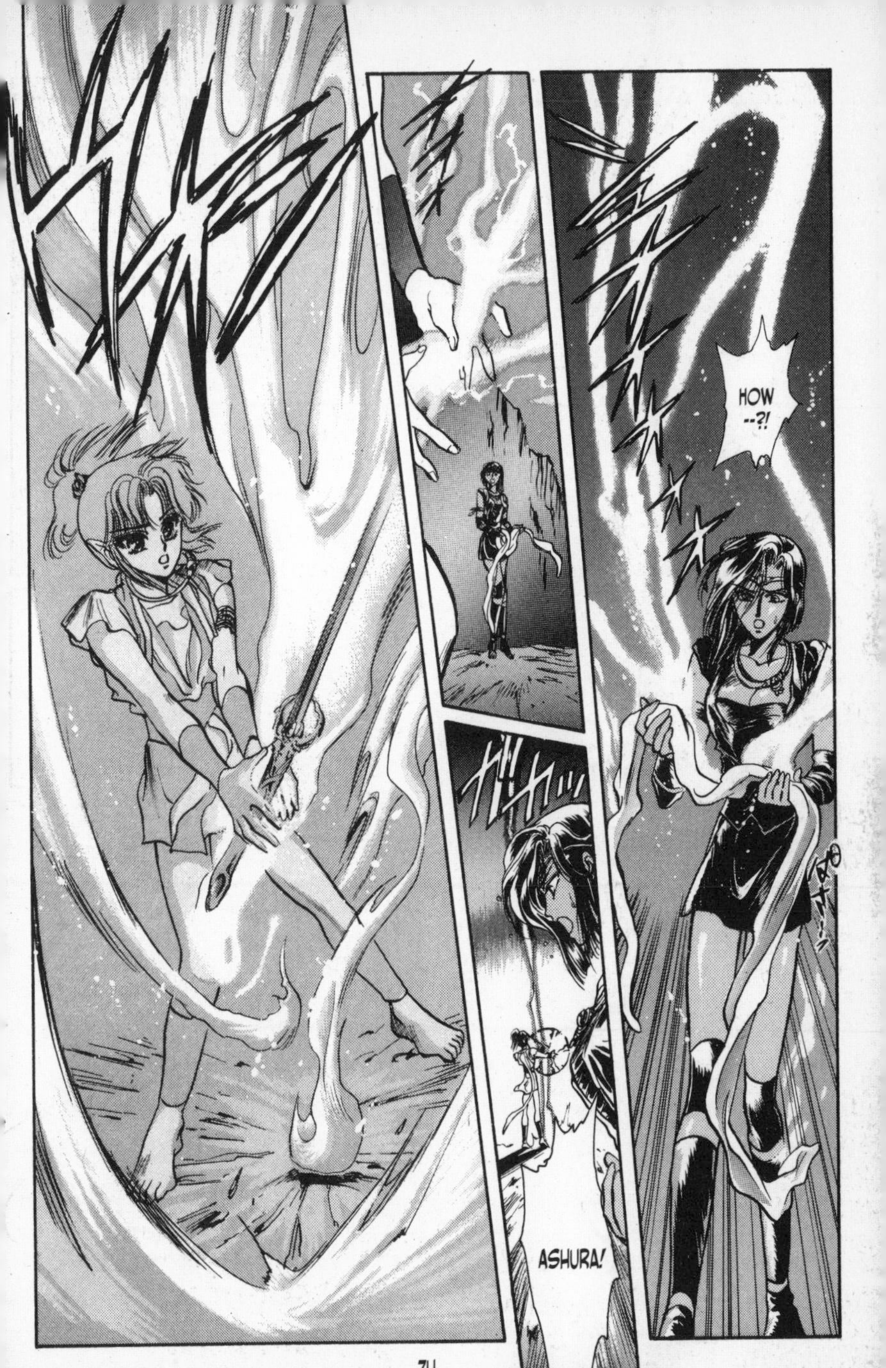
HOW --?!
ASHURA!

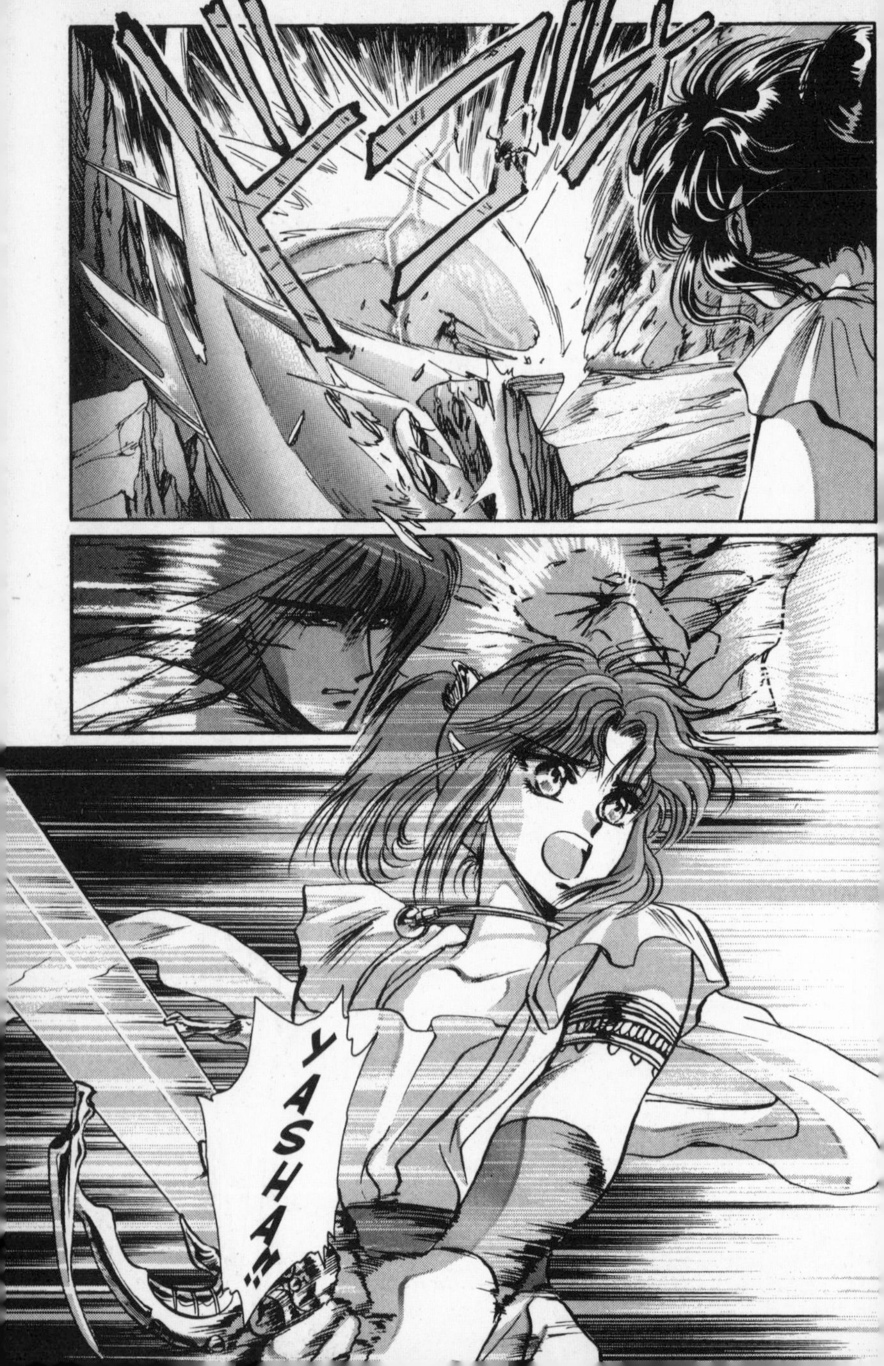
YASHA!!

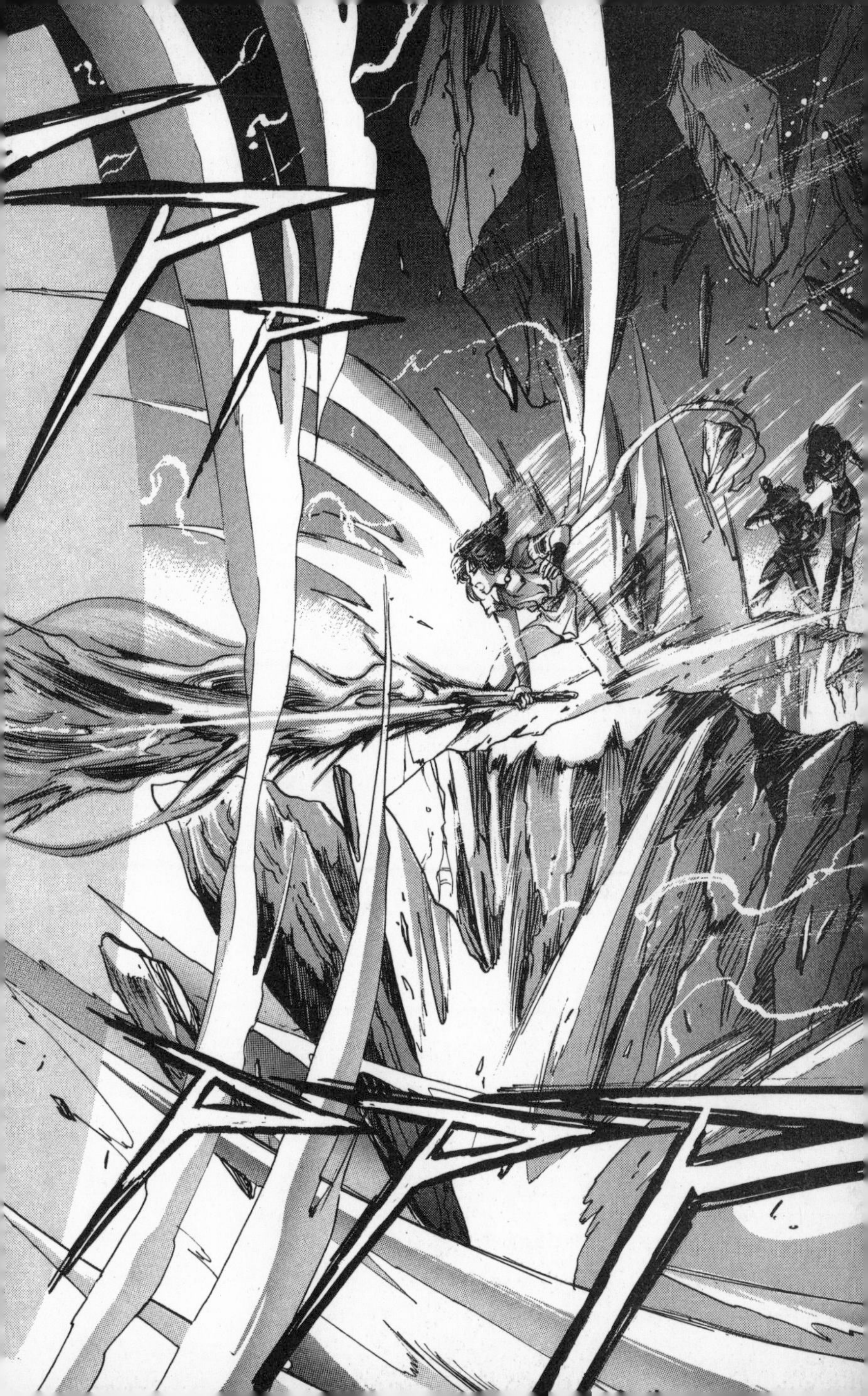

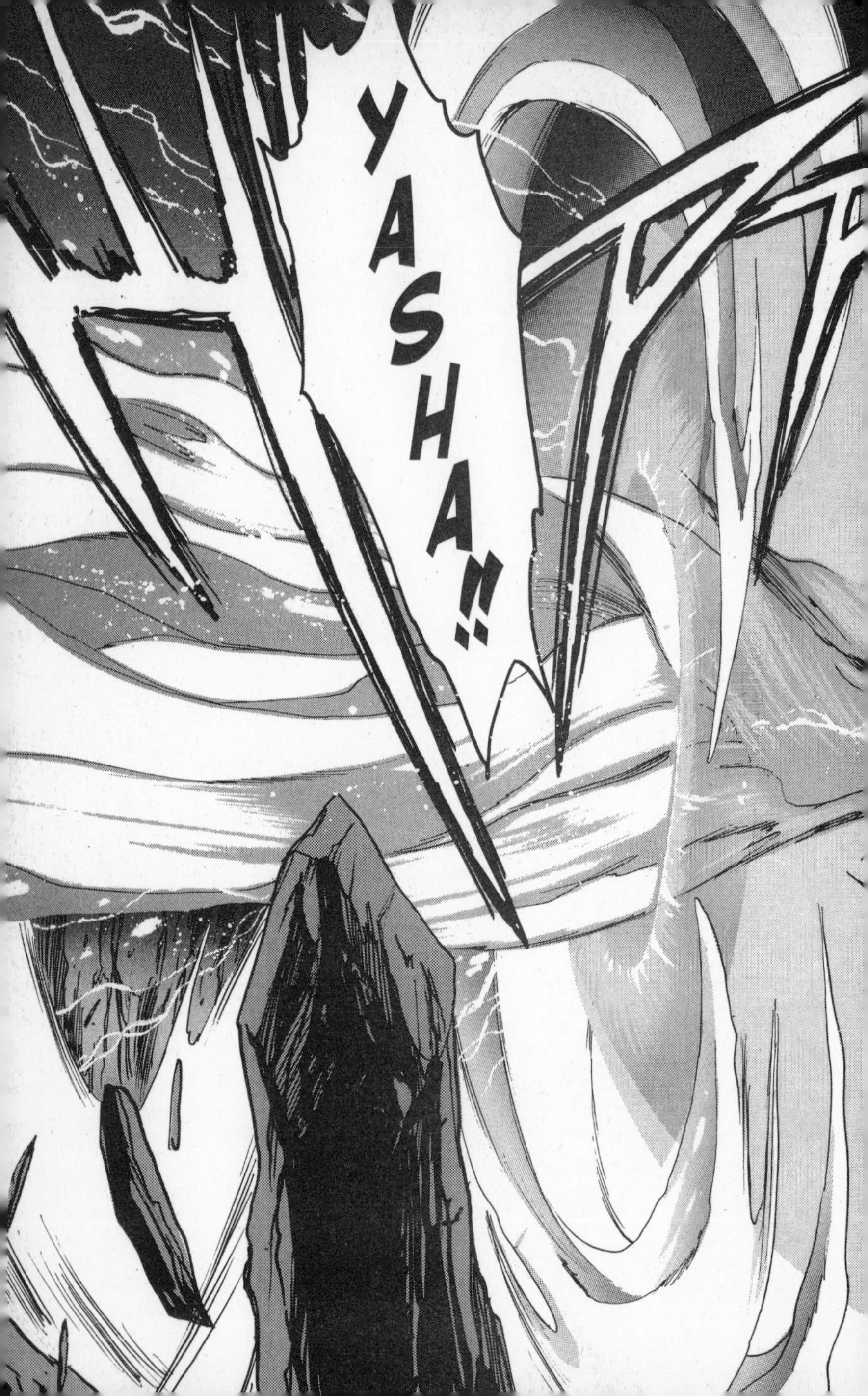
YASHA!!

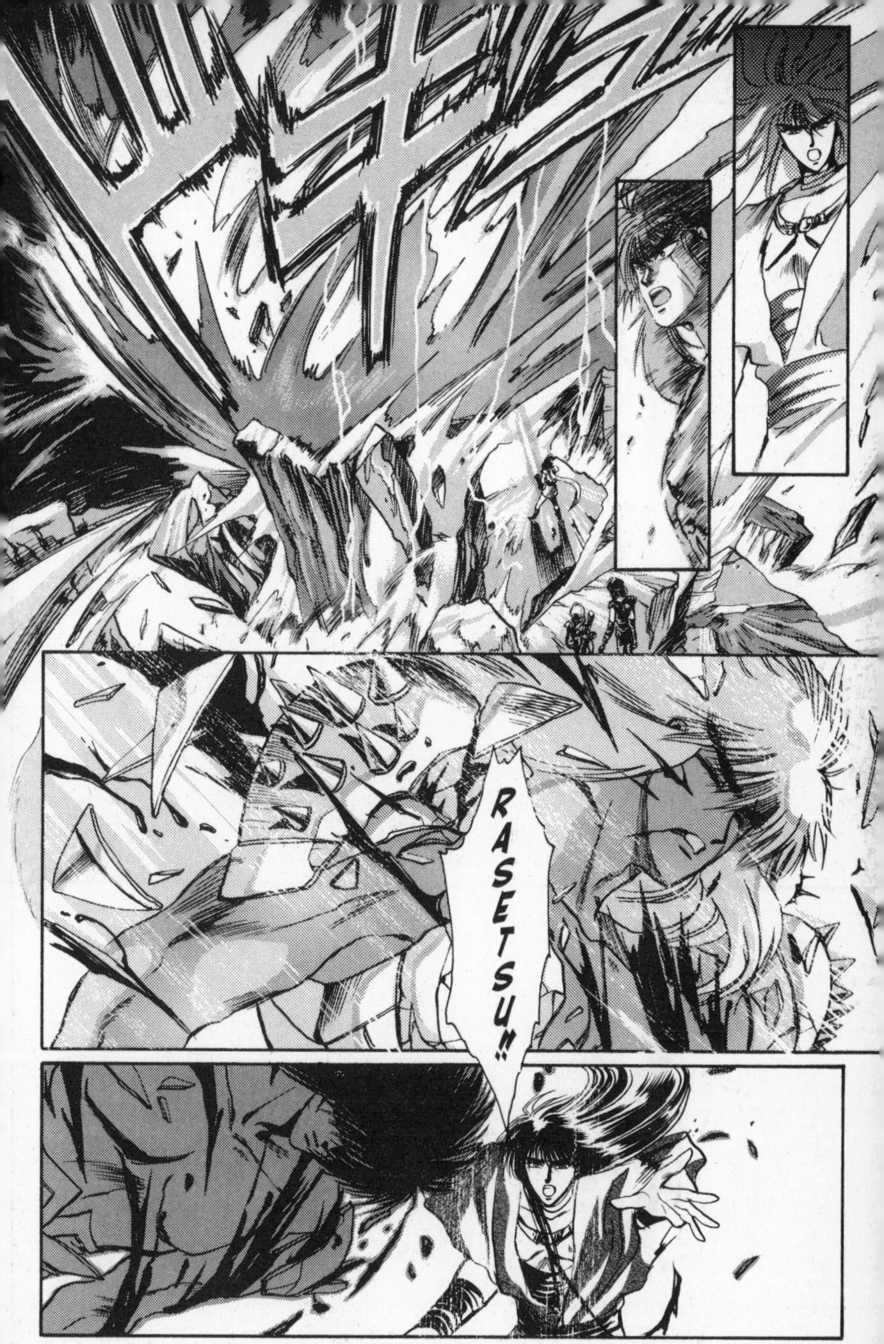
RASETSU!!

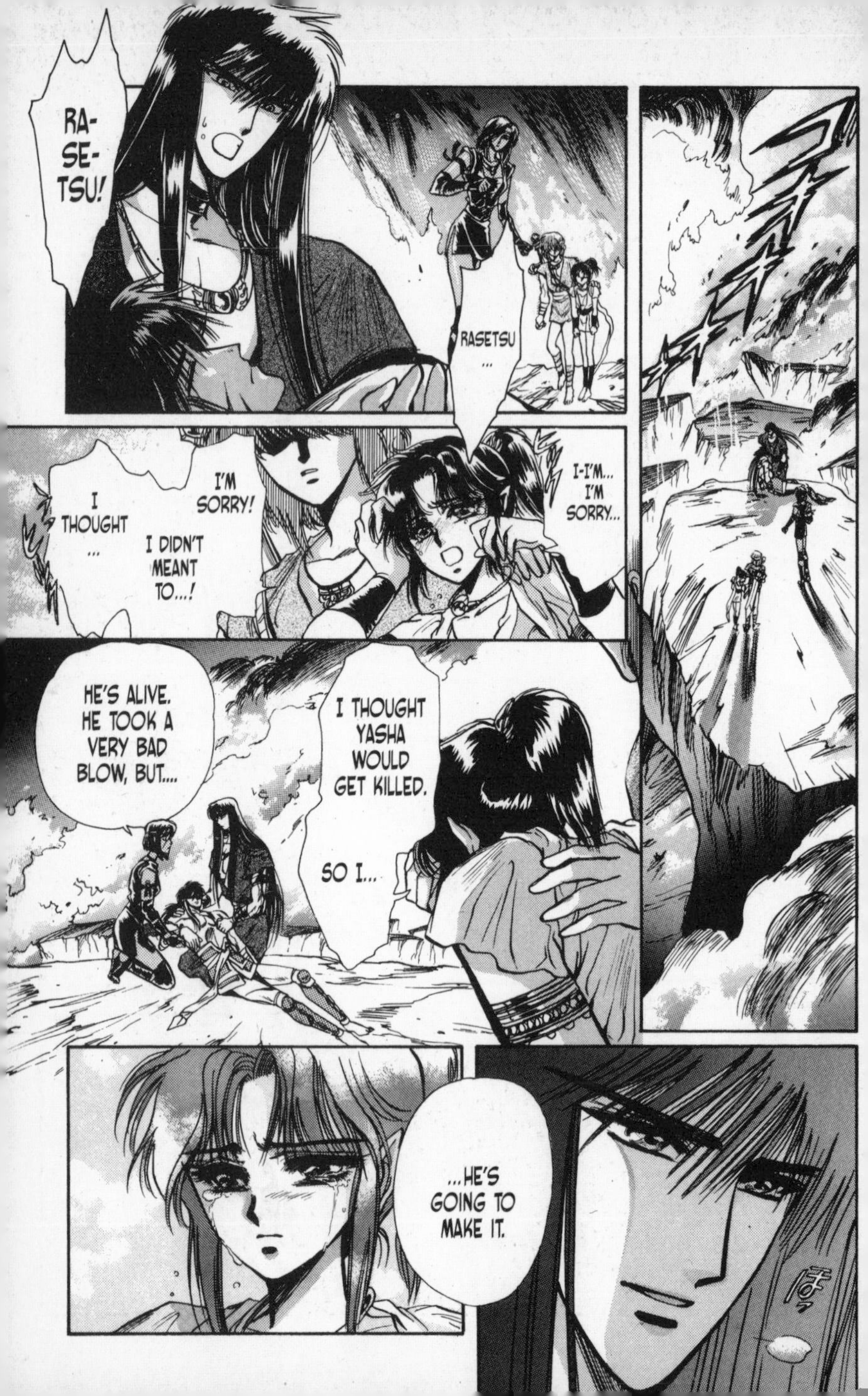
RA-SE-TSU!
RASETSU ...
I-I'M... I'M SORRY...
I'M SORRY!
I DIDN'T MEANT TO...!
I THOUGHT ...
I THOUGHT YASHA WOULD GET KILLED.
SO I...
HE'S ALIVE. HE TOOK A VERY BAD BLOW, BUT....
...HE'S GOING TO MAKE IT.
ほっ

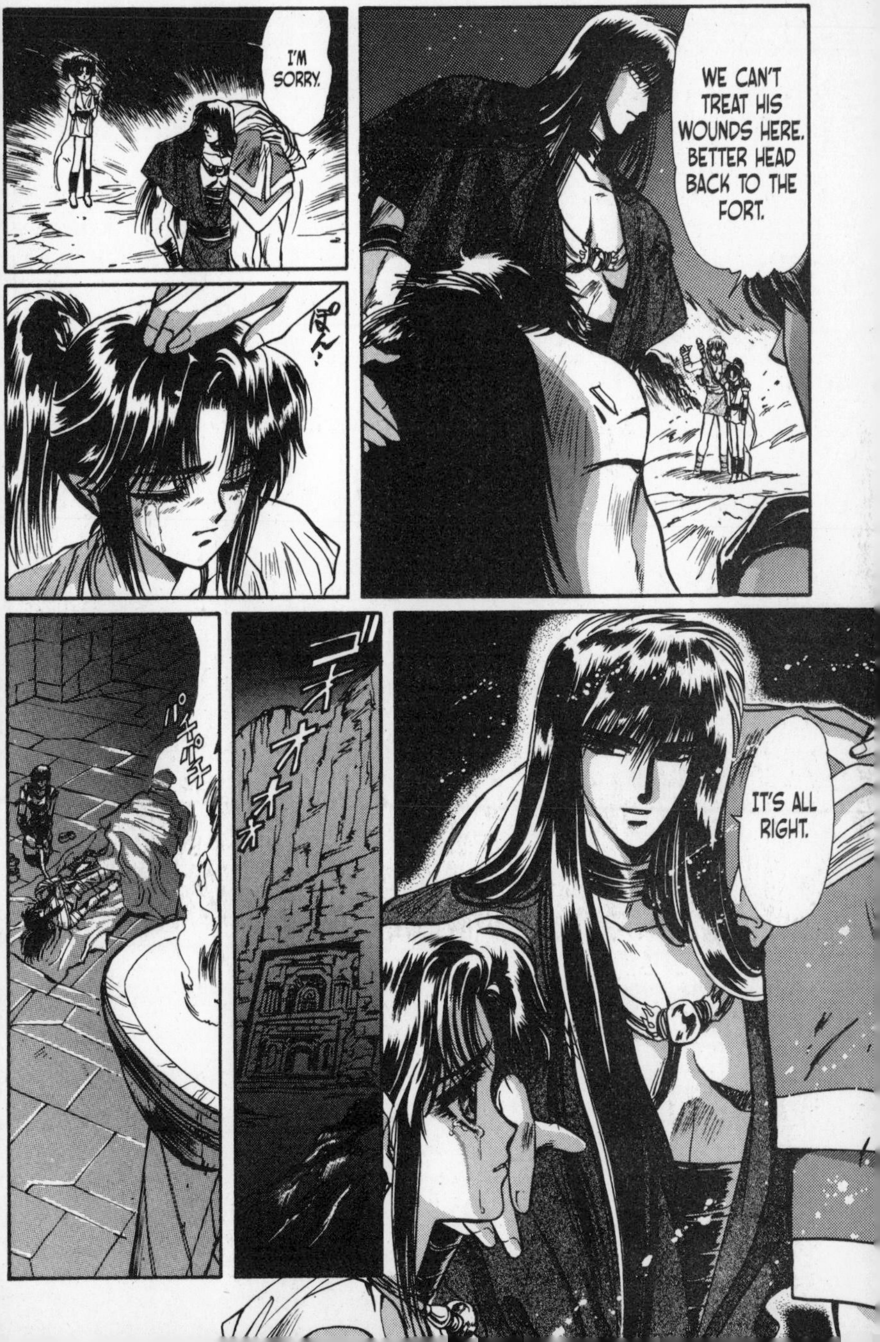
WE CAN'T TREAT HIS WOUNDS HERE. BETTER HEAD BACK TO THE FORT.
I'M SORRY.
ぽん
IT'S ALL RIGHT.
ゴオオオオ
パチパチ

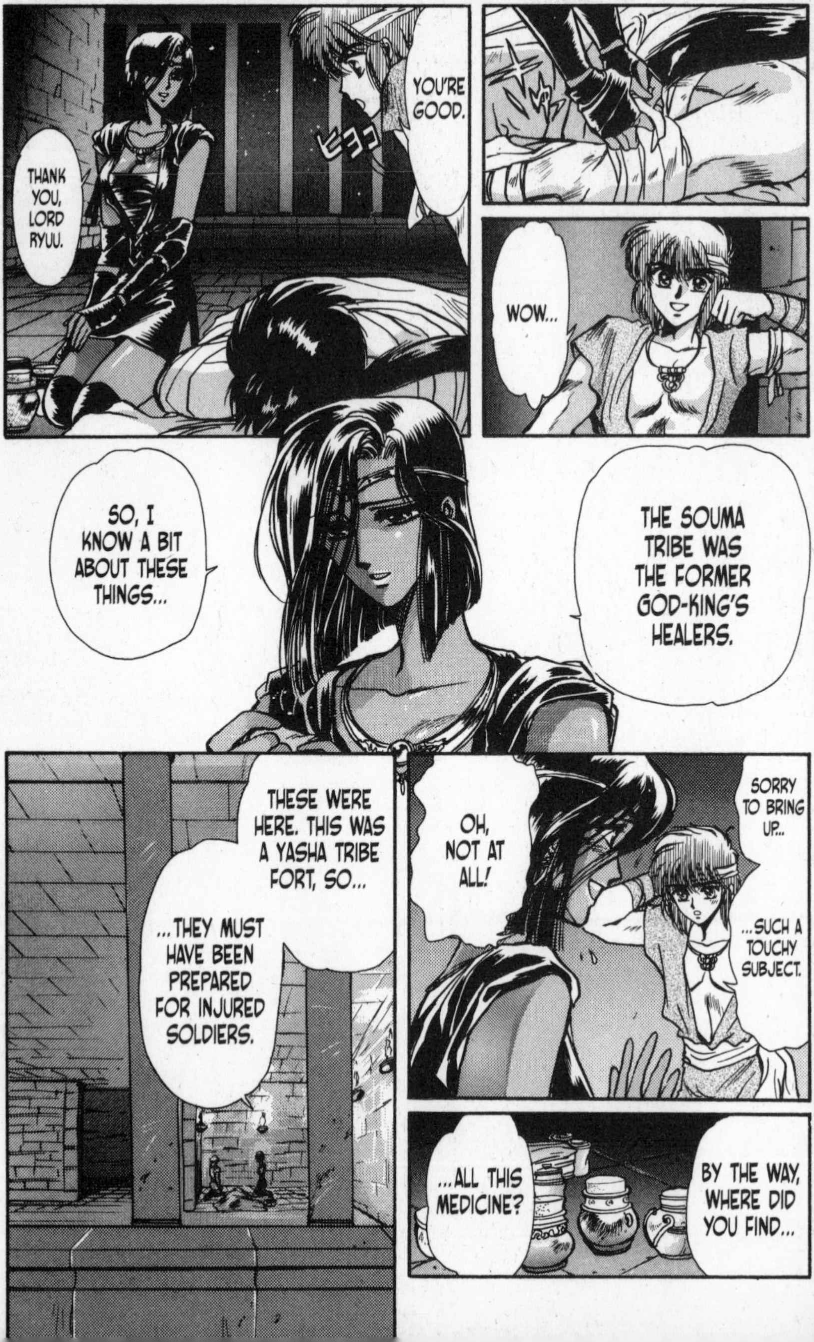
WOW...
YOU'RE GOOD.
THANK YOU, LORD RYUU.
THE SOUMA TRIBE WAS THE FORMER GOD-KING'S HEALERS.
SO, I KNOW A BIT ABOUT THESE THINGS...
SORRY TO BRING UP...
OH, NOT AT ALL!
...SUCH A TOUCHY SUBJECT.
BY THE WAY, WHERE DID YOU FIND...
...ALL THIS MEDICINE?
THESE WERE HERE. THIS WAS A YASHA TRIBE FORT, SO...
...THEY MUST HAVE BEEN PREPARED FOR INJURED SOLDIERS.

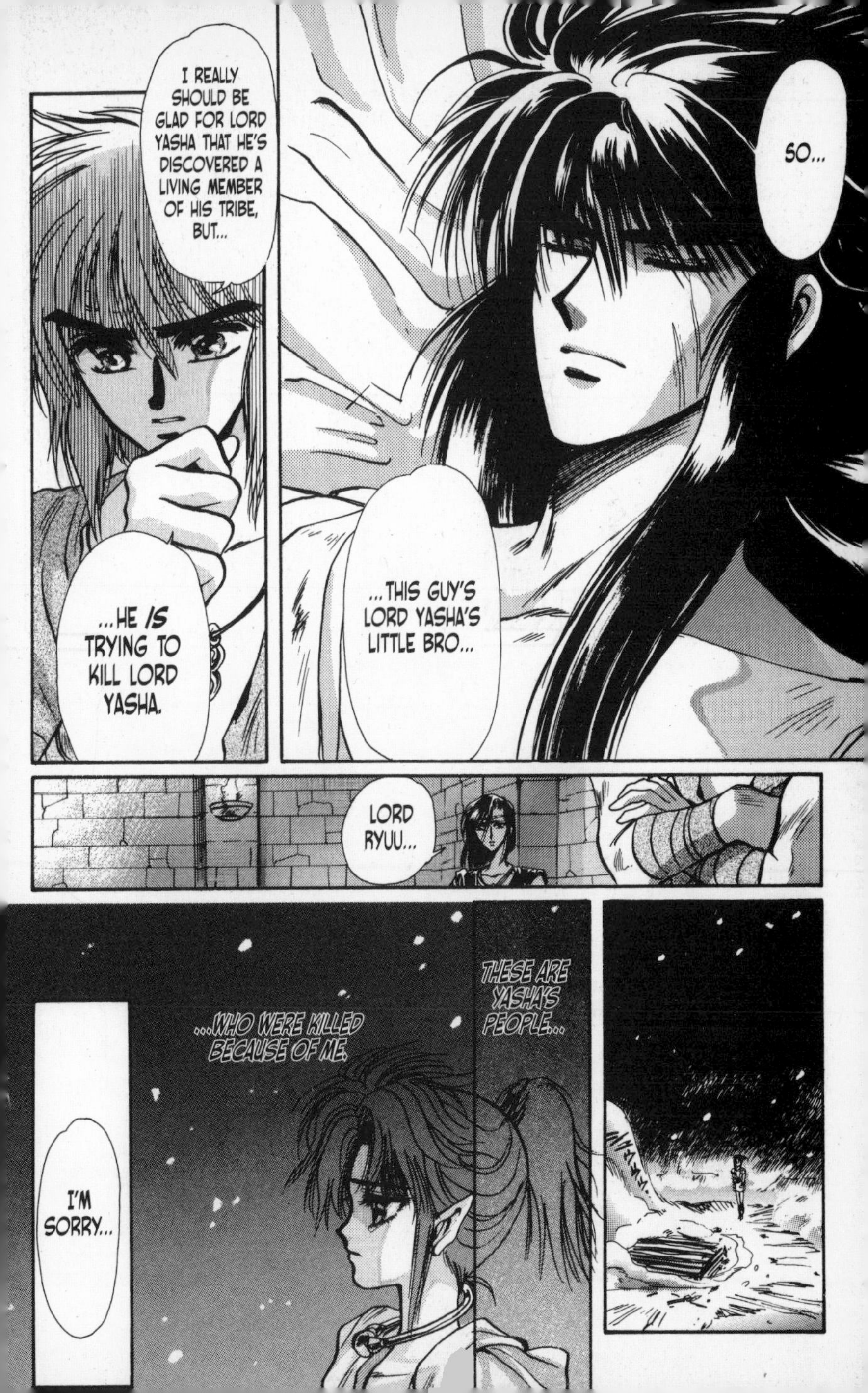
SO...
...THIS GUY'S LORD YASHA'S LITTLE BRO...
I REALLY SHOULD BE GLAD FOR LORD YASHA THAT HE'S DISCOVERED A LIVING MEMBER OF HIS TRIBE, BUT...
...HE *IS* TRYING TO KILL LORD YASHA.
LORD RYUU...
THESE ARE YASHA'S PEOPLE...
...WHO WERE KILLED BECAUSE OF ME.
I'M SORRY...

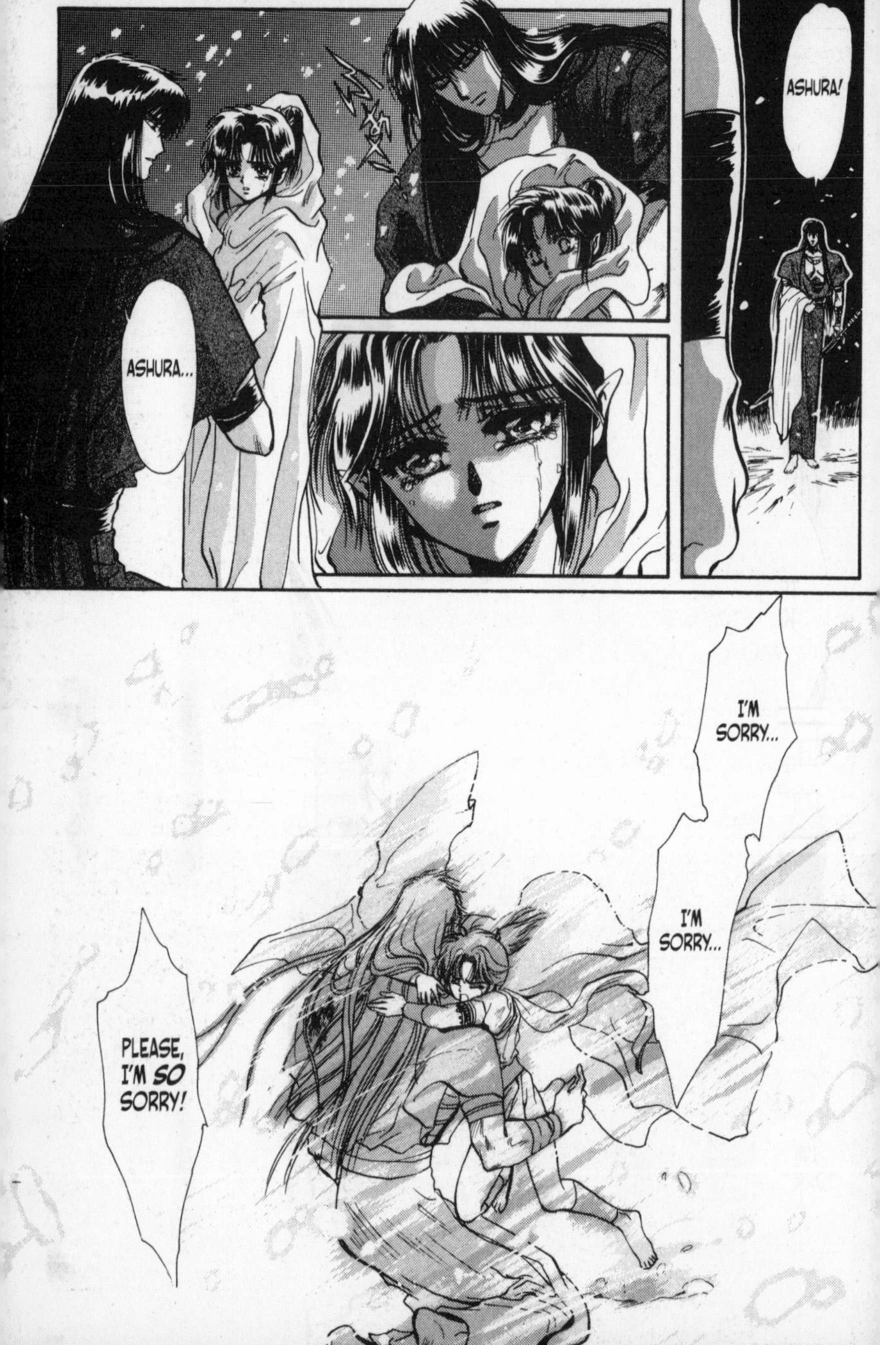
ASHURA!
ASHURA...
I'M SORRY...
I'M SORRY...
PLEASE, I'M SO SORRY!

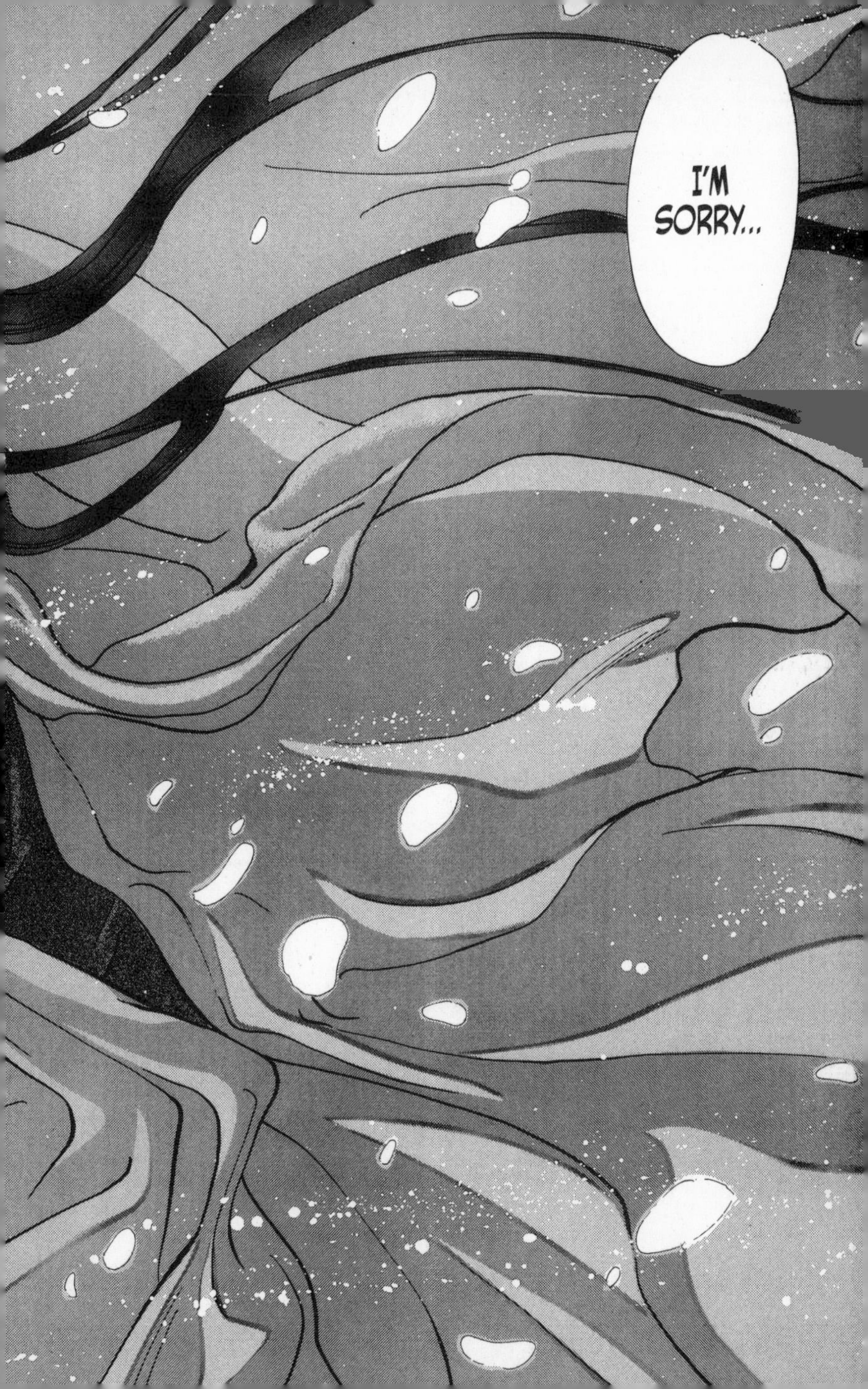
I'M SORRY...

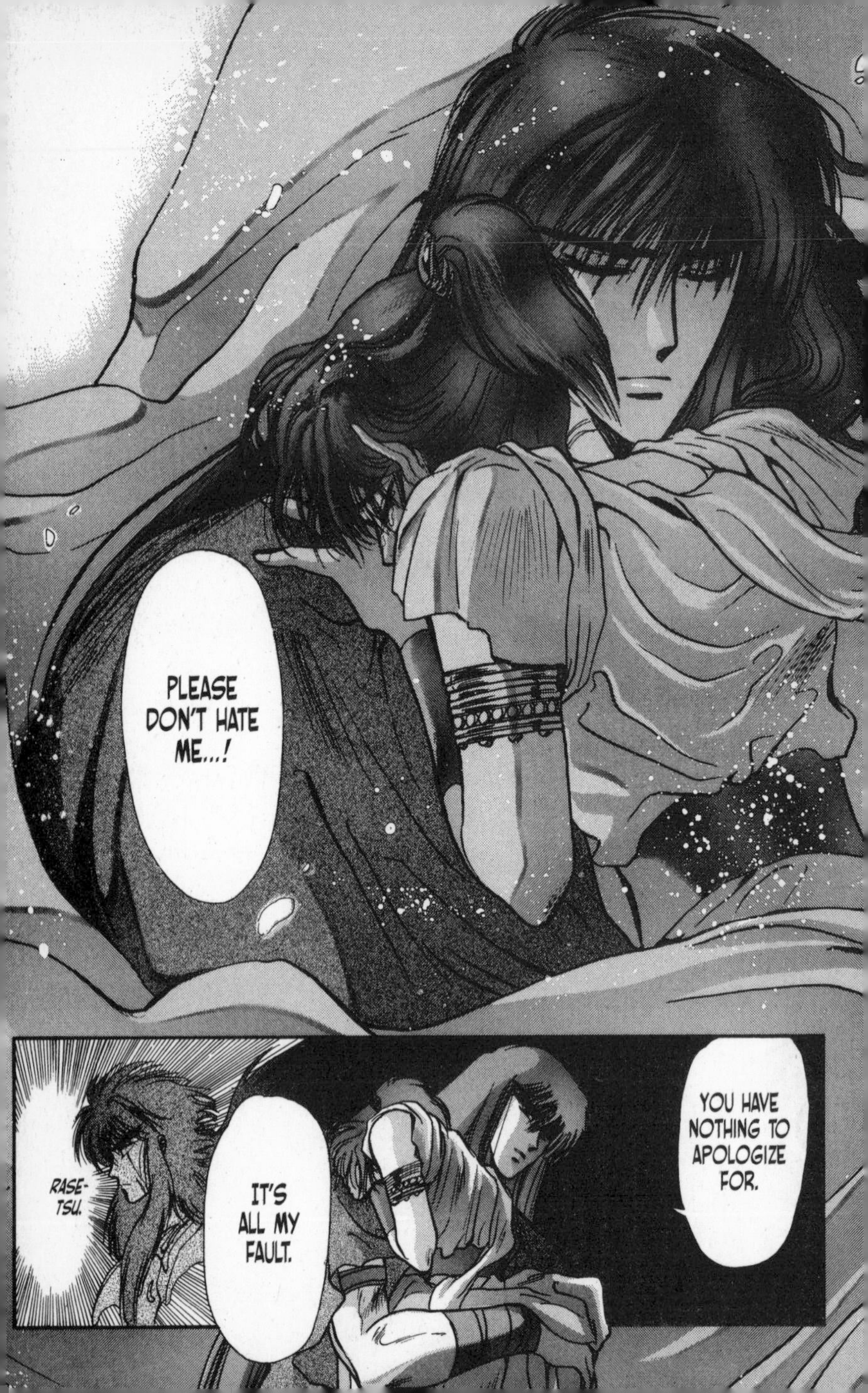
PLEASE DON'T HATE ME...!
YOU HAVE NOTHING TO APOLOGIZE FOR.
IT'S ALL MY FAULT.
RASE-TSU.

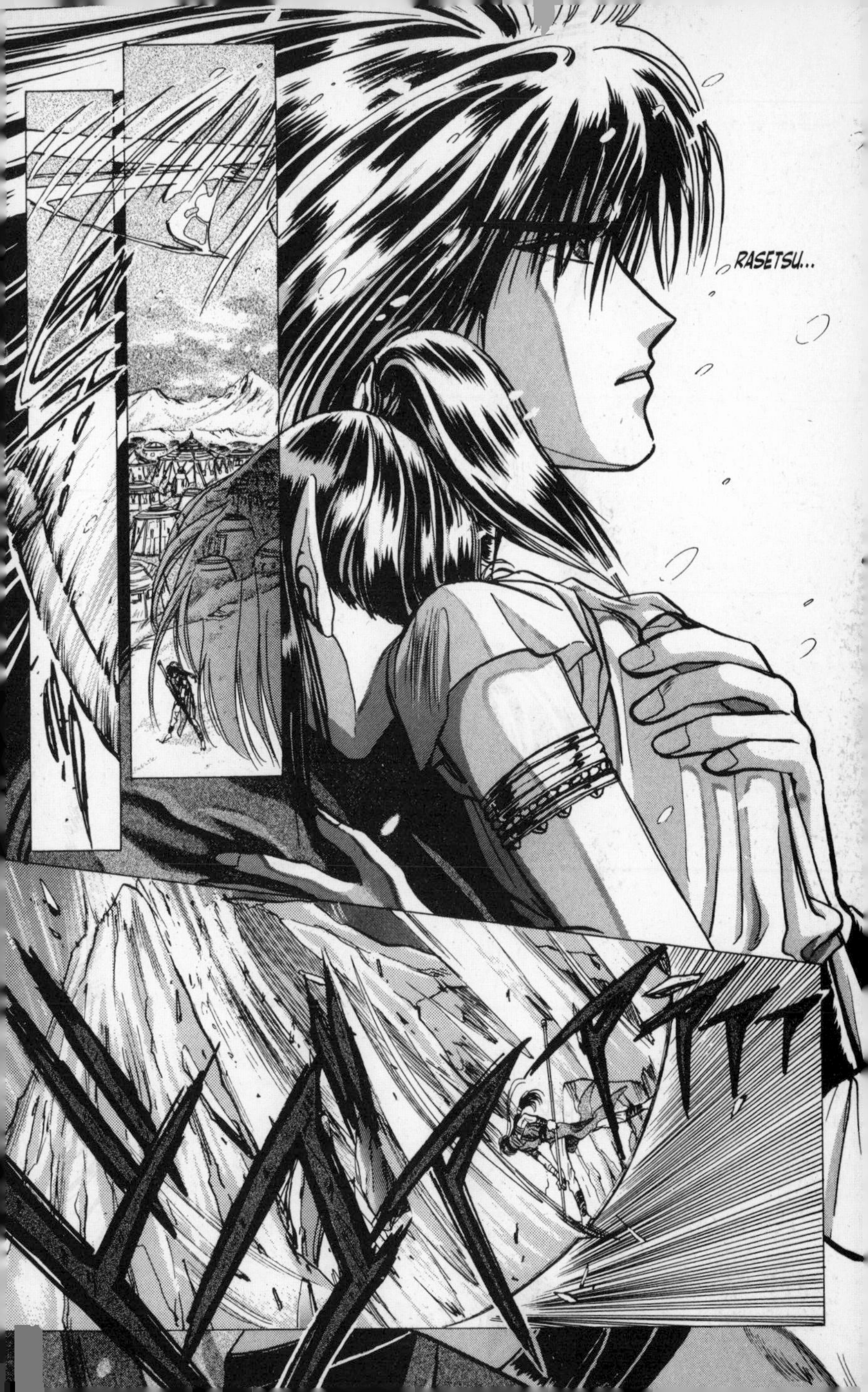
RASETSU...

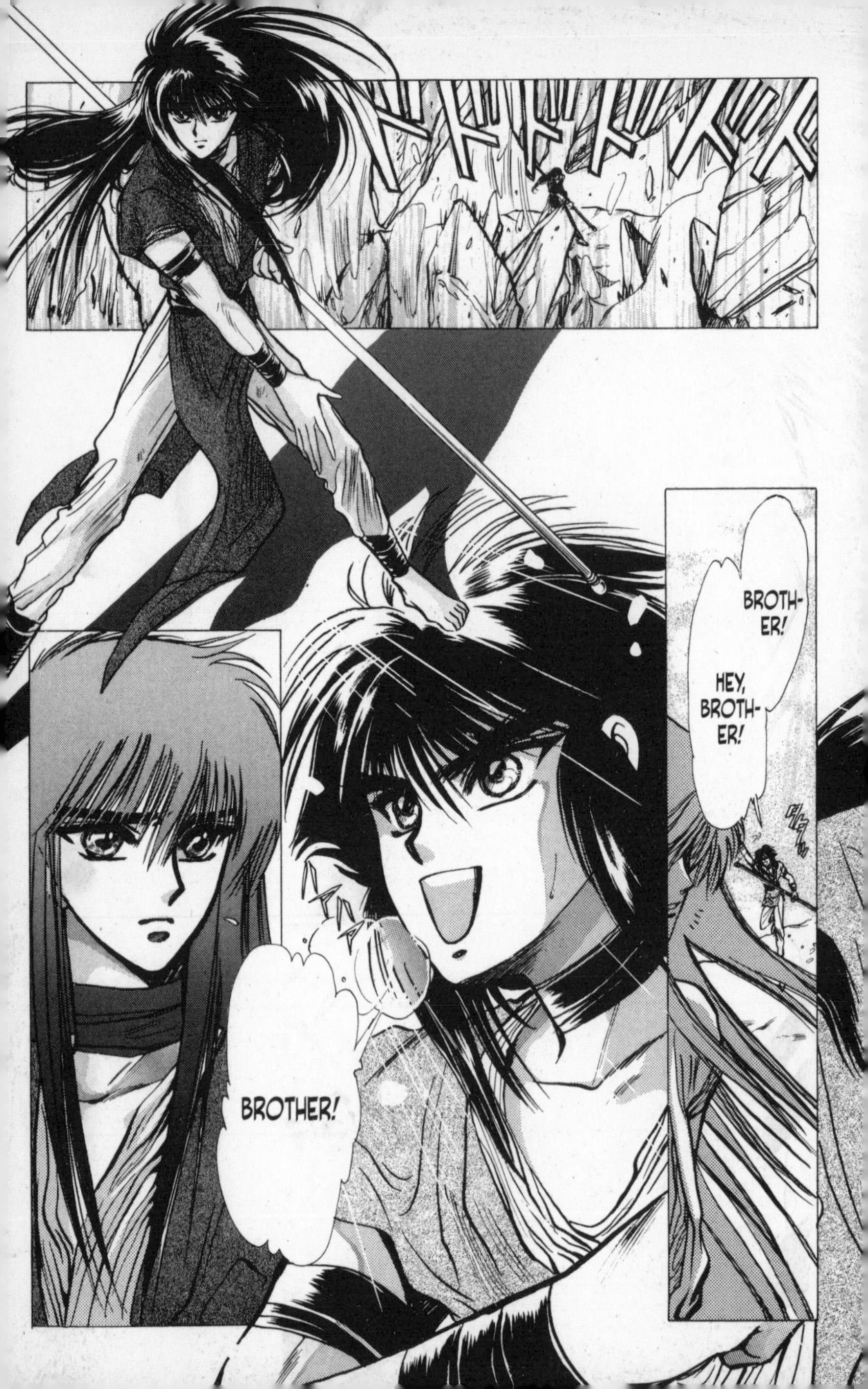
BROTH-ER!
HEY, BROTH-ER!
BROTHER!

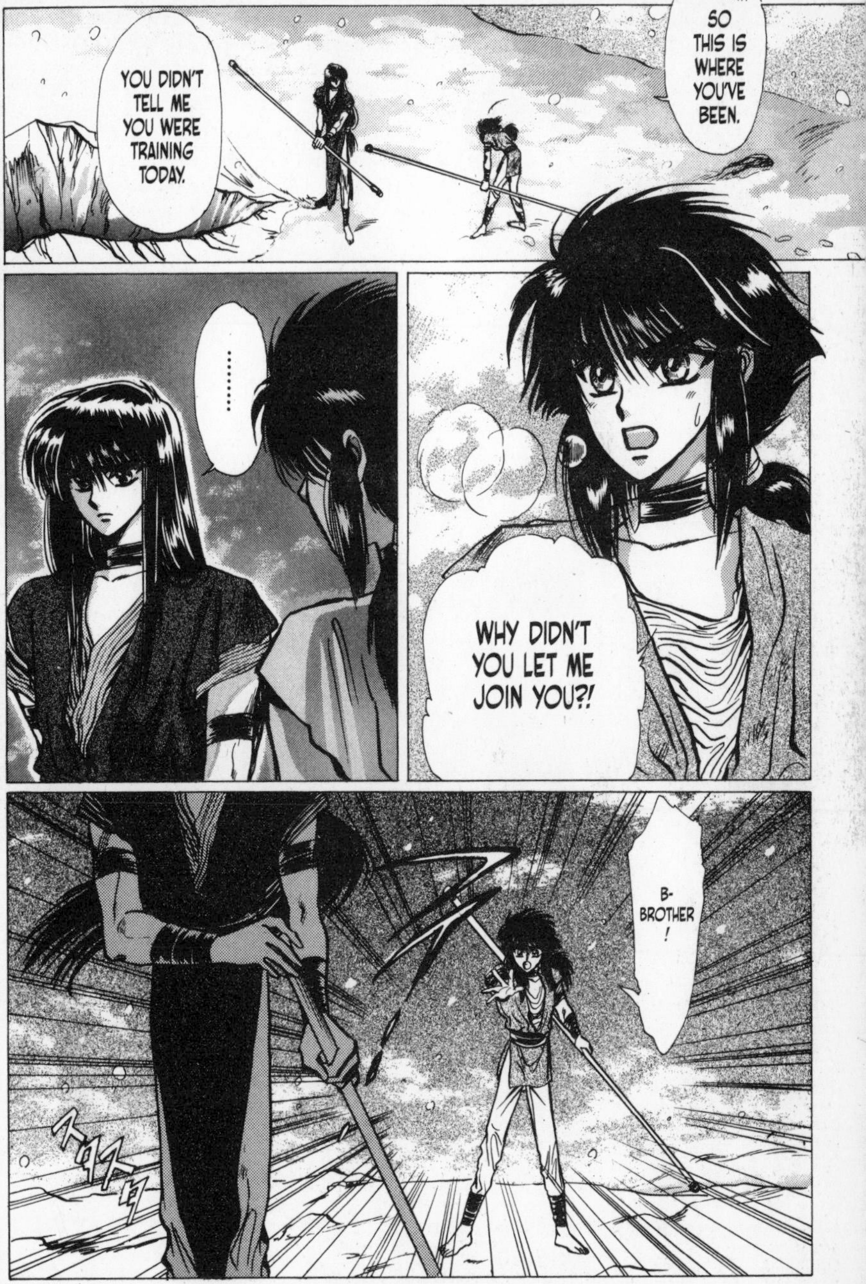
Huff! Huff!
SO THIS IS WHERE YOU'VE BEEN.
YOU DIDN'T TELL ME YOU WERE TRAINING TODAY.
WHY DIDN'T YOU LET ME JOIN YOU?!
......
B-BROTHER!

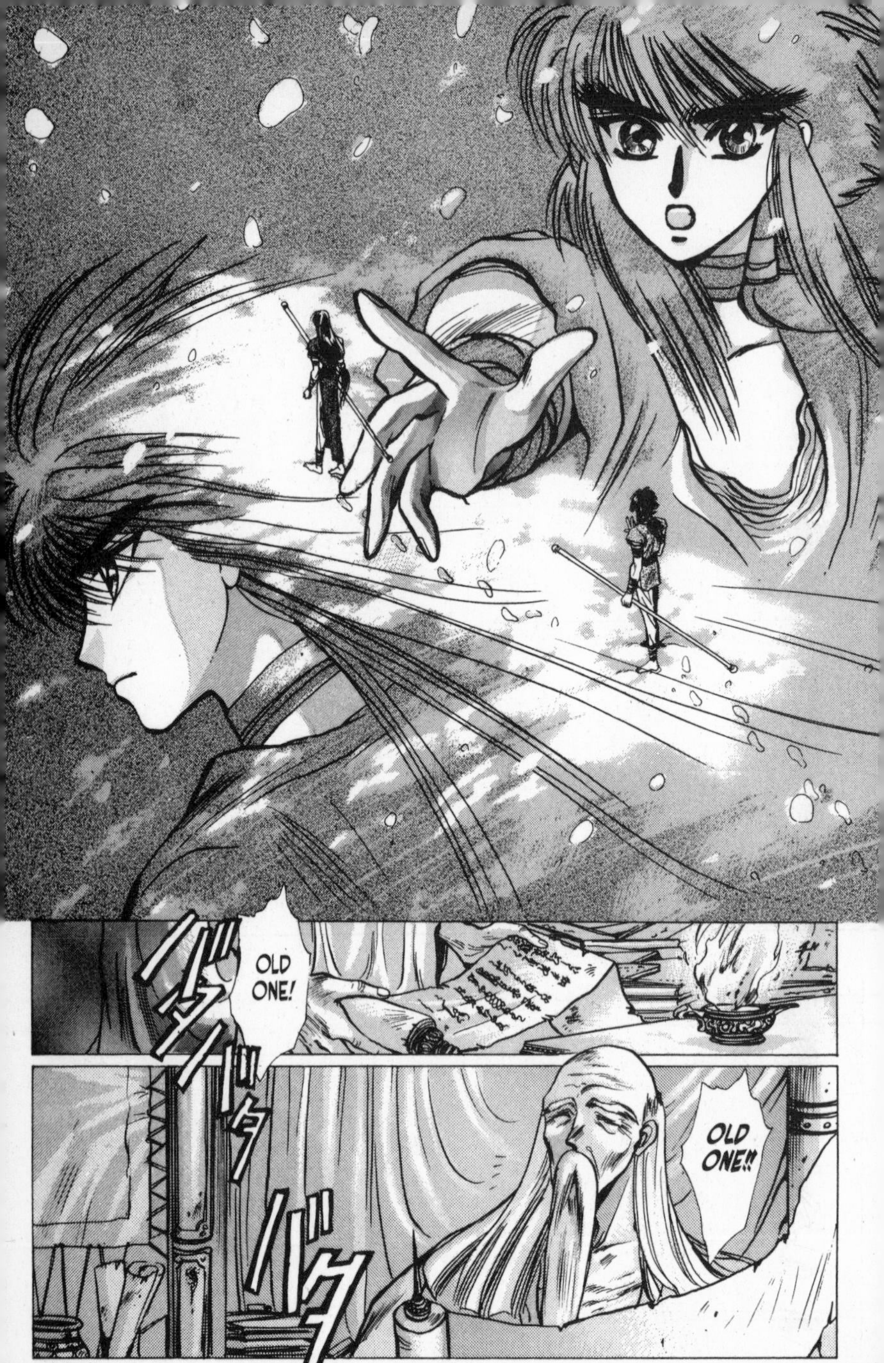
OLD ONE!
OLD ONE!!

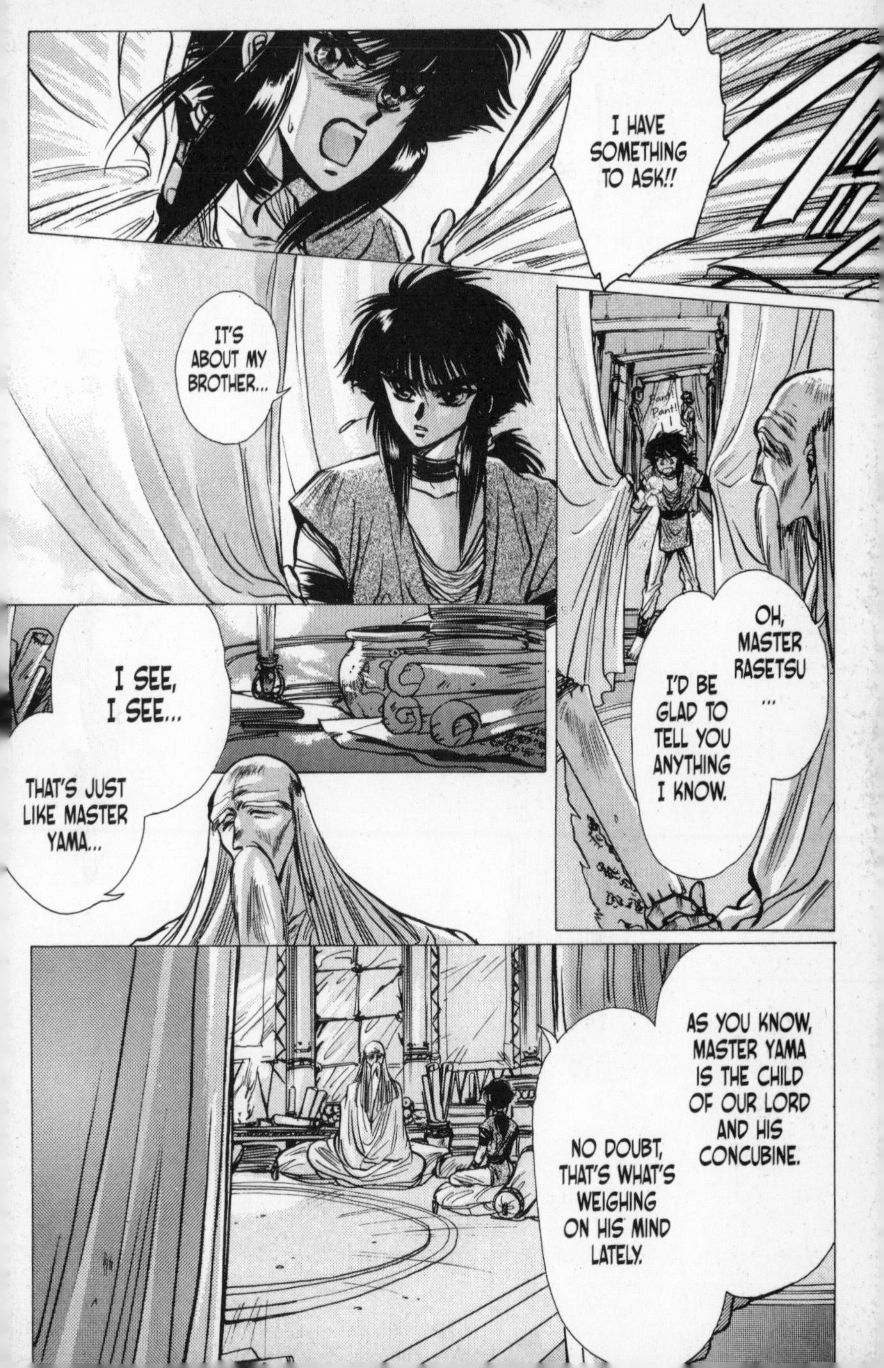
I HAVE SOMETHING TO ASK!!
Pant! Pant!!
OH, MASTER RASETSU...
I'D BE GLAD TO TELL YOU ANYTHING I KNOW.
IT'S ABOUT MY BROTHER...
I SEE, I SEE...
THAT'S JUST LIKE MASTER YAMA...
AS YOU KNOW, MASTER YAMA IS THE CHILD OF OUR LORD AND HIS CONCUBINE.
NO DOUBT, THAT'S WHAT'S WEIGHING ON HIS MIND LATELY.

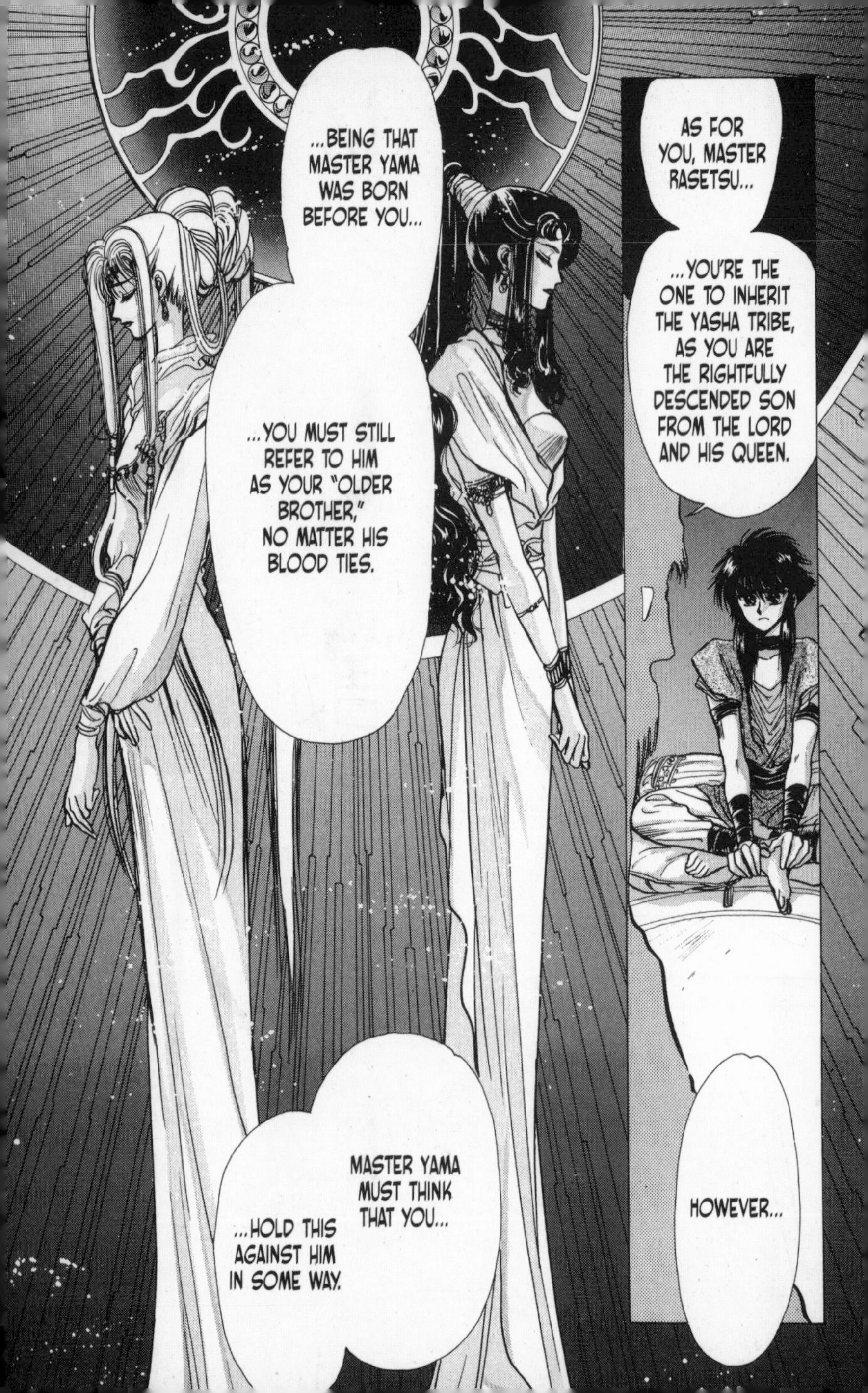
AS FOR YOU, MASTER RASETSU...
...YOU'RE THE ONE TO INHERIT THE YASHA TRIBE, AS YOU ARE THE RIGHTFULLY DESCENDED SON FROM THE LORD AND HIS QUEEN.
HOWEVER...
...BEING THAT MASTER YAMA WAS BORN BEFORE YOU...
...YOU MUST STILL REFER TO HIM AS YOUR "OLDER BROTHER," NO MATTER HIS BLOOD TIES.
MASTER YAMA MUST THINK THAT YOU...
...HOLD THIS AGAINST HIM IN SOME WAY.

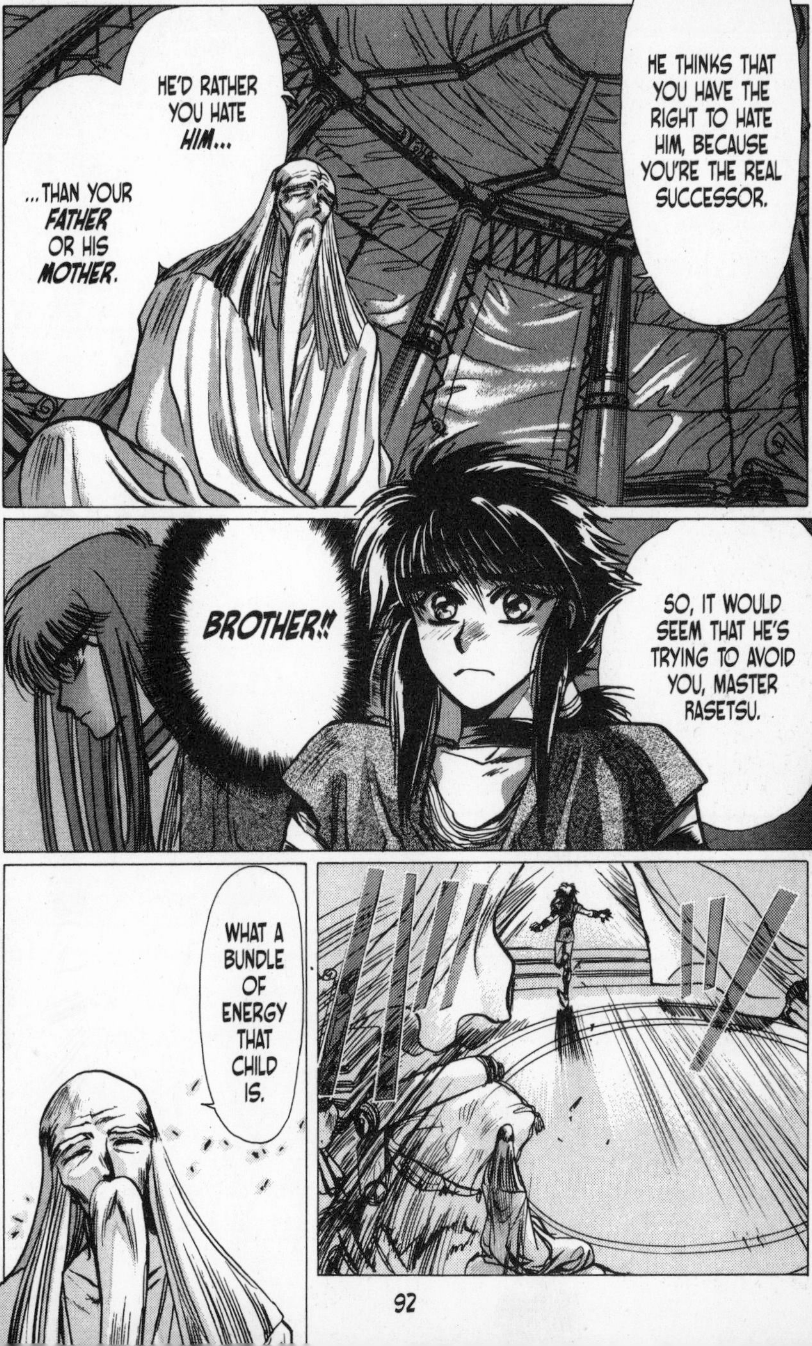
HE THINKS THAT YOU HAVE THE RIGHT TO HATE HIM, BECAUSE YOU'RE THE REAL SUCCESSOR.
HE'D RATHER YOU HATE *HIM*...
...THAN YOUR *FATHER* OR HIS *MOTHER*.
SO, IT WOULD SEEM THAT HE'S TRYING TO AVOID YOU, MASTER RASETSU.
*BROTHER!!*
WHAT A BUNDLE OF ENERGY THAT CHILD IS.

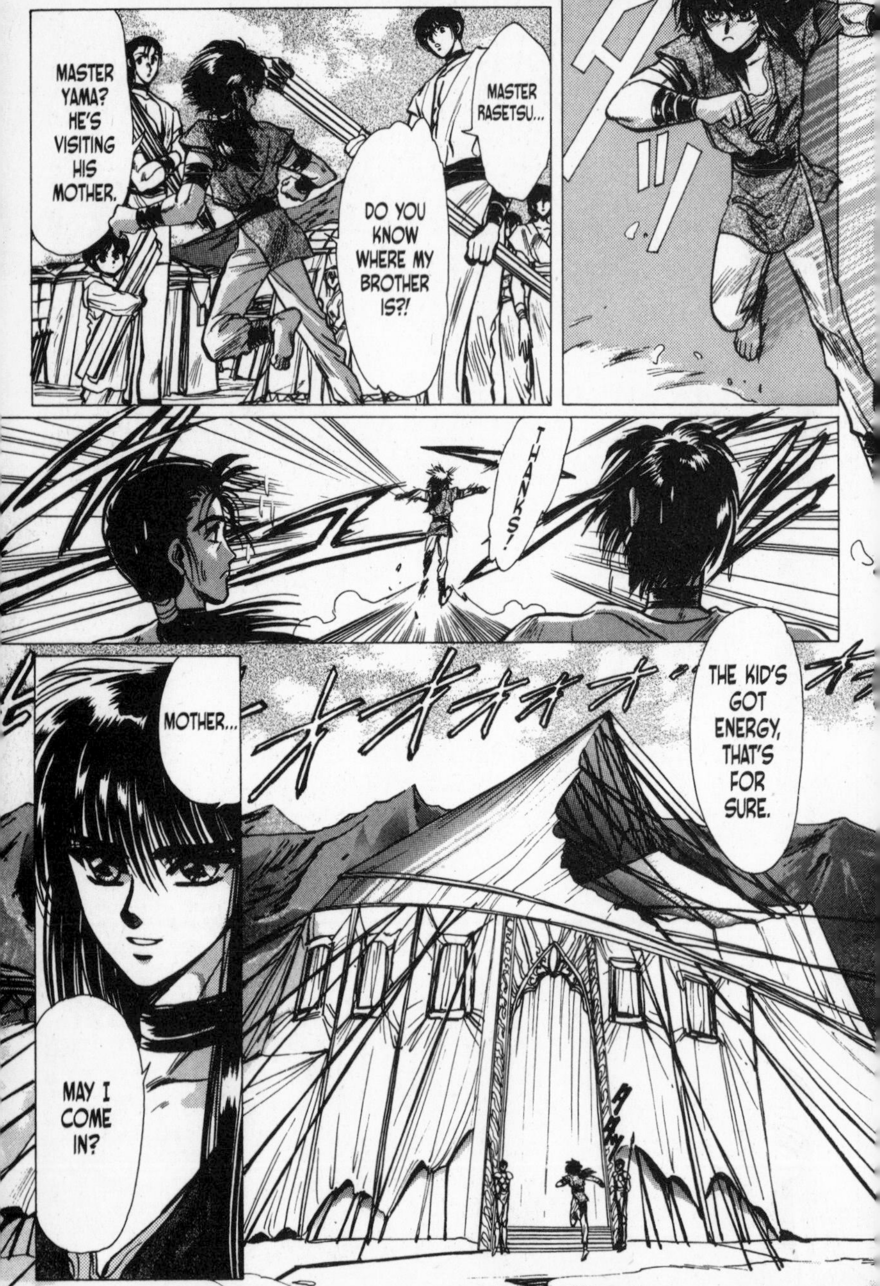
MASTER RASETSU...
DO YOU KNOW WHERE MY BROTHER IS?!
MASTER YAMA? HE'S VISITING HIS MOTHER.
THANKS!
THE KID'S GOT ENERGY, THAT'S FOR SURE.
MOTHER...
MAY I COME IN?

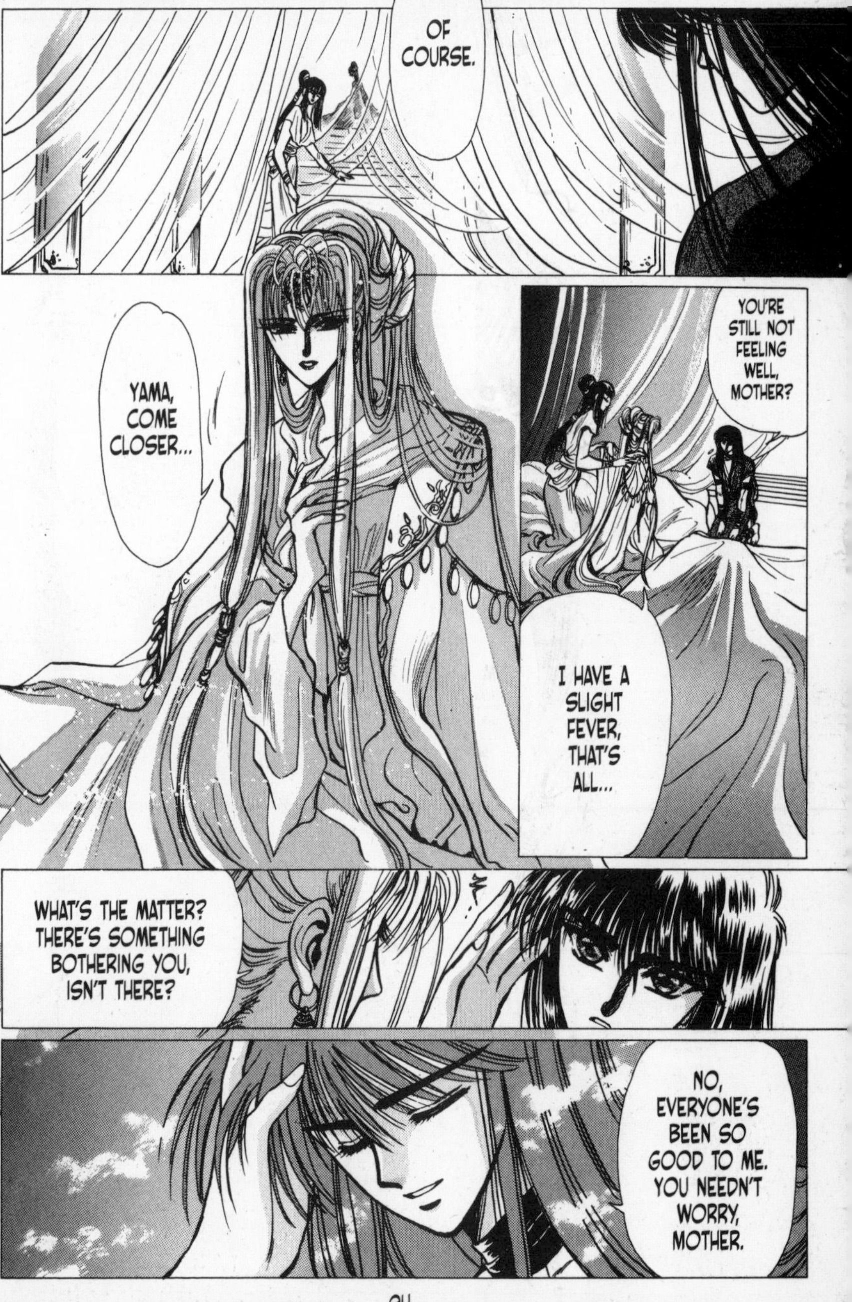
OF COURSE.
YOU'RE STILL NOT FEELING WELL, MOTHER?
I HAVE A SLIGHT FEVER, THAT'S ALL...
YAMA, COME CLOSER...
WHAT'S THE MATTER? THERE'S SOMETHING BOTHERING YOU, ISN'T THERE?
NO, EVERYONE'S BEEN SO GOOD TO ME. YOU NEEDN'T WORRY, MOTHER.

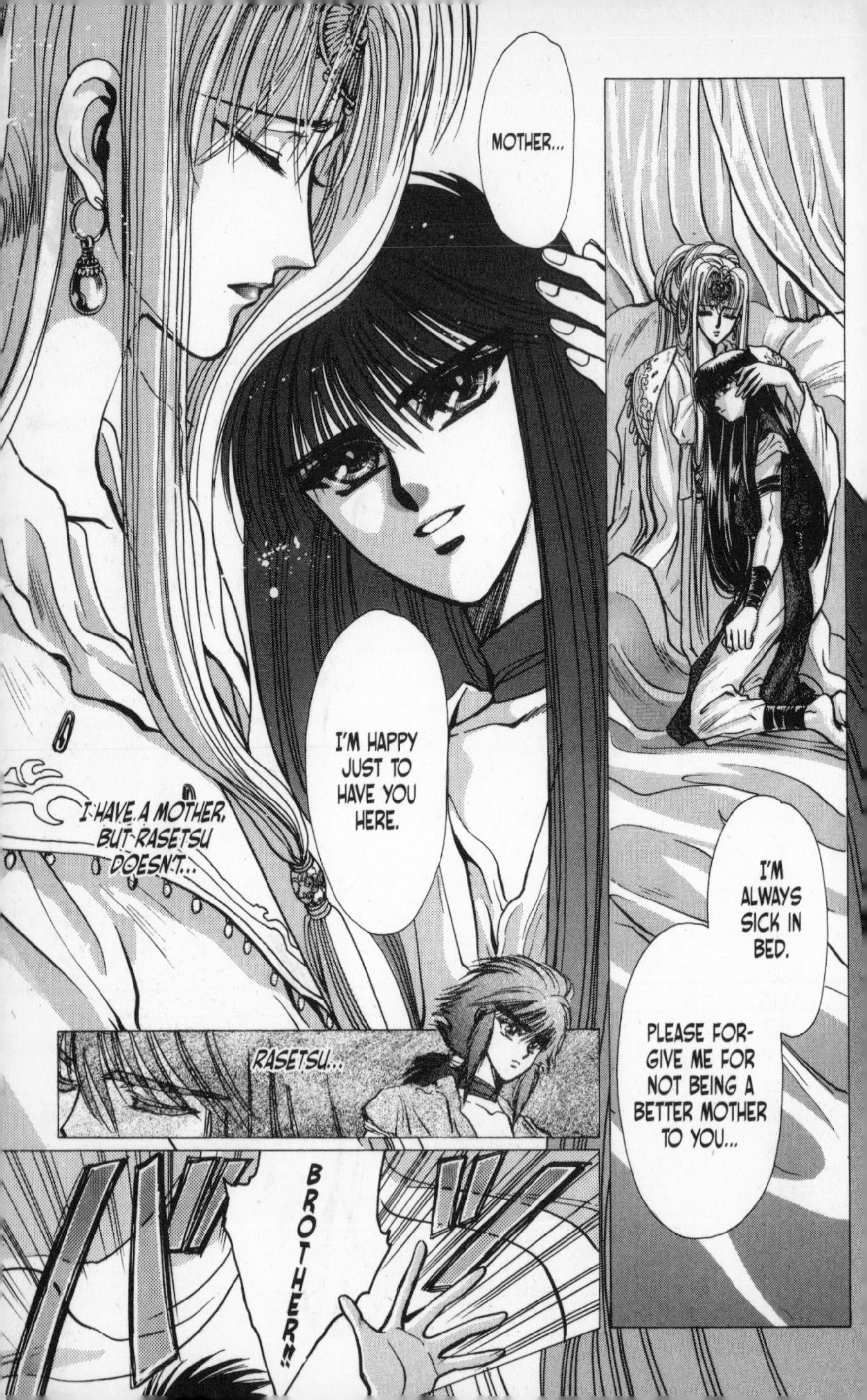
I'M ALWAYS SICK IN BED.
PLEASE FOR-GIVE ME FOR NOT BEING A BETTER MOTHER TO YOU...
MOTHER...
I'M HAPPY JUST TO HAVE YOU HERE.
I HAVE A MOTHER, BUT RASETSU DOESN'T...
RASETSU...
BROTHER!!

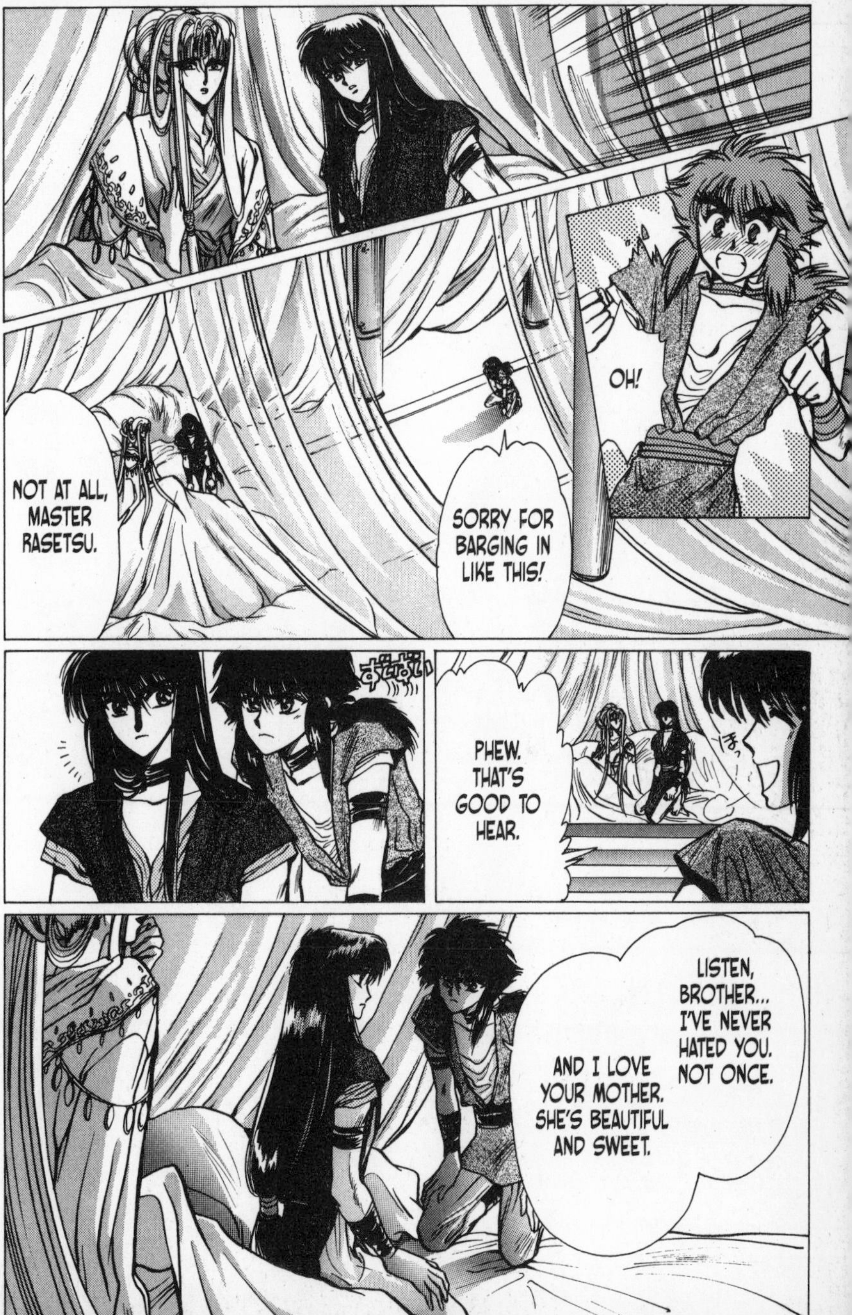
OH!
SORRY FOR BARGING IN LIKE THIS!
NOT AT ALL, MASTER RASETSU.
PHEW. THAT'S GOOD TO HEAR.
LISTEN, BROTHER... I'VE NEVER HATED YOU. NOT ONCE.
AND I LOVE YOUR MOTHER. SHE'S BEAUTIFUL AND SWEET.

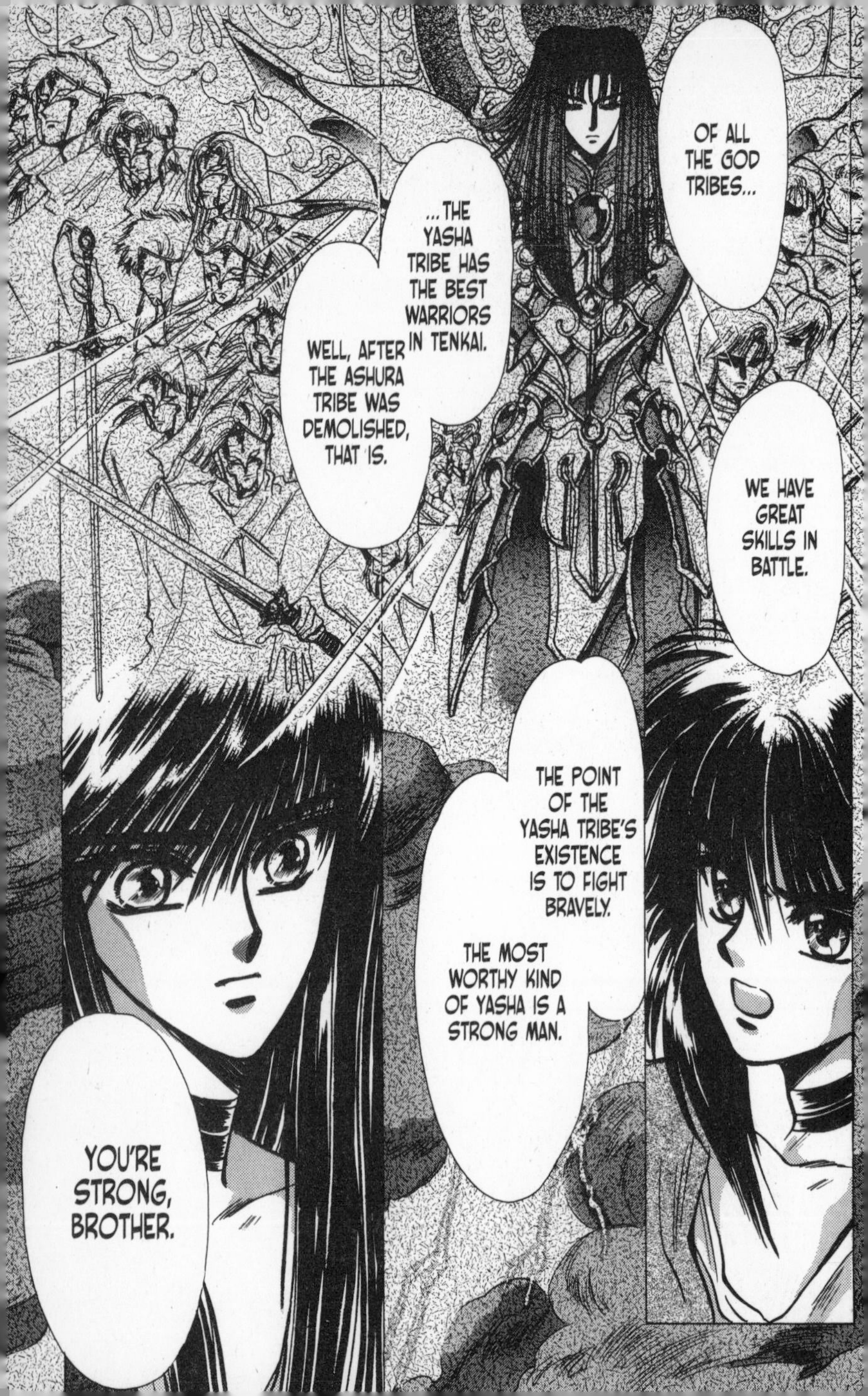
OF ALL THE GOD TRIBES...
...THE YASHA TRIBE HAS THE BEST WARRIORS IN TENKAI.
WELL, AFTER THE ASHURA TRIBE WAS DEMOLISHED, THAT IS.
WE HAVE GREAT SKILLS IN BATTLE.
THE POINT OF THE YASHA TRIBE'S EXISTENCE IS TO FIGHT BRAVELY.
THE MOST WORTHY KIND OF YASHA IS A STRONG MAN.
YOU'RE STRONG, BROTHER.

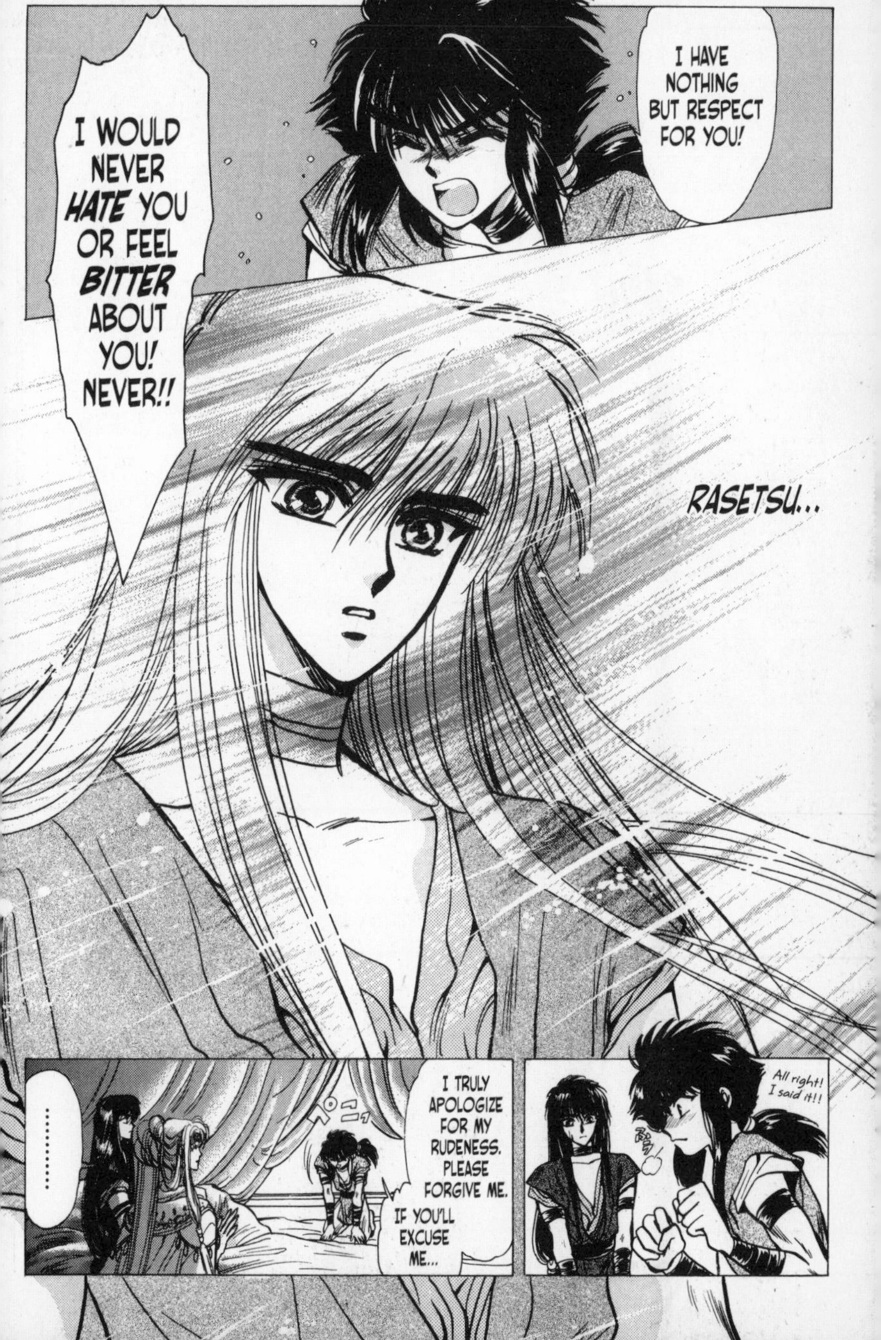
I HAVE NOTHING BUT RESPECT FOR YOU!
I WOULD NEVER HATE YOU OR FEEL BITTER ABOUT YOU! NEVER!!
RASETSU...
All right! I said it!!
I TRULY APOLOGIZE FOR MY RUDENESS. PLEASE FORGIVE ME.
IF YOU'LL EXCUSE ME...
......

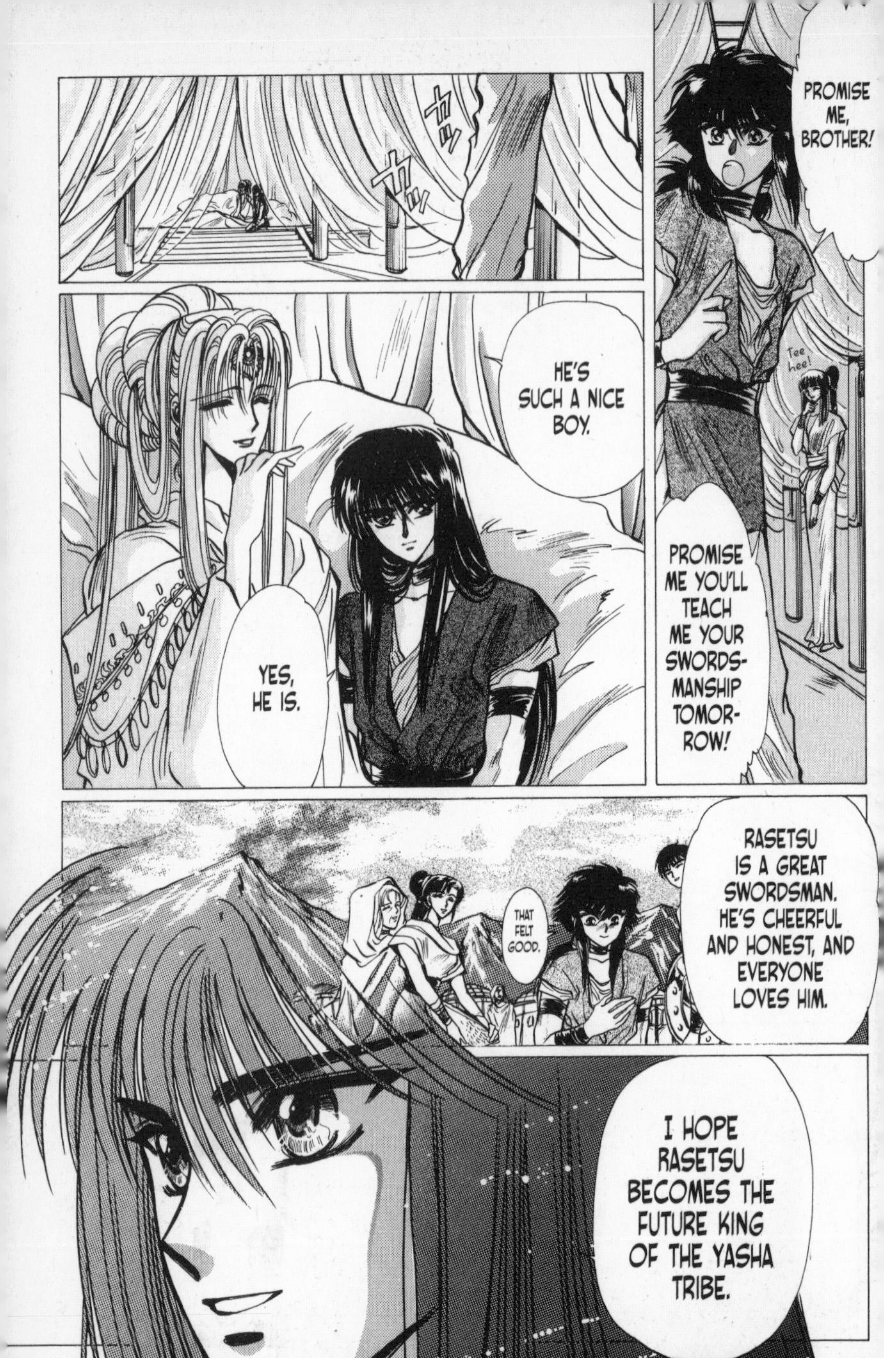
PROMISE ME, BROTHER!
PROMISE ME YOU'LL TEACH ME YOUR SWORDS-MANSHIP TOMOR-ROW!
Tee hee!
HE'S SUCH A NICE BOY.
YES, HE IS.
RASETSU IS A GREAT SWORDSMAN. HE'S CHEERFUL AND HONEST, AND EVERYONE LOVES HIM.
THAT FELT GOOD.
I HOPE RASETSU BECOMES THE FUTURE KING OF THE YASHA TRIBE.

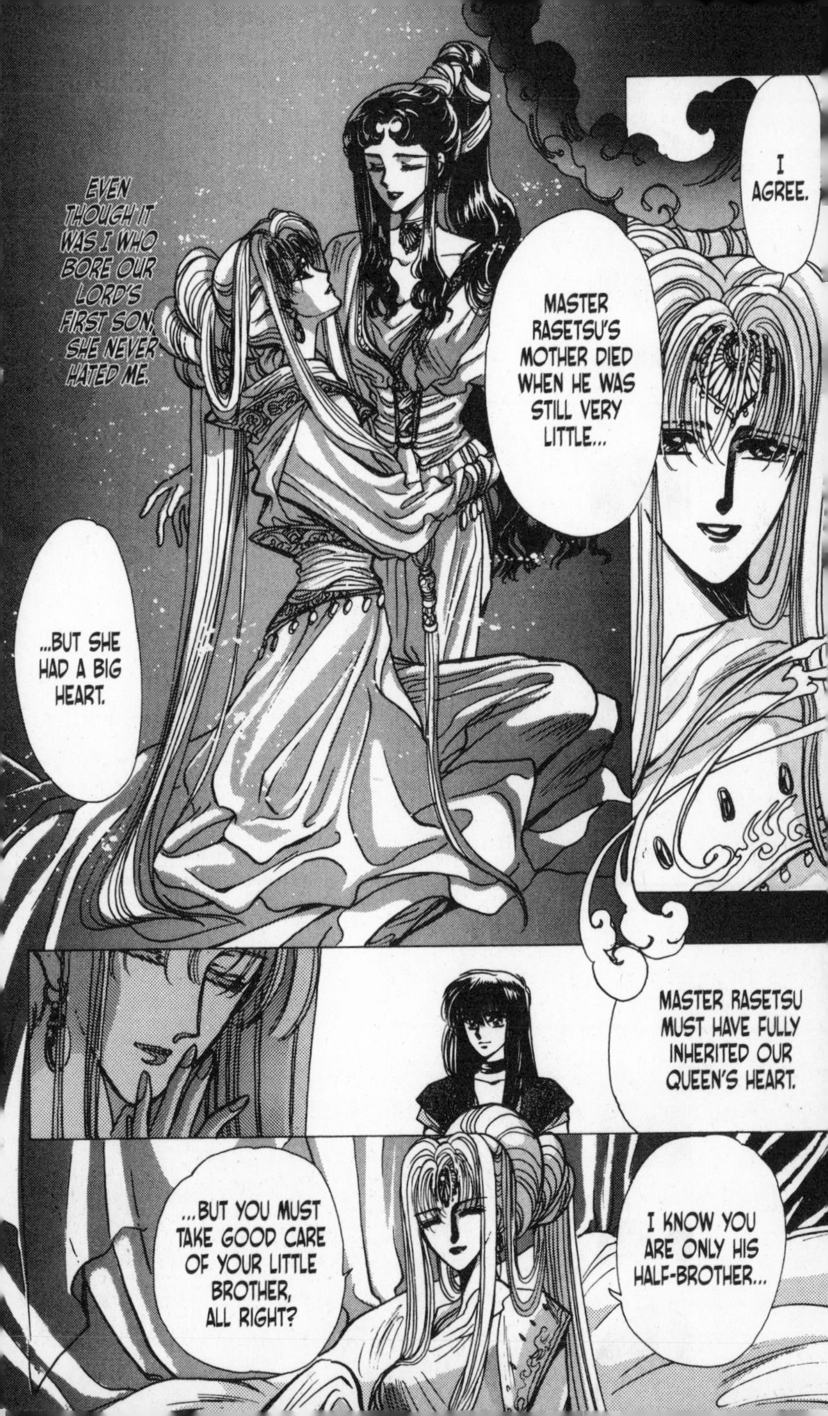
I AGREE.
MASTER RASETSU'S MOTHER DIED WHEN HE WAS STILL VERY LITTLE...
EVEN THOUGH IT WAS I WHO BORE OUR LORD'S FIRST SON, SHE NEVER HATED ME.
...BUT SHE HAD A BIG HEART.
MASTER RASETSU MUST HAVE FULLY INHERITED OUR QUEEN'S HEART.
I KNOW YOU ARE ONLY HIS HALF-BROTHER...
...BUT YOU MUST TAKE GOOD CARE OF YOUR LITTLE BROTHER, ALL RIGHT?

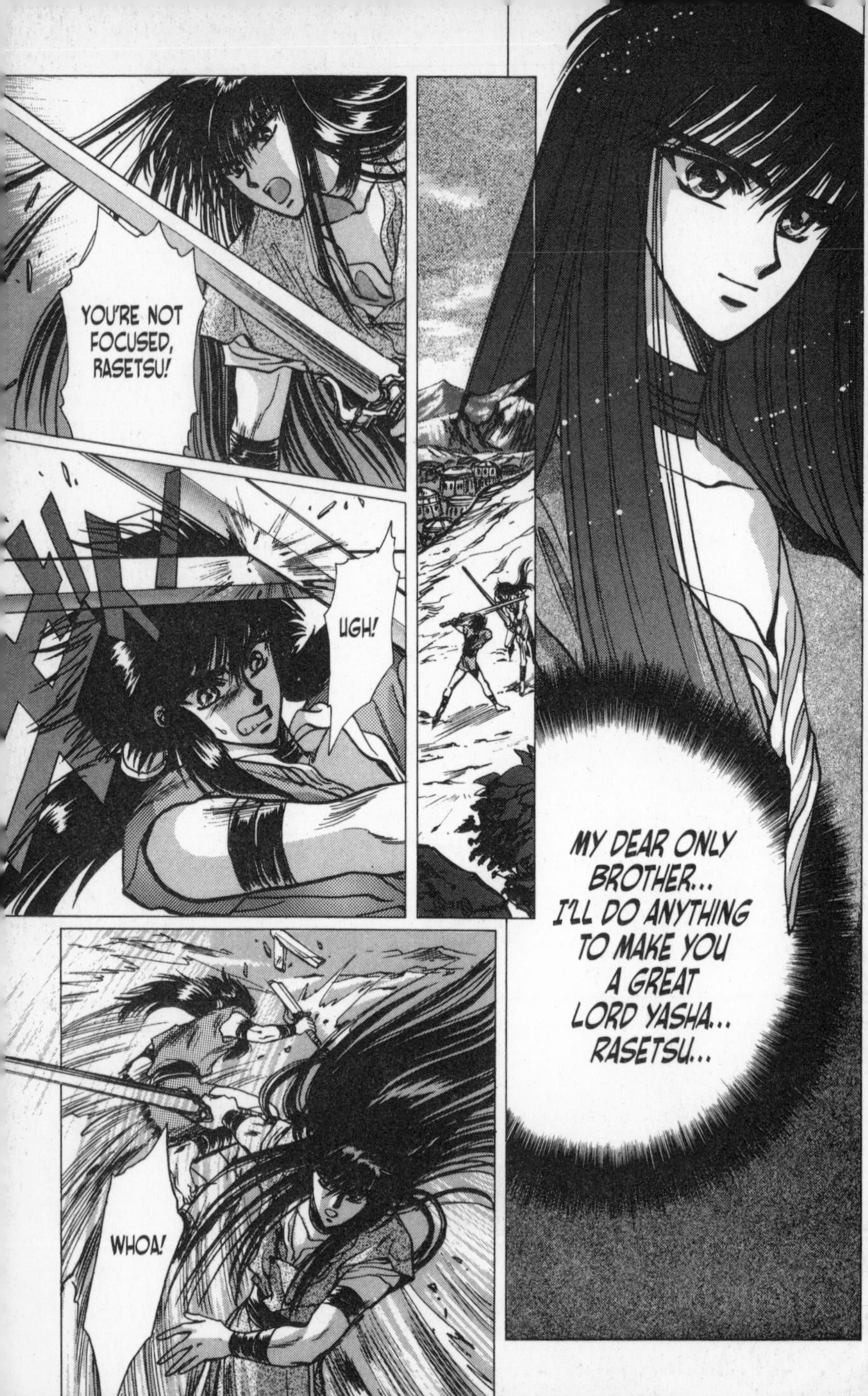
MY DEAR ONLY BROTHER... I'LL DO ANYTHING TO MAKE YOU A GREAT LORD YASHA... RASETSU...
YOU'RE NOT FOCUSED, RASETSU!
UGH!
WHOA!

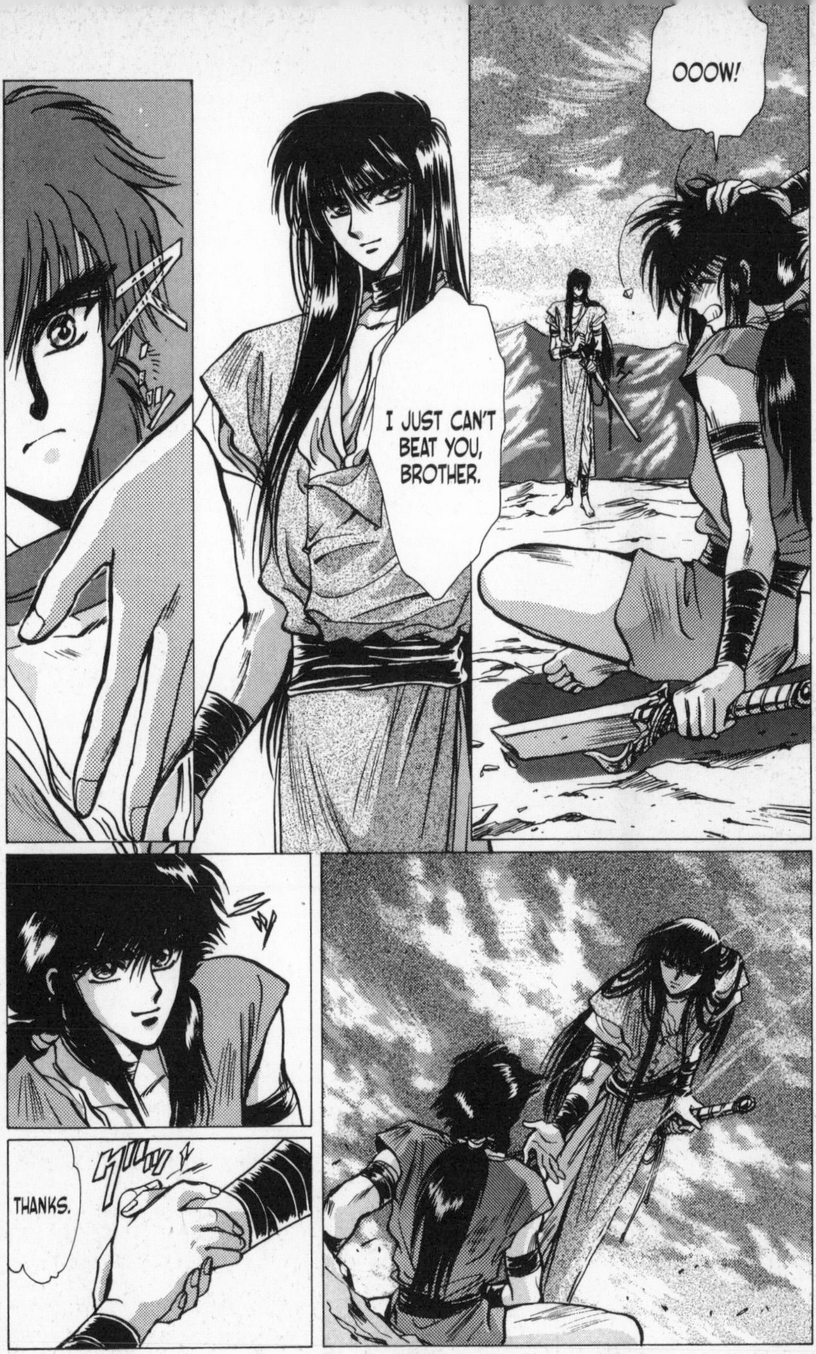
OOOW!
I JUST CAN'T BEAT YOU, BROTHER.
THANKS.

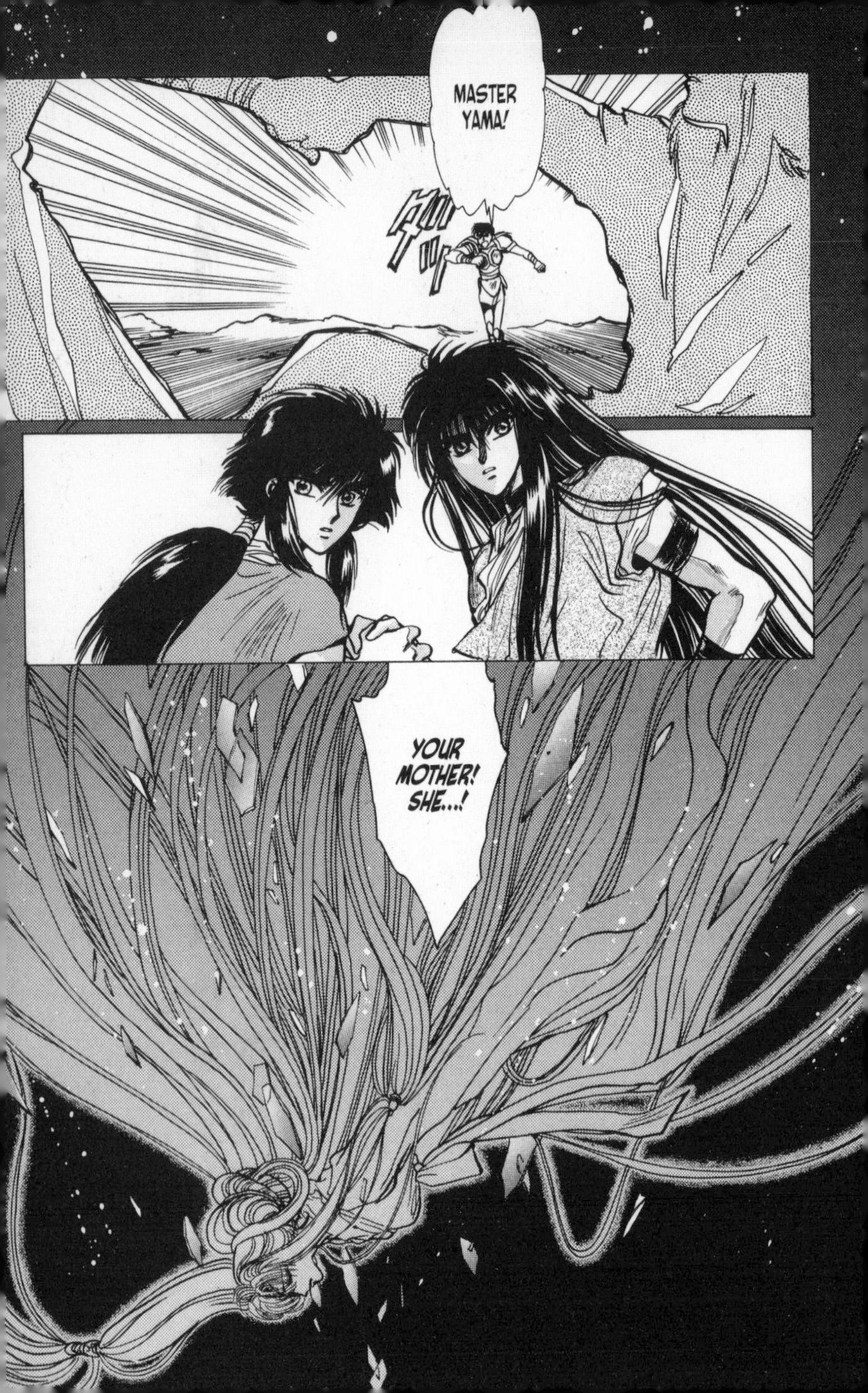
MASTER YAMA!
YOUR MOTHER! SHE...!

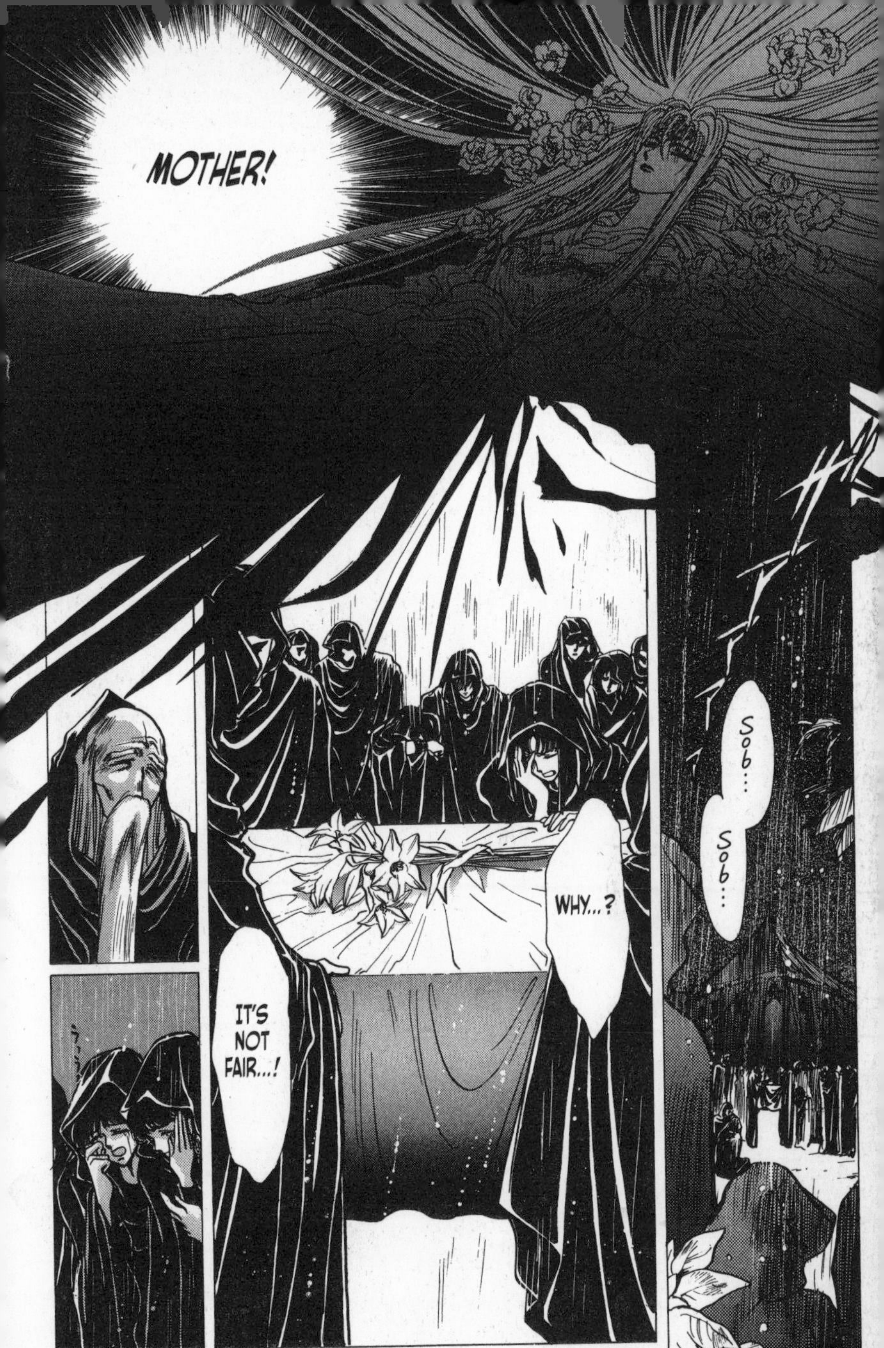
MOTHER!
Sob... Sob...
WHY...?
IT'S NOT FAIR...!

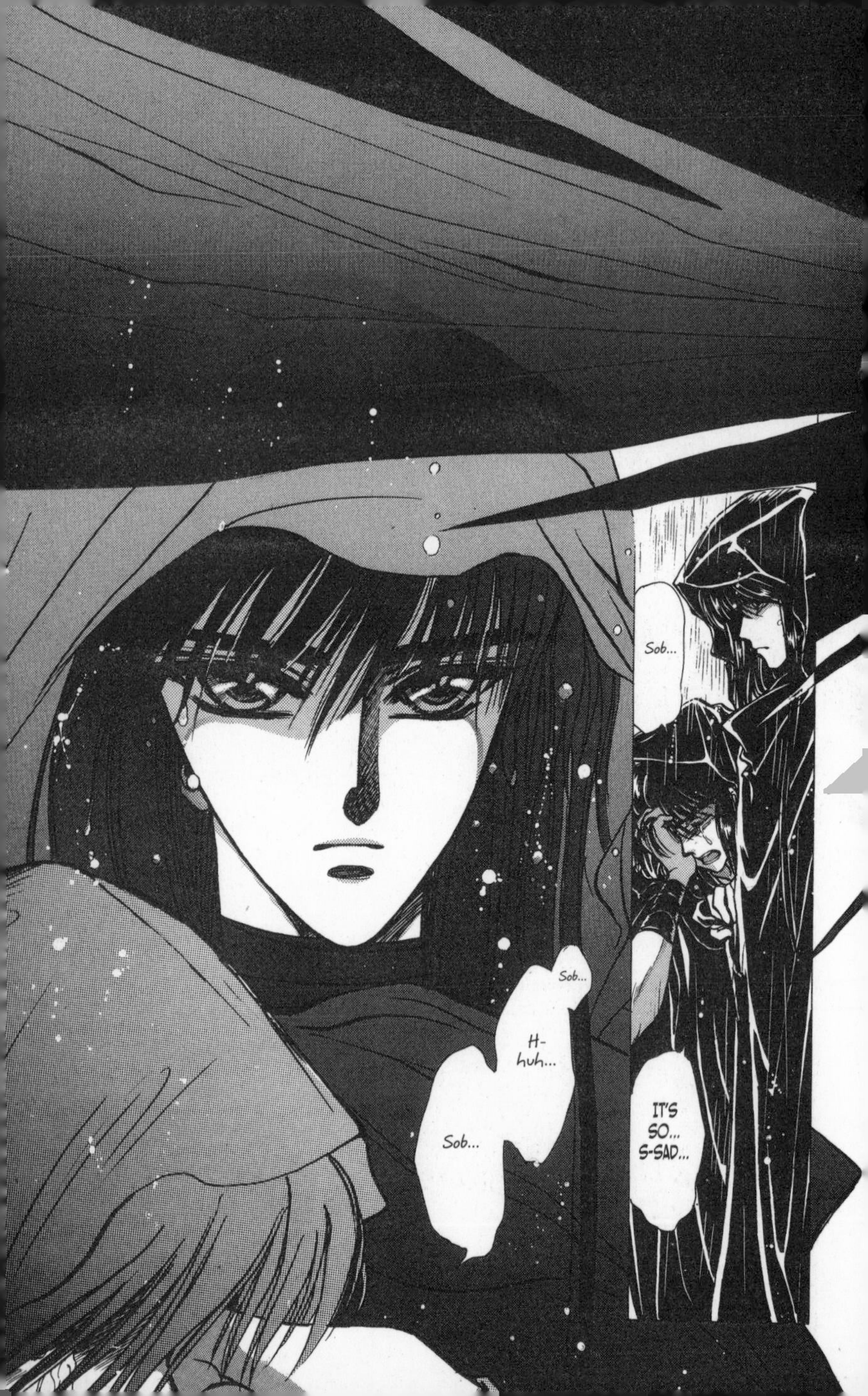
Sob...
IT'S SO... S-SAD...
Sob...
H-huh...
Sob...

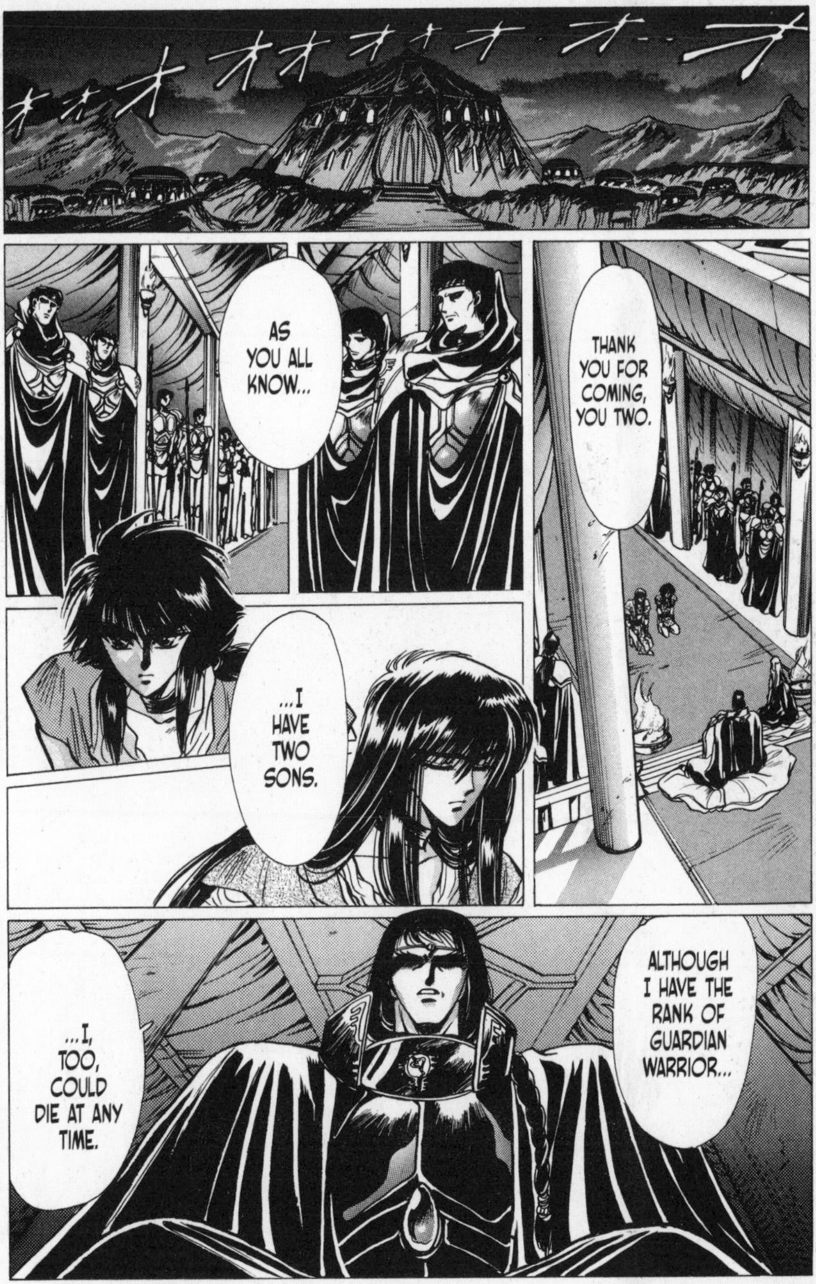
THANK YOU FOR COMING, YOU TWO.
AS YOU ALL KNOW...
...I HAVE TWO SONS.
ALTHOUGH I HAVE THE RANK OF GUARDIAN WARRIOR...
...I, TOO, COULD DIE AT ANY TIME.

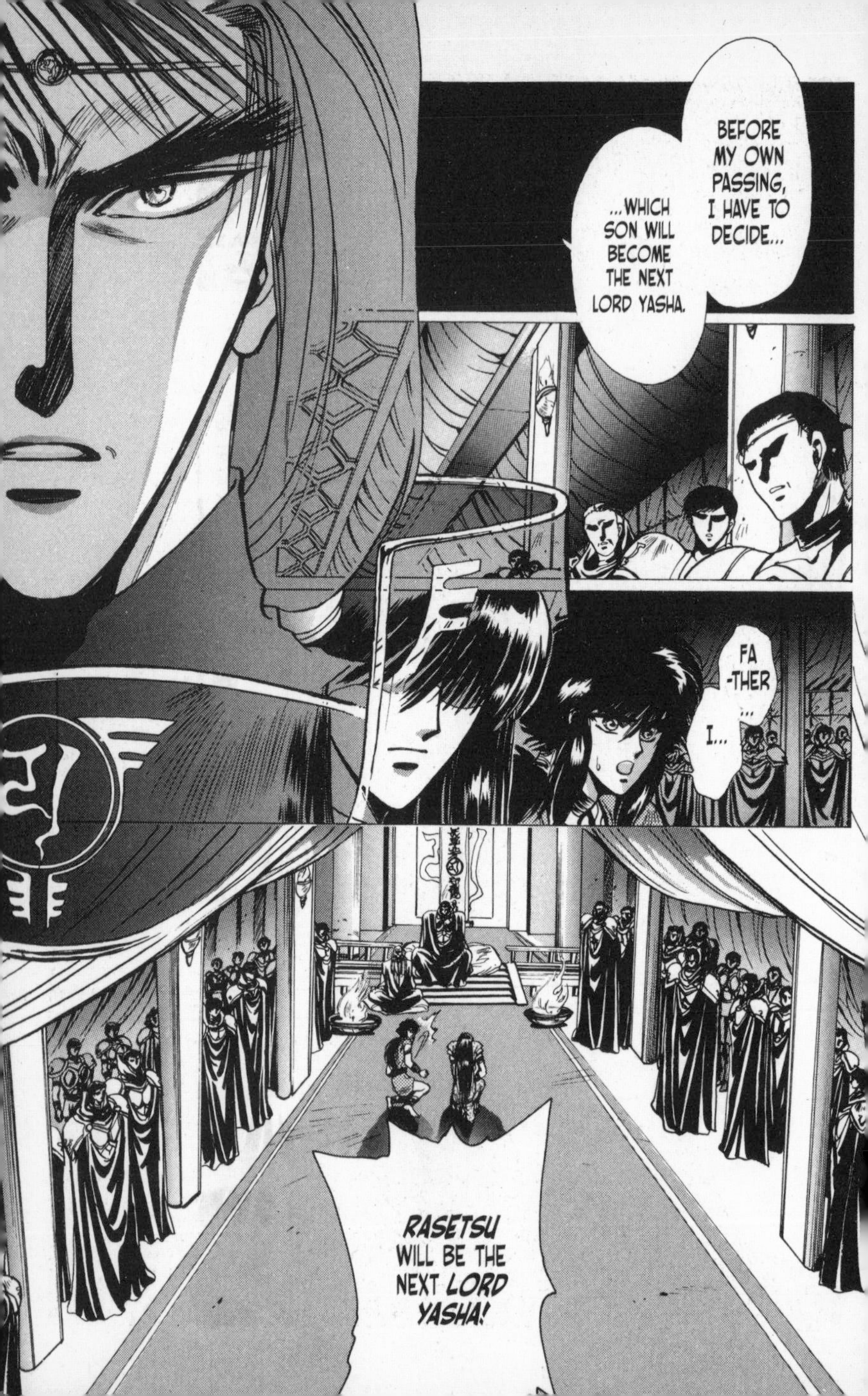
BEFORE MY OWN PASSING, I HAVE TO DECIDE...
...WHICH SON WILL BECOME THE NEXT LORD YASHA.
FA -THER ...
I...
*RASETSU* WILL BE THE NEXT *LORD YASHA!*

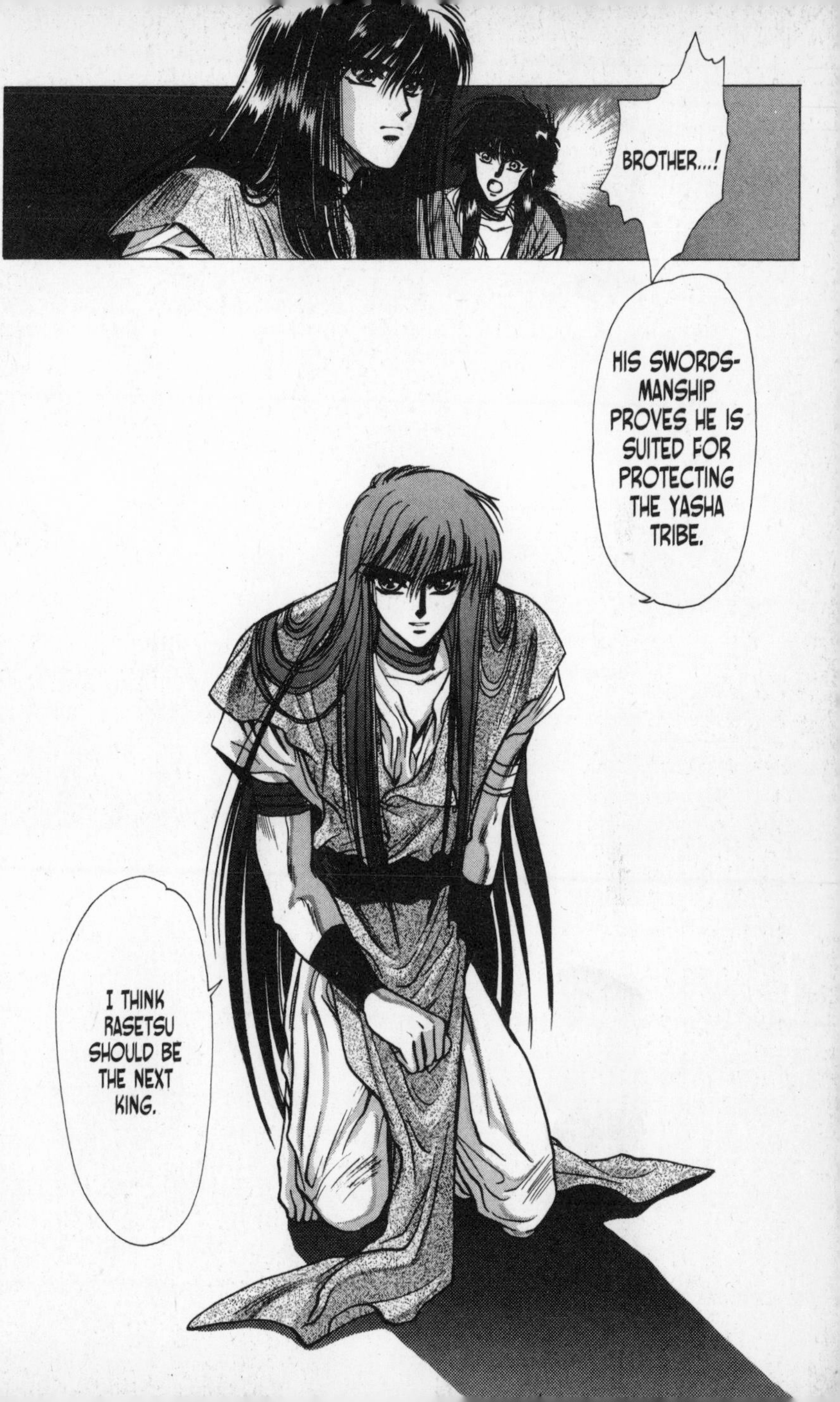
BROTHER...!
HIS SWORDS-MANSHIP PROVES HE IS SUITED FOR PROTECTING THE YASHA TRIBE.
I THINK RASETSU SHOULD BE THE NEXT KING.

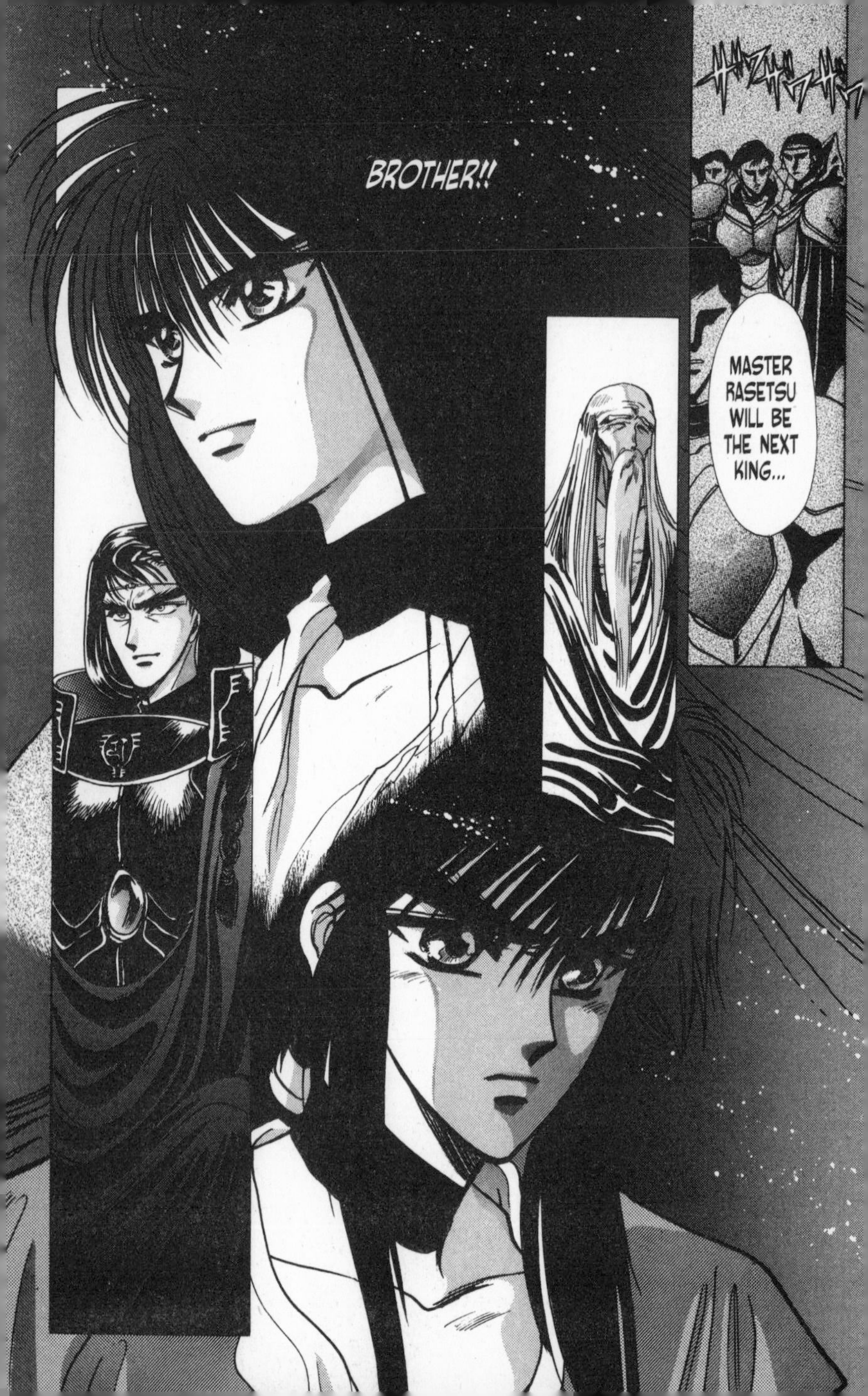
MASTER RASETSU WILL BE THE NEXT KING...
BROTHER!!

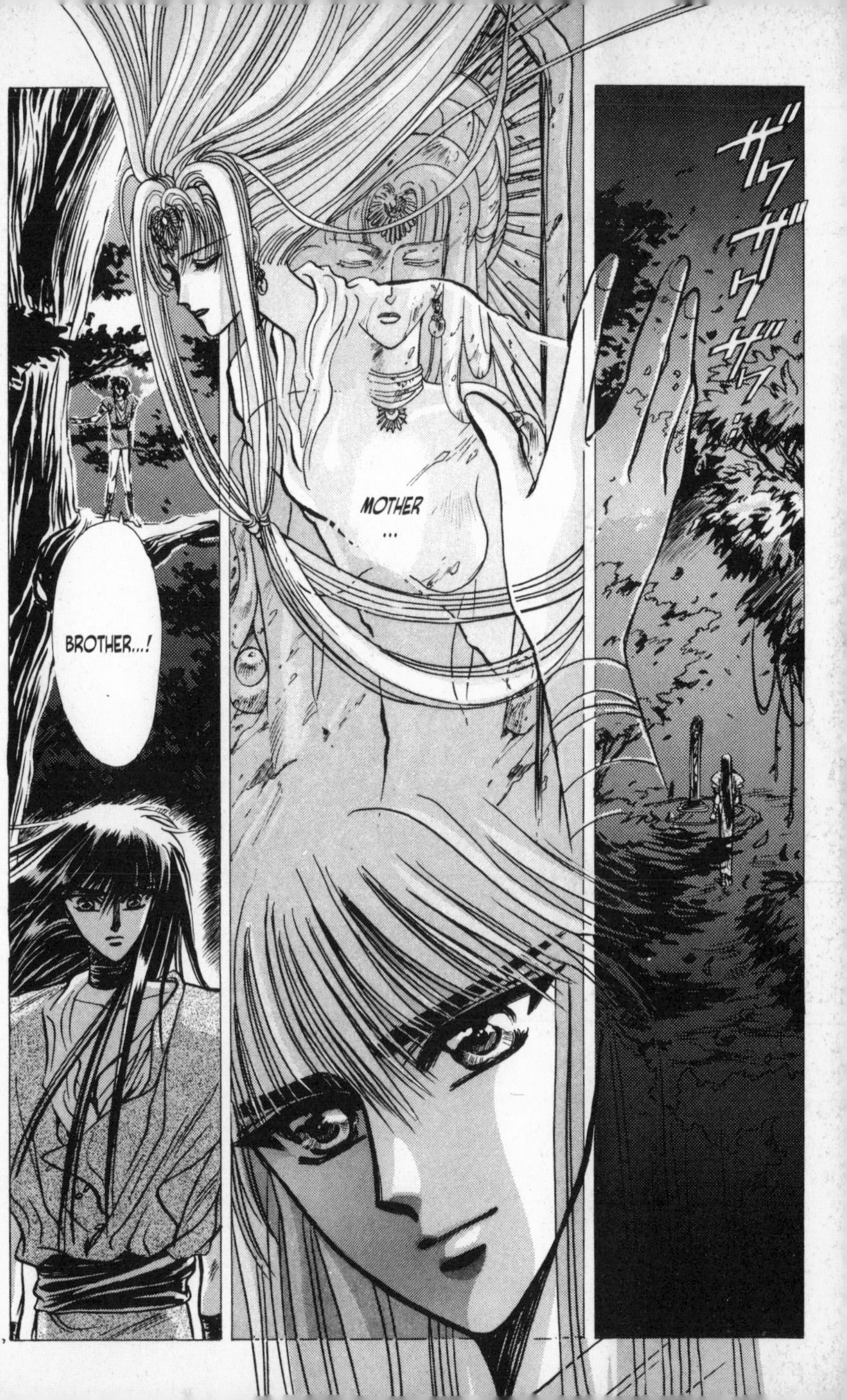
ザワザワザワ…
MOTHER ...
BROTHER...!

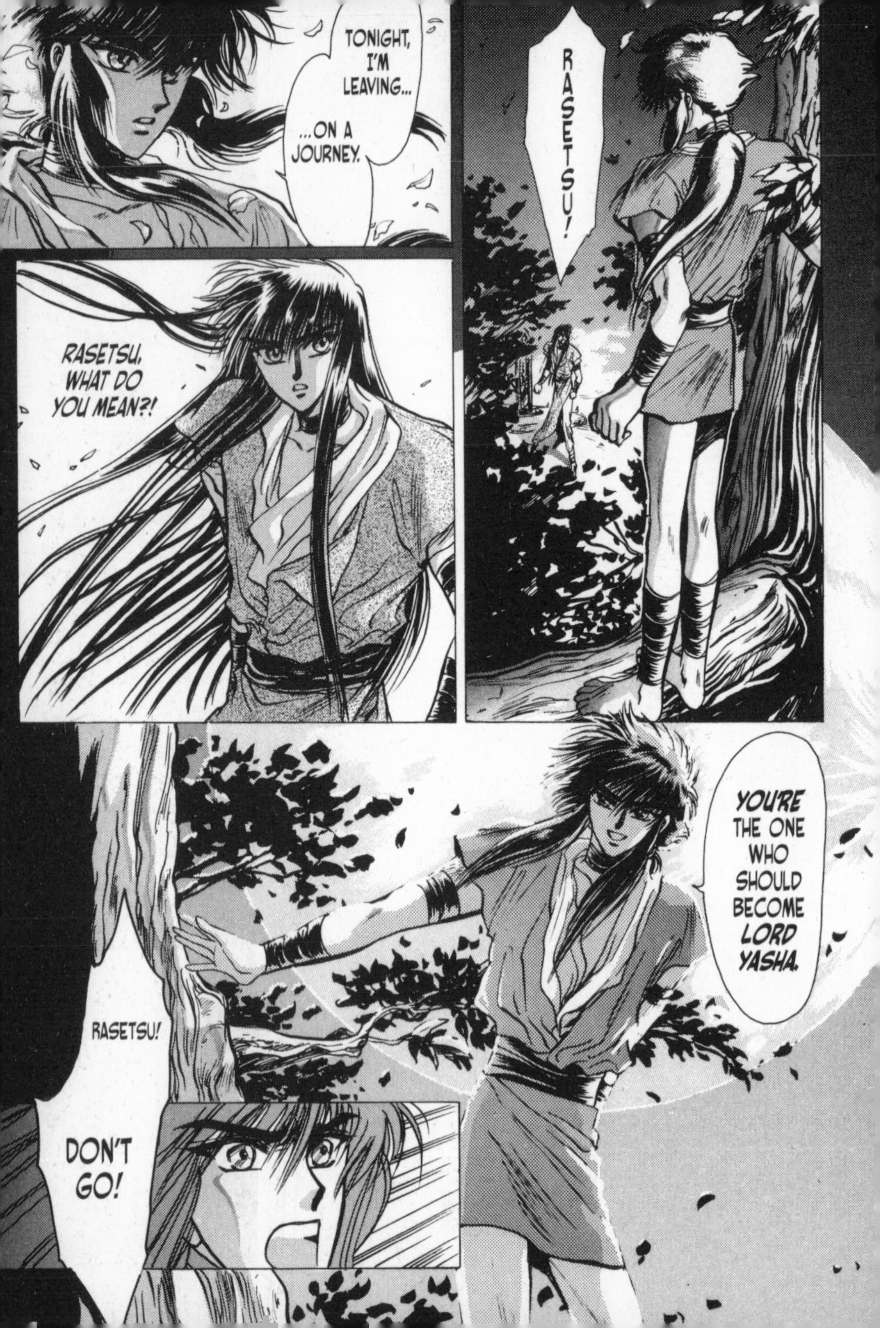
RASETSU!
TONIGHT, I'M LEAVING...
...ON A JOURNEY.
RASETSU, WHAT DO YOU MEAN?!
YOU'RE THE ONE WHO SHOULD BECOME LORD YASHA.
RASETSU!
DON'T GO!

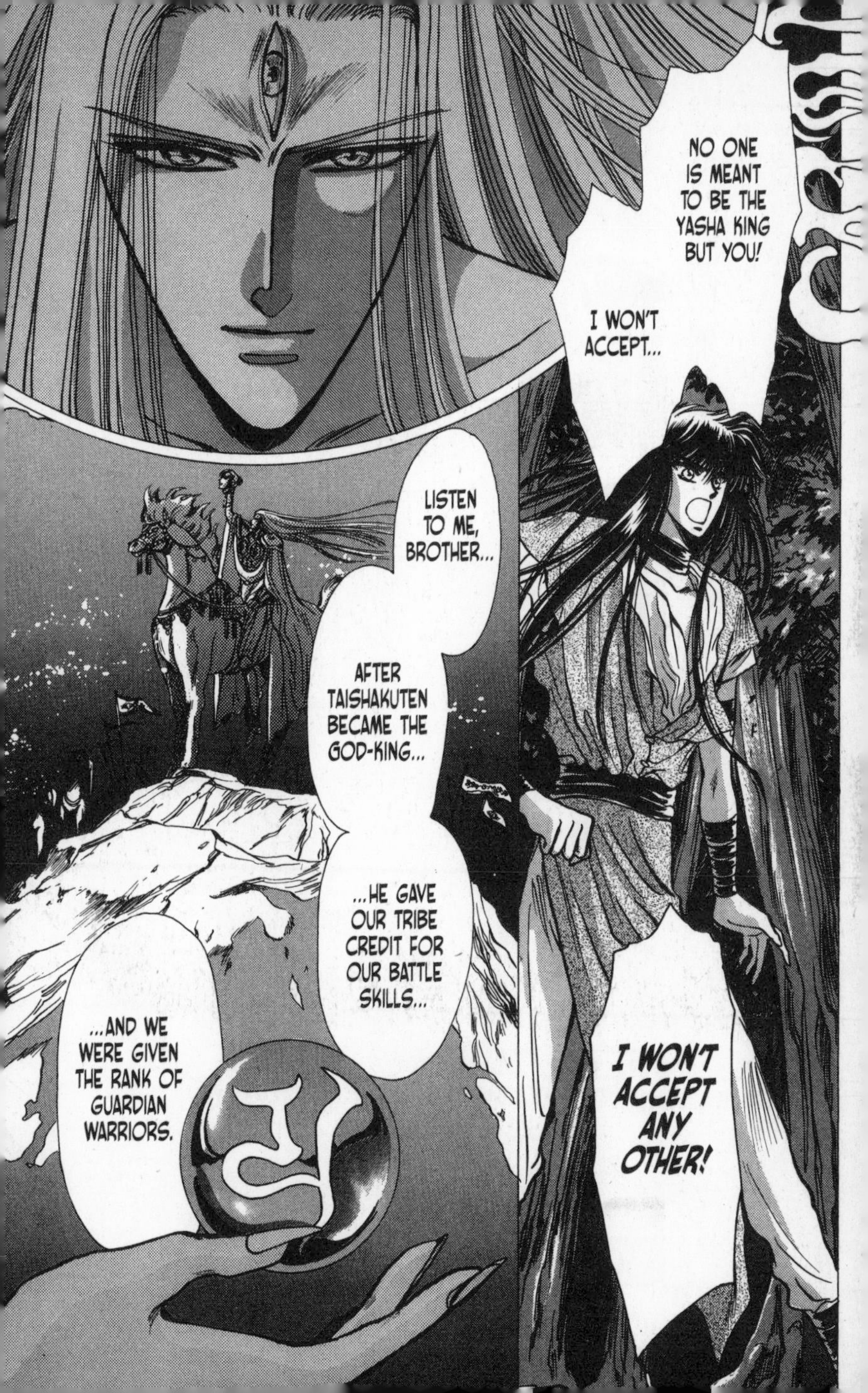
NO ONE IS MEANT TO BE THE YASHA KING BUT YOU!
I WON'T ACCEPT...
I WON'T ACCEPT ANY OTHER!
LISTEN TO ME, BROTHER...
AFTER TAISHAKUTEN BECAME THE GOD-KING...
...HE GAVE OUR TRIBE CREDIT FOR OUR BATTLE SKILLS...
...AND WE WERE GIVEN THE RANK OF GUARDIAN WARRIORS.

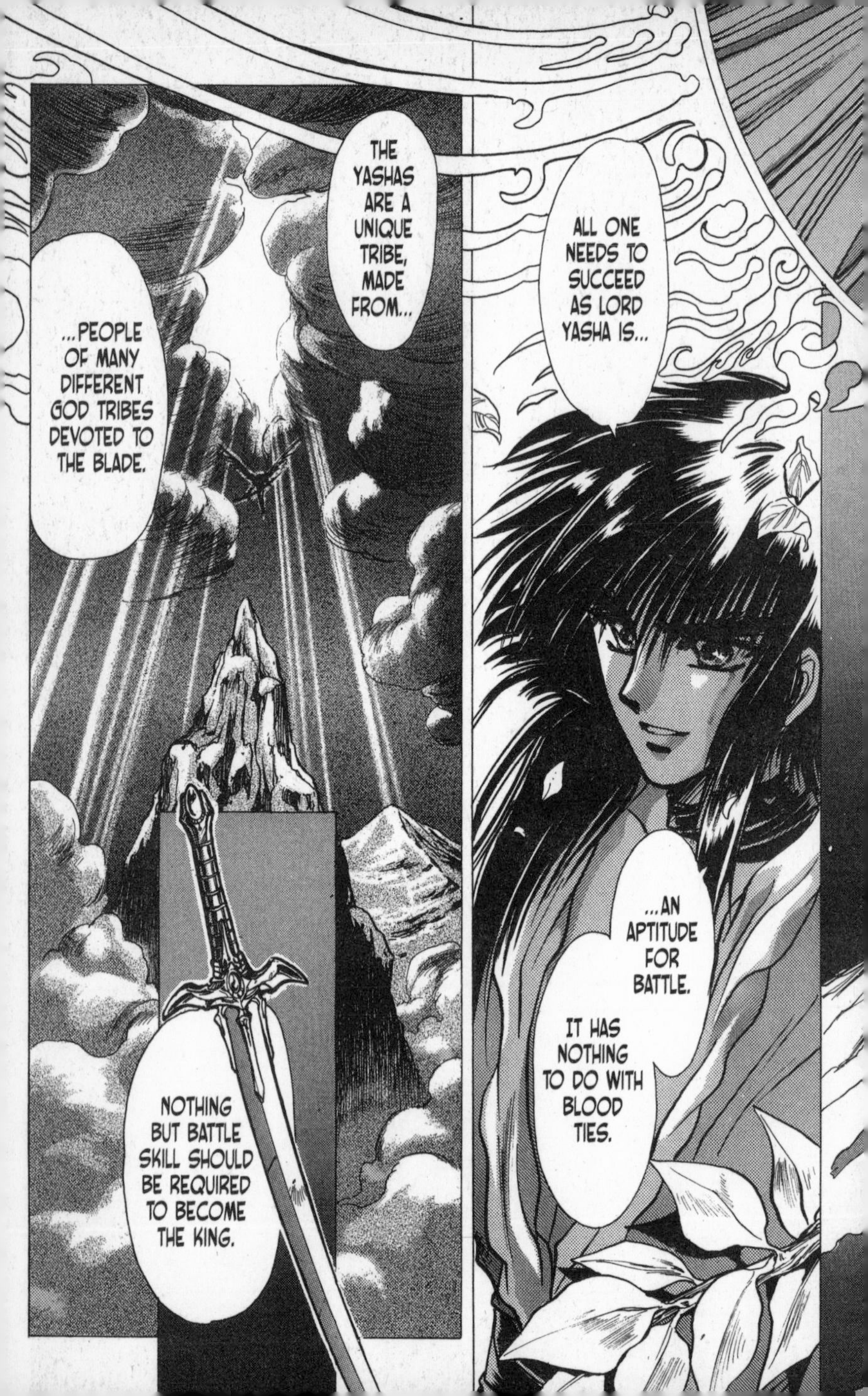
ALL ONE NEEDS TO SUCCEED AS LORD YASHA IS...
...AN APTITUDE FOR BATTLE.
IT HAS NOTHING TO DO WITH BLOOD TIES.
THE YASHAS ARE A UNIQUE TRIBE, MADE FROM...
...PEOPLE OF MANY DIFFERENT GOD TRIBES DEVOTED TO THE BLADE.
NOTHING BUT BATTLE SKILL SHOULD BE REQUIRED TO BECOME THE KING.

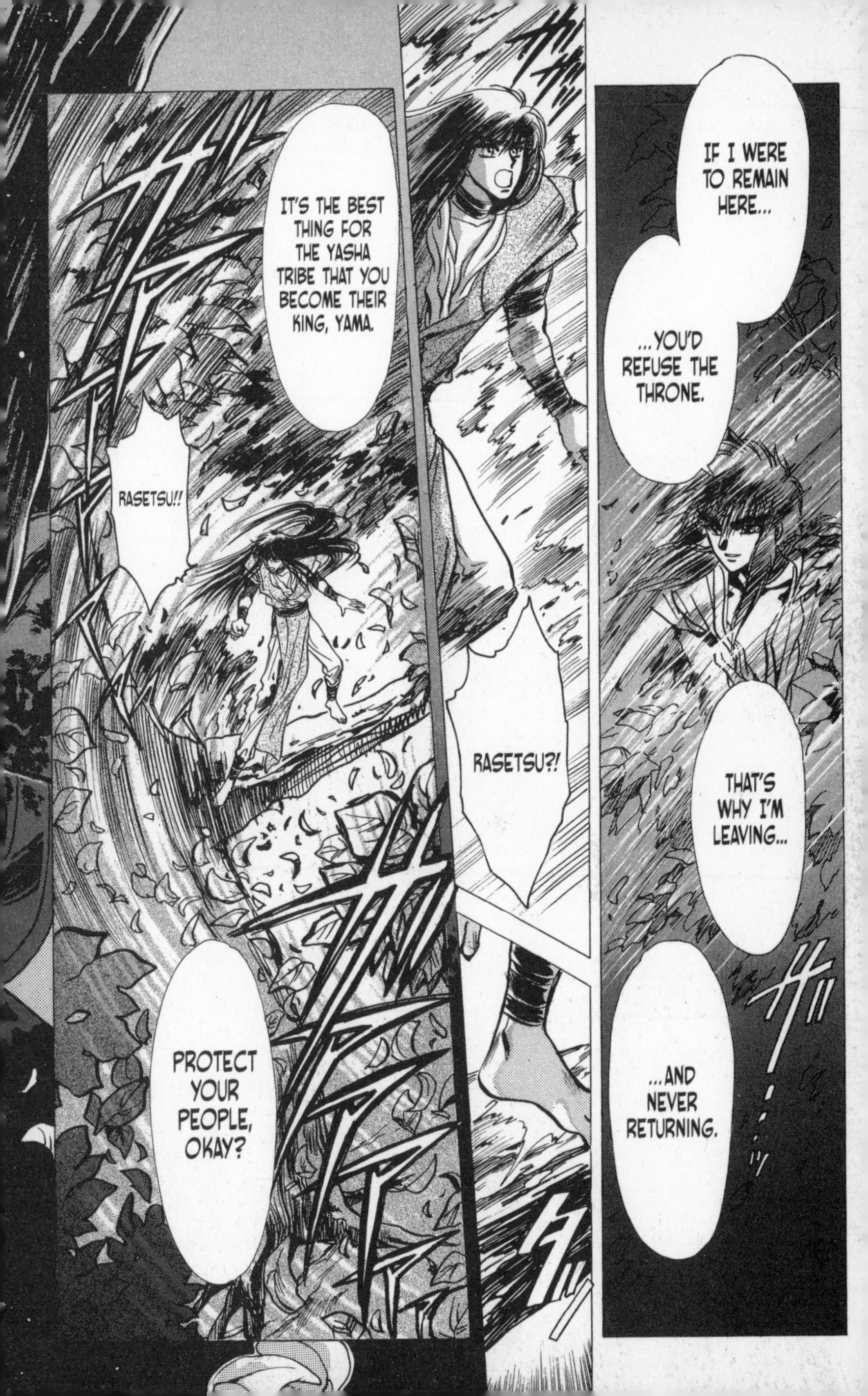
IF I WERE TO REMAIN HERE...
...YOU'D REFUSE THE THRONE.
THAT'S WHY I'M LEAVING...
...AND NEVER RETURNING.
RASETSU?!
IT'S THE BEST THING FOR THE YASHA TRIBE THAT YOU BECOME THEIR KING, YAMA.
RASETSU!!
PROTECT YOUR PEOPLE, OKAY?

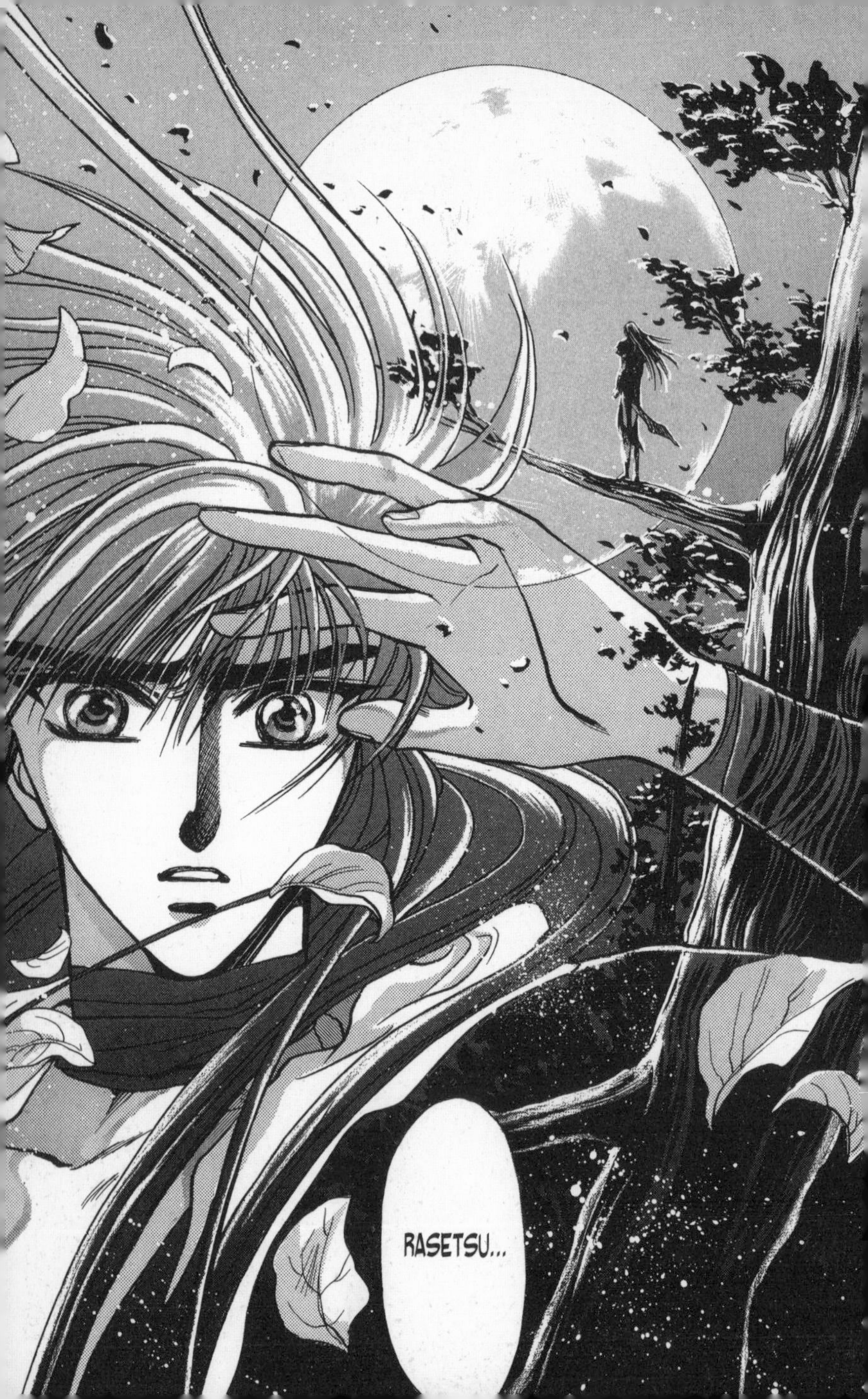
RASETSU...

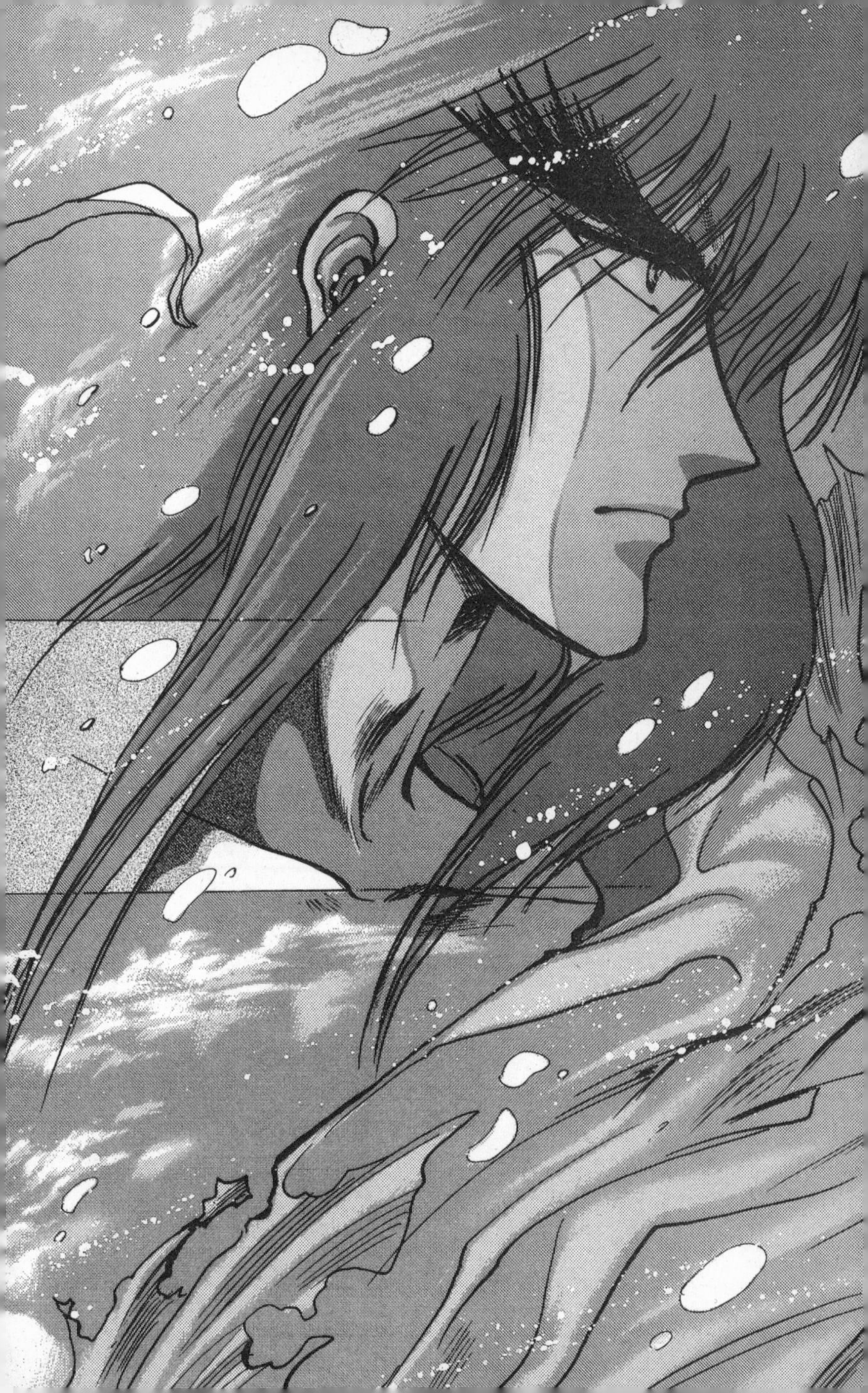

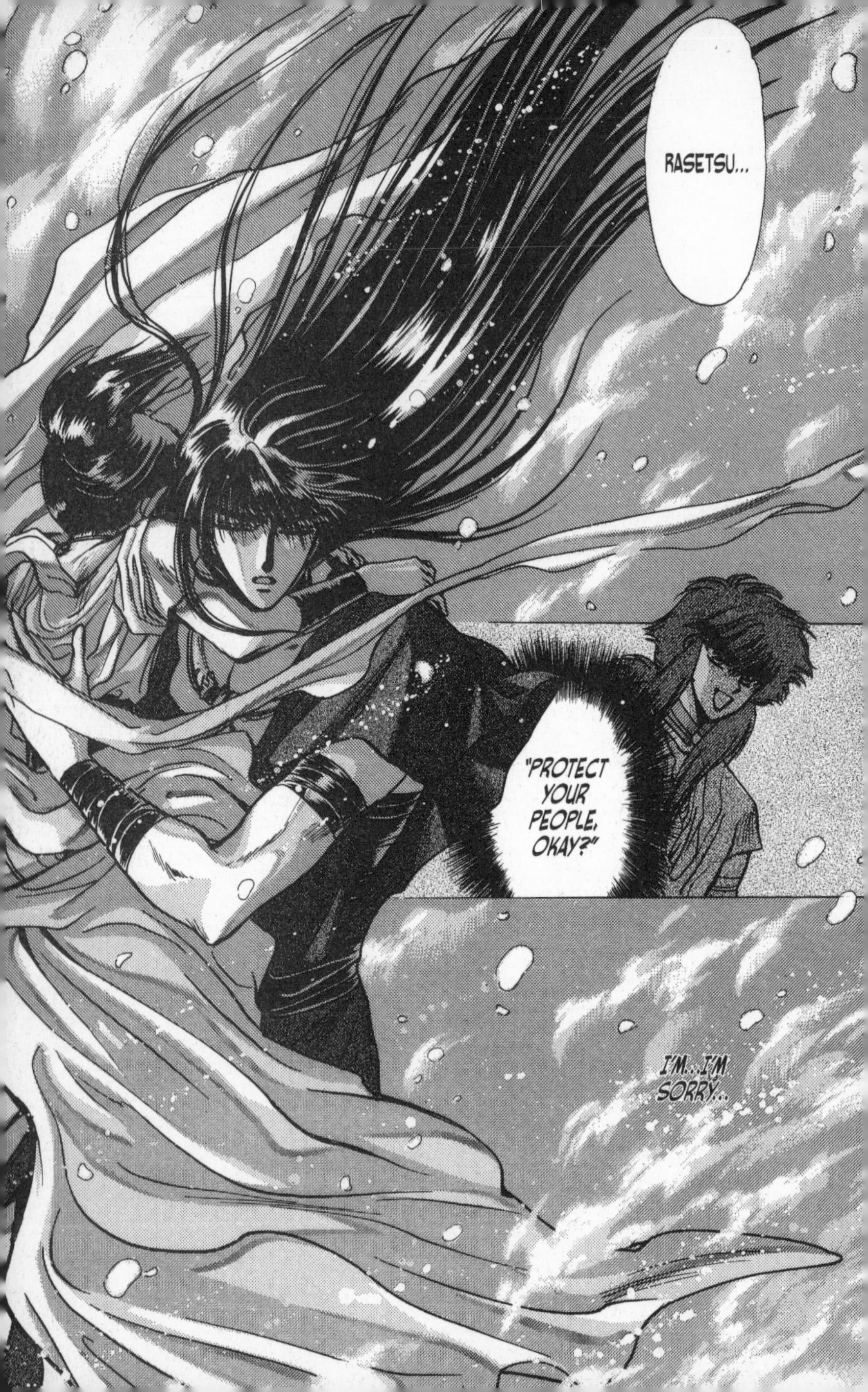
RASETSU...
"PROTECT YOUR PEOPLE, OKAY?"
I'M...I'M SORRY...

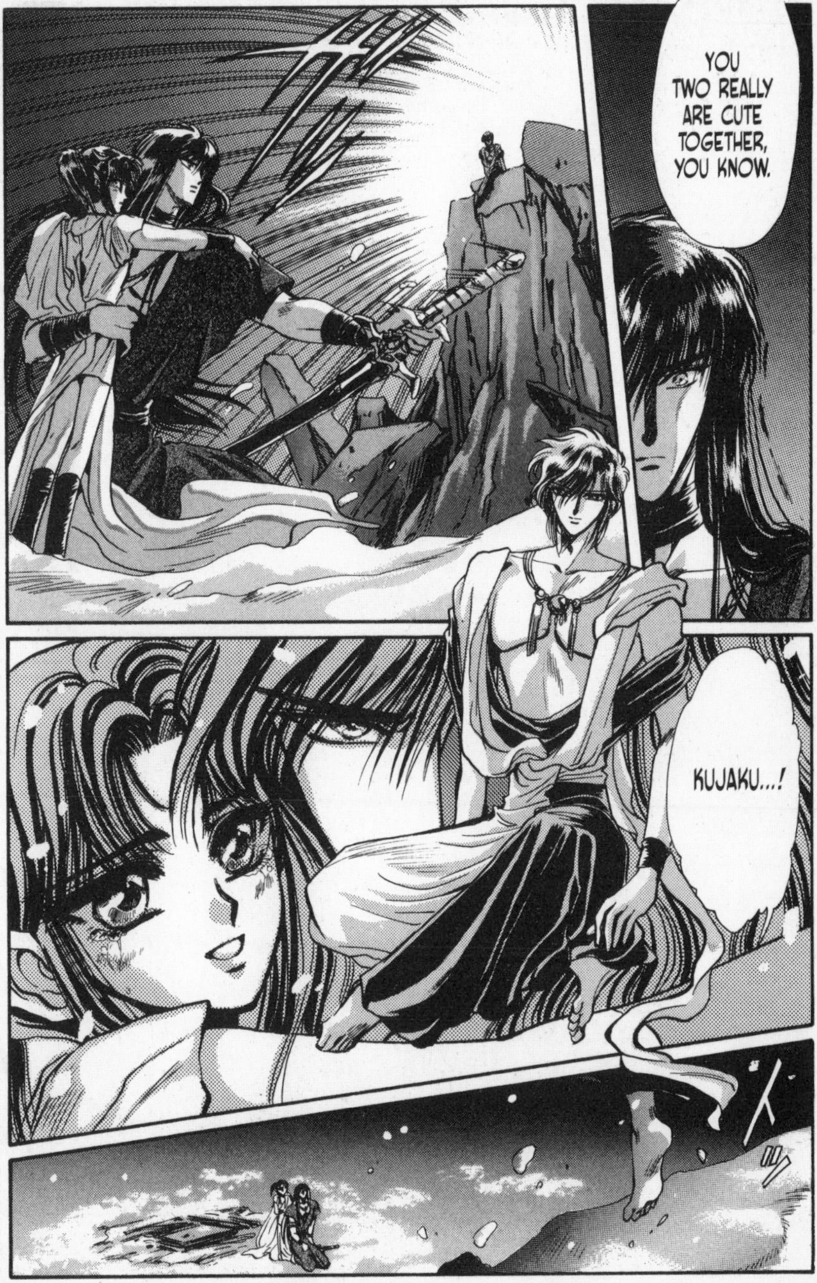
YOU TWO REALLY ARE CUTE TOGETHER, YOU KNOW.
KUJAKU...!

WHAT'S WRONG?
HAS LORD YASHA BEEN BULLYING YOU?
IF SO, THAT'S NO WAY FOR A FATHER TO ACT.

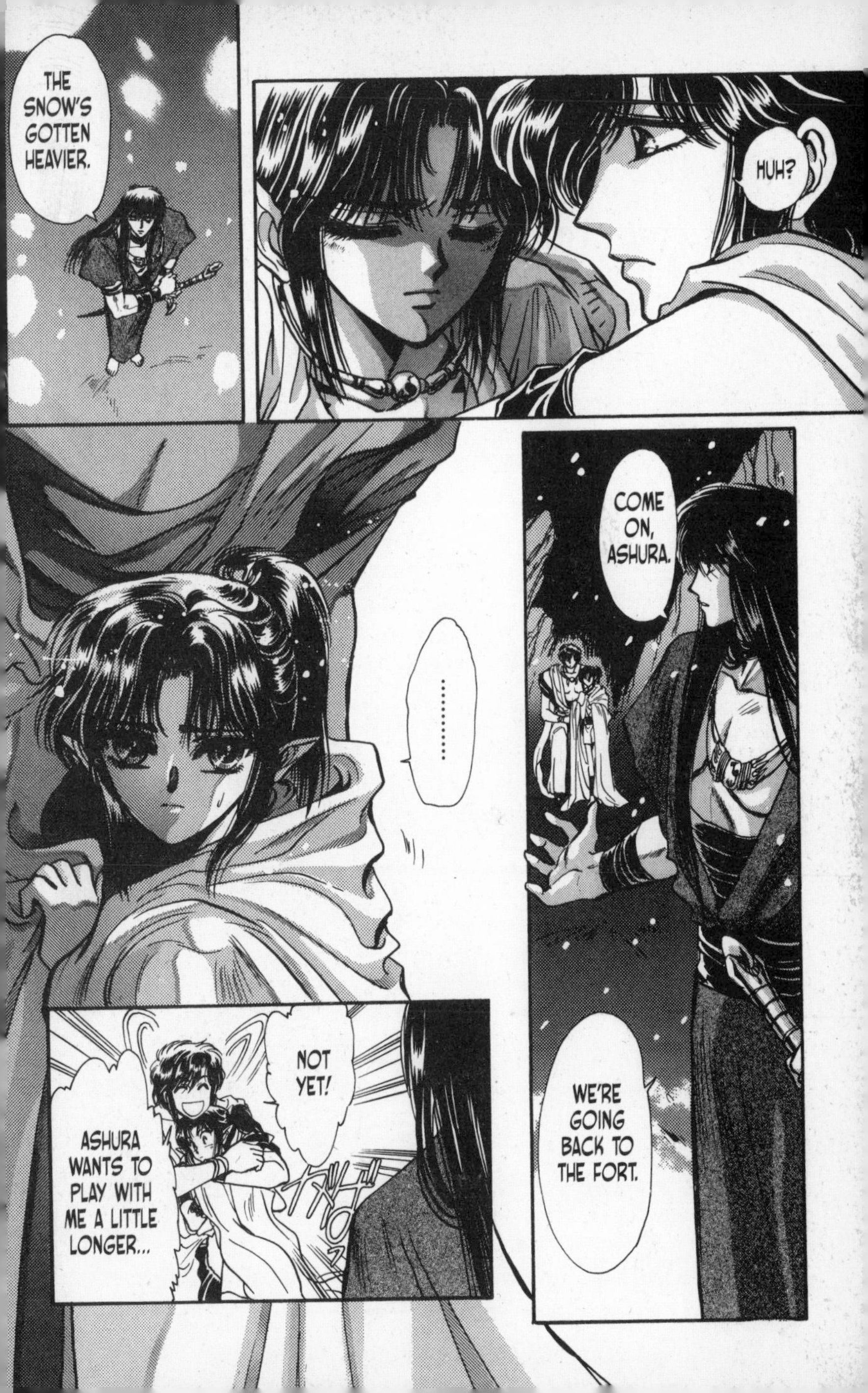
HUH?
THE SNOW'S GOTTEN HEAVIER.
COME ON, ASHURA.
WE'RE GOING BACK TO THE FORT.
......
NOT YET!
ASHURA WANTS TO PLAY WITH ME A LITTLE LONGER...

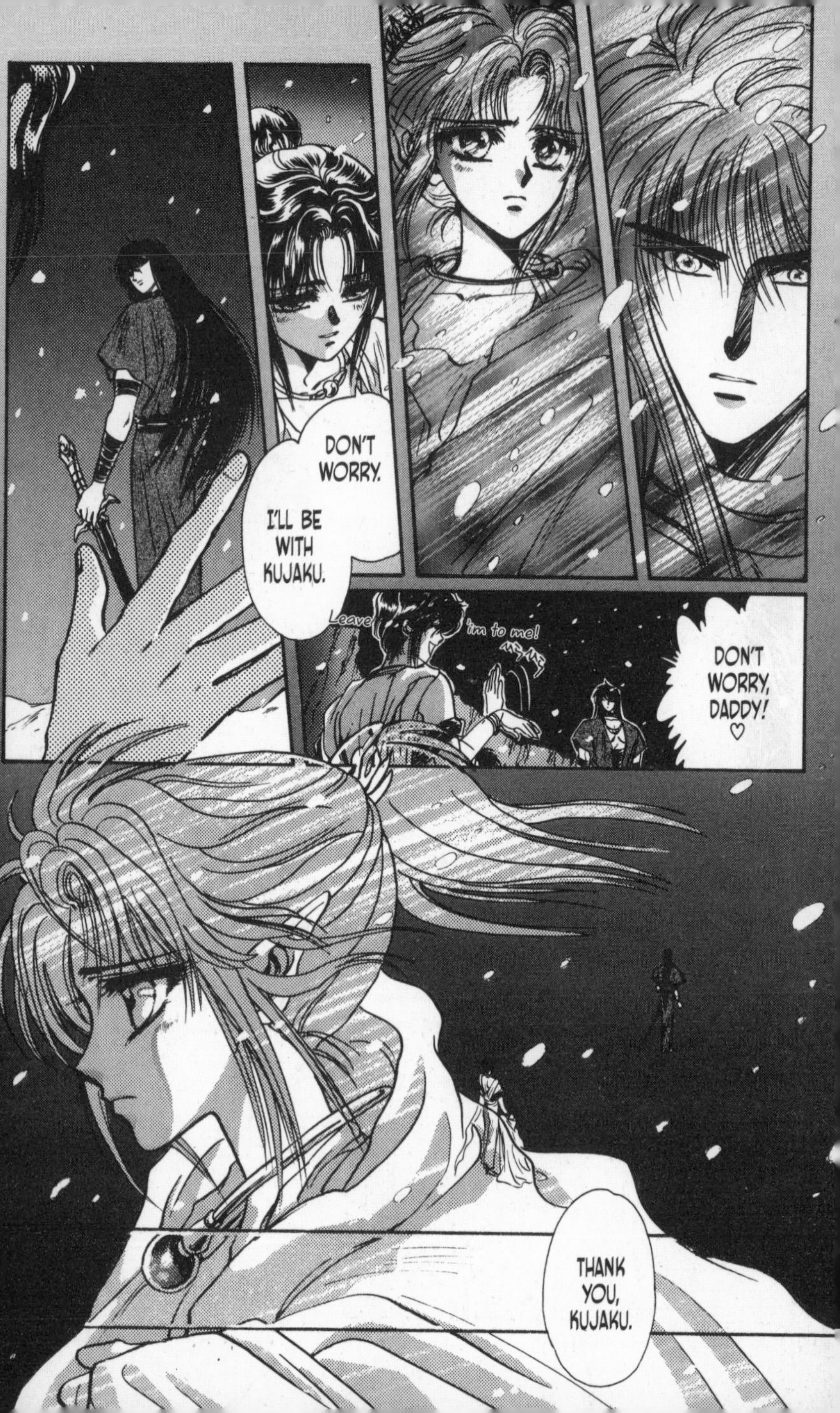
DON'T WORRY.
I'LL BE WITH KUJAKU.
DON'T WORRY, DADDY! ♡
Leave 'im to me!
THANK YOU, KUJAKU.

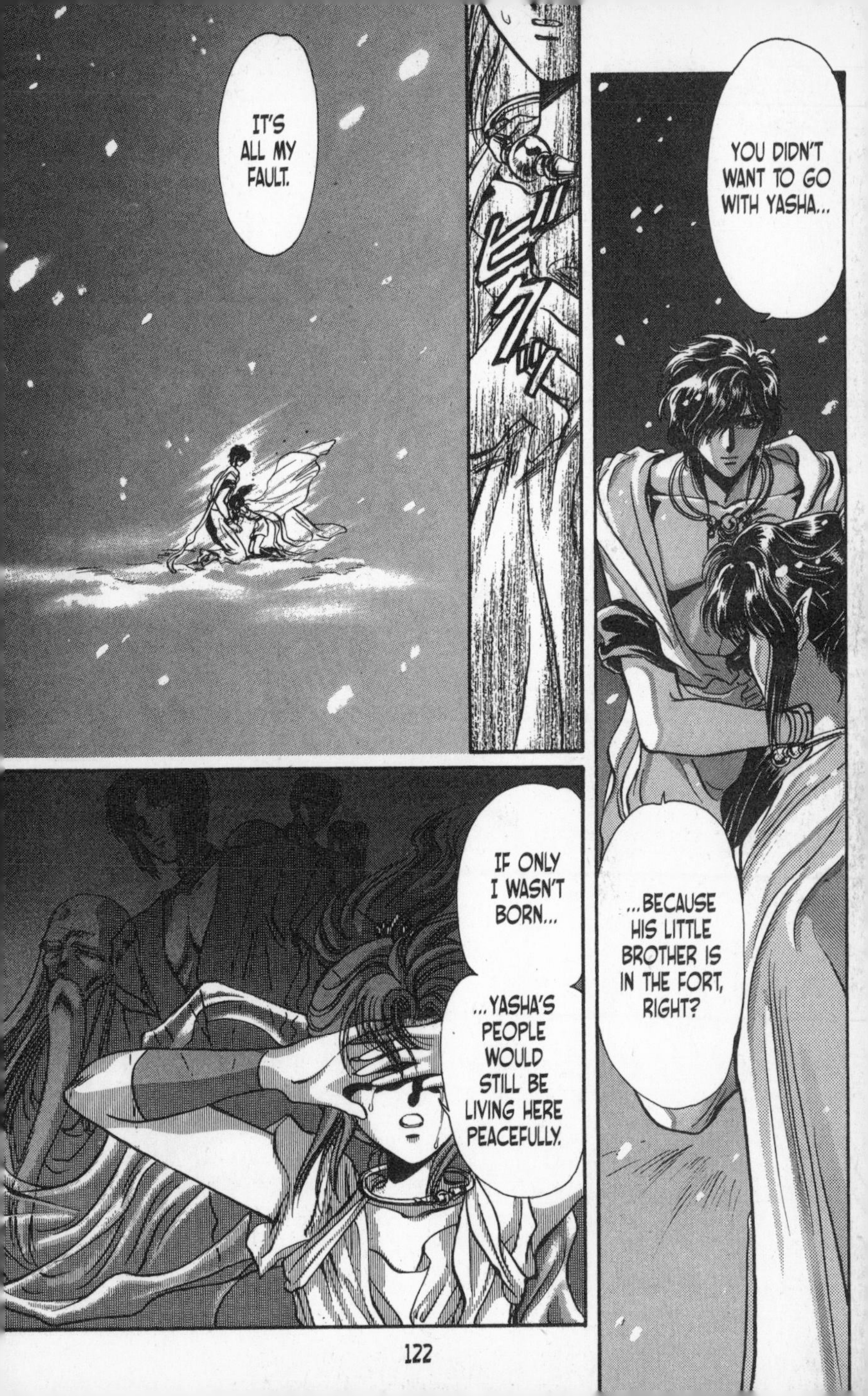
YOU DIDN'T WANT TO GO WITH YASHA...
...BECAUSE HIS LITTLE BROTHER IS IN THE FORT, RIGHT?
IT'S ALL MY FAULT.
IF ONLY I WASN'T BORN...
...YASHA'S PEOPLE WOULD STILL BE LIVING HERE PEACEFULLY.

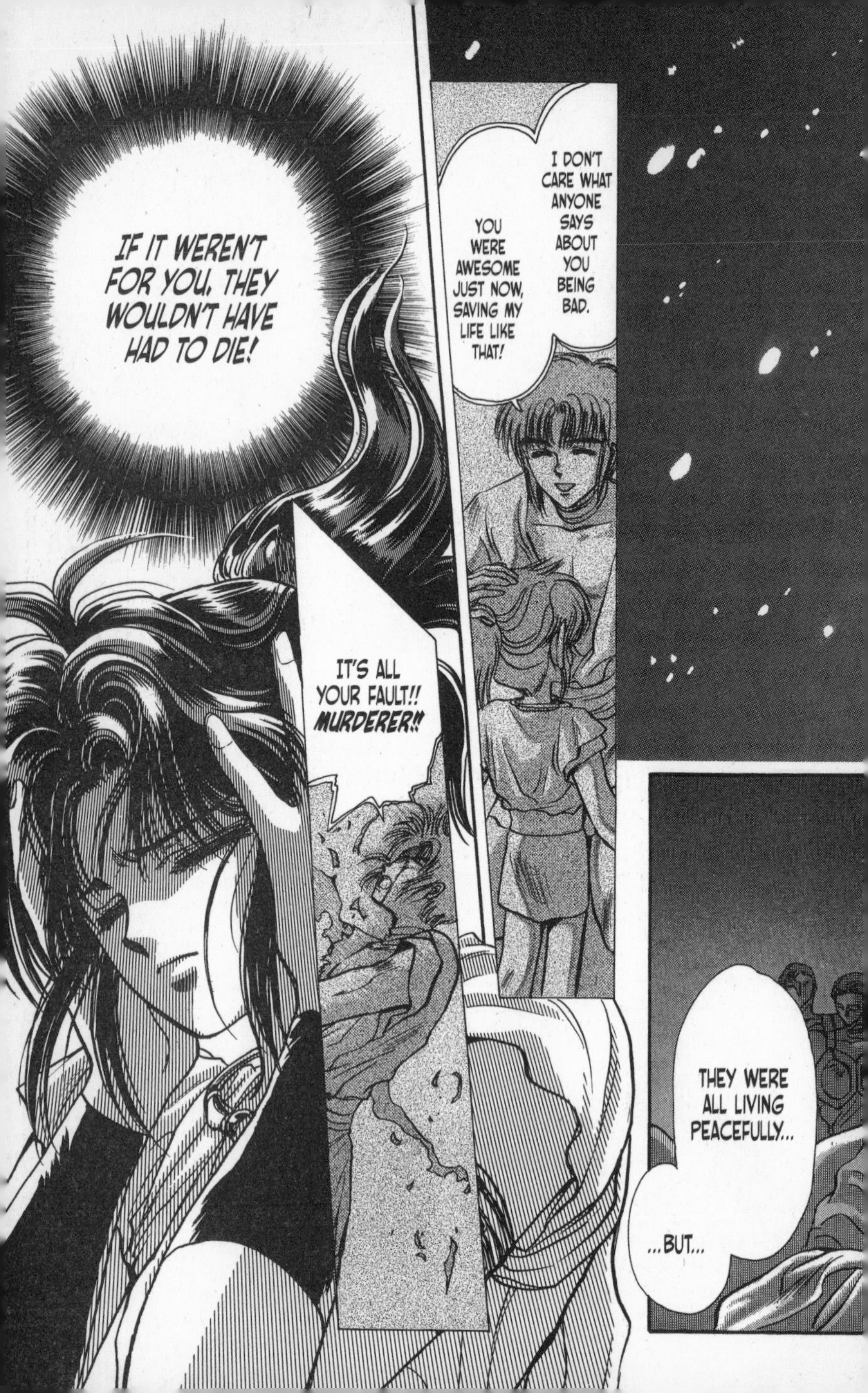
I DON'T CARE WHAT ANYONE SAYS ABOUT YOU BEING BAD.
YOU WERE AWESOME JUST NOW, SAVING MY LIFE LIKE THAT!
THEY WERE ALL LIVING PEACEFULLY...
...BUT...
IF IT WEREN'T FOR YOU, THEY WOULDN'T HAVE HAD TO DIE!
IT'S ALL YOUR FAULT!! MURDERER!!

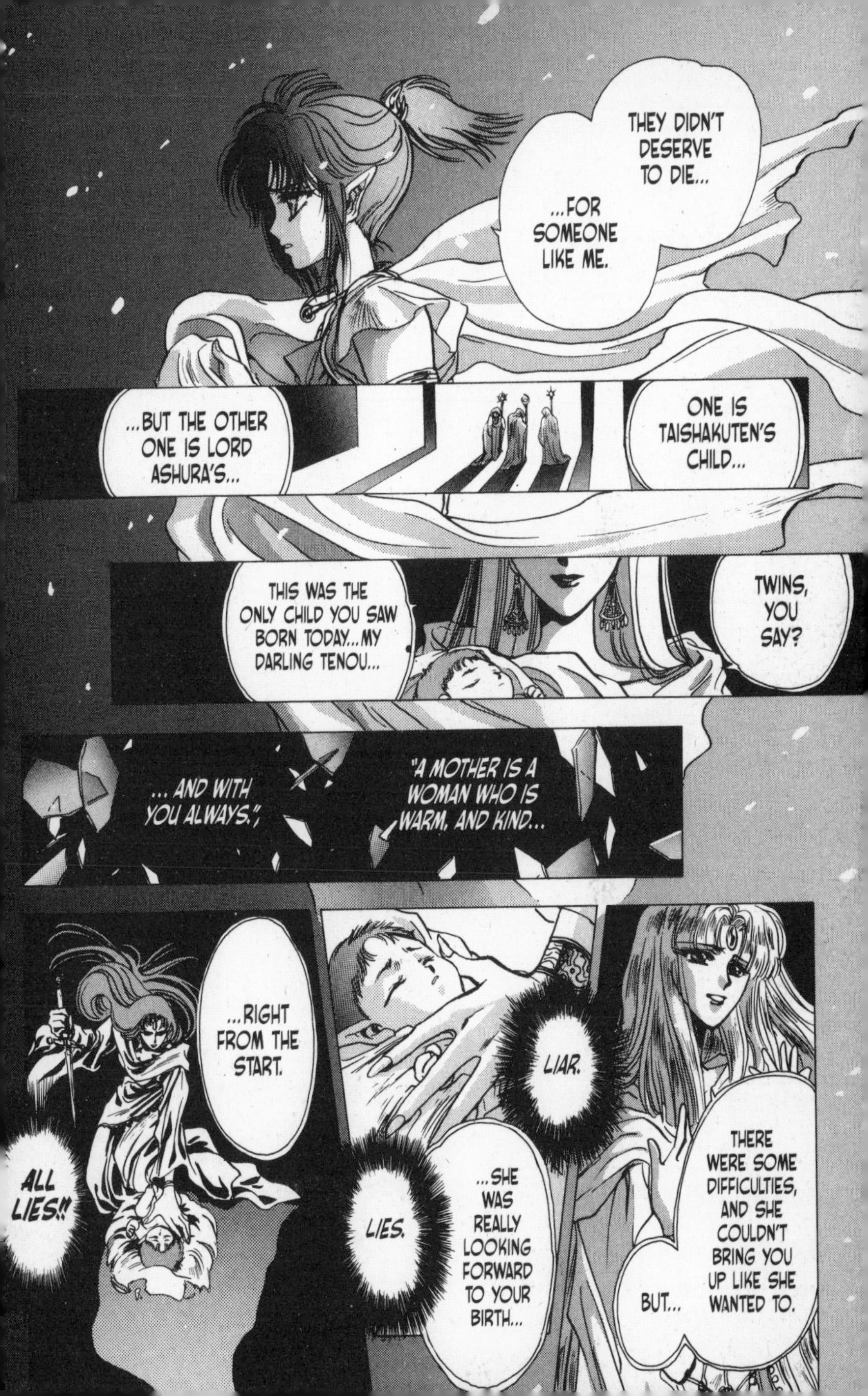
THEY DIDN'T DESERVE TO DIE...
...FOR SOMEONE LIKE ME.
ONE IS TAISHAKUTEN'S CHILD...
...BUT THE OTHER ONE IS LORD ASHURA'S...
TWINS, YOU SAY?
THIS WAS THE ONLY CHILD YOU SAW BORN TODAY...MY DARLING TENOU...
"A MOTHER IS A WOMAN WHO IS WARM, AND KIND...
... AND WITH YOU ALWAYS.",
THERE WERE SOME DIFFICULTIES, AND SHE COULDN'T BRING YOU UP LIKE SHE WANTED TO.
BUT...
LIAR.
...SHE WAS REALLY LOOKING FORWARD TO YOUR BIRTH...
LIES.
...RIGHT FROM THE START.
ALL LIES!!

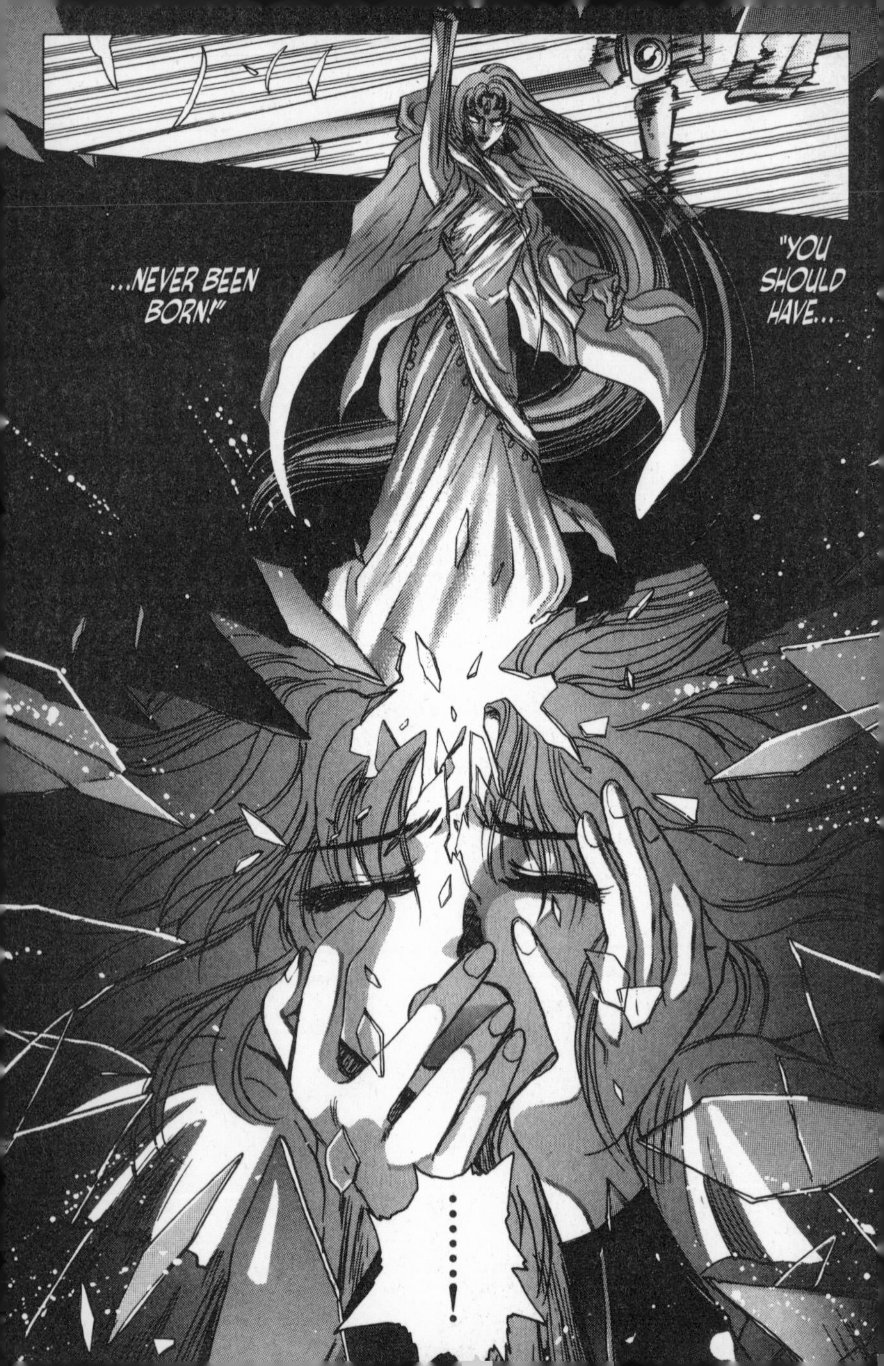
"YOU SHOULD HAVE...
...NEVER BEEN BORN!"
......!

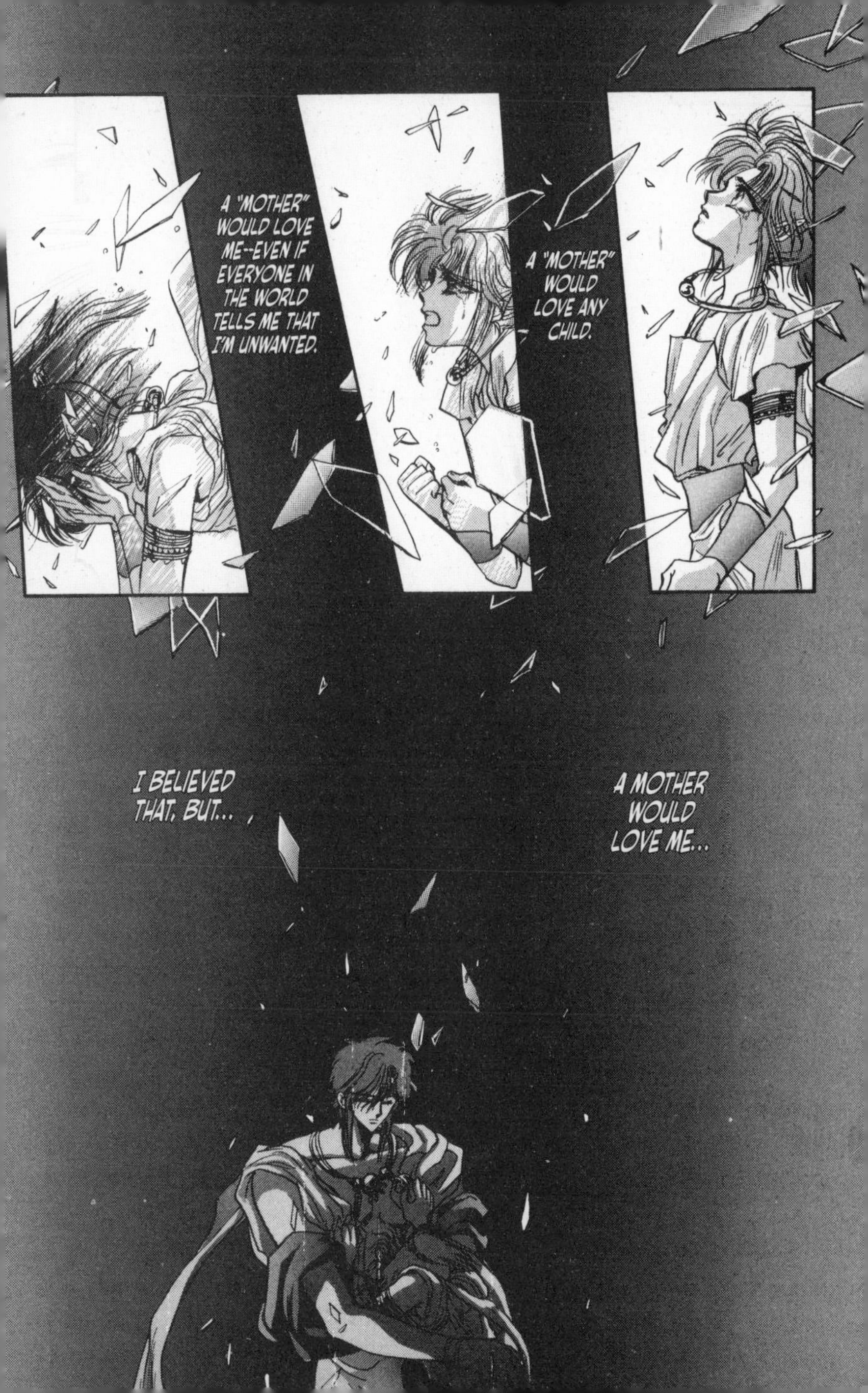
A "MOTHER" WOULD LOVE ANY CHILD.
A "MOTHER" WOULD LOVE ME--EVEN IF EVERYONE IN THE WORLD TELLS ME THAT I'M UNWANTED.
A MOTHER WOULD LOVE ME...
I BELIEVED THAT, BUT...

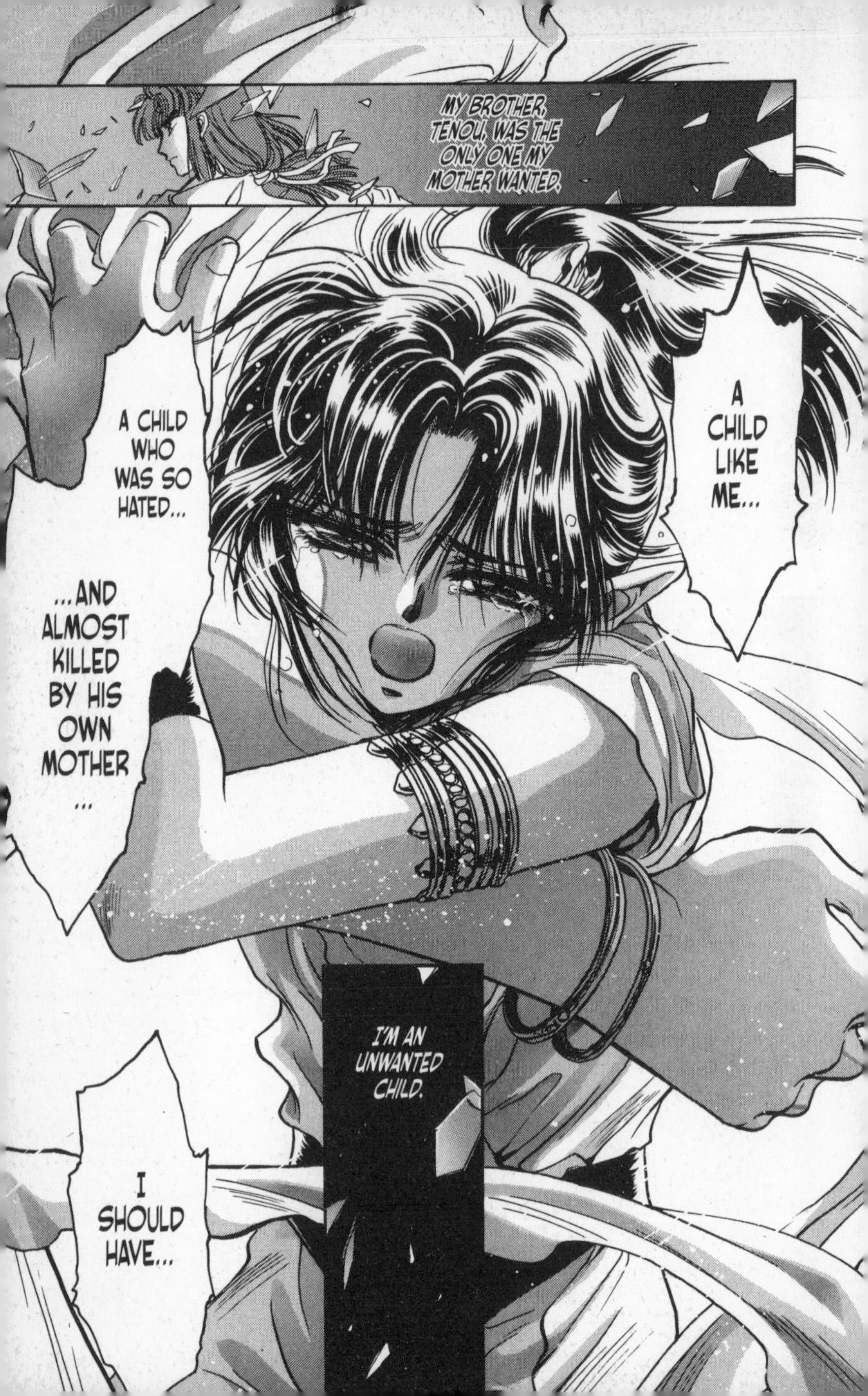
MY BROTHER, TENOU, WAS THE ONLY ONE MY MOTHER WANTED.
A CHILD LIKE ME...
A CHILD WHO WAS SO HATED...
...AND ALMOST KILLED BY HIS OWN MOTHER...
I'M AN UNWANTED CHILD.
I SHOULD HAVE...

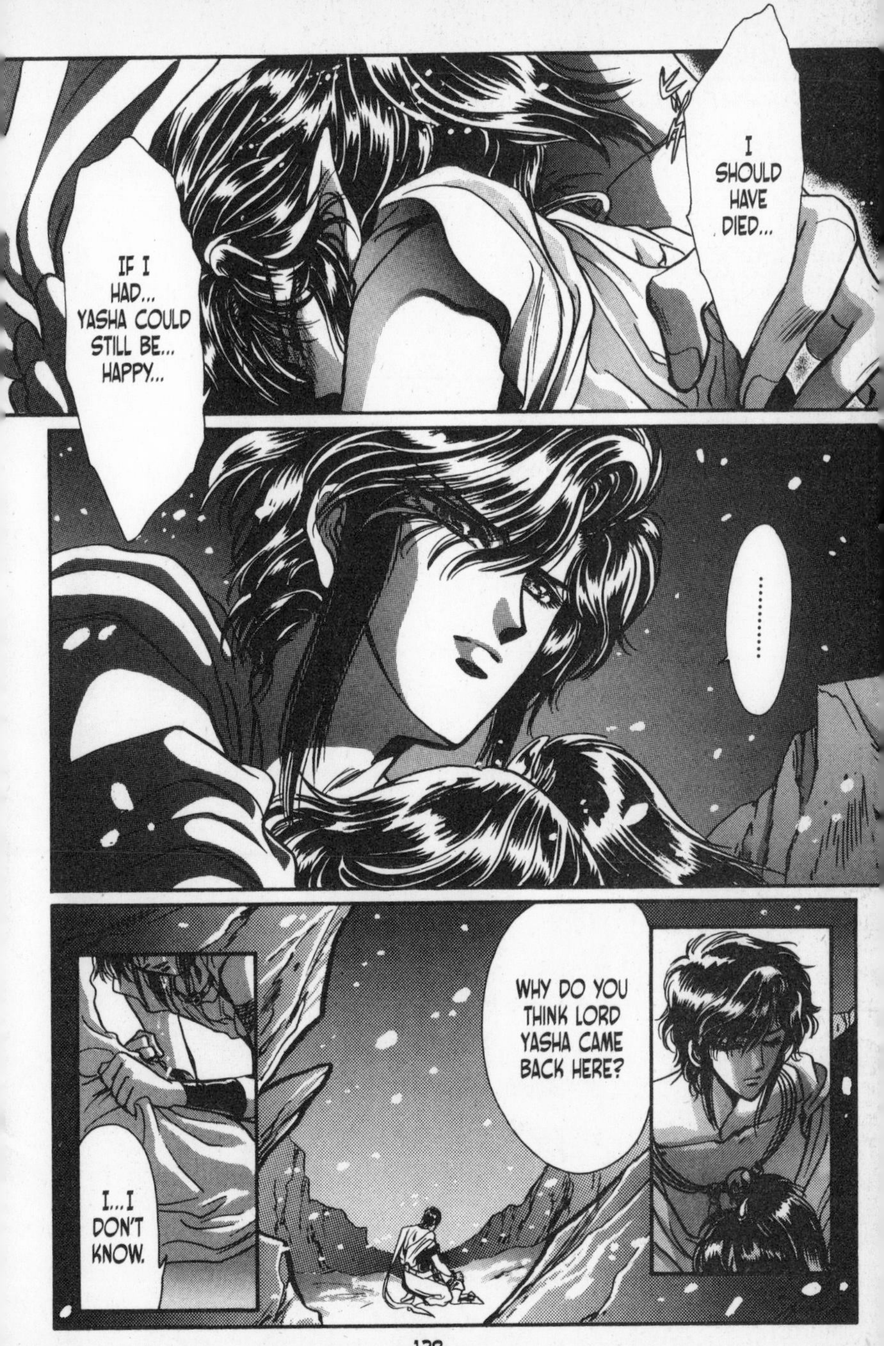
I SHOULD HAVE DIED...
IF I HAD... YASHA COULD STILL BE... HAPPY...
......
WHY DO YOU THINK LORD YASHA CAME BACK HERE?
I...I DON'T KNOW.

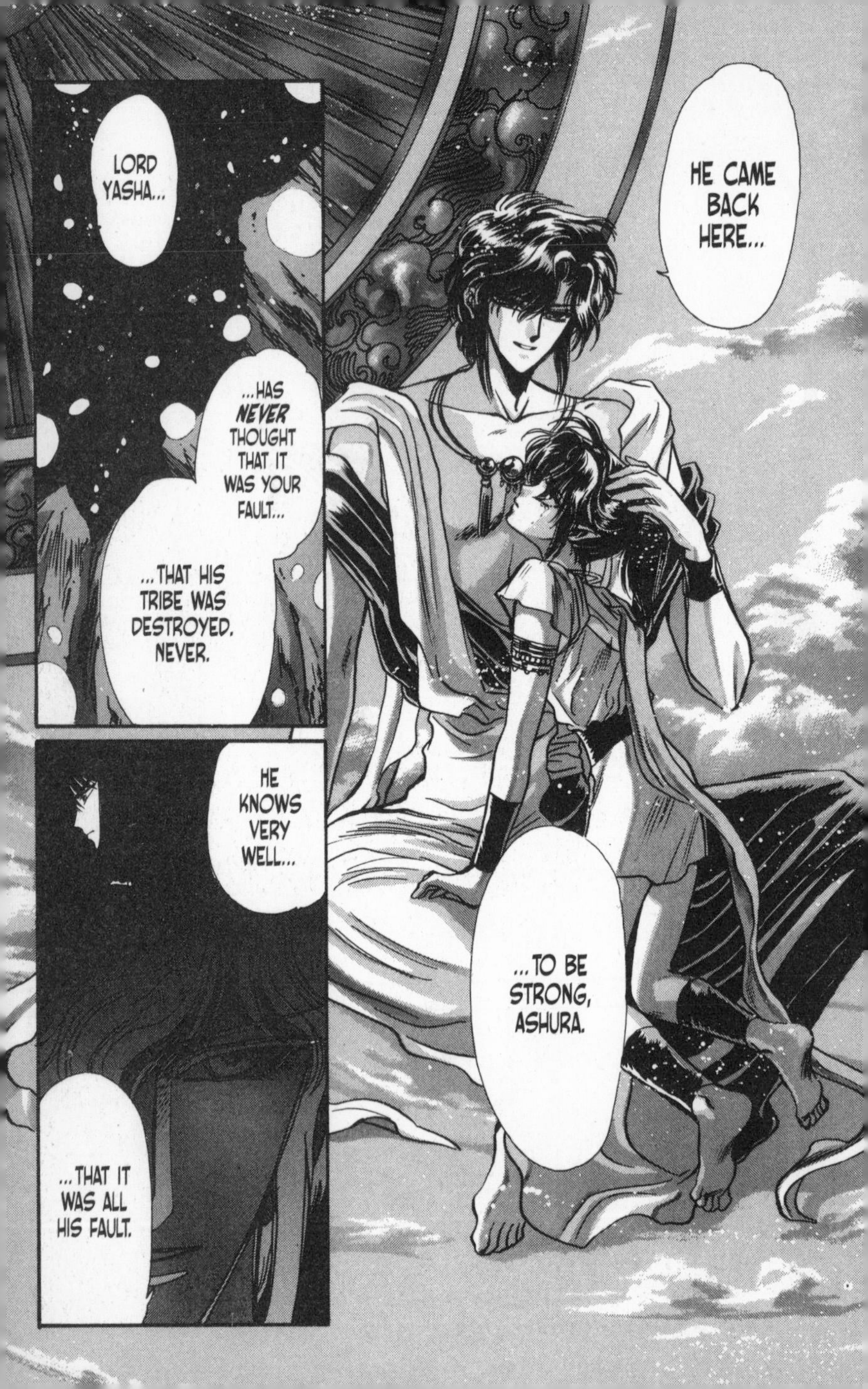
HE CAME BACK HERE...
...TO BE STRONG, ASHURA.
LORD YASHA...
...HAS *NEVER* THOUGHT THAT IT WAS YOUR FAULT...
...THAT HIS TRIBE WAS DESTROYED. NEVER.
HE KNOWS VERY WELL...
...THAT IT WAS ALL HIS FAULT.

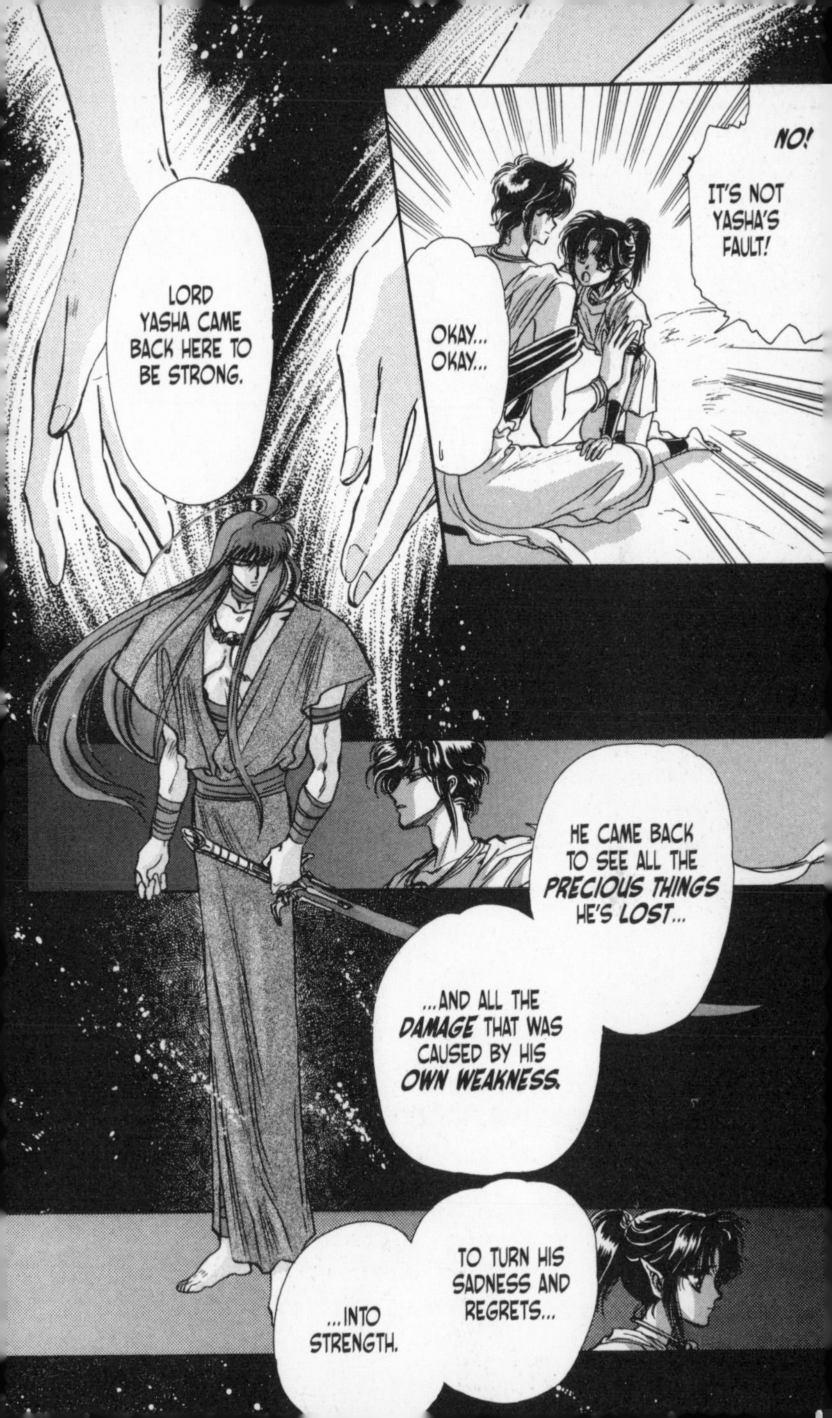
NO!
IT'S NOT YASHA'S FAULT!
OKAY... OKAY...
LORD YASHA CAME BACK HERE TO BE STRONG.
HE CAME BACK TO SEE ALL THE *PRECIOUS THINGS* HE'S *LOST*...
...AND ALL THE *DAMAGE* THAT WAS CAUSED BY HIS *OWN WEAKNESS.*
TO TURN HIS SADNESS AND REGRETS...
...INTO STRENGTH.

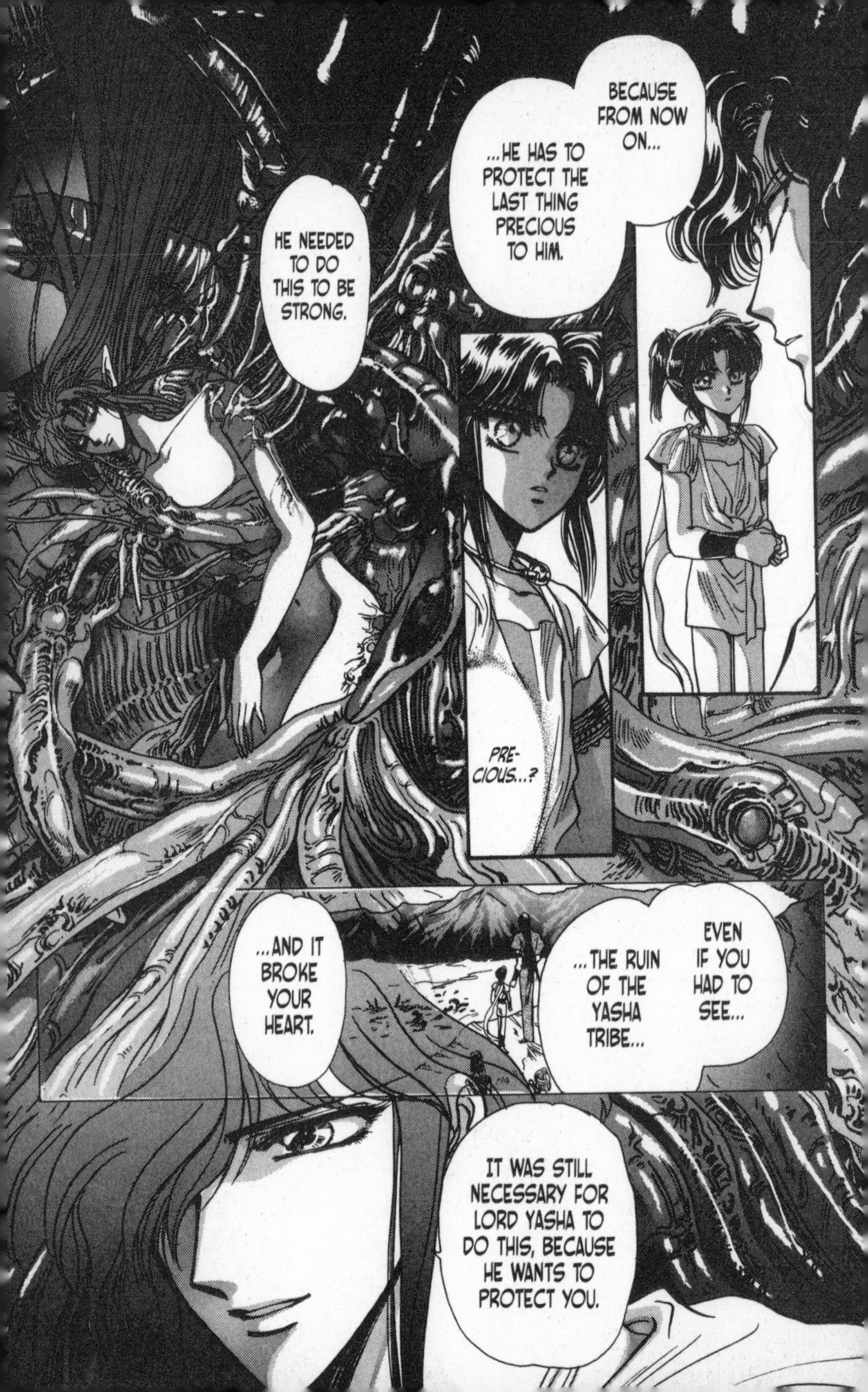
HE NEEDED TO DO THIS TO BE STRONG.
BECAUSE FROM NOW ON...
...HE HAS TO PROTECT THE LAST THING PRECIOUS TO HIM.
PRE-CIOUS...?
EVEN IF YOU HAD TO SEE...
...THE RUIN OF THE YASHA TRIBE...
...AND IT BROKE YOUR HEART.
IT WAS STILL NECESSARY FOR LORD YASHA TO DO THIS, BECAUSE HE WANTS TO PROTECT YOU.

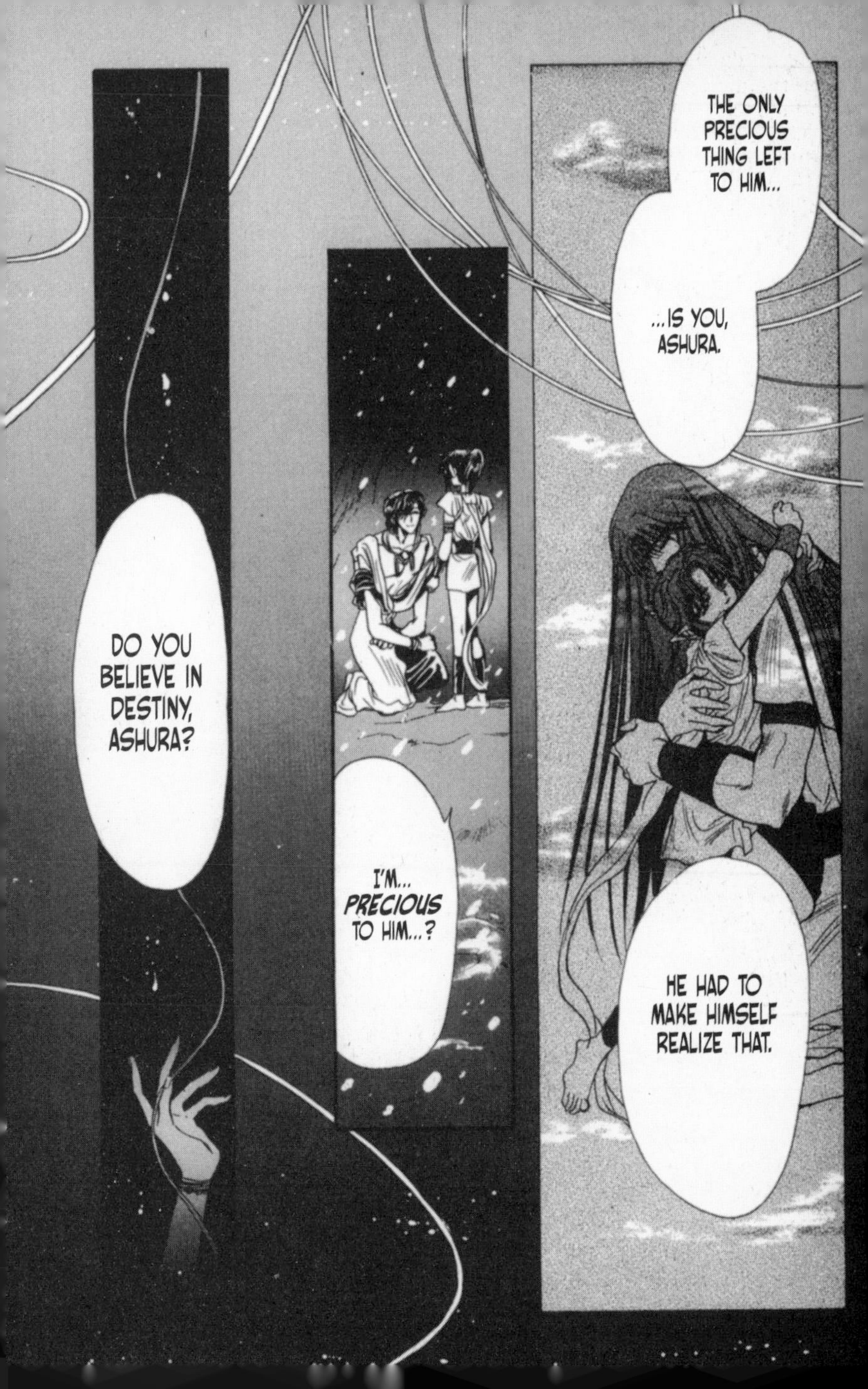
THE ONLY PRECIOUS THING LEFT TO HIM...
...IS YOU, ASHURA.
HE HAD TO MAKE HIMSELF REALIZE THAT.
I'M... *PRECIOUS* TO HIM...?
DO YOU BELIEVE IN DESTINY, ASHURA?

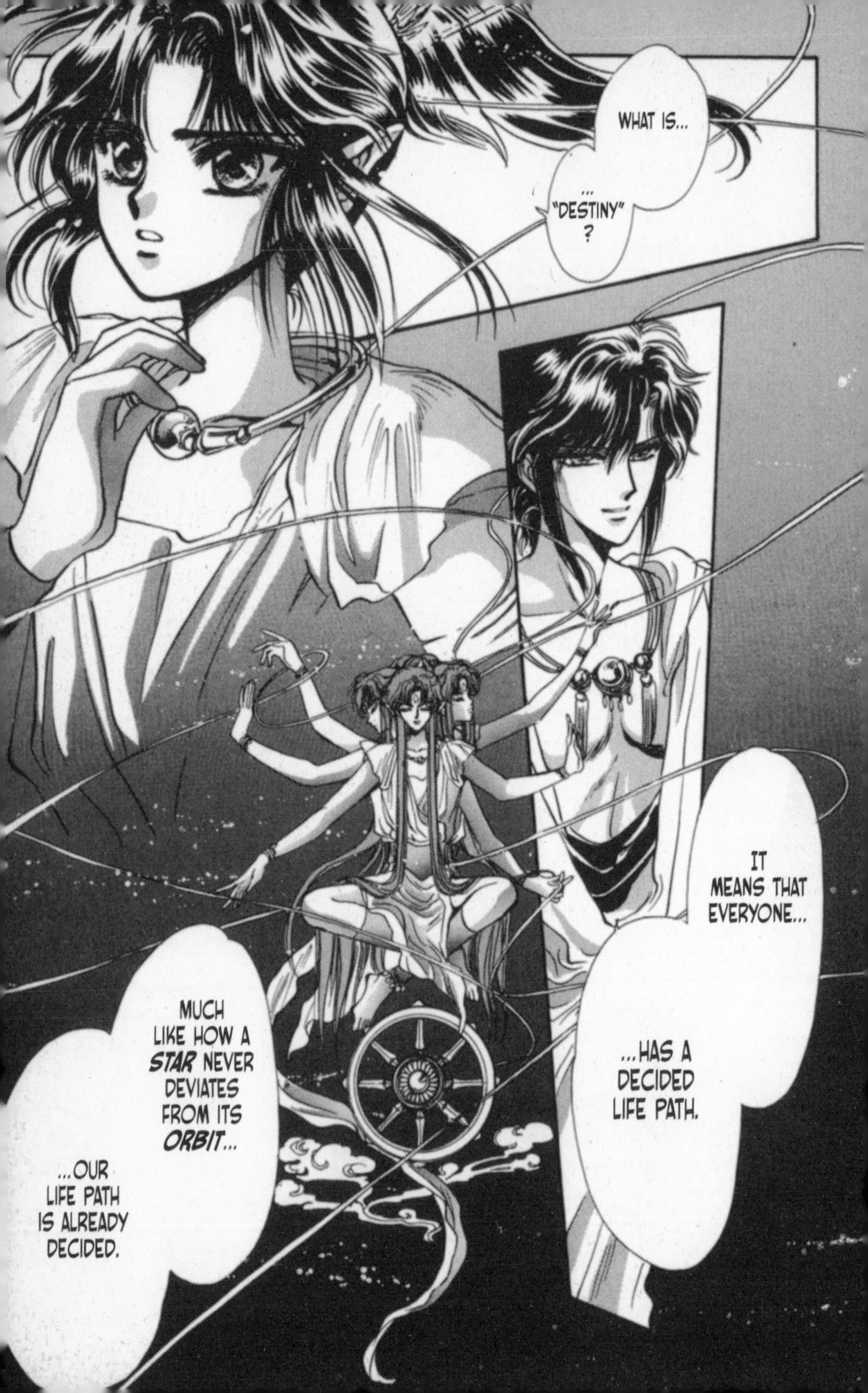
WHAT IS...
... "DESTINY" ?
IT MEANS THAT EVERYONE...
...HAS A DECIDED LIFE PATH.
MUCH LIKE HOW A STAR NEVER DEVIATES FROM ITS ORBIT...
...OUR LIFE PATH IS ALREADY DECIDED.

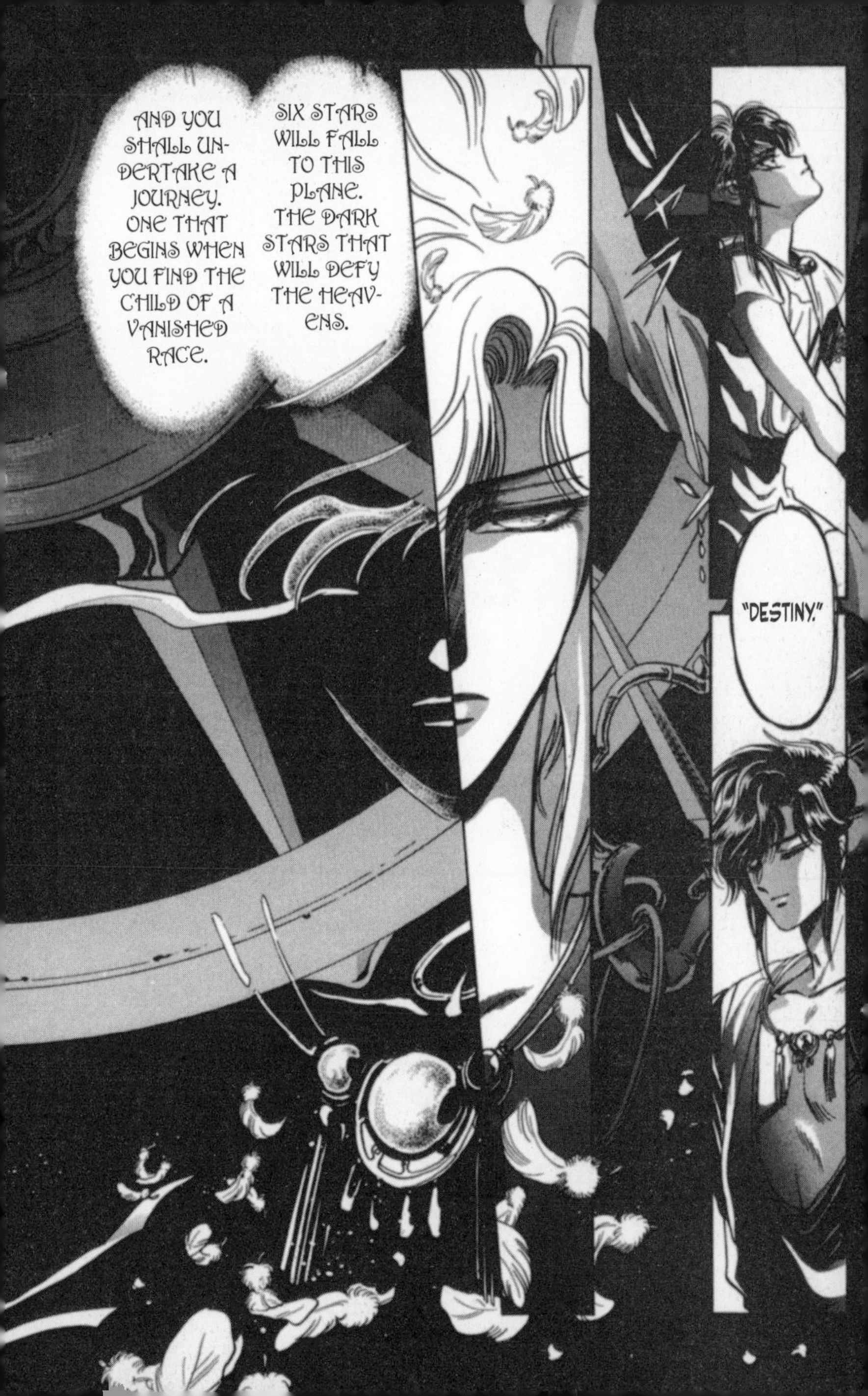
"DESTINY."
SIX STARS WILL FALL TO THIS PLANE. THE DARK STARS THAT WILL DEFY THE HEAV-ENS.
AND YOU SHALL UN-DERTAKE A JOURNEY. ONE THAT BEGINS WHEN YOU FIND THE CHILD OF A VANISHED RACE.

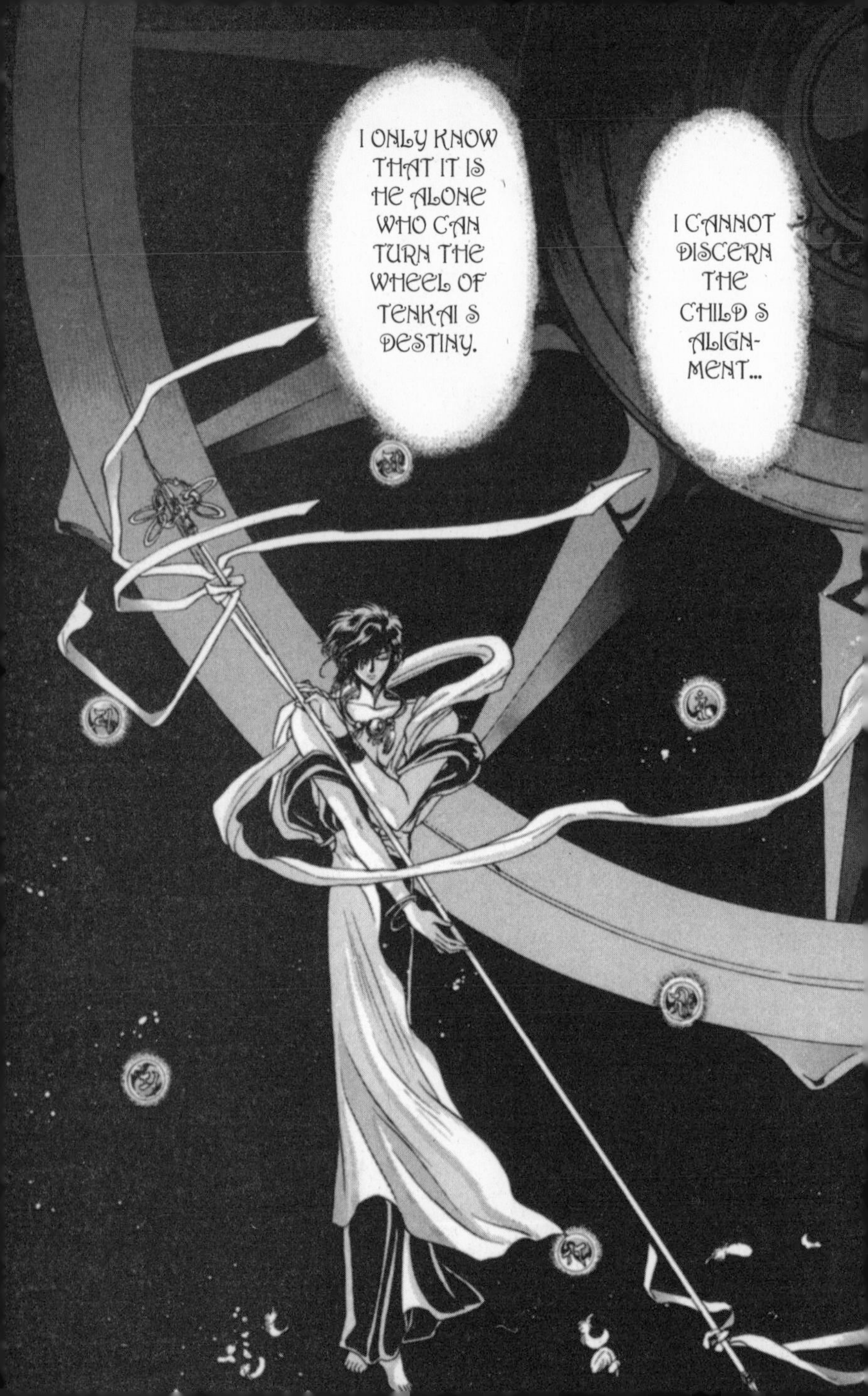
I CANNOT DISCERN THE CHILD S ALIGN-MENT...
I ONLY KNOW THAT IT IS HE ALONE WHO CAN TURN THE WHEEL OF TENKAI S DESTINY.

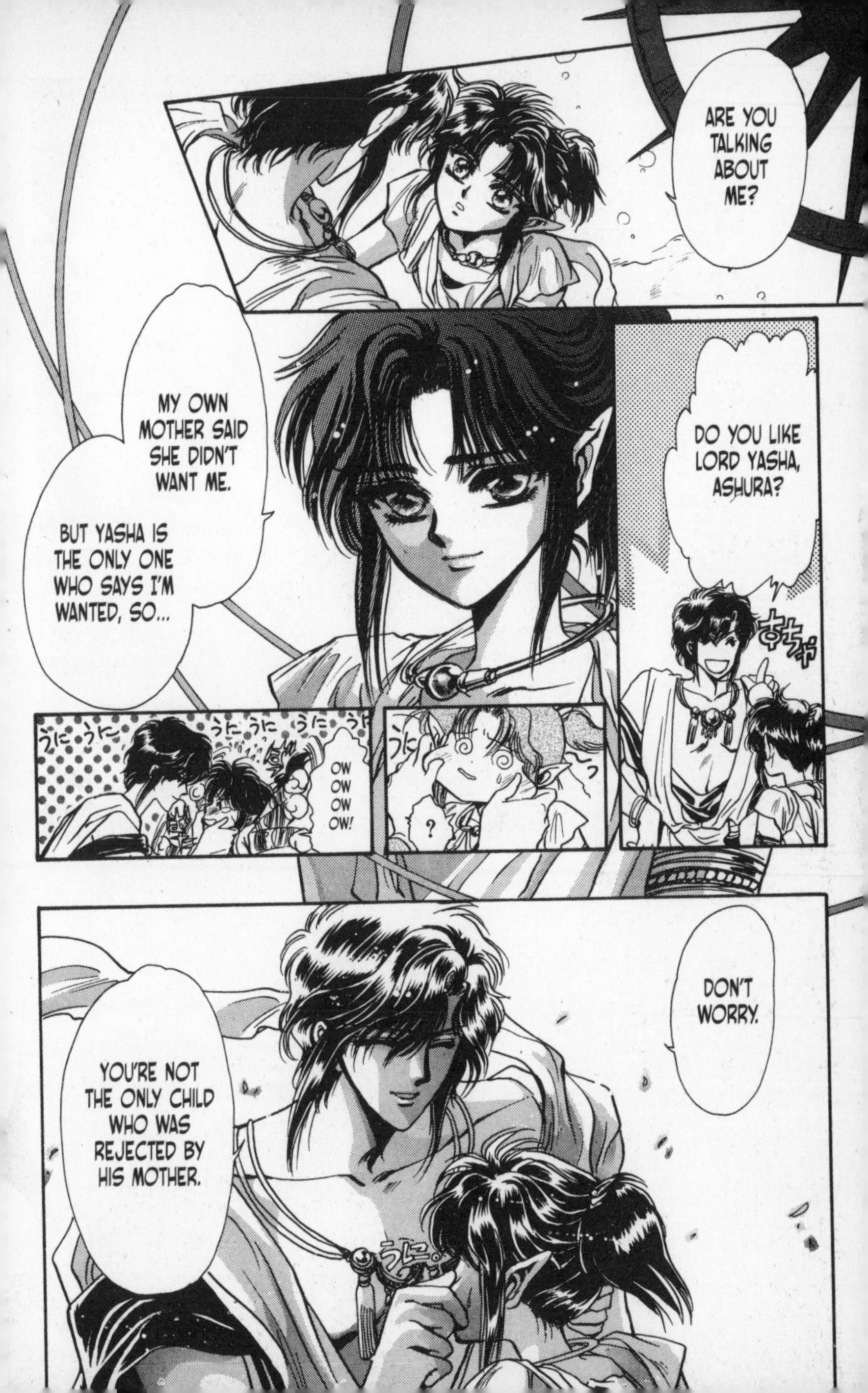
ARE YOU TALKING ABOUT ME?
DO YOU LIKE LORD YASHA, ASHURA?
MY OWN MOTHER SAID SHE DIDN'T WANT ME.
BUT YASHA IS THE ONLY ONE WHO SAYS I'M WANTED, SO...
?
OW OW OW OW!
DON'T WORRY.
YOU'RE NOT THE ONLY CHILD WHO WAS REJECTED BY HIS MOTHER.

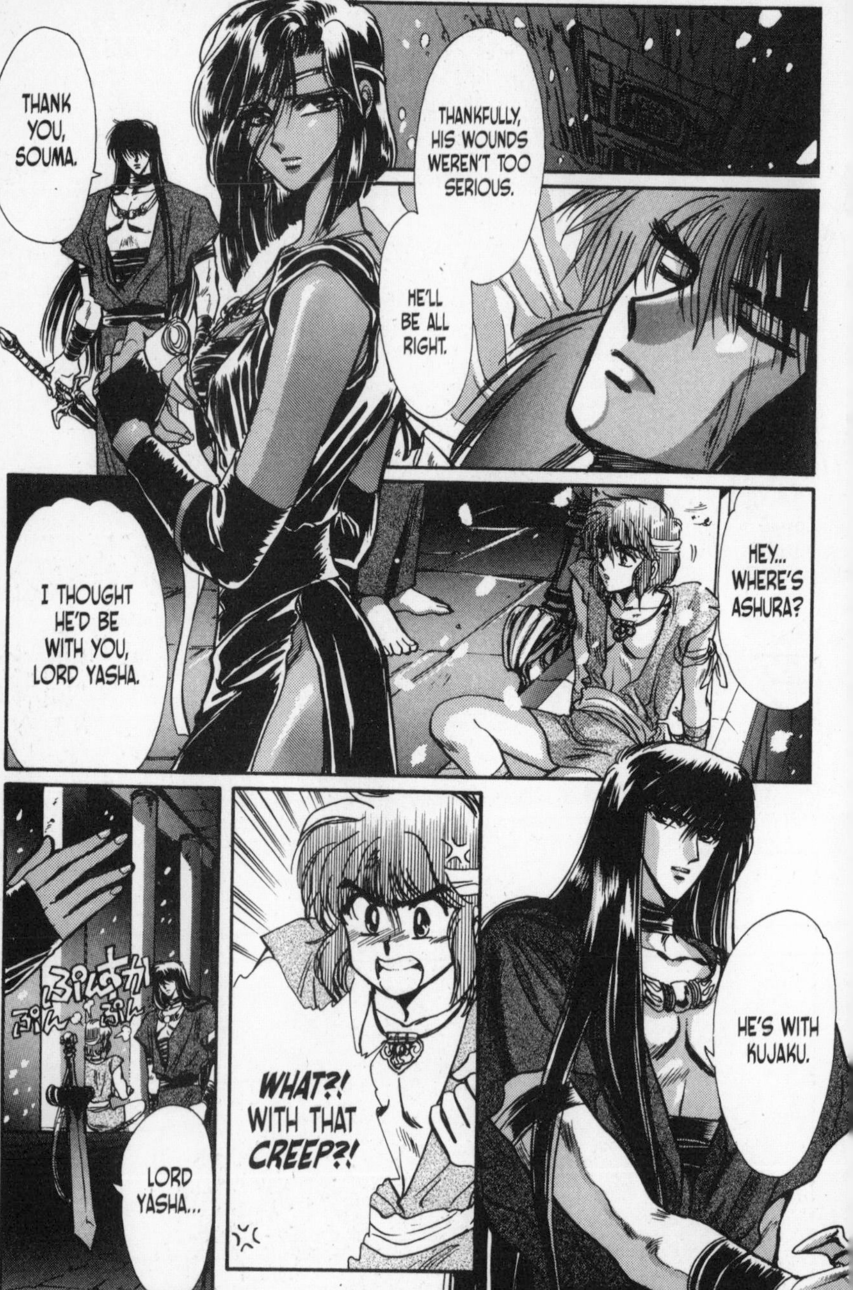
THANKFULLY, HIS WOUNDS WEREN'T TOO SERIOUS.
HE'LL BE ALL RIGHT.
THANK YOU, SOUMA.
HEY... WHERE'S ASHURA?
I THOUGHT HE'D BE WITH YOU, LORD YASHA.
HE'S WITH KUJAKU.
WHAT?! WITH THAT CREEP?!
ぷんすか
ぷん ぷん
LORD YASHA...

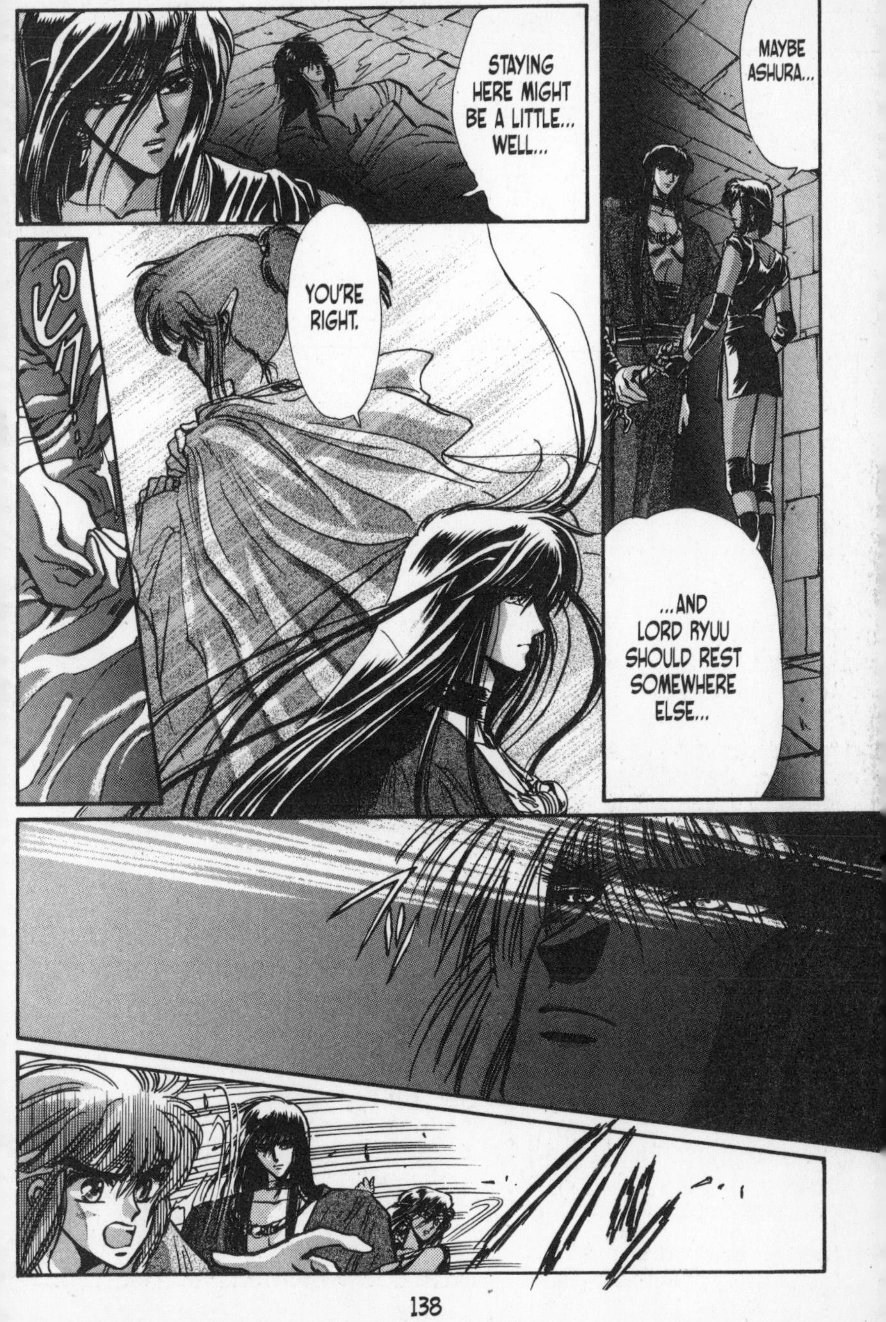
MAYBE ASHURA...
...AND LORD RYUU SHOULD REST SOMEWHERE ELSE...
STAYING HERE MIGHT BE A LITTLE... WELL...
YOU'RE RIGHT.

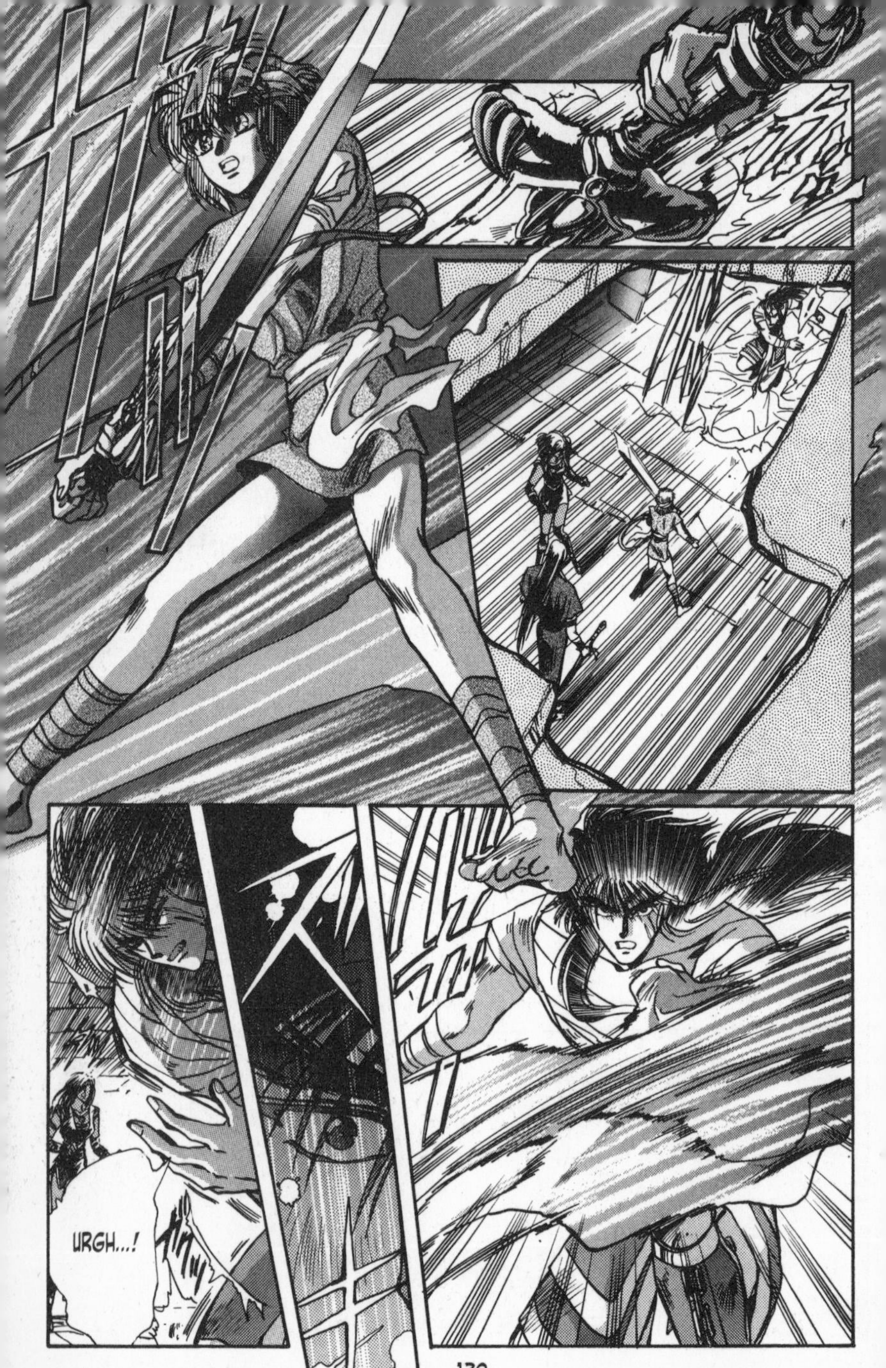
URGH...!

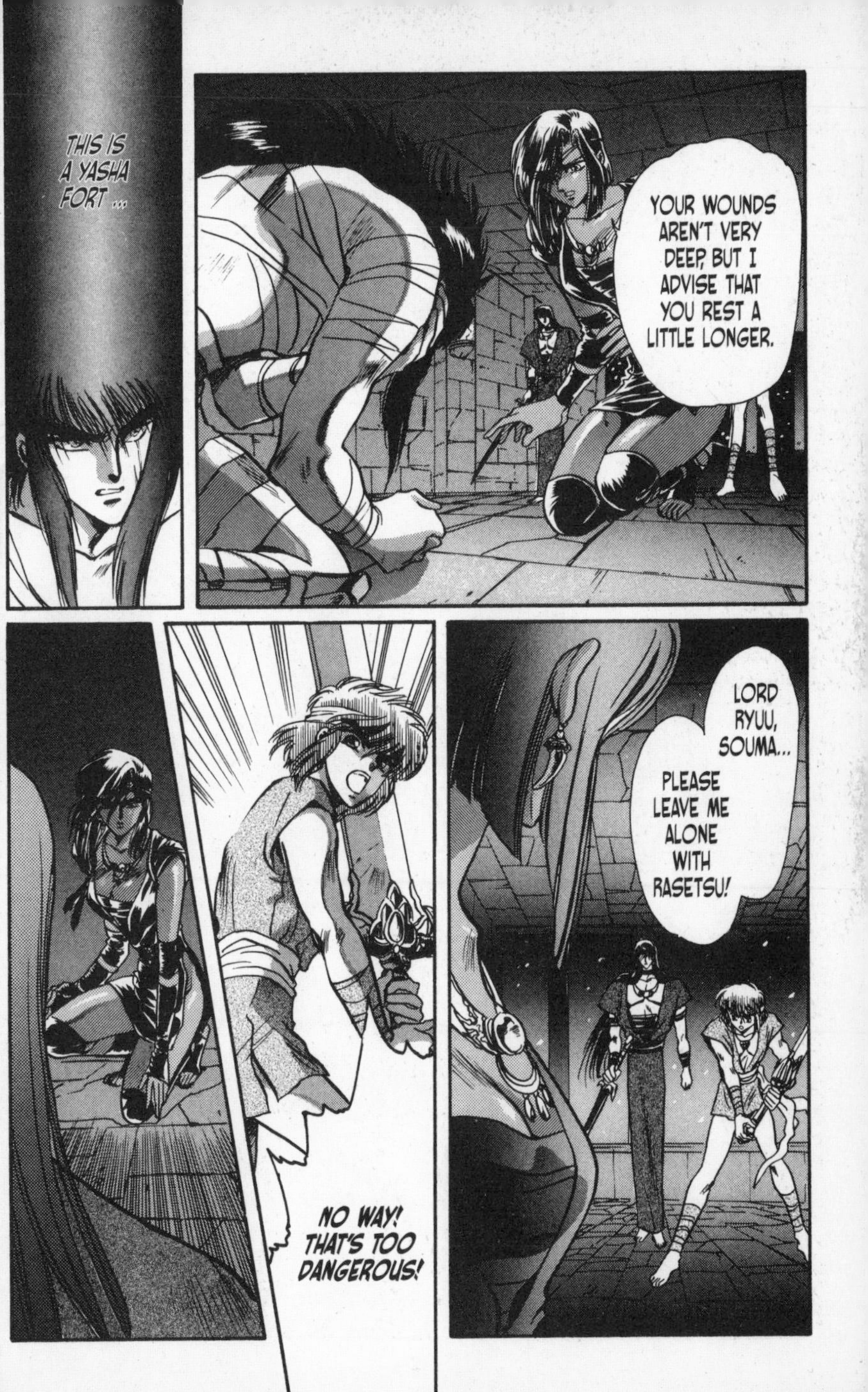
YOUR WOUNDS AREN'T VERY DEEP, BUT I ADVISE THAT YOU REST A LITTLE LONGER.
THIS IS A YASHA FORT ...
LORD RYUU, SOUMA...
PLEASE LEAVE ME ALONE WITH RASETSU!
NO WAY! THAT'S TOO DANGEROUS!

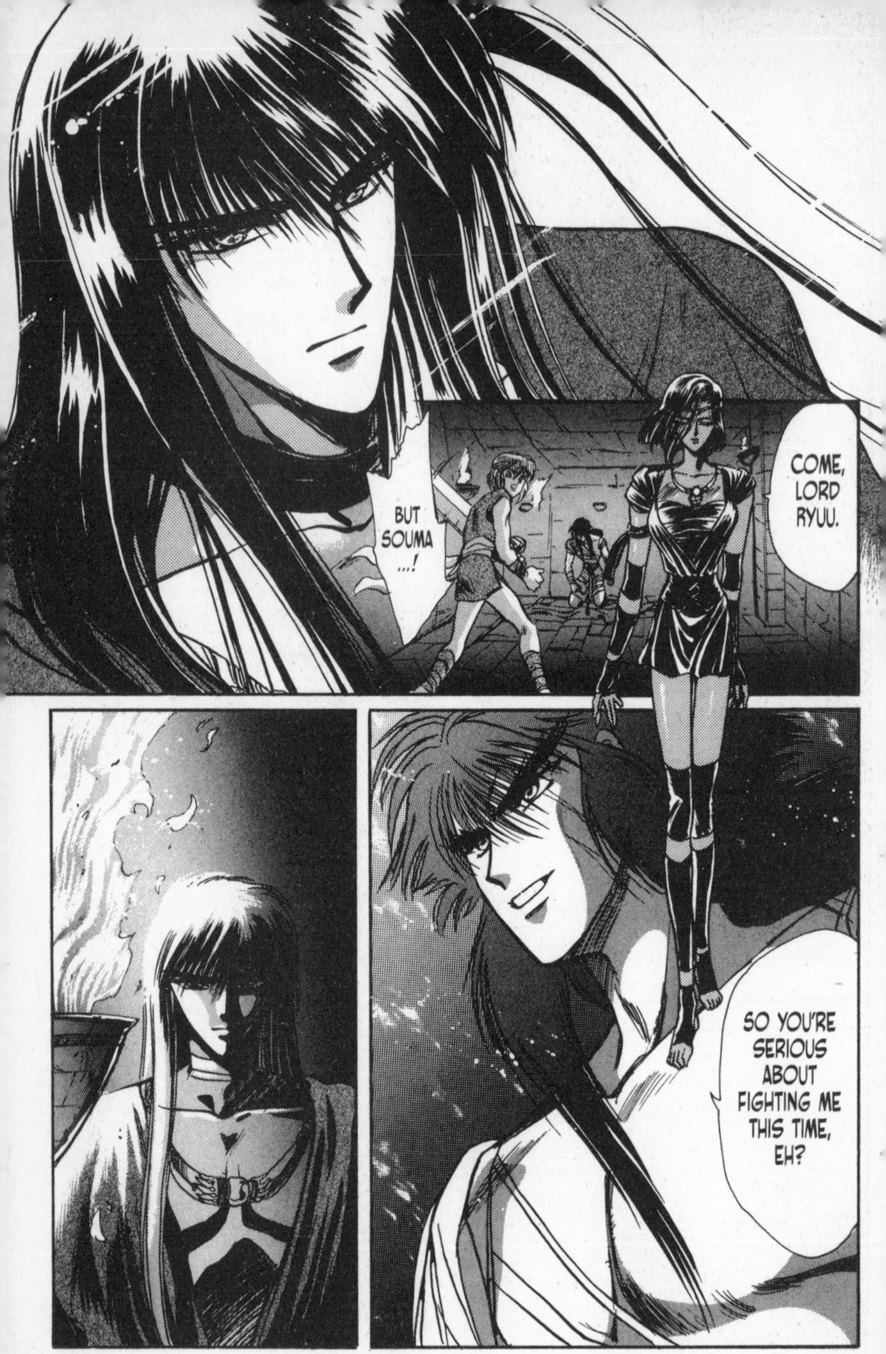
COME, LORD RYUU.
BUT SOUMA ...!
SO YOU'RE SERIOUS ABOUT FIGHTING ME THIS TIME, EH?

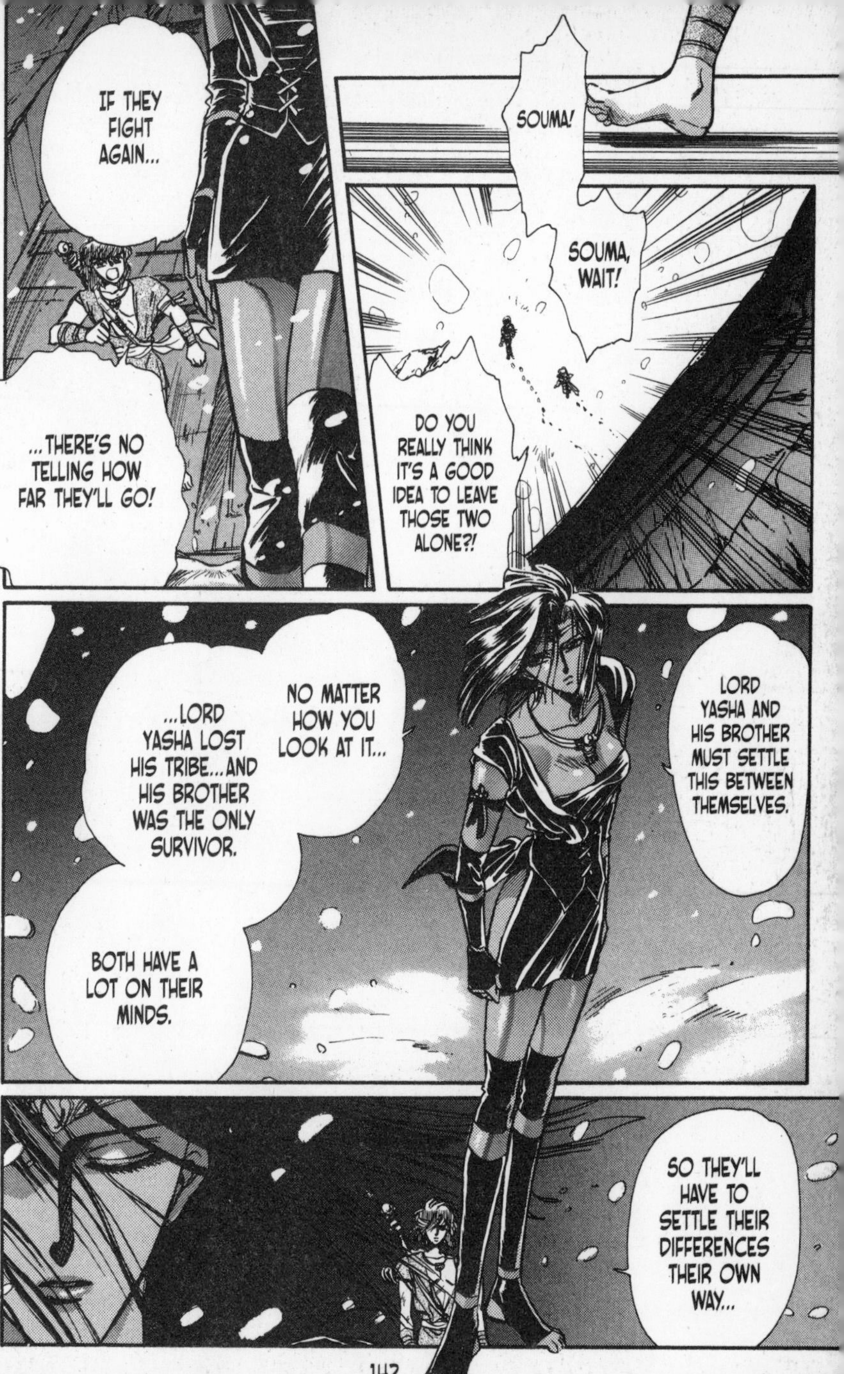
SOUMA!
SOUMA, WAIT!
DO YOU REALLY THINK IT'S A GOOD IDEA TO LEAVE THOSE TWO ALONE?!
IF THEY FIGHT AGAIN...
...THERE'S NO TELLING HOW FAR THEY'LL GO!
LORD YASHA AND HIS BROTHER MUST SETTLE THIS BETWEEN THEMSELVES.
NO MATTER HOW YOU LOOK AT IT...
...LORD YASHA LOST HIS TRIBE...AND HIS BROTHER WAS THE ONLY SURVIVOR.
BOTH HAVE A LOT ON THEIR MINDS.
SO THEY'LL HAVE TO SETTLE THEIR DIFFERENCES THEIR OWN WAY...

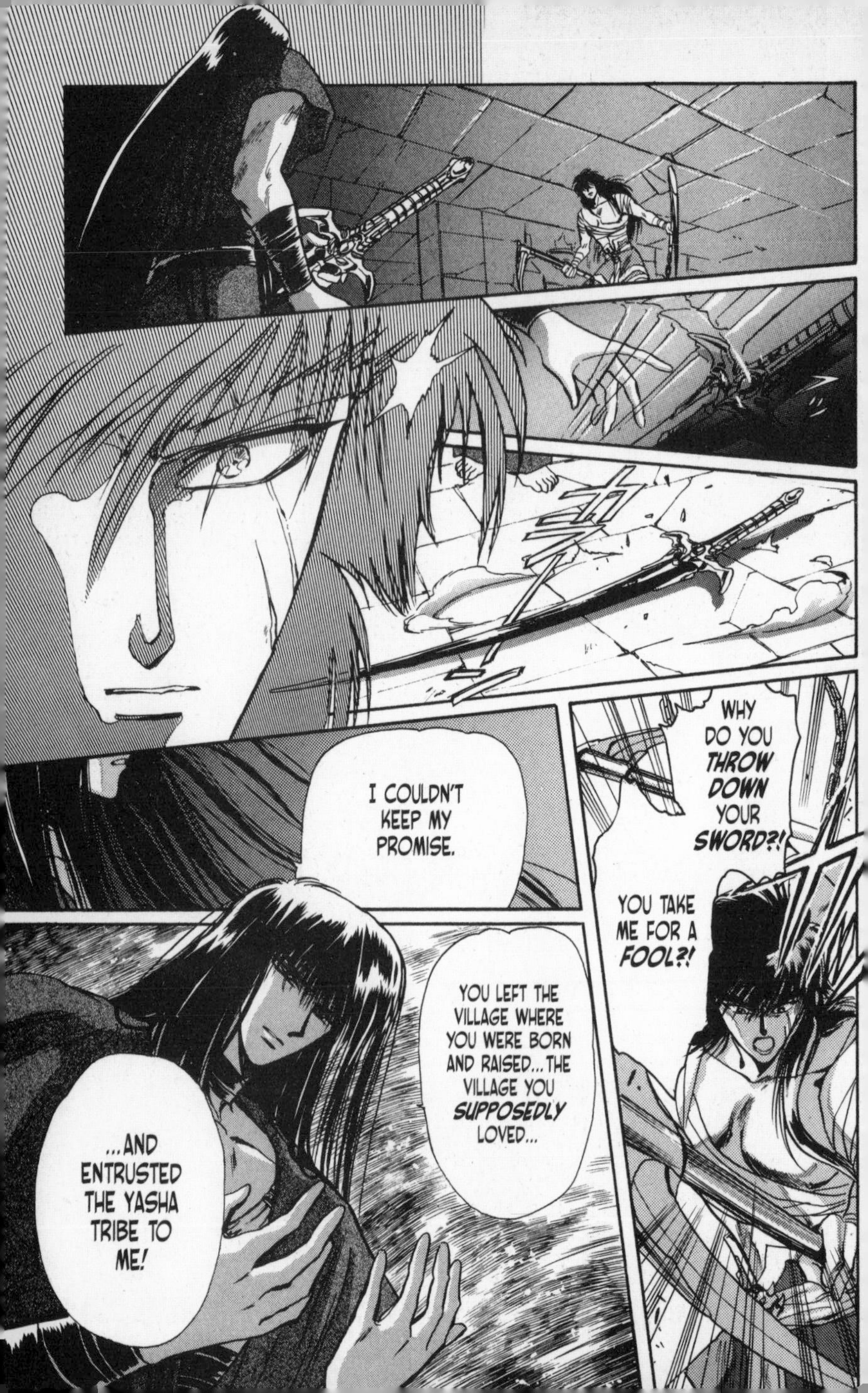
WHY DO YOU THROW DOWN YOUR SWORD?!
YOU TAKE ME FOR A FOOL?!
I COULDN'T KEEP MY PROMISE.
YOU LEFT THE VILLAGE WHERE YOU WERE BORN AND RAISED...THE VILLAGE YOU SUPPOSEDLY LOVED...
...AND ENTRUSTED THE YASHA TRIBE TO ME!

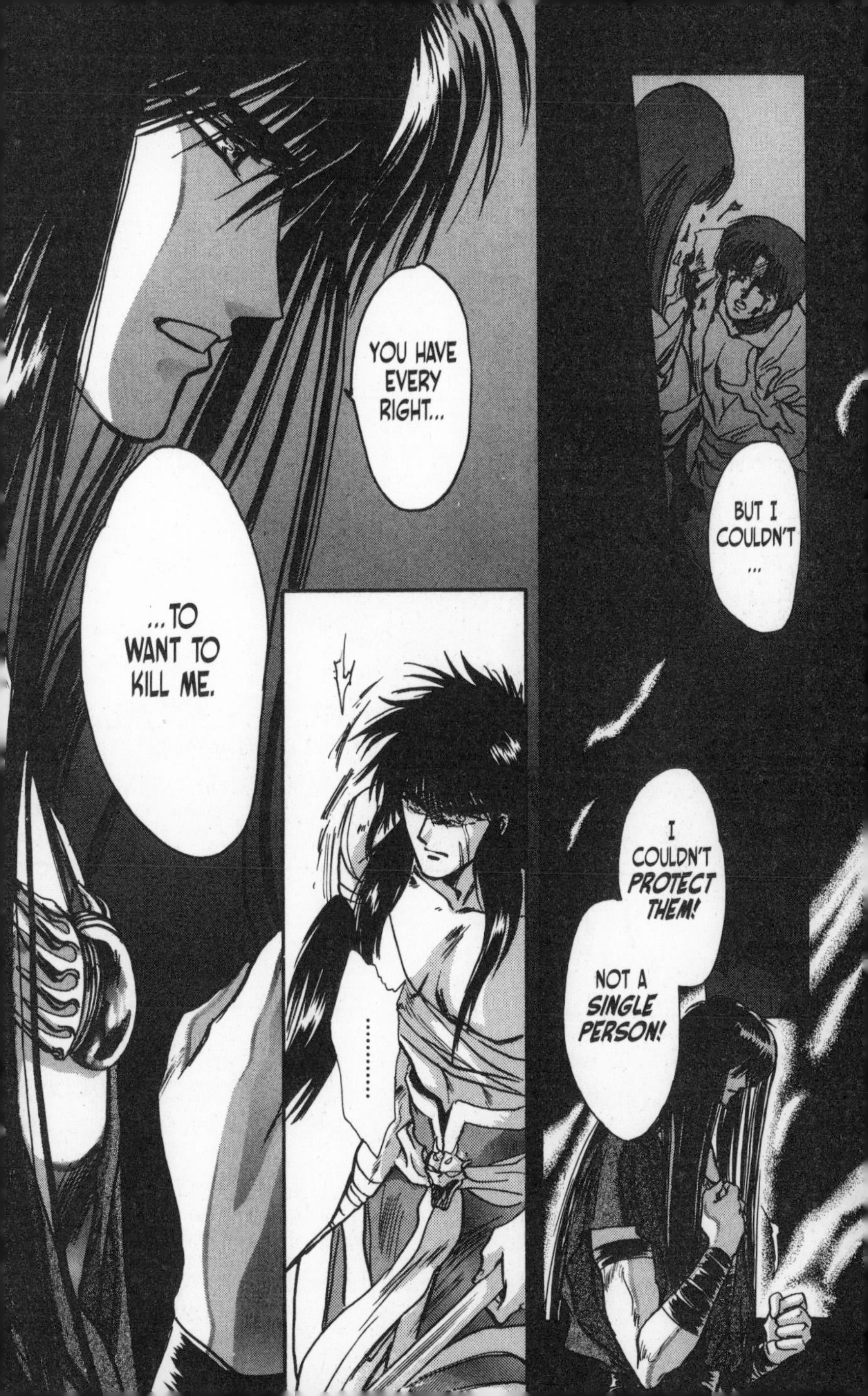
BUT I COULDN'T ...
I COULDN'T PROTECT THEM!
NOT A SINGLE PERSON!
YOU HAVE EVERY RIGHT...
...TO WANT TO KILL ME.
......

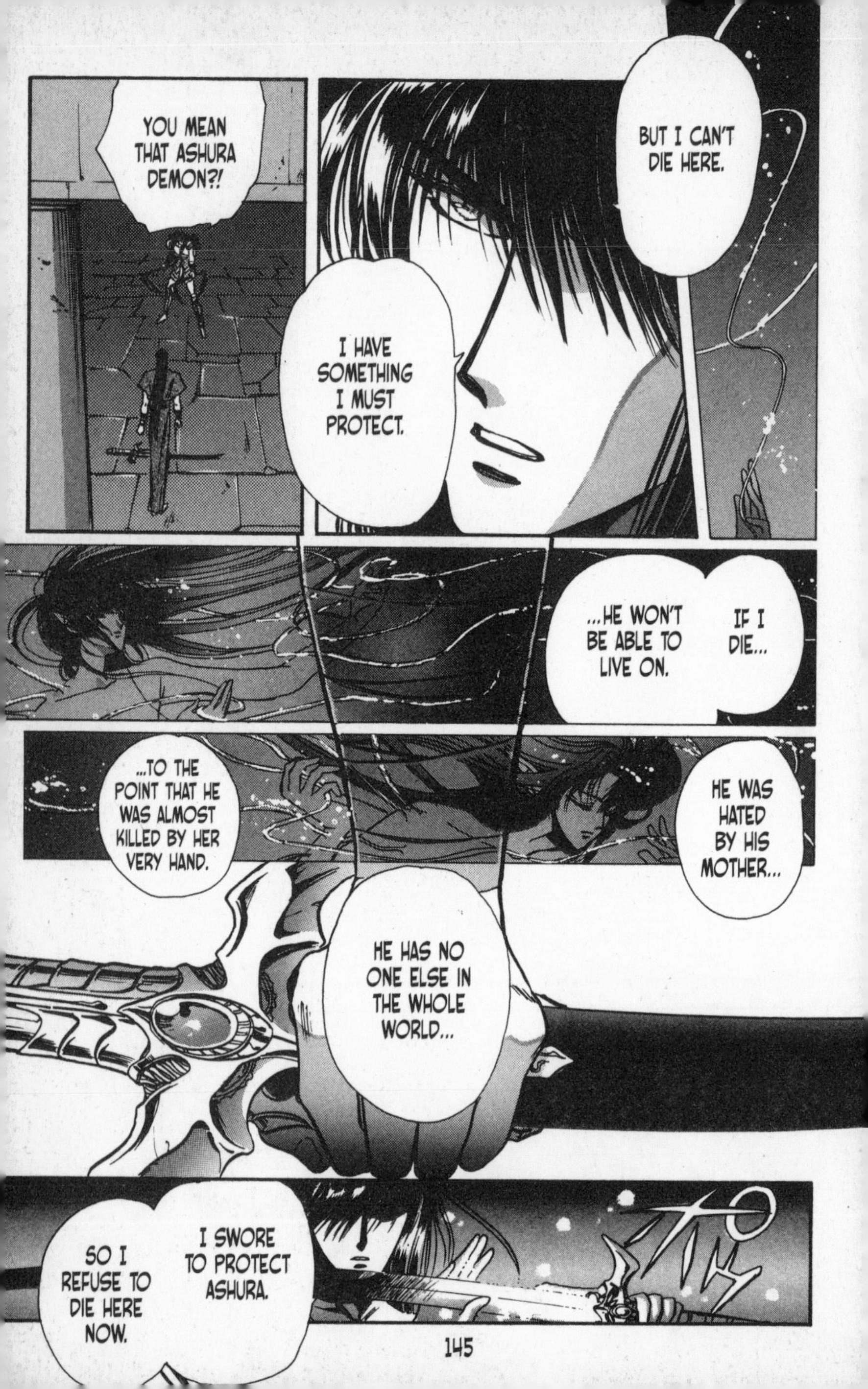
BUT I CAN'T DIE HERE.
I HAVE SOMETHING I MUST PROTECT.
YOU MEAN THAT ASHURA DEMON?!
IF I DIE...
...HE WON'T BE ABLE TO LIVE ON.
HE WAS HATED BY HIS MOTHER...
...TO THE POINT THAT HE WAS ALMOST KILLED BY HER VERY HAND.
HE HAS NO ONE ELSE IN THE WHOLE WORLD...
I SWORE TO PROTECT ASHURA.
SO I REFUSE TO DIE HERE NOW.

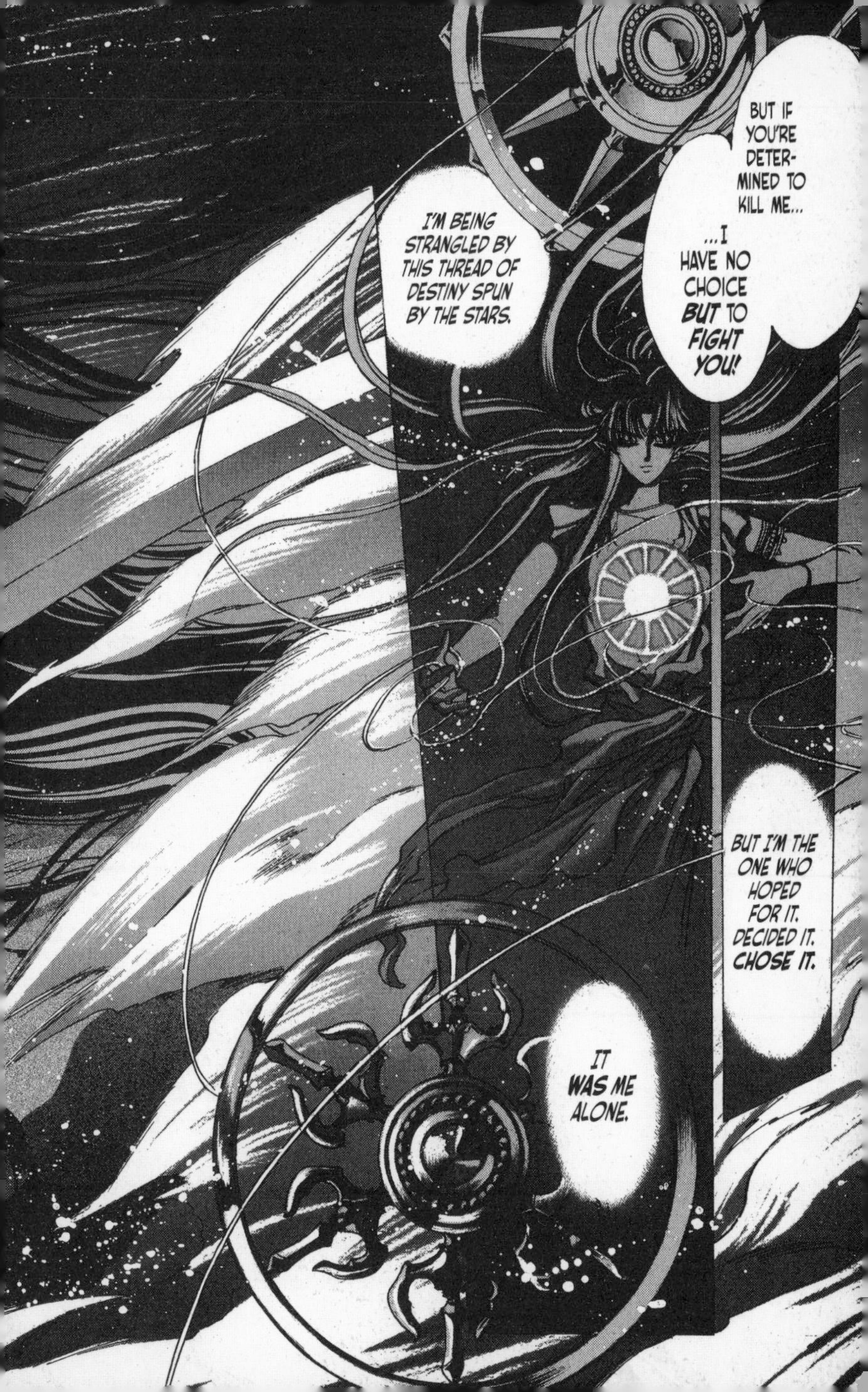
BUT IF YOU'RE DETERMINED TO KILL ME...
...I HAVE NO CHOICE BUT TO FIGHT YOU!
I'M BEING STRANGLED BY THIS THREAD OF DESTINY SPUN BY THE STARS.
BUT I'M THE ONE WHO HOPED FOR IT. DECIDED IT. CHOSE IT.
IT WAS ME ALONE.

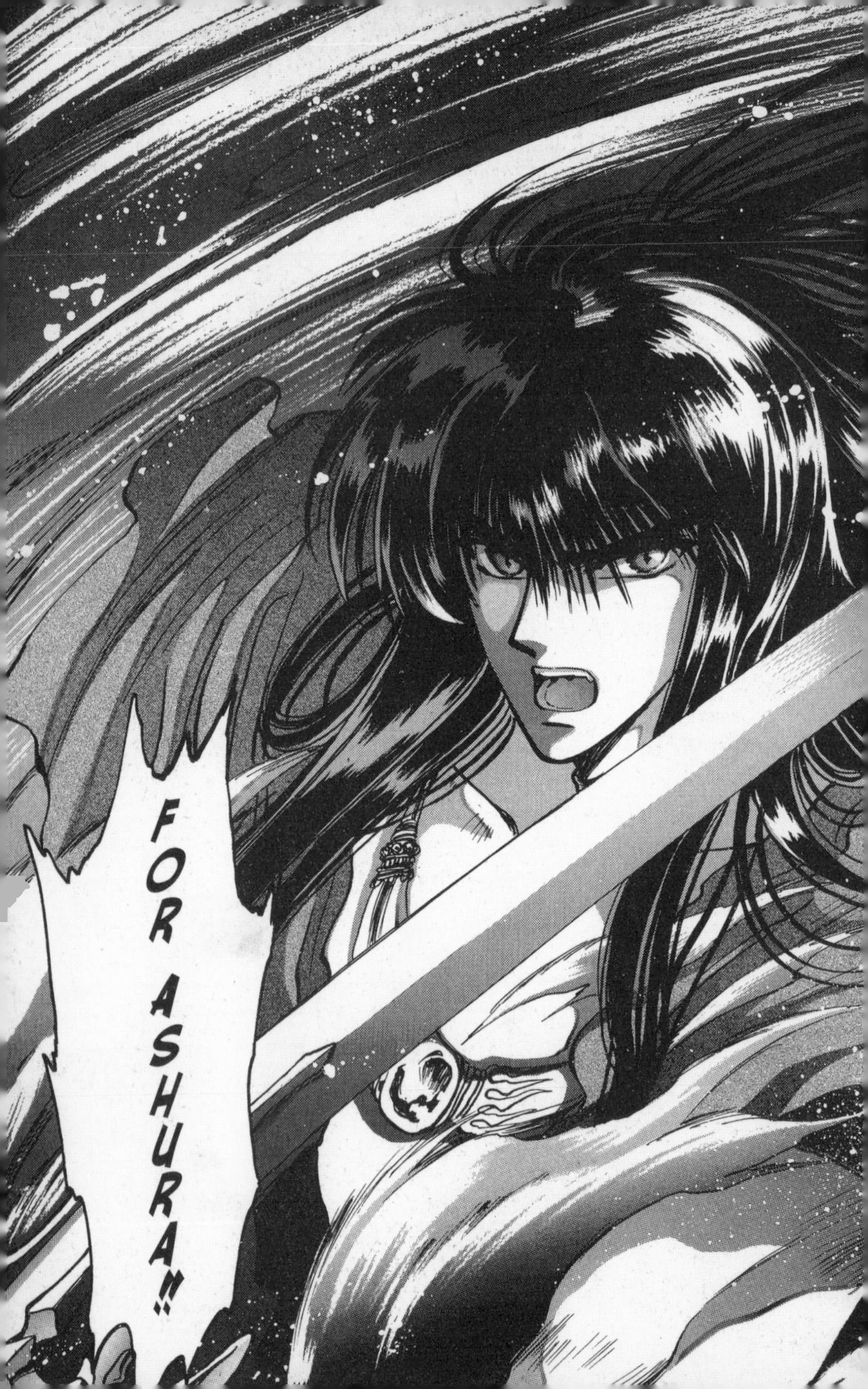
FOR ASHURA!!

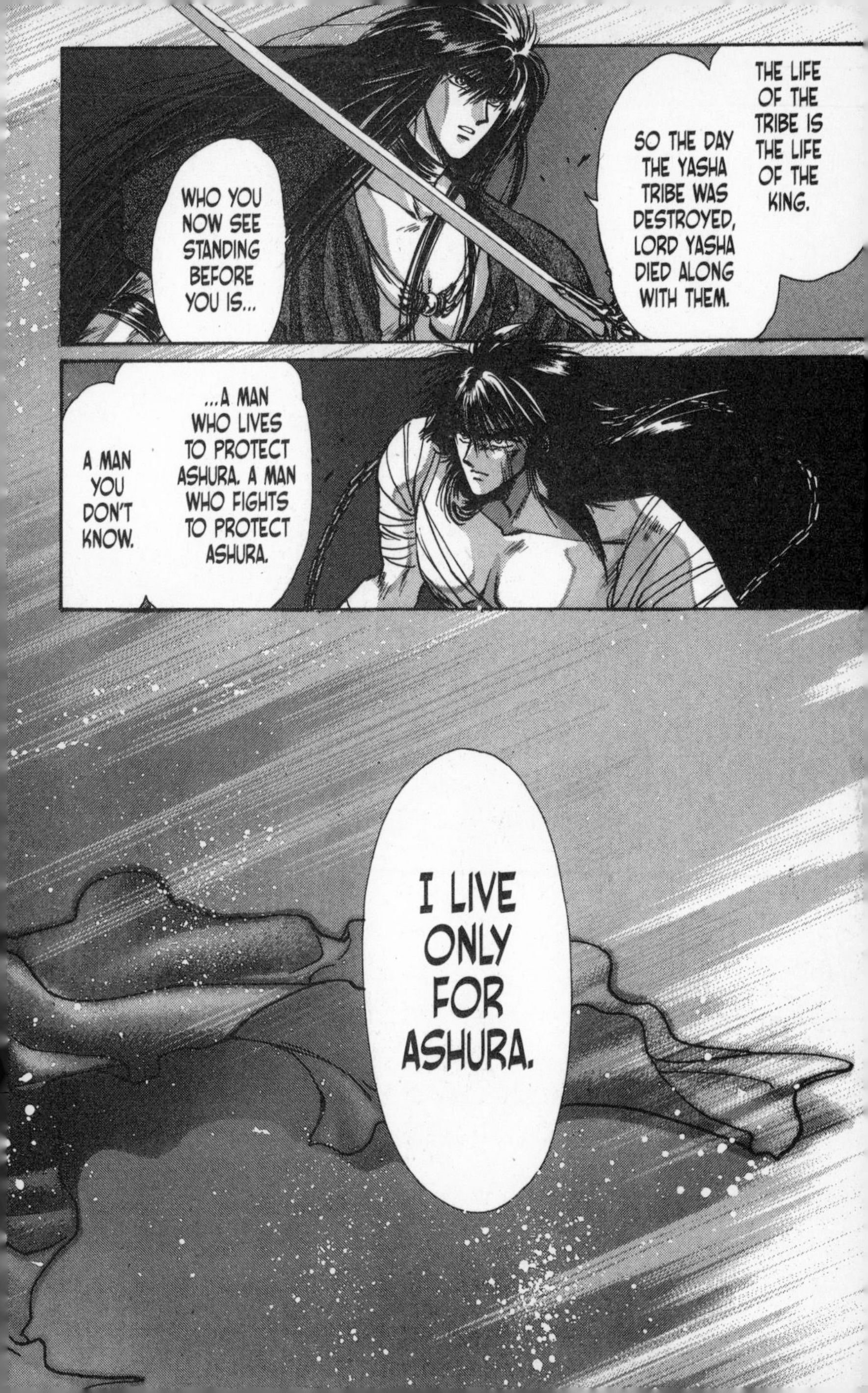
THE LIFE OF THE TRIBE IS THE LIFE OF THE KING.
SO THE DAY THE YASHA TRIBE WAS DESTROYED, LORD YASHA DIED ALONG WITH THEM.
WHO YOU NOW SEE STANDING BEFORE YOU IS...
...A MAN WHO LIVES TO PROTECT ASHURA. A MAN WHO FIGHTS TO PROTECT ASHURA.
A MAN YOU DON'T KNOW.
I LIVE ONLY FOR ASHURA.

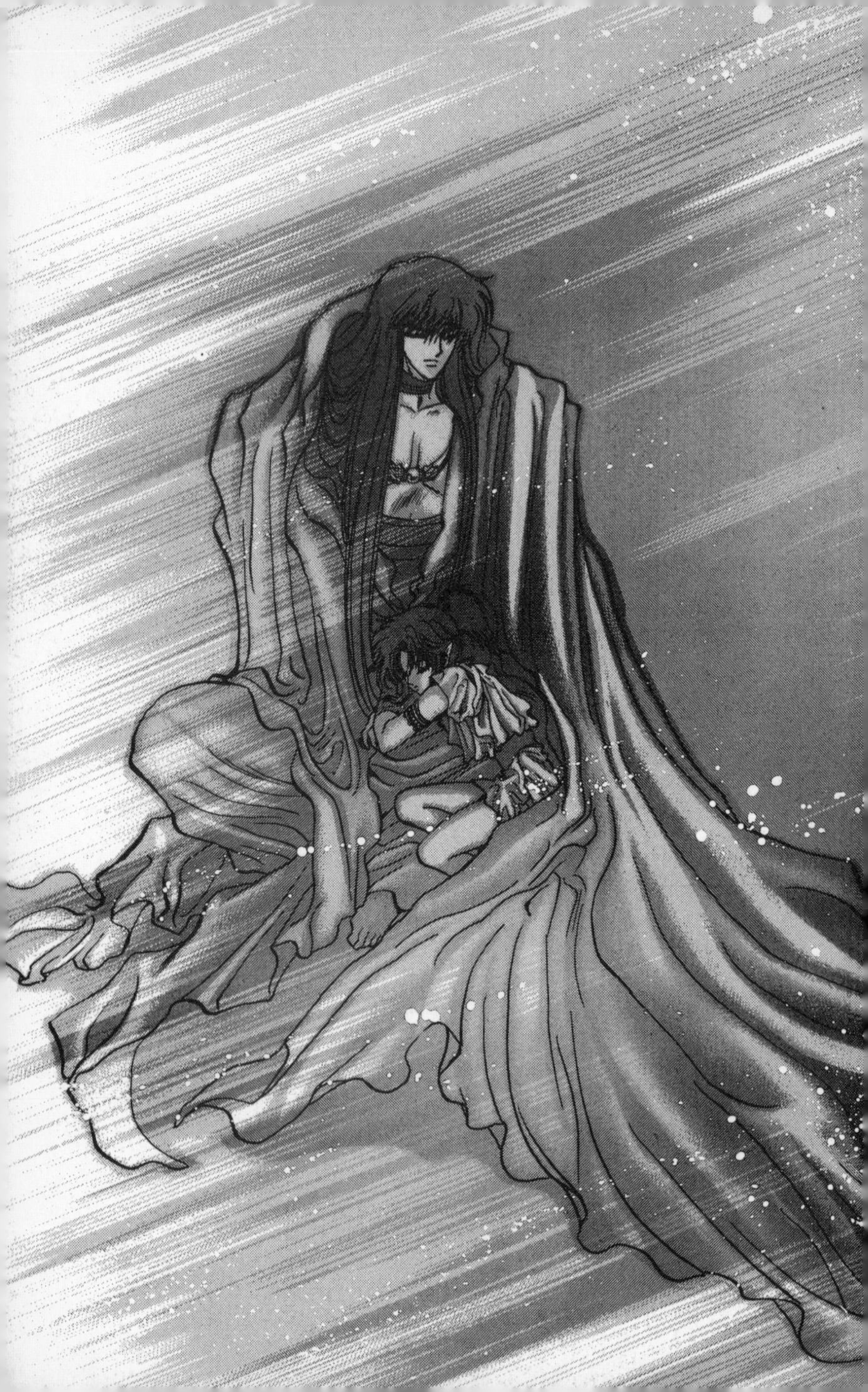

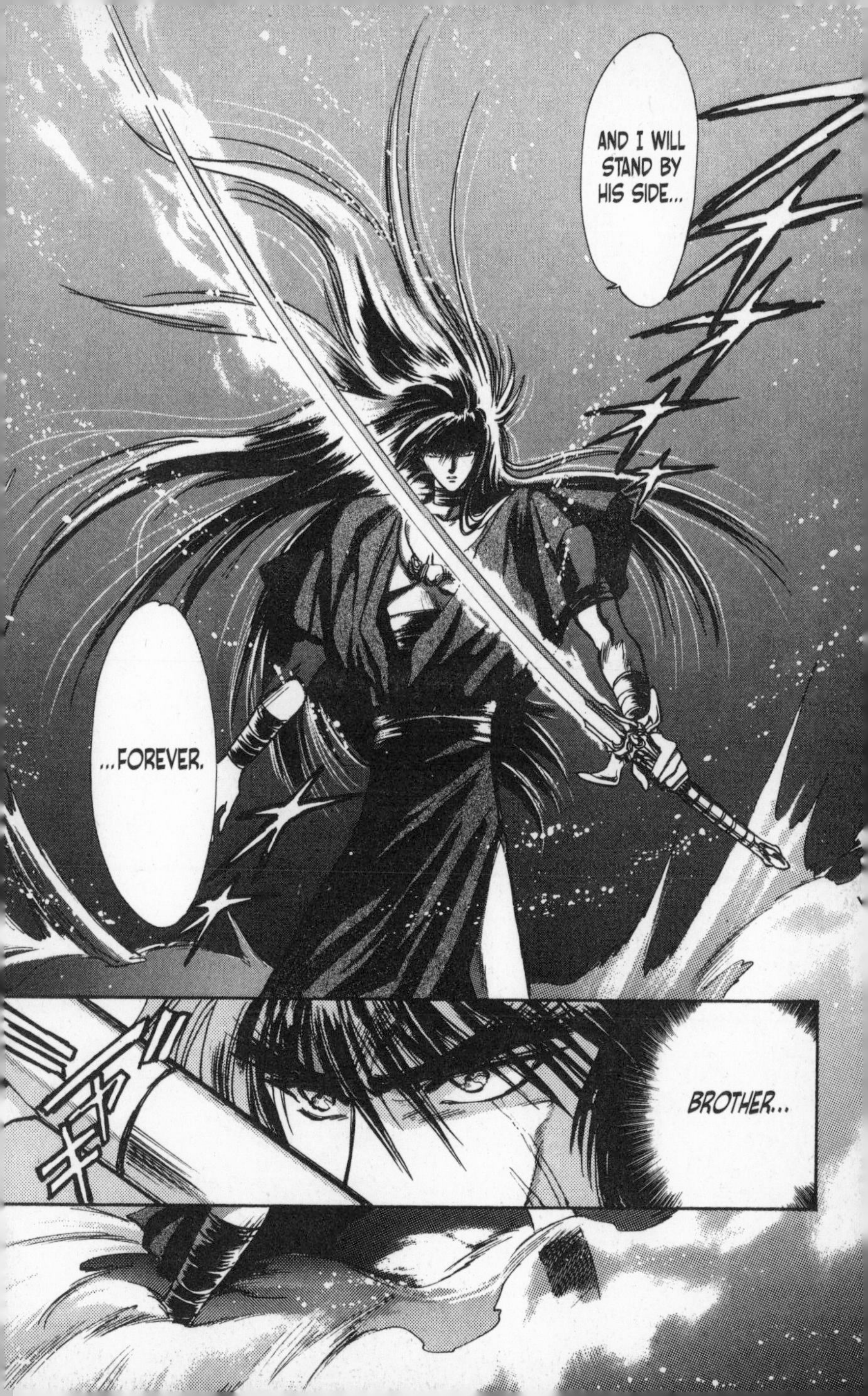
AND I WILL STAND BY HIS SIDE...
...FOREVER.
BROTHER...

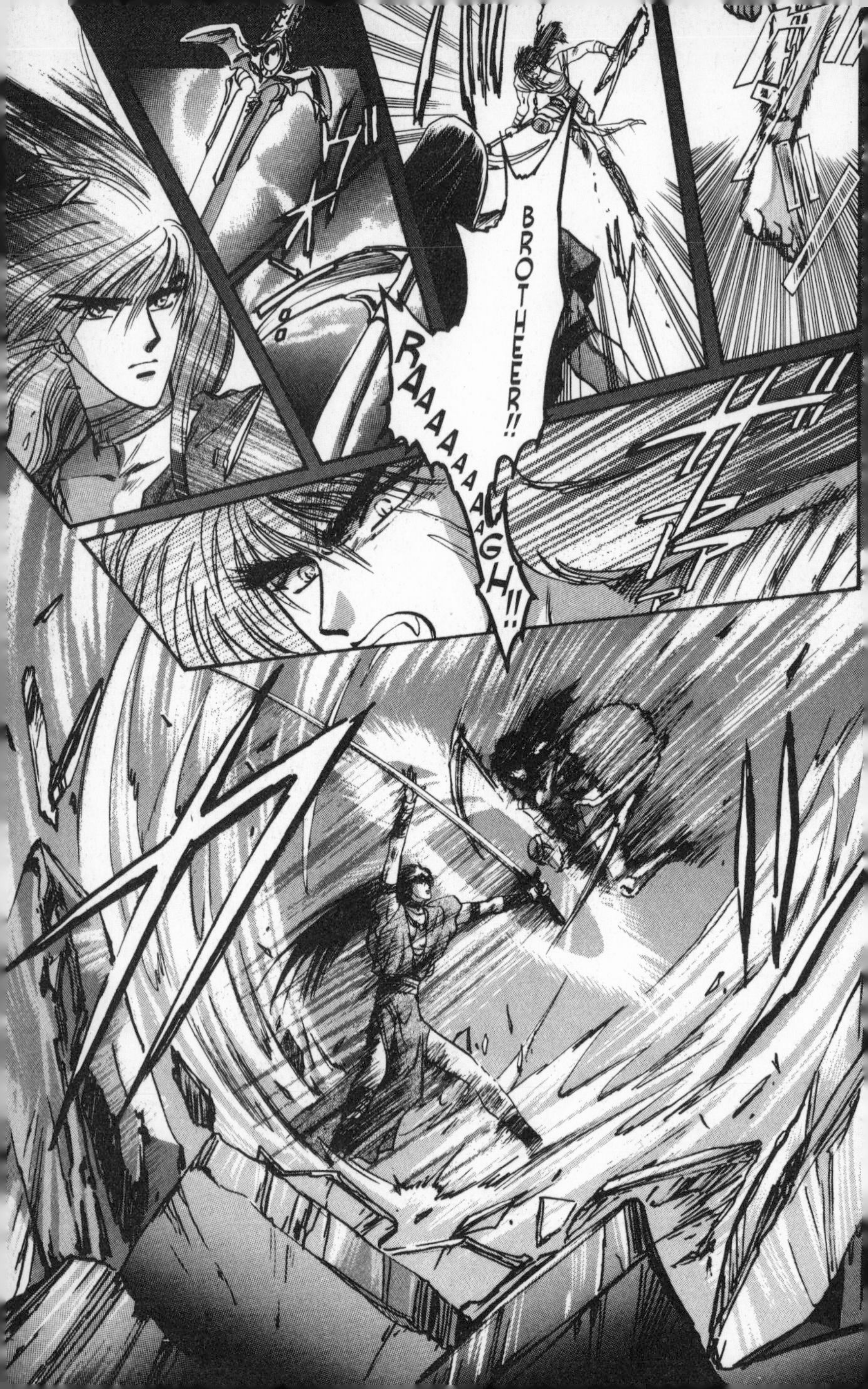
BROTHEER!!
RAAAAAAAAGH!!!

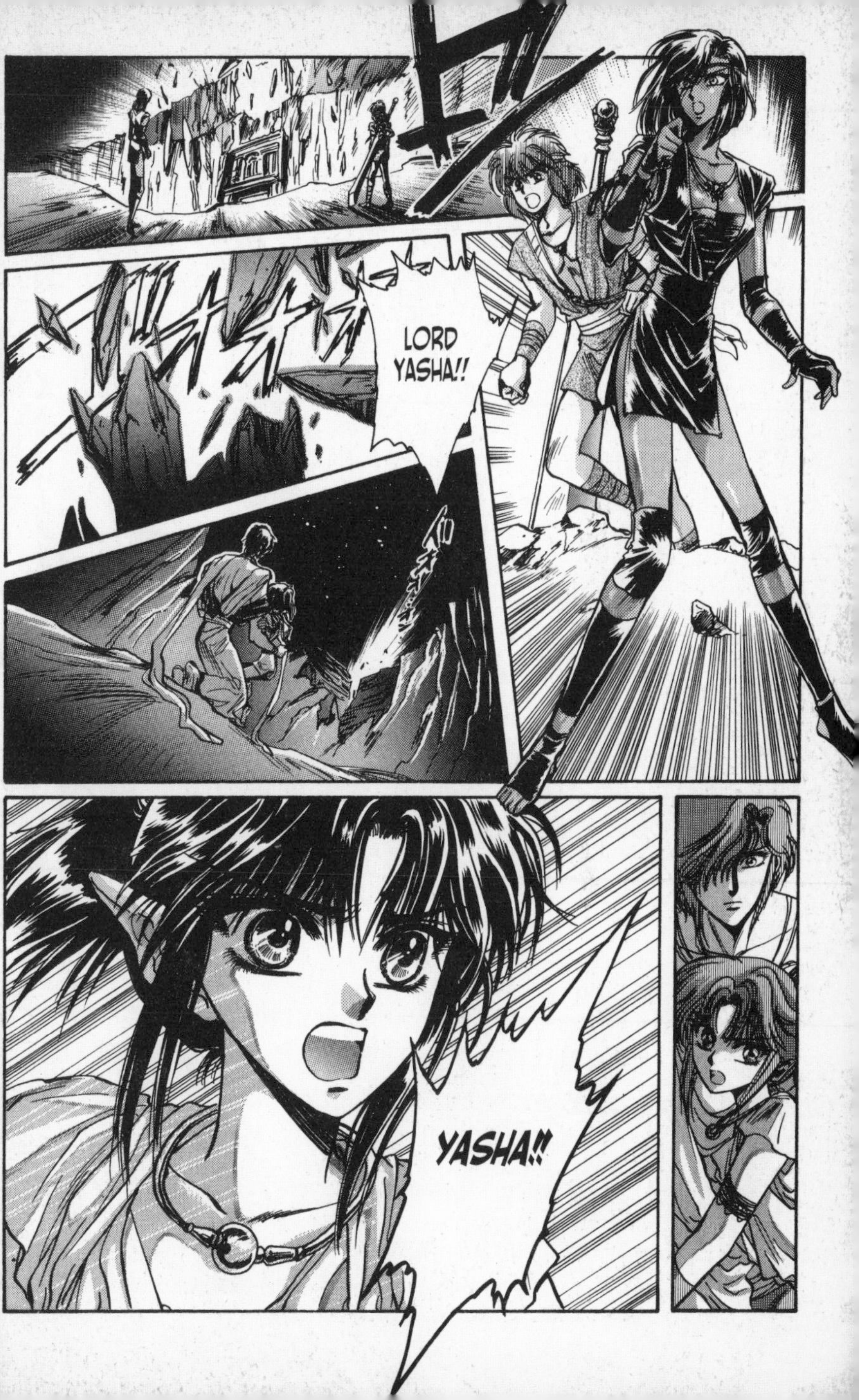
LORD YASHA!!
YASHA!!

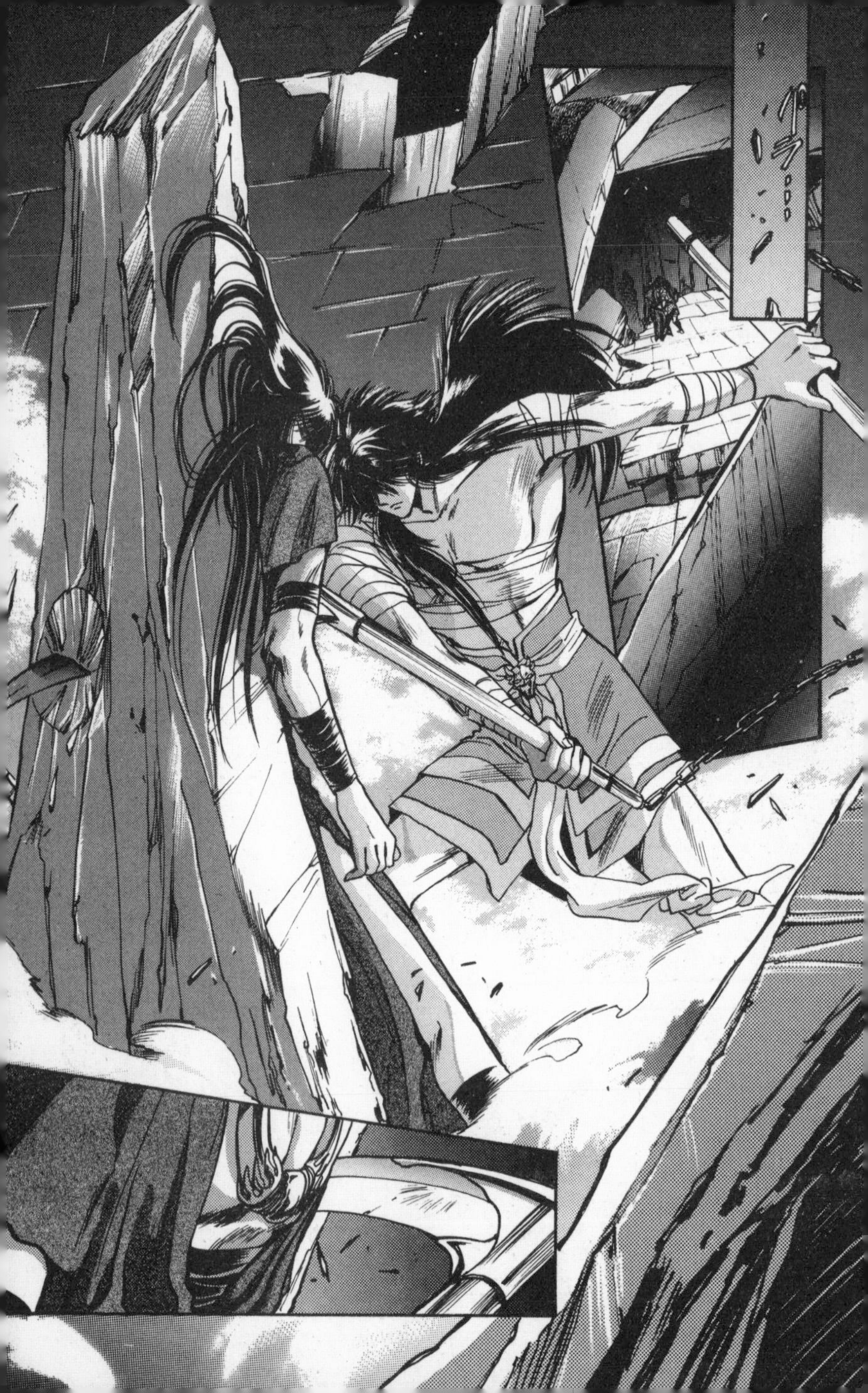
パラ…

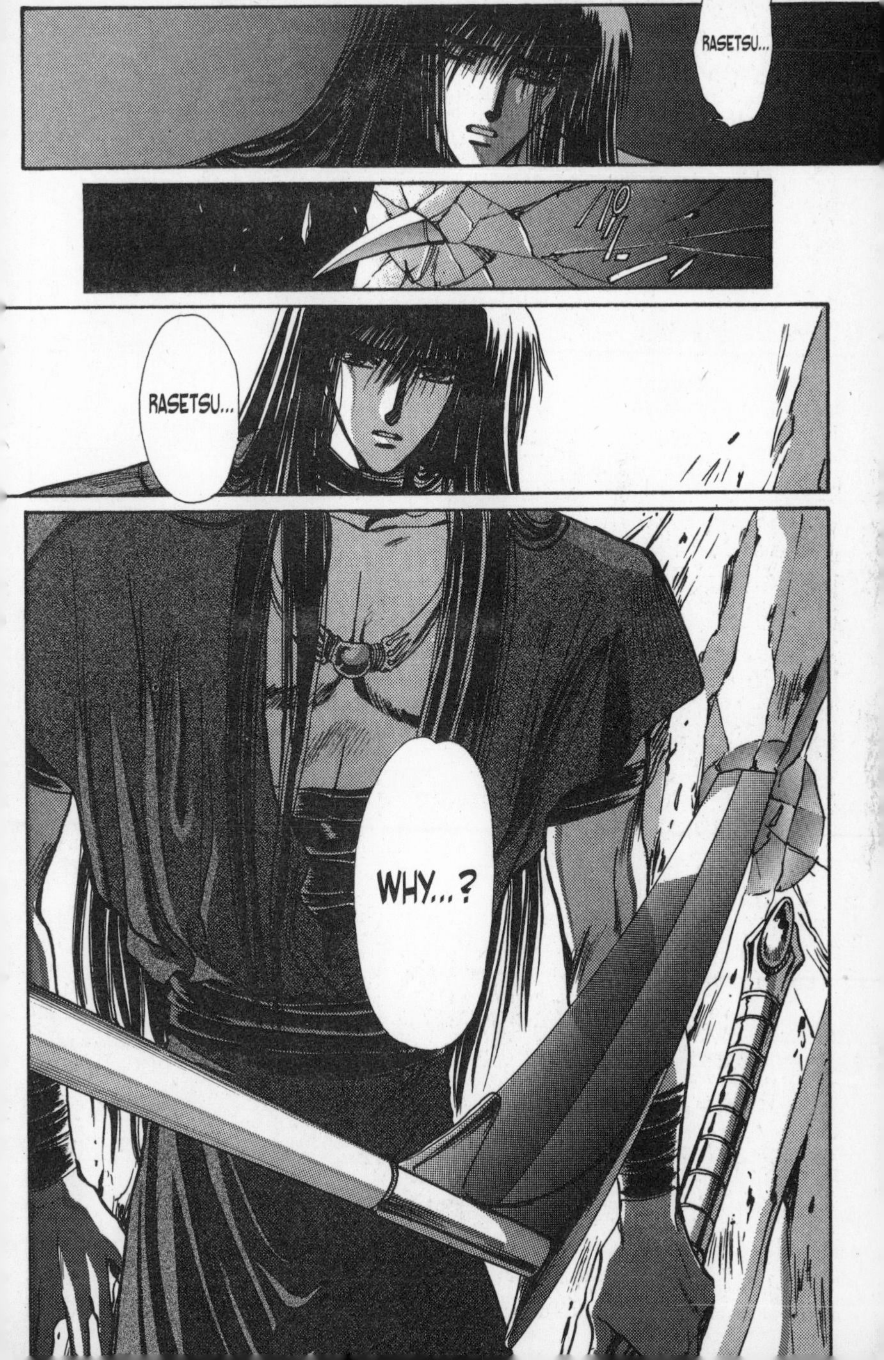
RASETSU...
RASETSU...
WHY...?

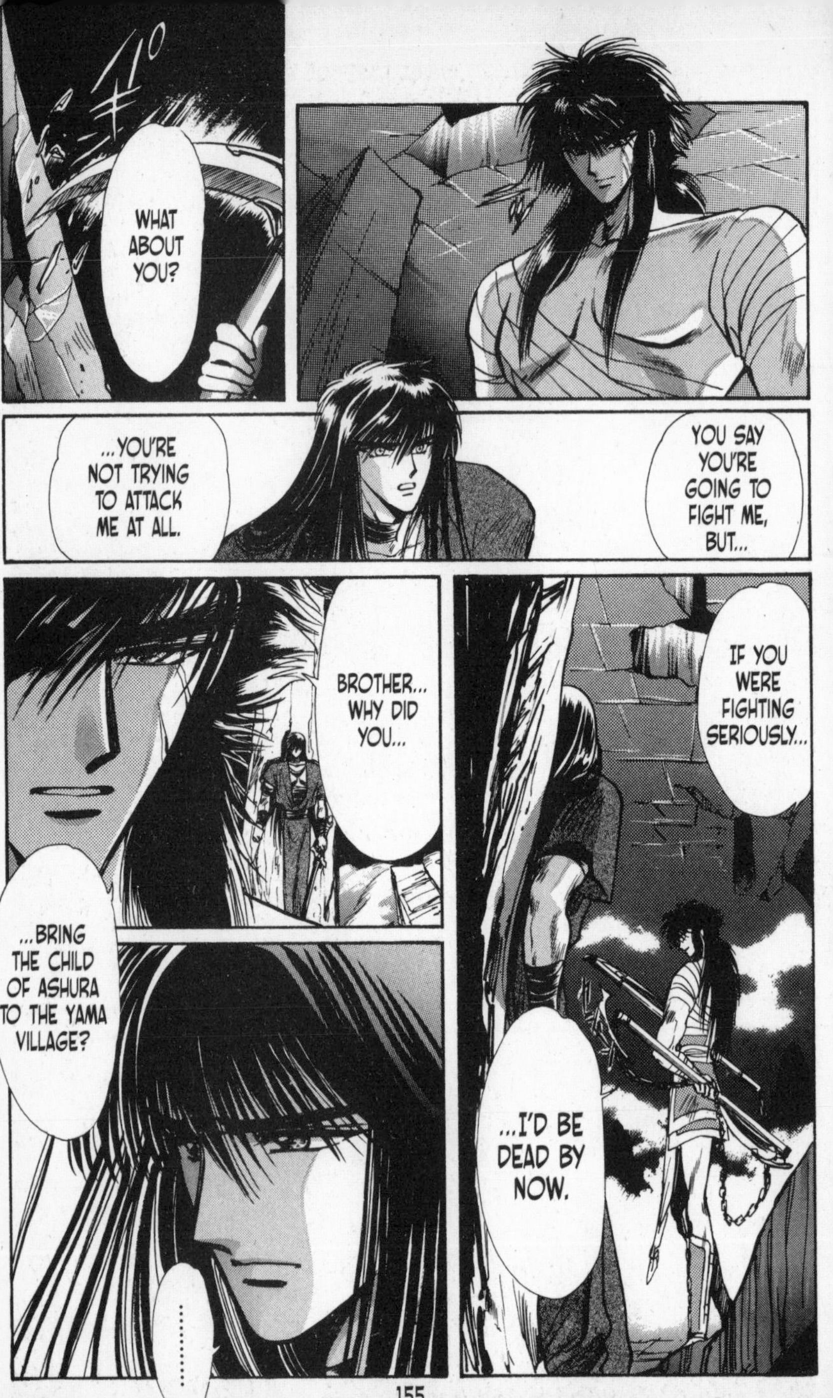
WHAT ABOUT YOU?
YOU SAY YOU'RE GOING TO FIGHT ME, BUT...
...YOU'RE NOT TRYING TO ATTACK ME AT ALL.
IF YOU WERE FIGHTING SERIOUSLY...
...I'D BE DEAD BY NOW.
BROTHER... WHY DID YOU...
...BRING THE CHILD OF ASHURA TO THE YAMA VILLAGE?
.......

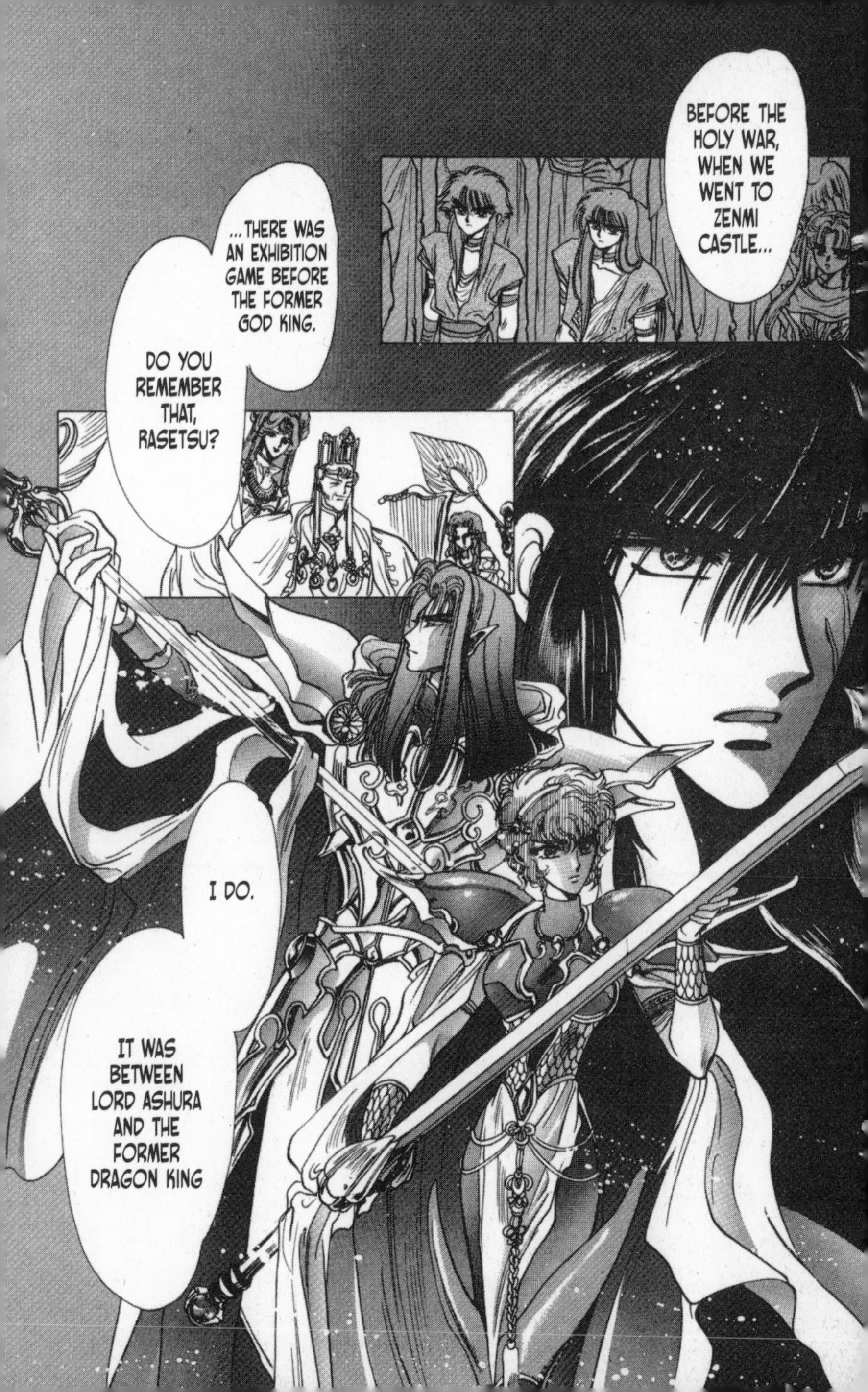
BEFORE THE HOLY WAR, WHEN WE WENT TO ZENMI CASTLE...
...THERE WAS AN EXHIBITION GAME BEFORE THE FORMER GOD KING.
DO YOU REMEMBER THAT, RASETSU?
I DO.
IT WAS BETWEEN LORD ASHURA AND THE FORMER DRAGON KING

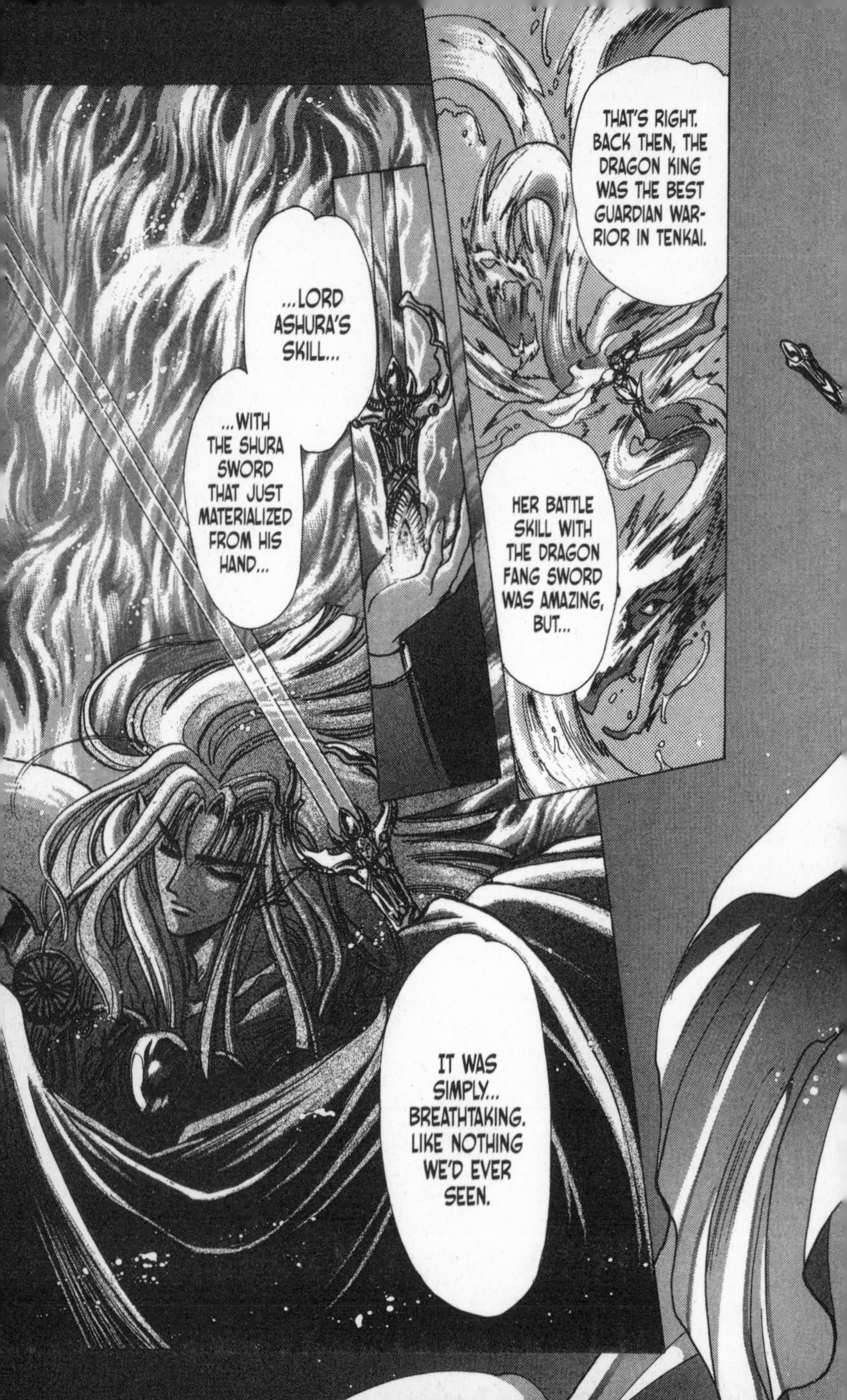
THAT'S RIGHT. BACK THEN, THE DRAGON KING WAS THE BEST GUARDIAN WAR-RIOR IN TENKAI.
HER BATTLE SKILL WITH THE DRAGON FANG SWORD WAS AMAZING, BUT...
...LORD ASHURA'S SKILL...
...WITH THE SHURA SWORD THAT JUST MATERIALIZED FROM HIS HAND...
IT WAS SIMPLY... BREATHTAKING. LIKE NOTHING WE'D EVER SEEN.

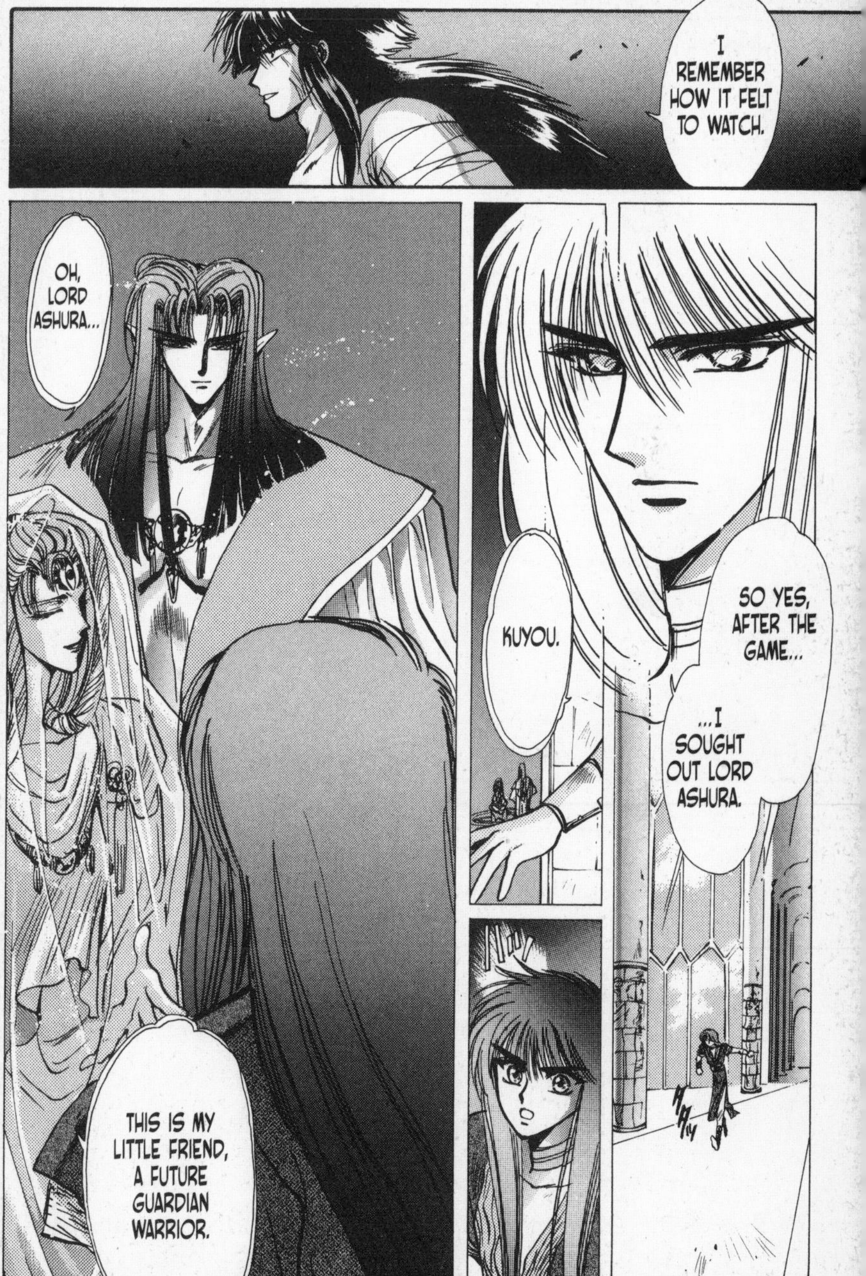
I REMEMBER HOW IT FELT TO WATCH.
SO YES, AFTER THE GAME...
...I SOUGHT OUT LORD ASHURA.
KUYOU.
OH, LORD ASHURA...
THIS IS MY LITTLE FRIEND, A FUTURE GUARDIAN WARRIOR.

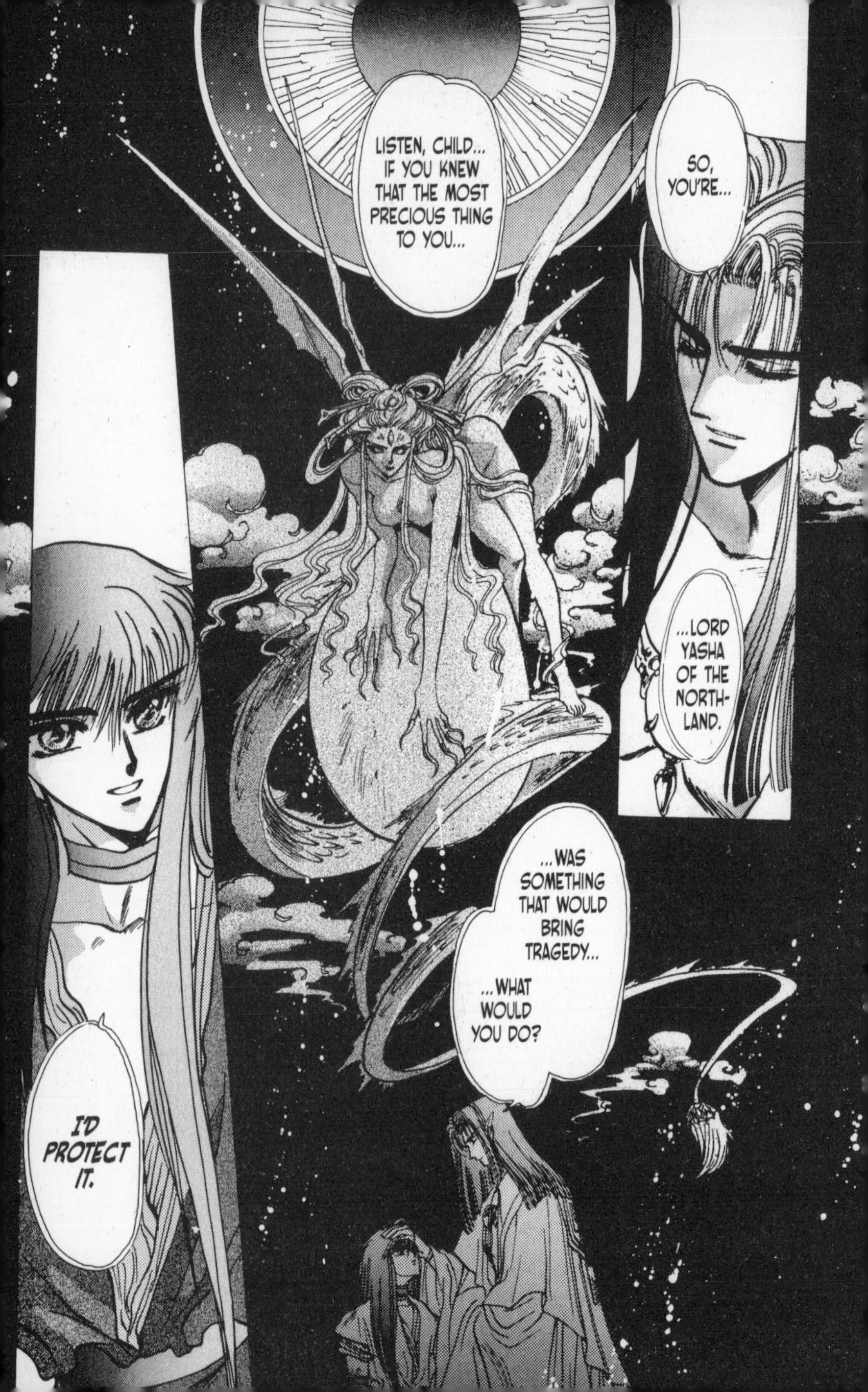
SO, YOU'RE...
...LORD YASHA OF THE NORTH-LAND.
LISTEN, CHILD... IF YOU KNEW THAT THE MOST PRECIOUS THING TO YOU...
...WAS SOMETHING THAT WOULD BRING TRAGEDY...
...WHAT WOULD YOU DO?
I'D PROTECT IT.

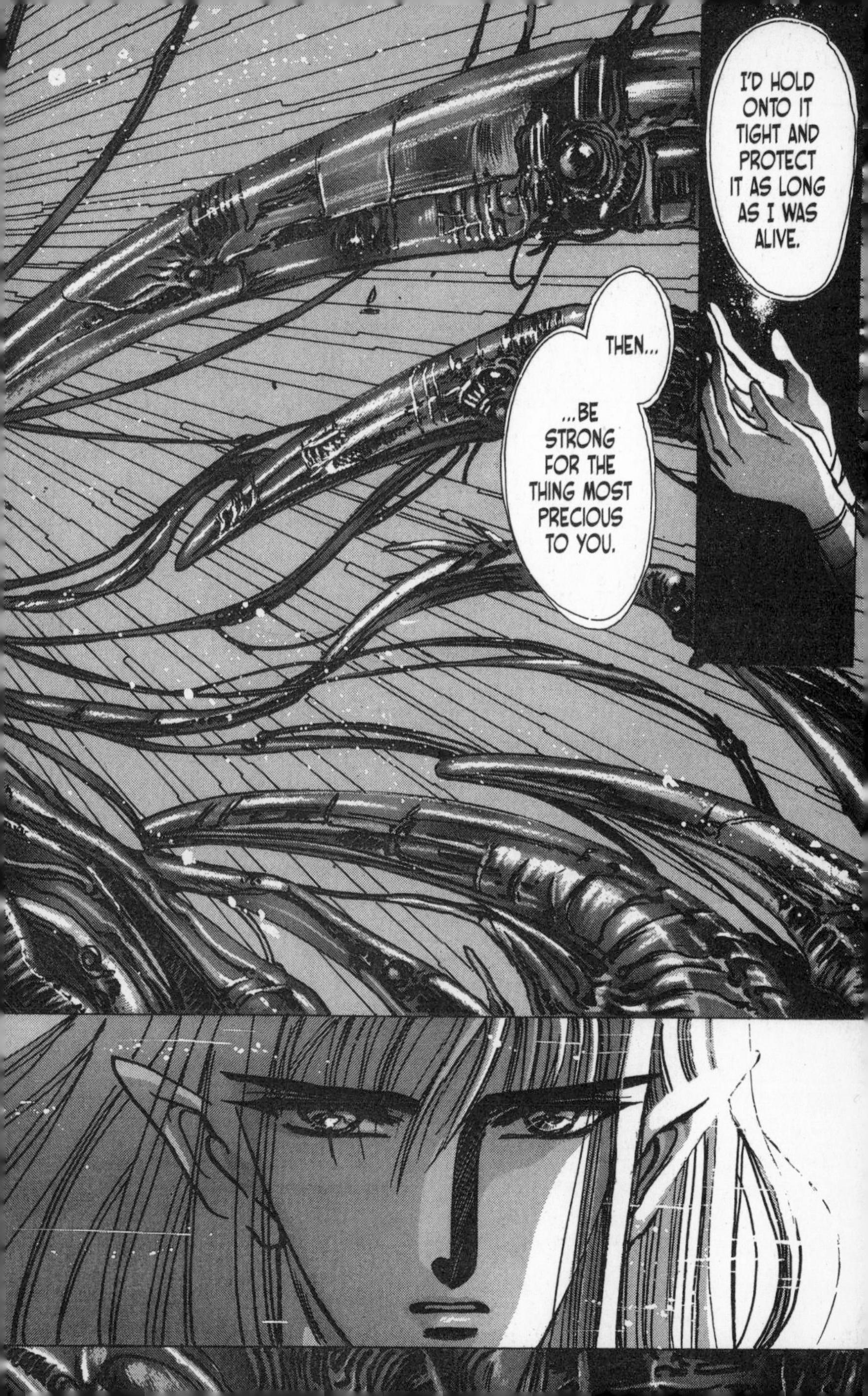
I'D HOLD ONTO IT TIGHT AND PROTECT IT AS LONG AS I WAS ALIVE.
THEN...
...BE STRONG FOR THE THING MOST PRECIOUS TO YOU.

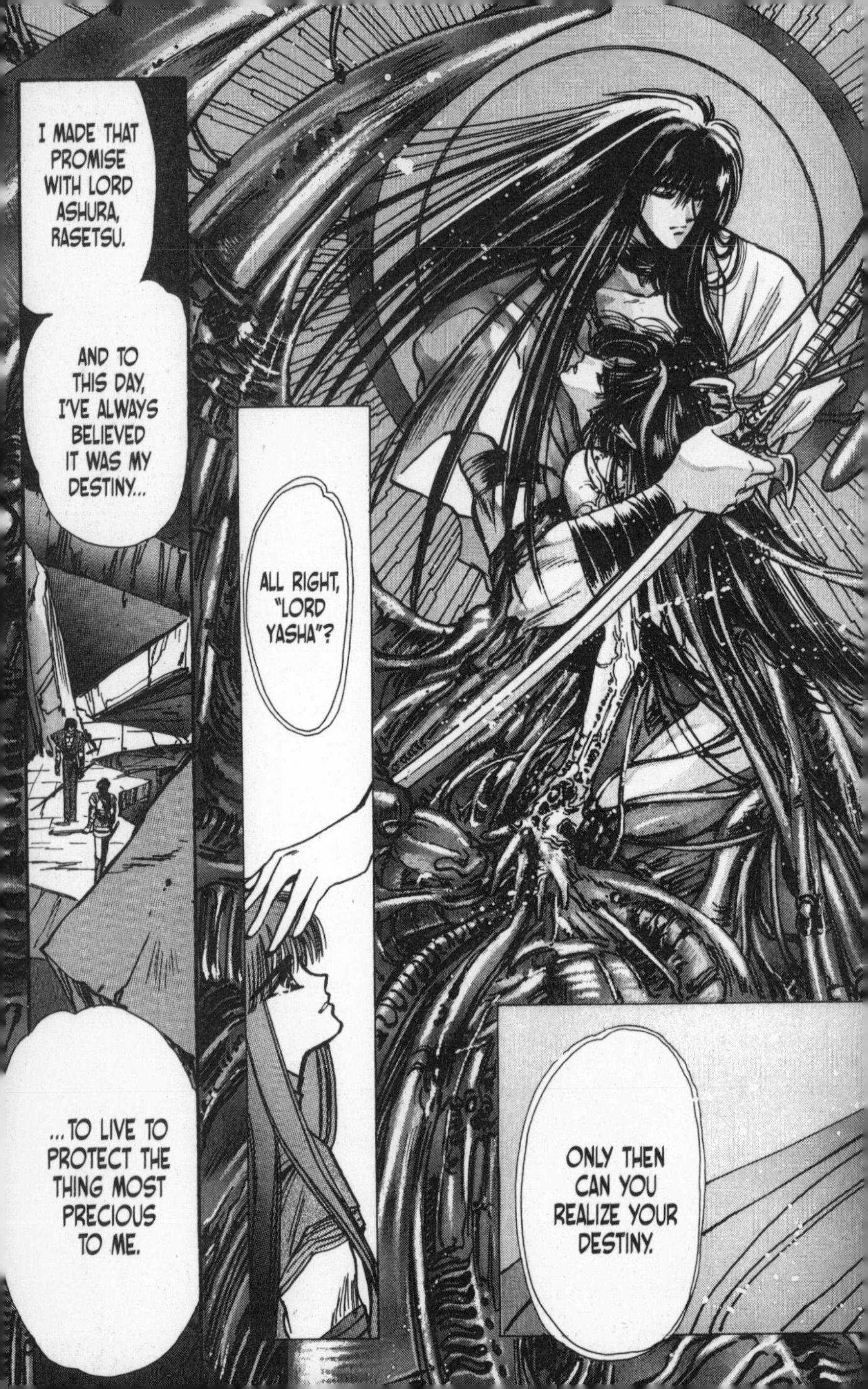
ONLY THEN CAN YOU REALIZE YOUR DESTINY.
ALL RIGHT, "LORD YASHA"?
I MADE THAT PROMISE WITH LORD ASHURA, RASETSU.
AND TO THIS DAY, I'VE ALWAYS BELIEVED IT WAS MY DESTINY...
...TO LIVE TO PROTECT THE THING MOST PRECIOUS TO ME.

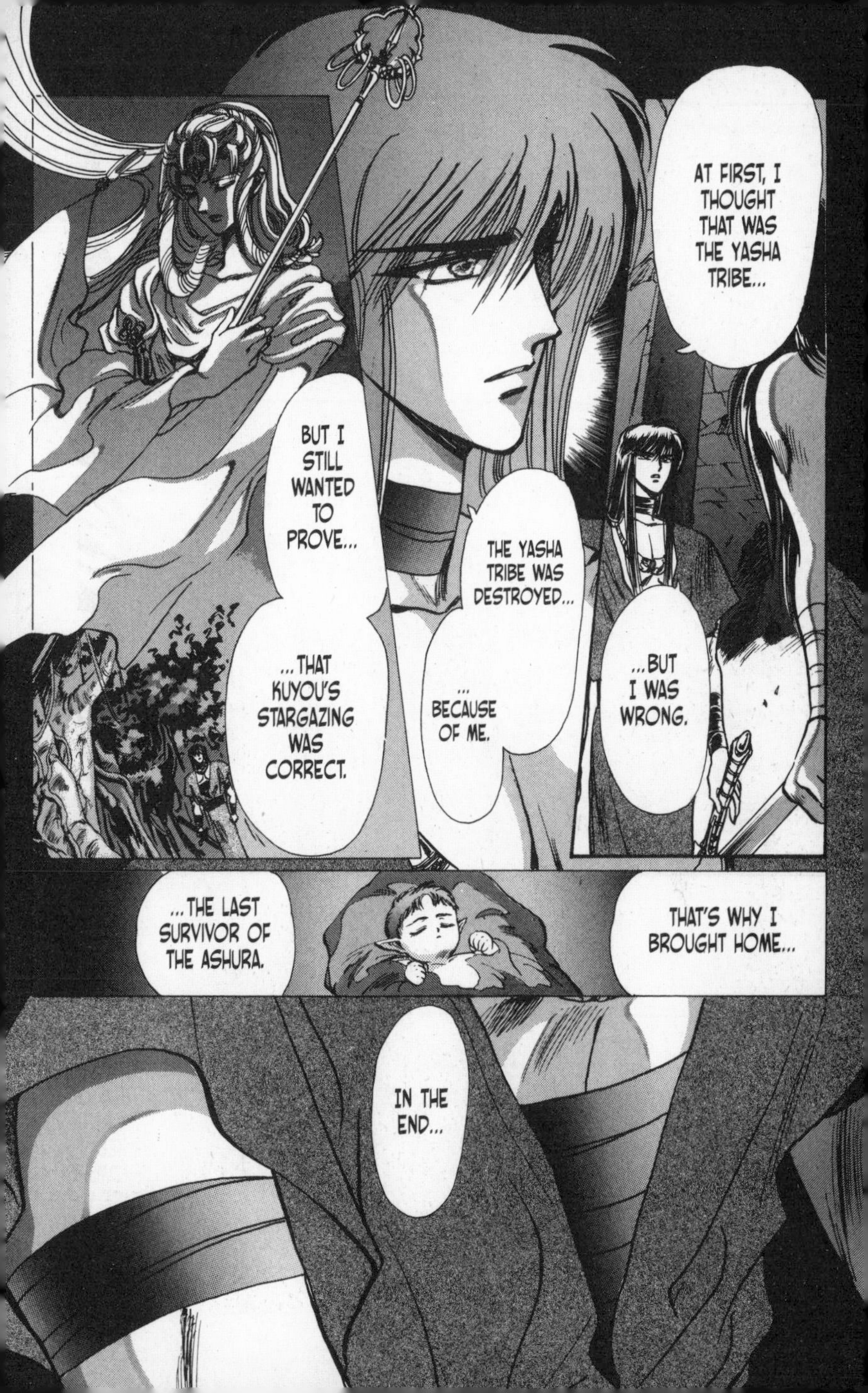
AT FIRST, I THOUGHT THAT WAS THE YASHA TRIBE...
...BUT I WAS WRONG.
THE YASHA TRIBE WAS DESTROYED...
...BECAUSE OF ME.
BUT I STILL WANTED TO PROVE...
...THAT KUYOU'S STARGAZING WAS CORRECT.
THAT'S WHY I BROUGHT HOME...
...THE LAST SURVIVOR OF THE ASHURA.
IN THE END...

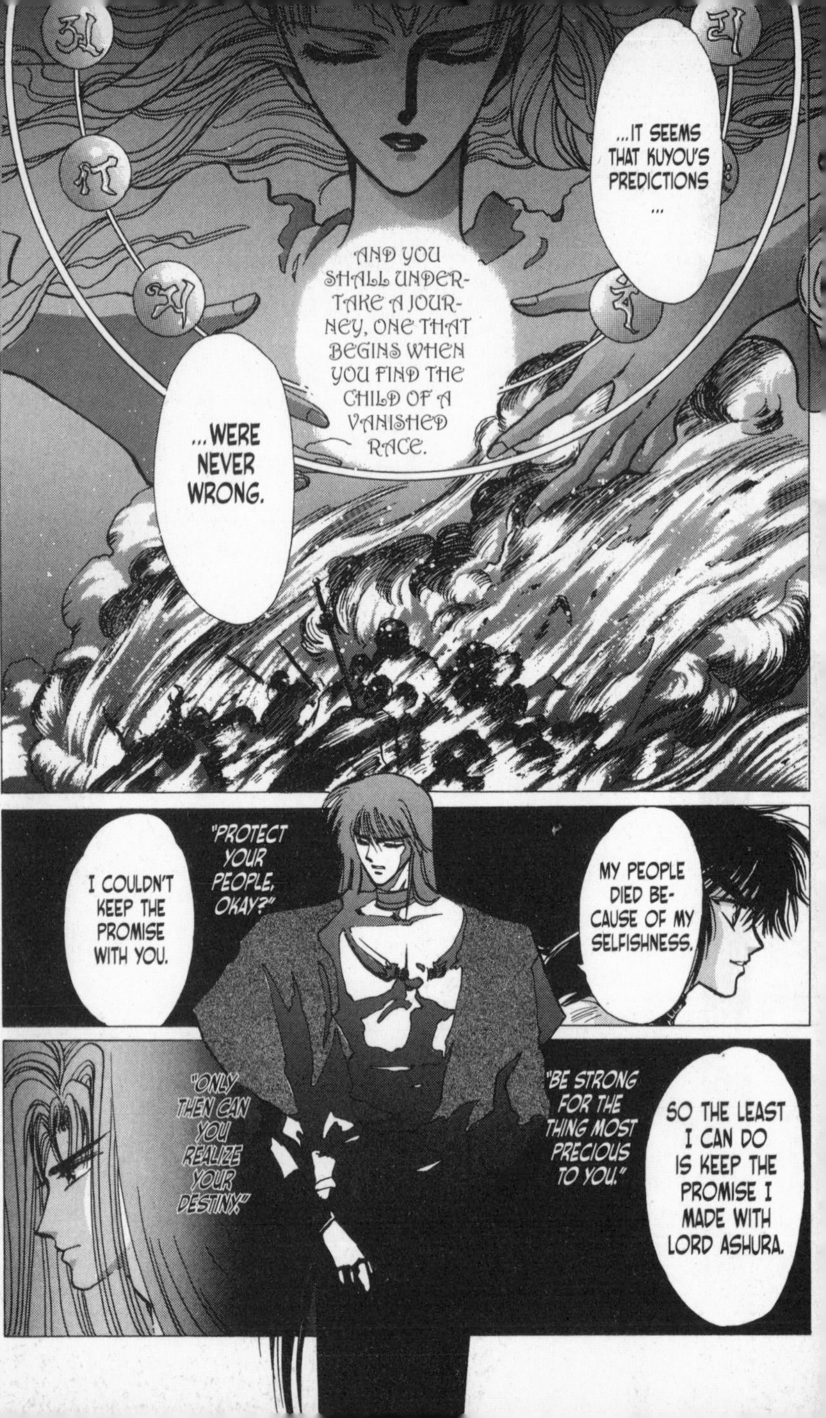
...IT SEEMS THAT KUYOU'S PREDICTIONS ...
AND YOU SHALL UNDERTAKE A JOURNEY, ONE THAT BEGINS WHEN YOU FIND THE CHILD OF A VANISHED RACE.
...WERE NEVER WRONG.
MY PEOPLE DIED BECAUSE OF MY SELFISHNESS.
"PROTECT YOUR PEOPLE, OKAY?"
I COULDN'T KEEP THE PROMISE WITH YOU.
SO THE LEAST I CAN DO IS KEEP THE PROMISE I MADE WITH LORD ASHURA.
"BE STRONG FOR THE THING MOST PRECIOUS TO YOU."
"ONLY THEN CAN YOU REALIZE YOUR DESTINY."

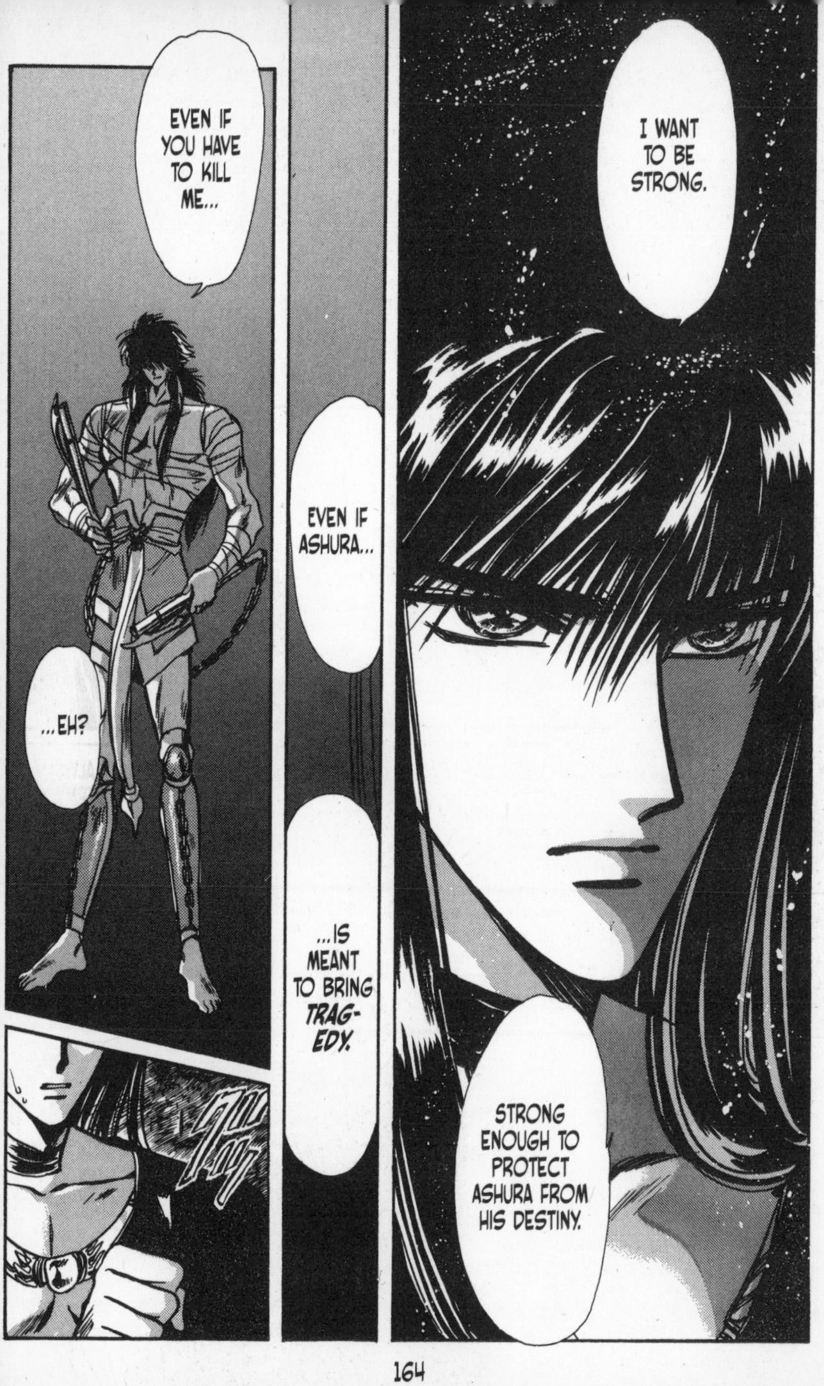
I WANT TO BE STRONG.
STRONG ENOUGH TO PROTECT ASHURA FROM HIS DESTINY.
EVEN IF ASHURA...
...IS MEANT TO BRING TRAG-EDY.
EVEN IF YOU HAVE TO KILL ME...
...EH?

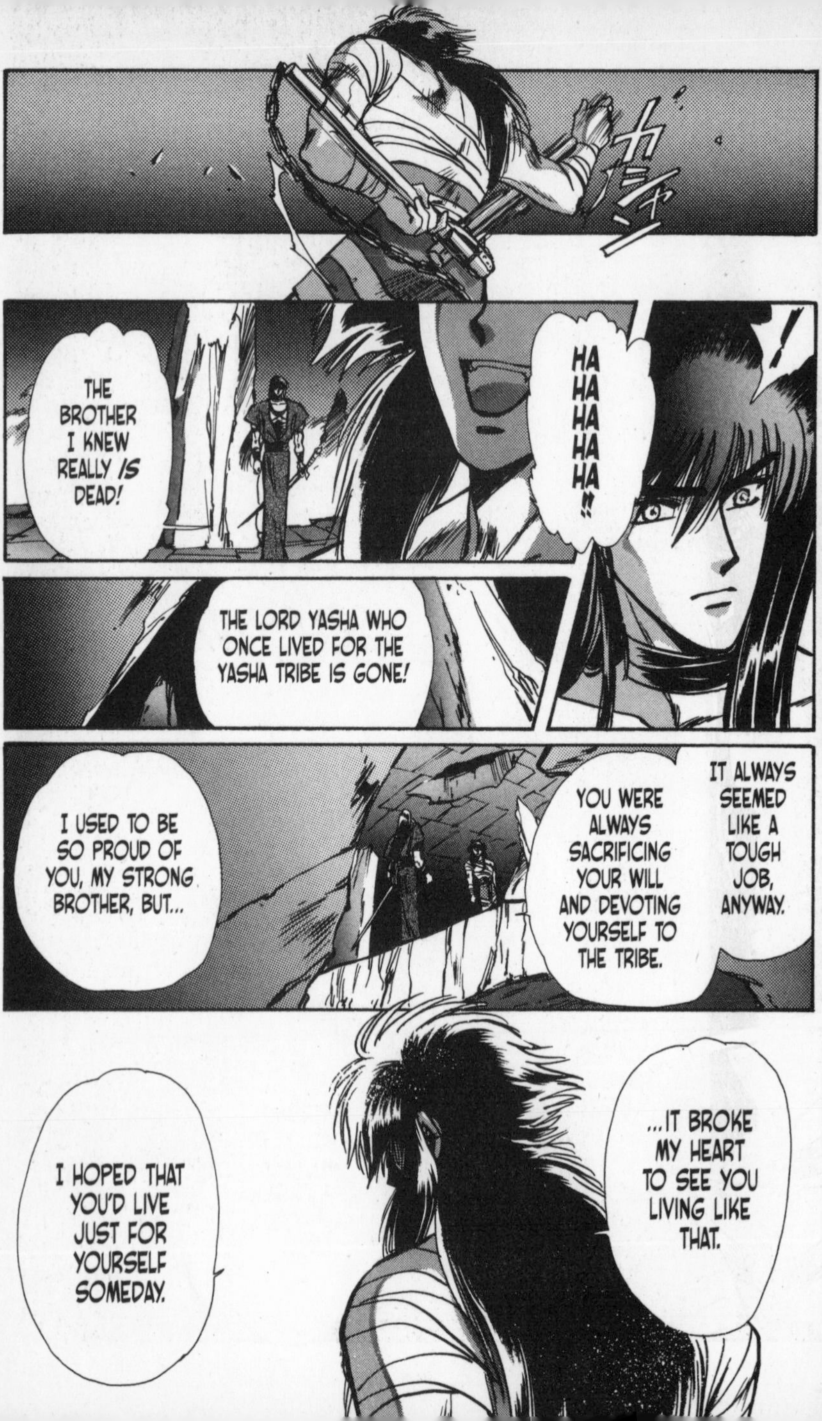
!
HA HA HA HA HA!!
THE BROTHER I KNEW REALLY *IS* DEAD!
THE LORD YASHA WHO ONCE LIVED FOR THE YASHA TRIBE IS GONE!
IT ALWAYS SEEMED LIKE A TOUGH JOB, ANYWAY.
YOU WERE ALWAYS SACRIFICING YOUR WILL AND DEVOTING YOURSELF TO THE TRIBE.
I USED TO BE SO PROUD OF YOU, MY STRONG BROTHER, BUT...
...IT BROKE MY HEART TO SEE YOU LIVING LIKE THAT.
I HOPED THAT YOU'D LIVE JUST FOR YOURSELF SOMEDAY.

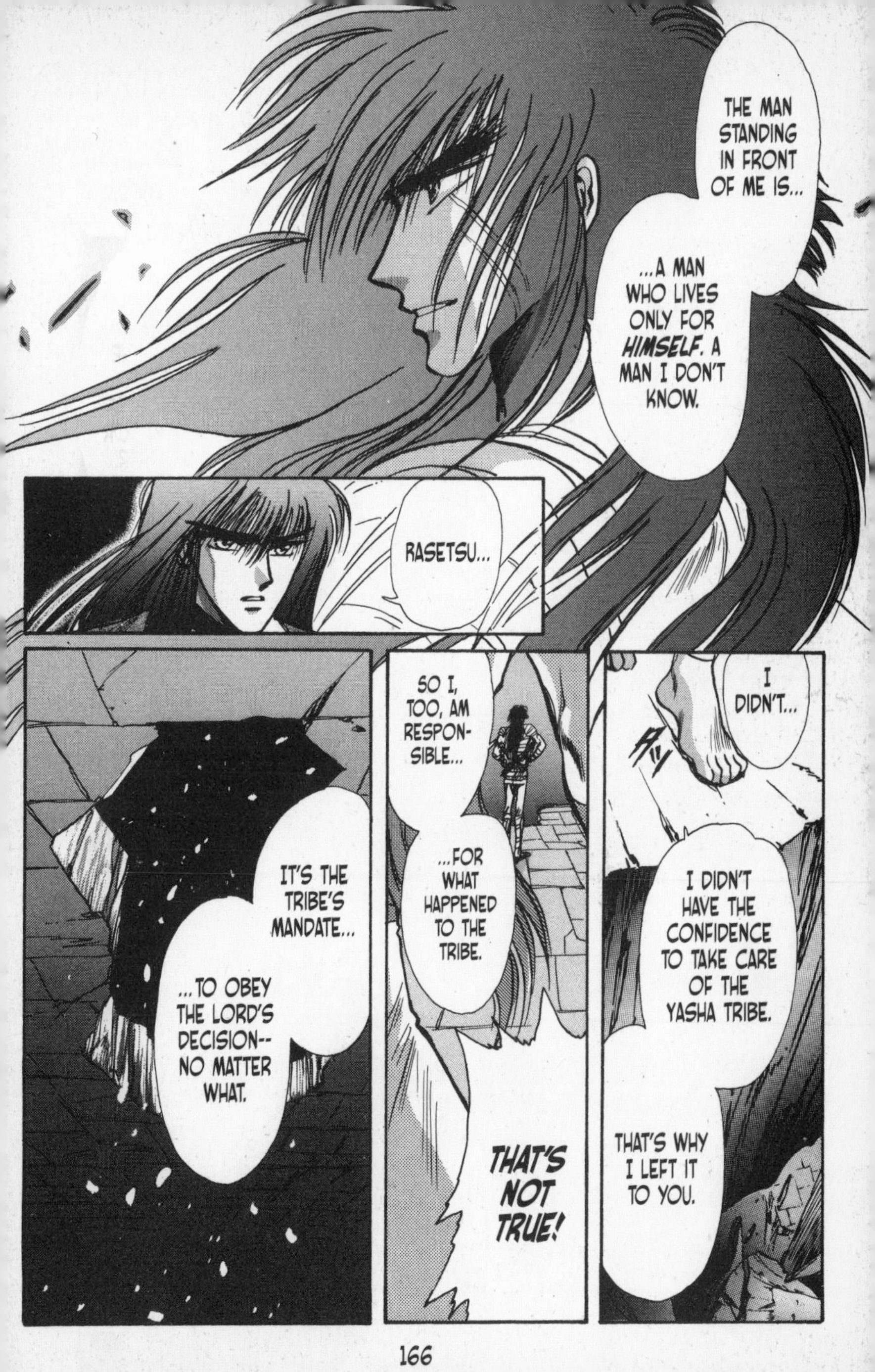
THE MAN STANDING IN FRONT OF ME IS...
...A MAN WHO LIVES ONLY FOR ***HIMSELF***. A MAN I DON'T KNOW.
RASETSU...
I DIDN'T...
I DIDN'T HAVE THE CONFIDENCE TO TAKE CARE OF THE YASHA TRIBE.
THAT'S WHY I LEFT IT TO YOU.
SO I, TOO, AM RESPONSIBLE...
...FOR WHAT HAPPENED TO THE TRIBE.
***THAT'S NOT TRUE!***
IT'S THE TRIBE'S MANDATE...
...TO OBEY THE LORD'S DECISION-- NO MATTER WHAT.

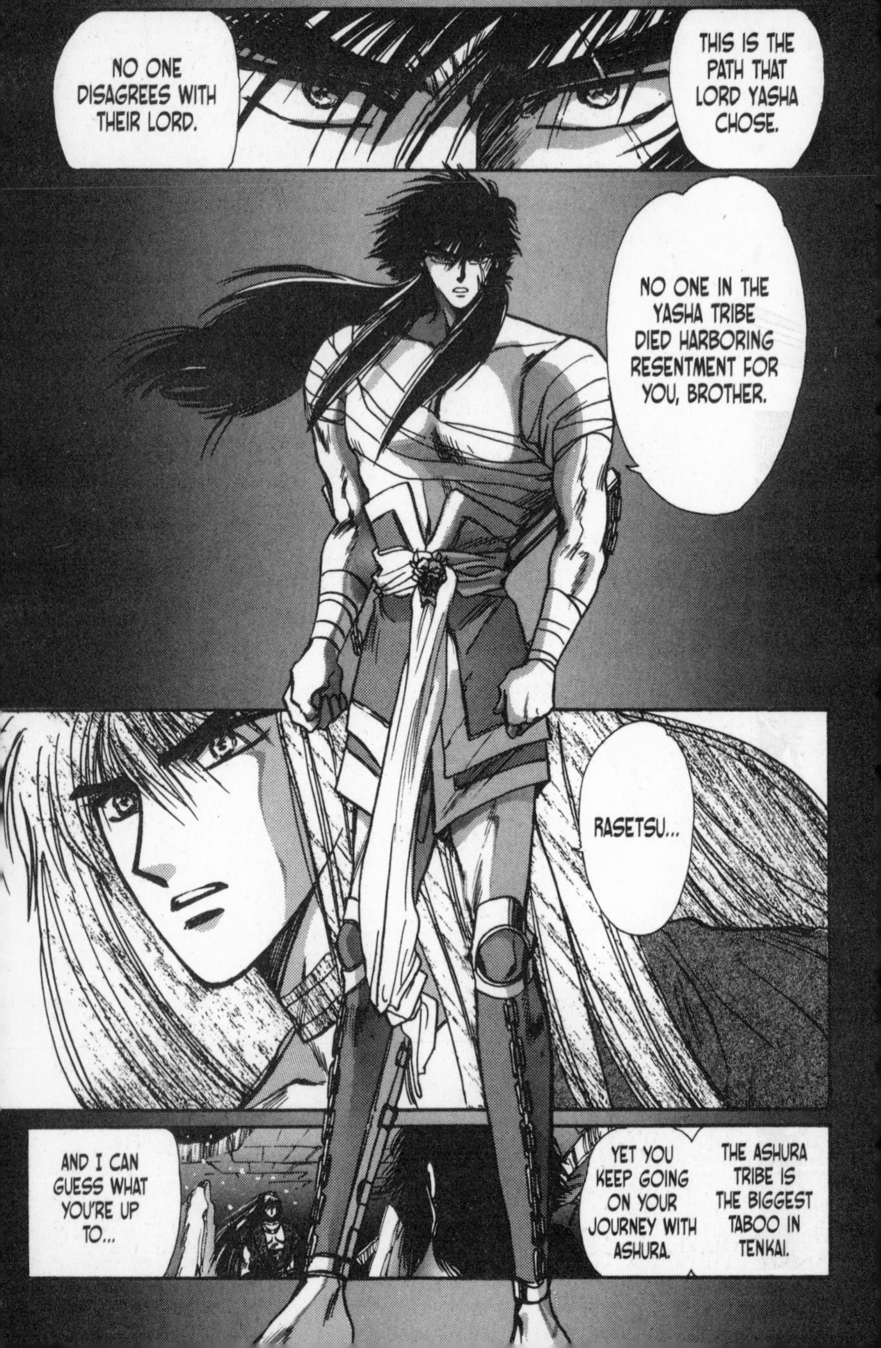
THIS IS THE PATH THAT LORD YASHA CHOSE.
NO ONE DISAGREES WITH THEIR LORD.
NO ONE IN THE YASHA TRIBE DIED HARBORING RESENTMENT FOR YOU, BROTHER.
RASETSU...
THE ASHURA TRIBE IS THE BIGGEST TABOO IN TENKAI.
YET YOU KEEP GOING ON YOUR JOURNEY WITH ASHURA.
AND I CAN GUESS WHAT YOU'RE UP TO...

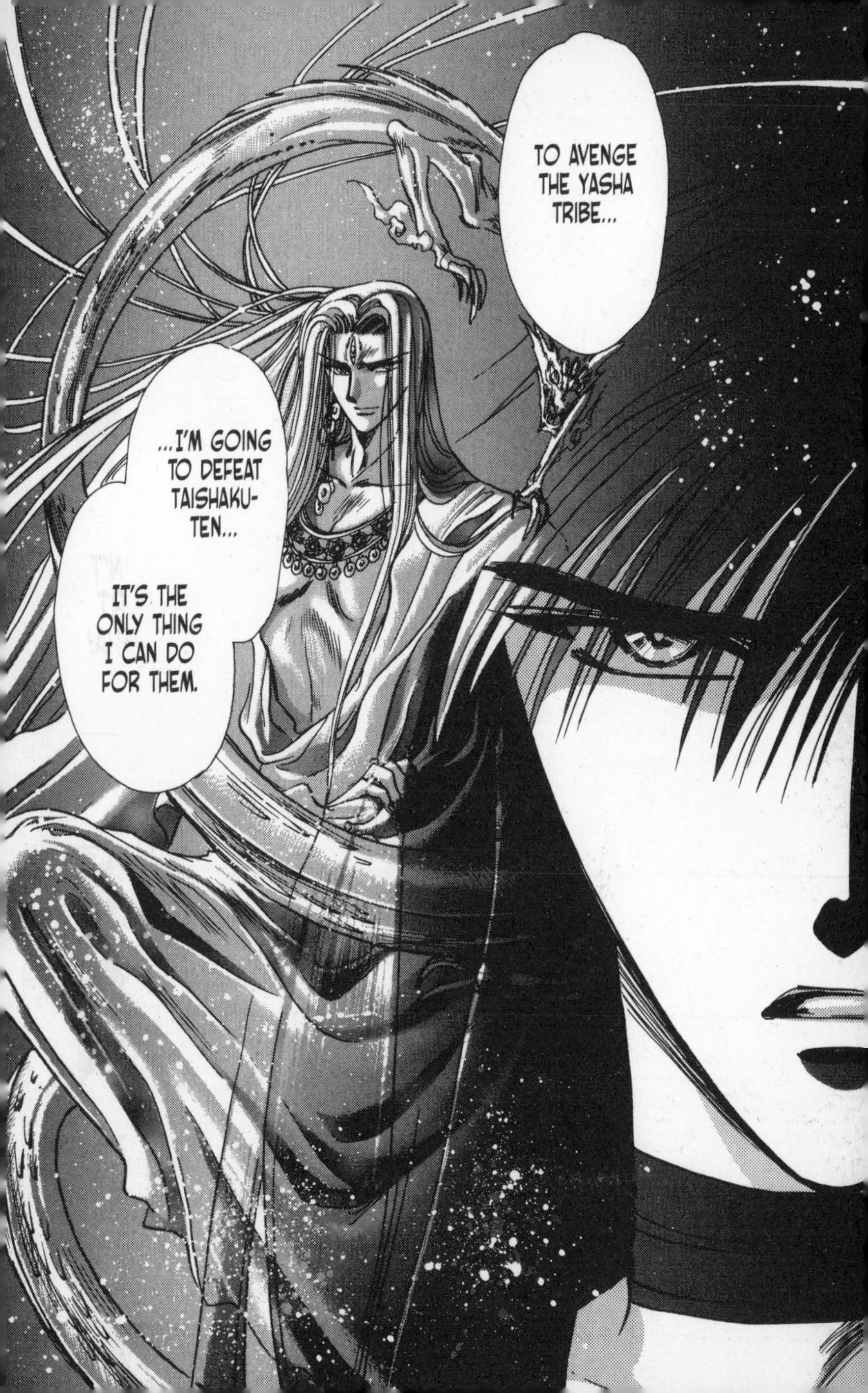
TO AVENGE THE YASHA TRIBE...
...I'M GOING TO DEFEAT TAISHAKU-TEN...
IT'S THE ONLY THING I CAN DO FOR THEM.

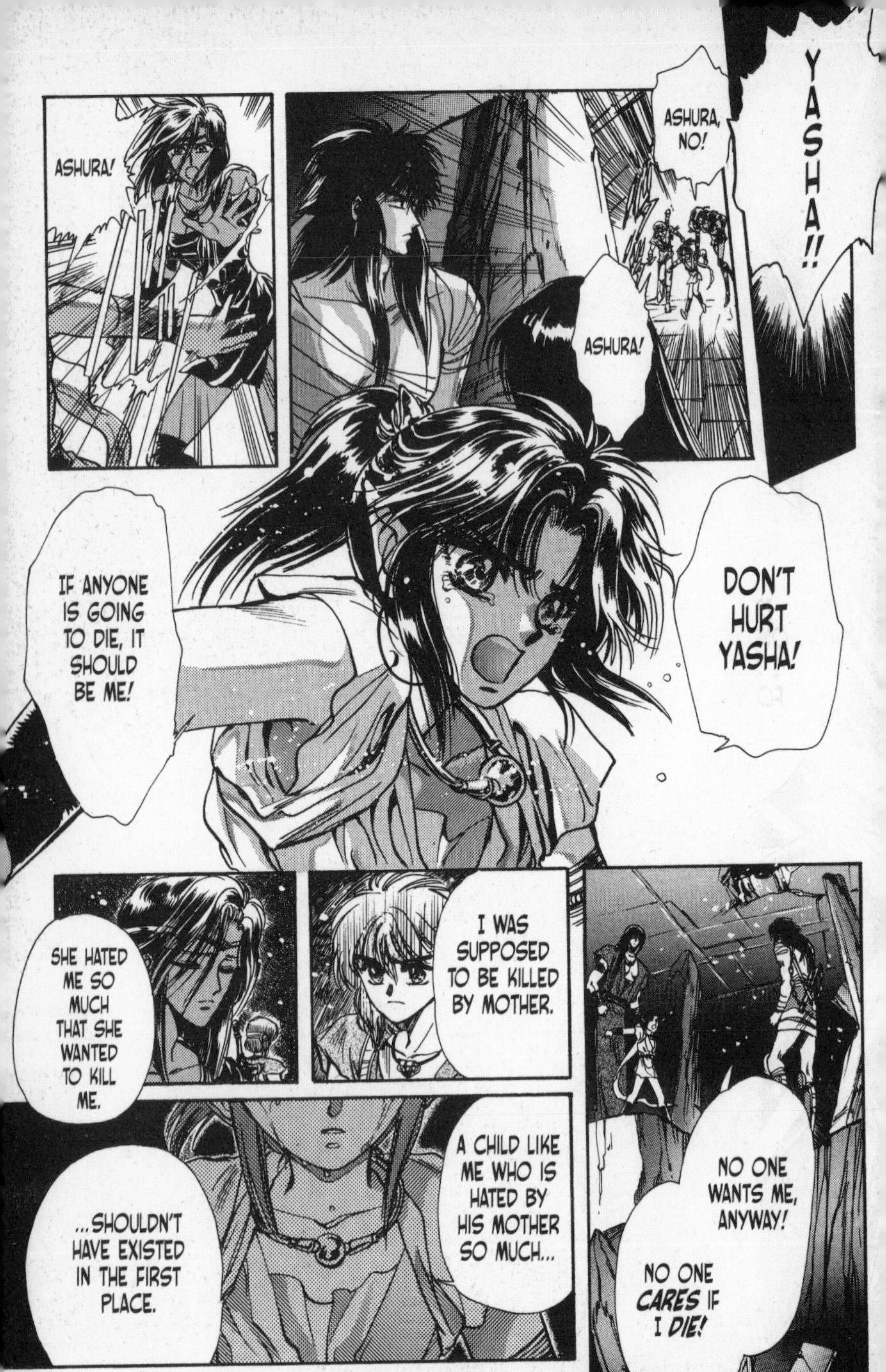
YASHA!!
ASHURA, NO!
ASHURA!
ASHURA!
DON'T HURT YASHA!
IF ANYONE IS GOING TO DIE, IT SHOULD BE ME!
NO ONE WANTS ME, ANYWAY!
NO ONE *CARES* IF I *DIE*!
I WAS SUPPOSED TO BE KILLED BY MOTHER.
SHE HATED ME SO MUCH THAT SHE WANTED TO KILL ME.
A CHILD LIKE ME WHO IS HATED BY HIS MOTHER SO MUCH...
...SHOULDN'T HAVE EXISTED IN THE FIRST PLACE.

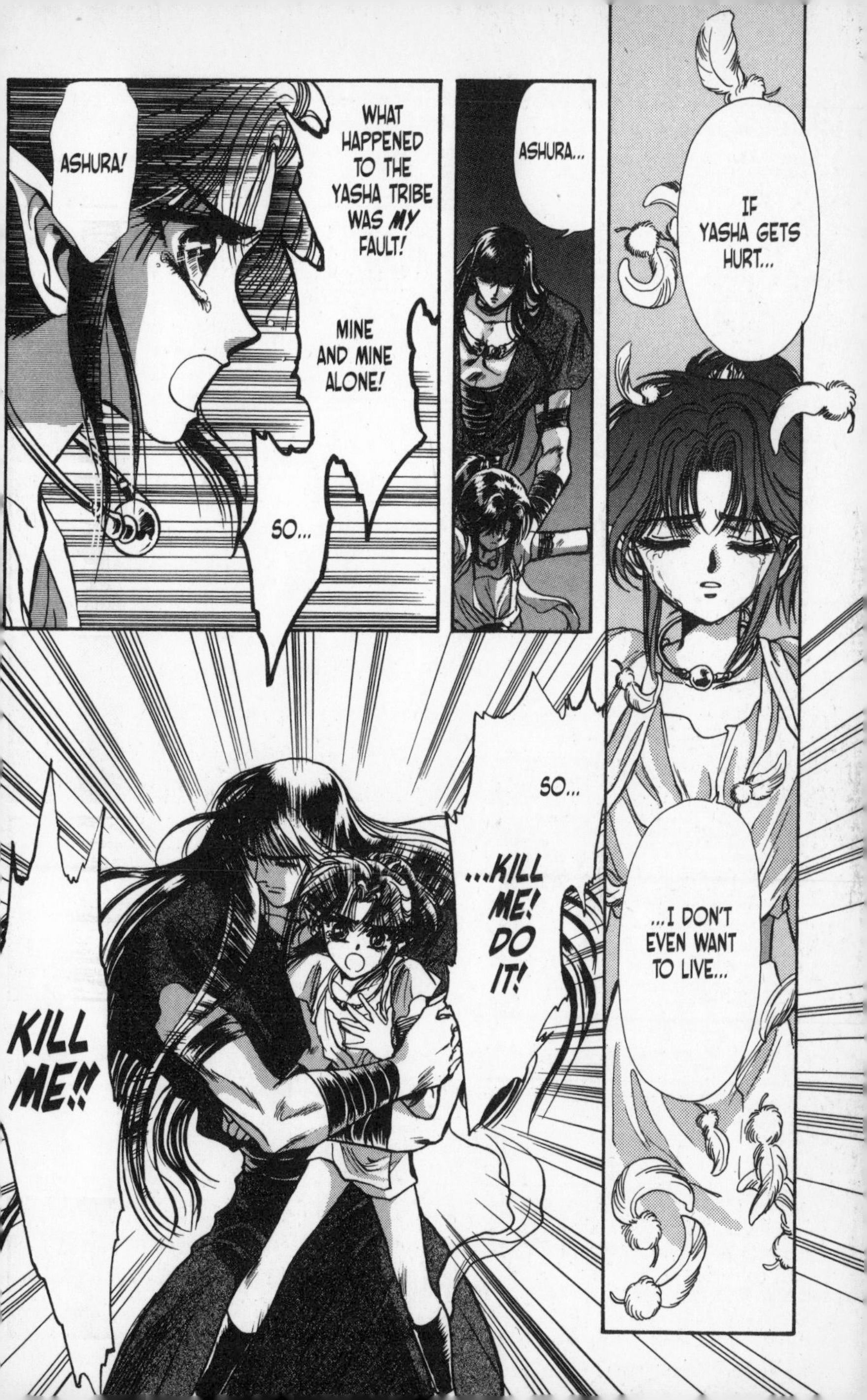

IF YASHA GETS HURT...
...I DON'T EVEN WANT TO LIVE...
ASHURA...
ASHURA!
WHAT HAPPENED TO THE YASHA TRIBE WAS *MY* FAULT!
MINE AND MINE ALONE!
SO...
SO...
...KILL ME! DO IT!
KILL ME!!

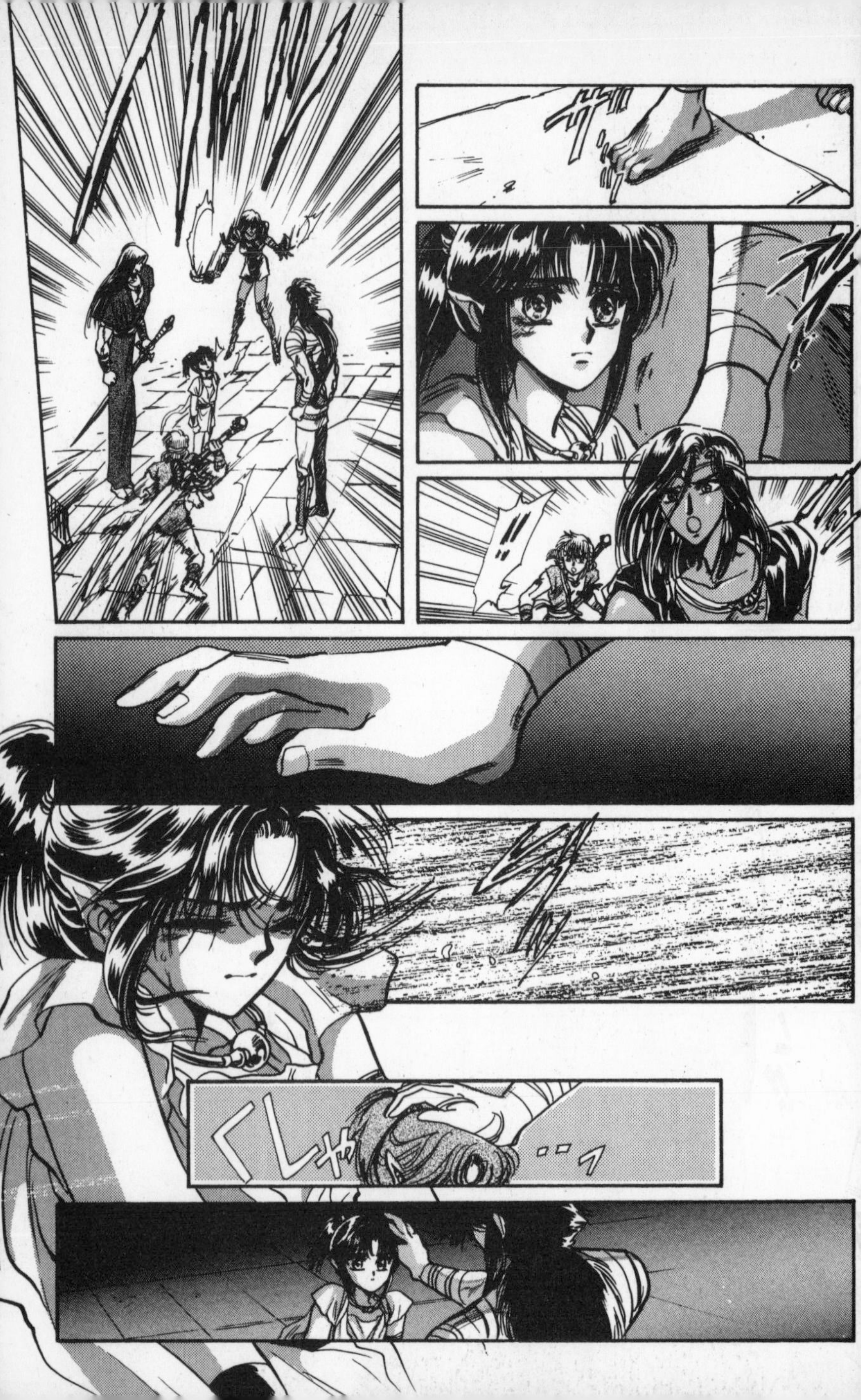
!!
くしゃ…っ

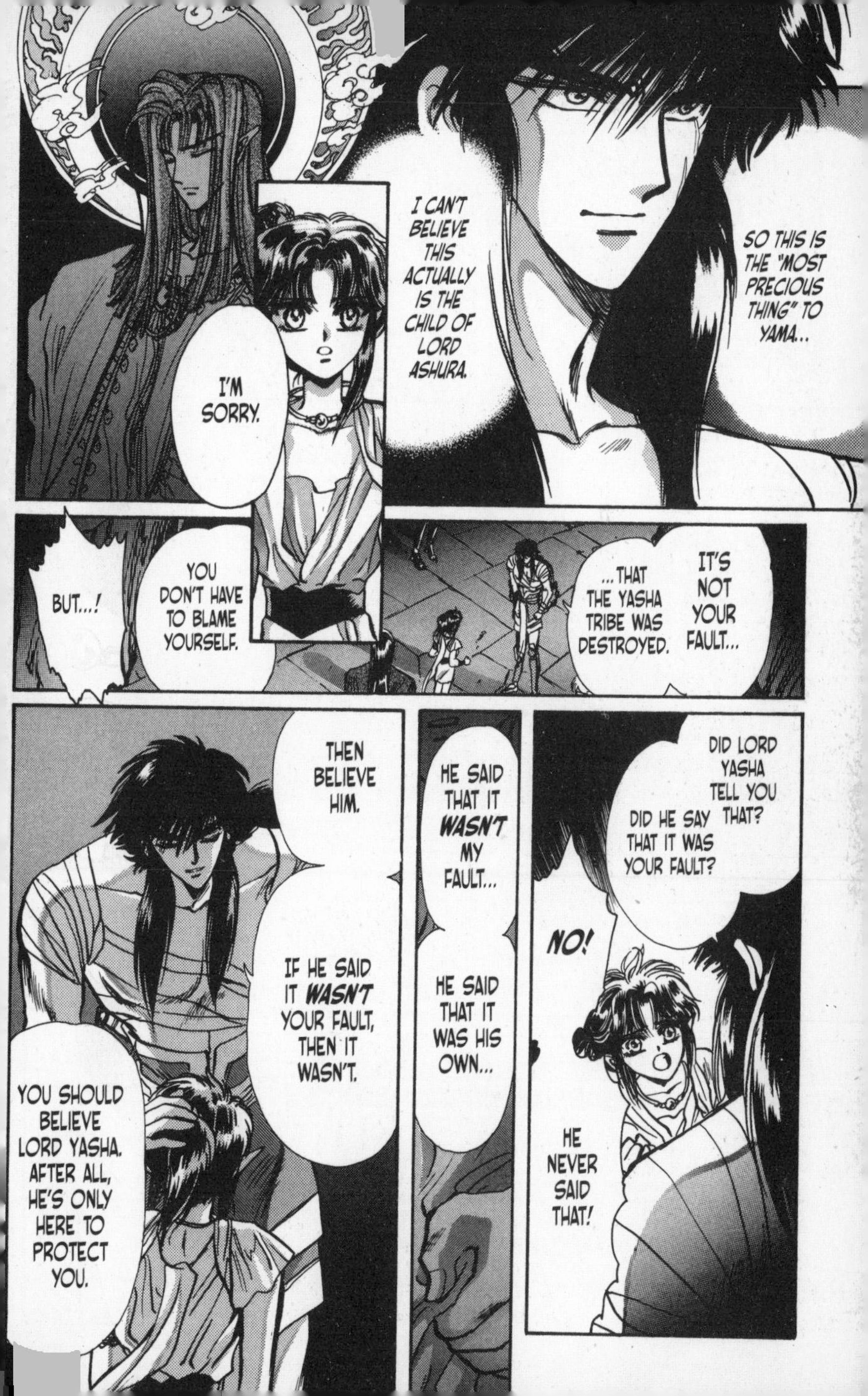
SO THIS IS THE "MOST PRECIOUS THING" TO YAMA...
I CAN'T BELIEVE THIS ACTUALLY IS THE CHILD OF LORD ASHURA.
I'M SORRY.
IT'S NOT YOUR FAULT...
...THAT THE YASHA TRIBE WAS DESTROYED.
YOU DON'T HAVE TO BLAME YOURSELF.
BUT...!
DID LORD YASHA TELL YOU THAT?
DID HE SAY THAT IT WAS YOUR FAULT?
NO!
HE NEVER SAID THAT!
HE SAID THAT IT *WASN'T* MY FAULT...
HE SAID THAT IT WAS HIS OWN...
THEN BELIEVE HIM.
IF HE SAID IT *WASN'T* YOUR FAULT, THEN IT WASN'T.
YOU SHOULD BELIEVE LORD YASHA. AFTER ALL, HE'S ONLY HERE TO PROTECT YOU.

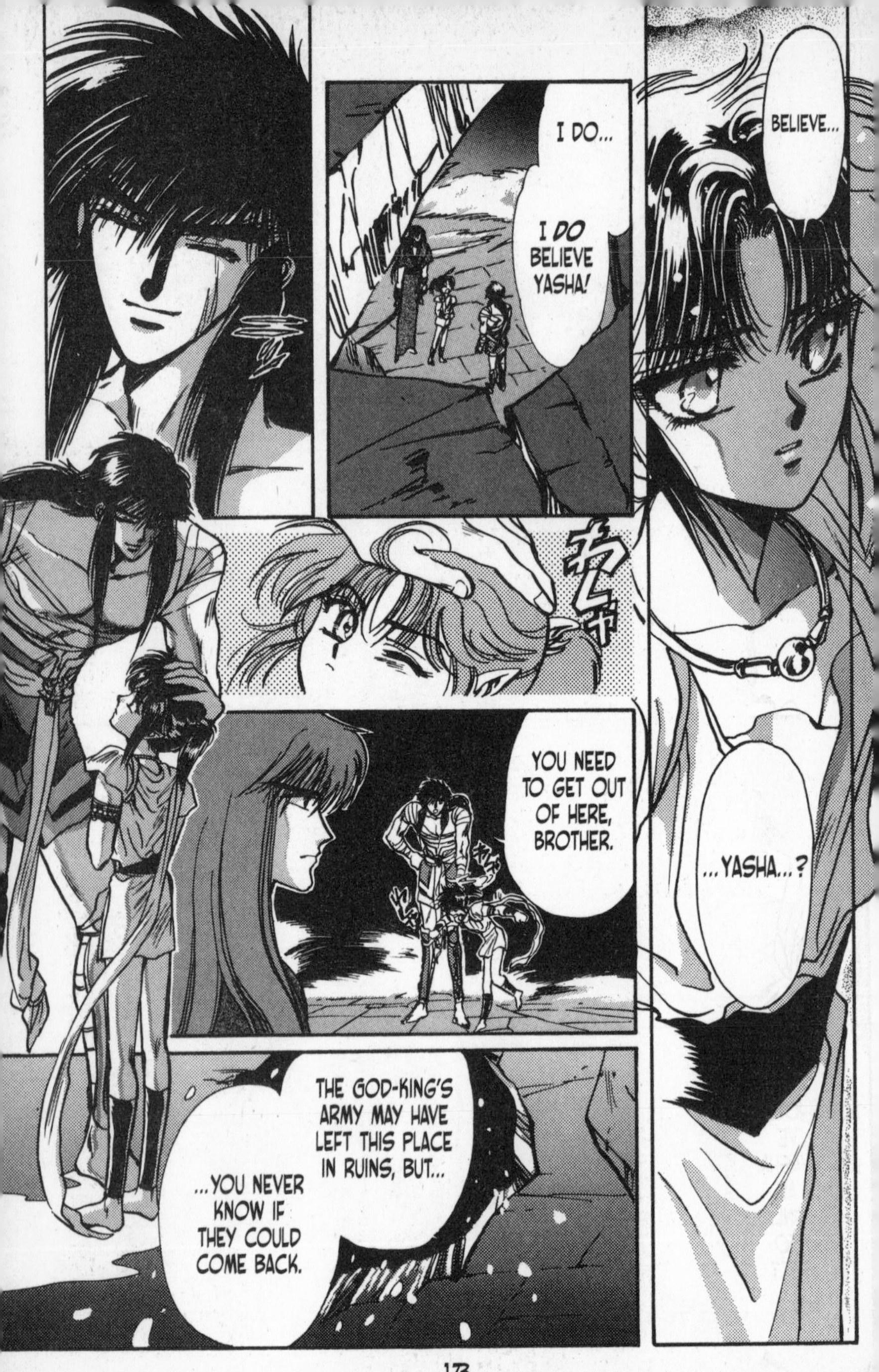
BELIEVE...
...YASHA...?
I DO...
I DO BELIEVE YASHA!
YOU NEED TO GET OUT OF HERE, BROTHER.
THE GOD-KING'S ARMY MAY HAVE LEFT THIS PLACE IN RUINS, BUT...
...YOU NEVER KNOW IF THEY COULD COME BACK.

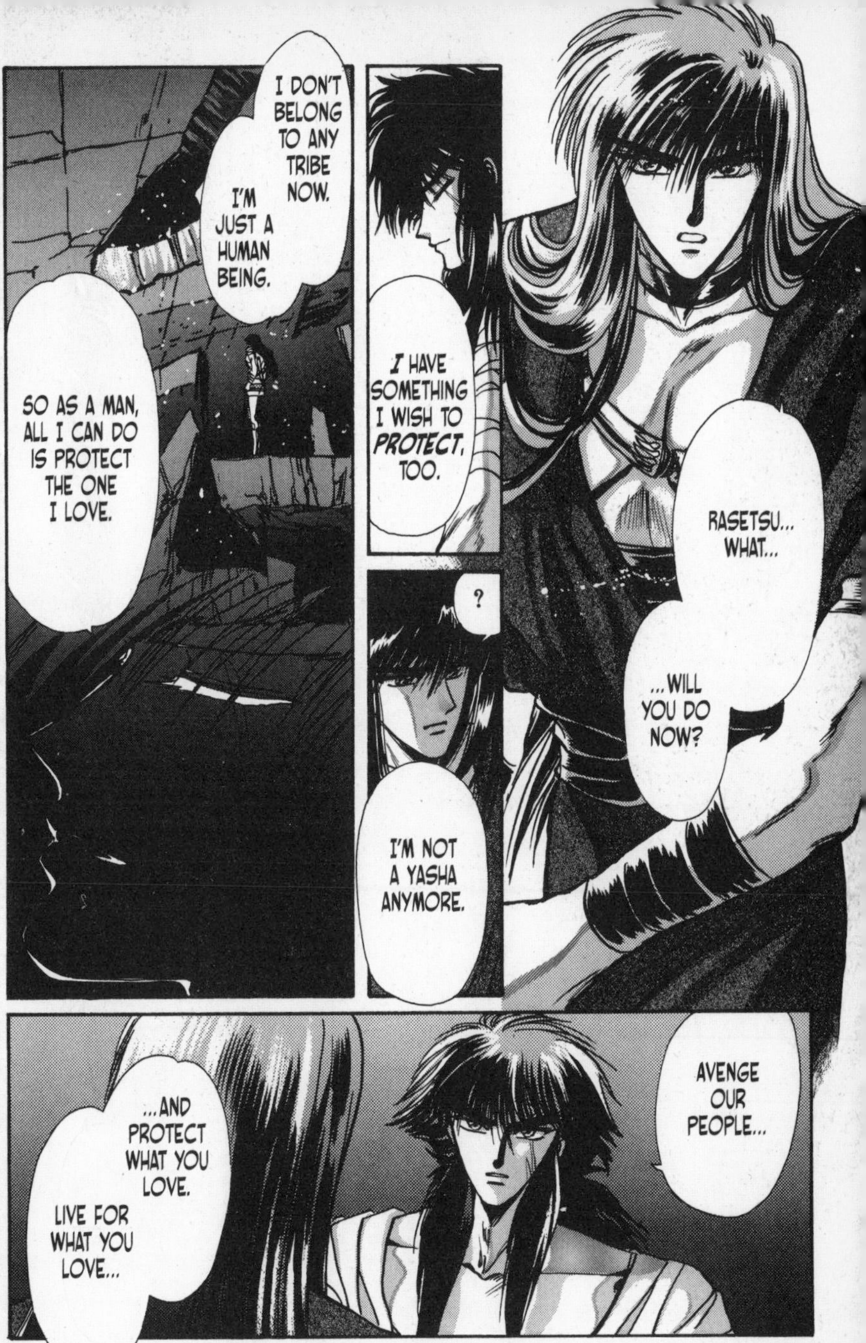
RASETSU... WHAT...
...WILL YOU DO NOW?
*I* HAVE SOMETHING I WISH TO *PROTECT*, TOO.
?
I'M NOT A YASHA ANYMORE.
I DON'T BELONG TO ANY TRIBE NOW.
I'M JUST A HUMAN BEING.
SO AS A MAN, ALL I CAN DO IS PROTECT THE ONE I LOVE.
AVENGE OUR PEOPLE...
...AND PROTECT WHAT YOU LOVE.
LIVE FOR WHAT YOU LOVE...

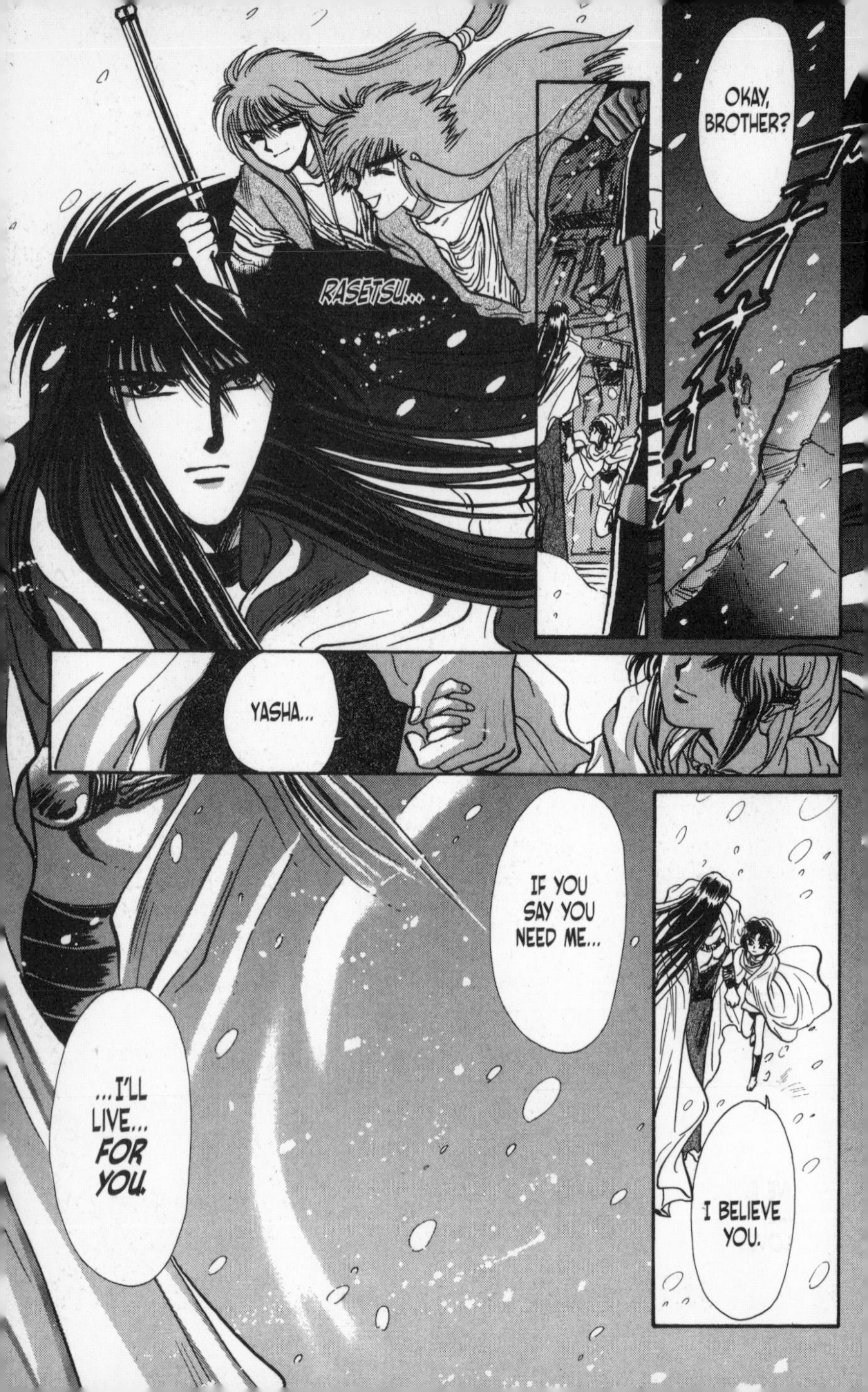
OKAY, BROTHER?
RASETSU...
YASHA...
I BELIEVE YOU.
IF YOU SAY YOU NEED ME...
...I'LL LIVE... FOR YOU.

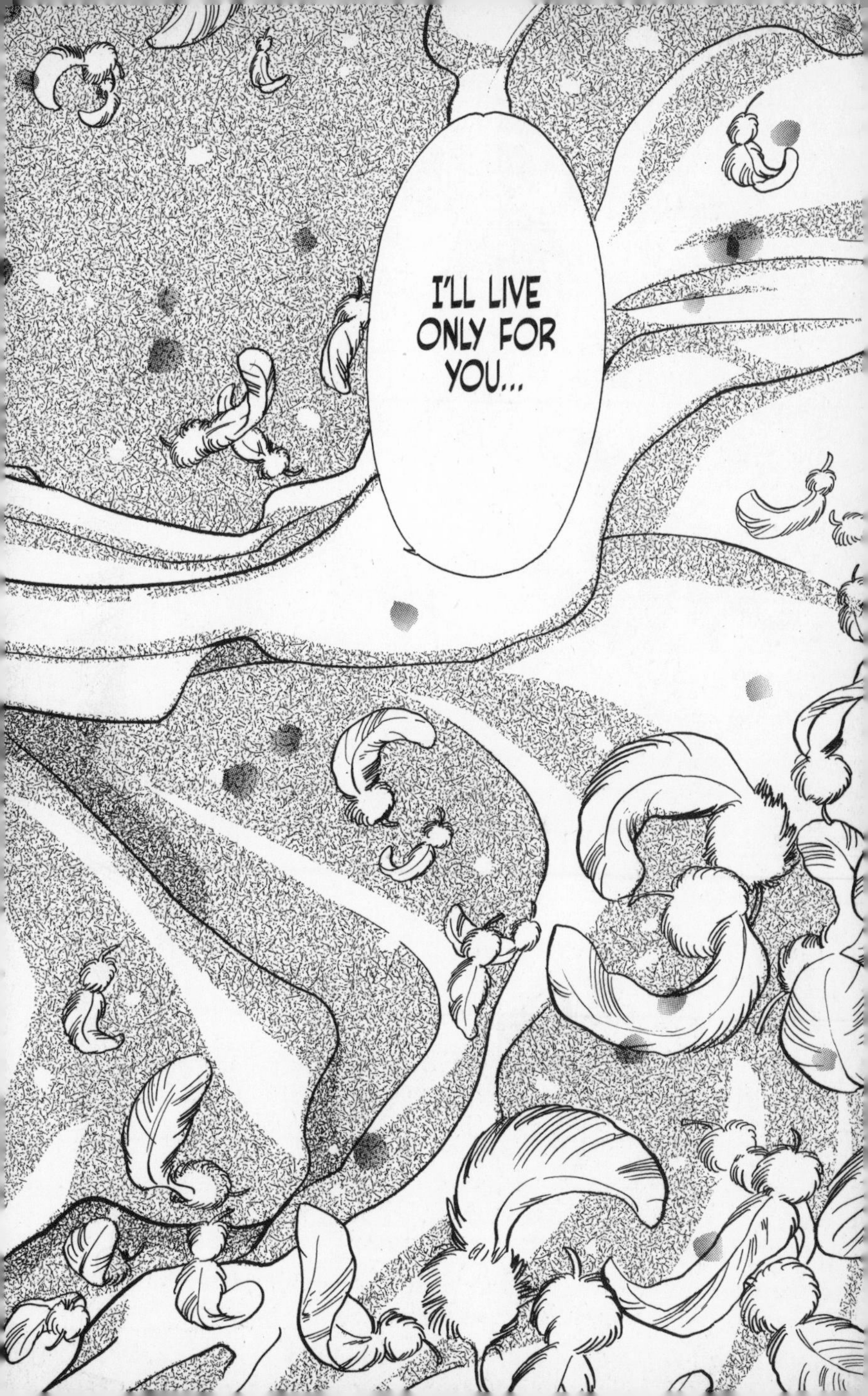
I'LL LIVE ONLY FOR YOU...

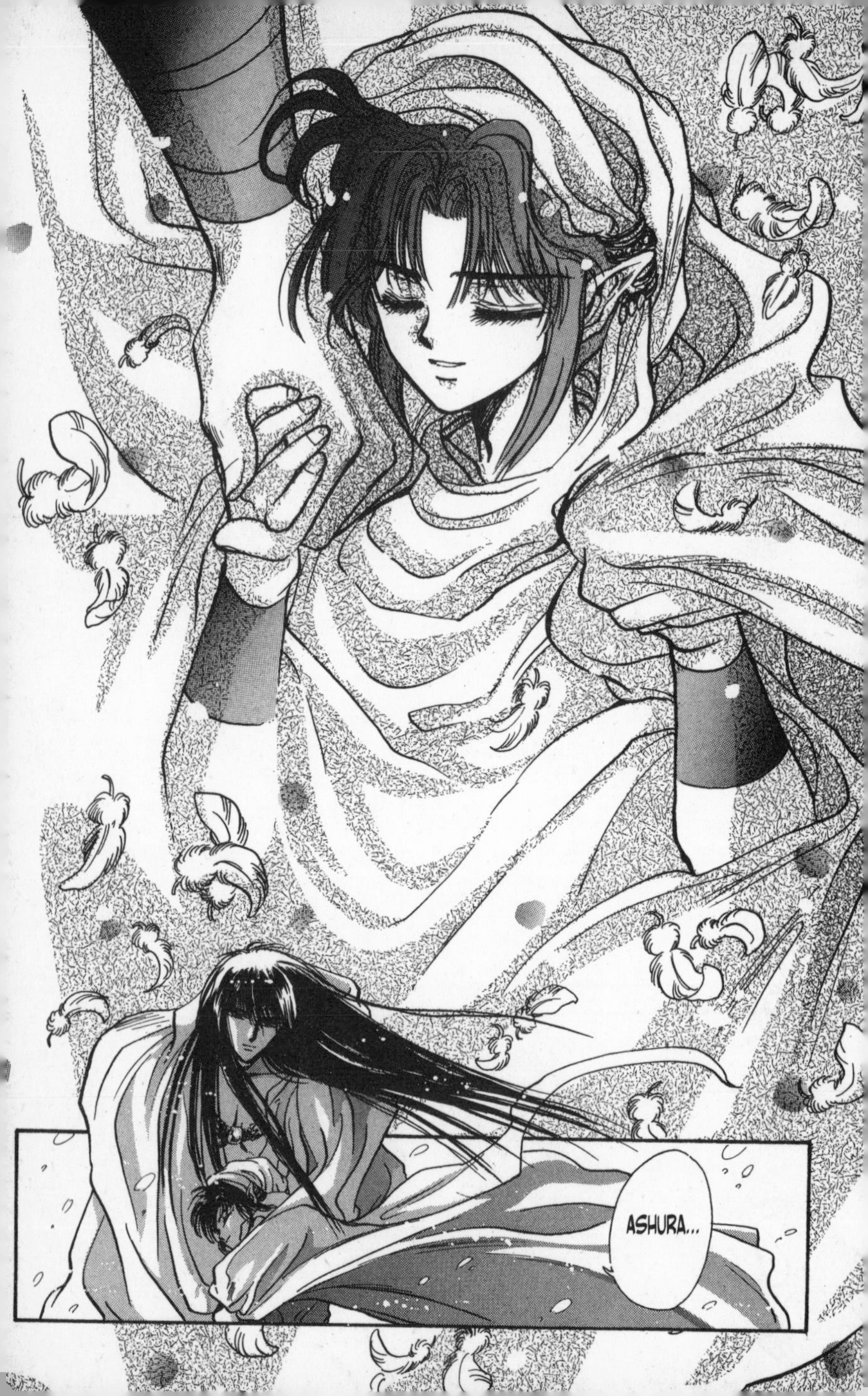
ASHURA...

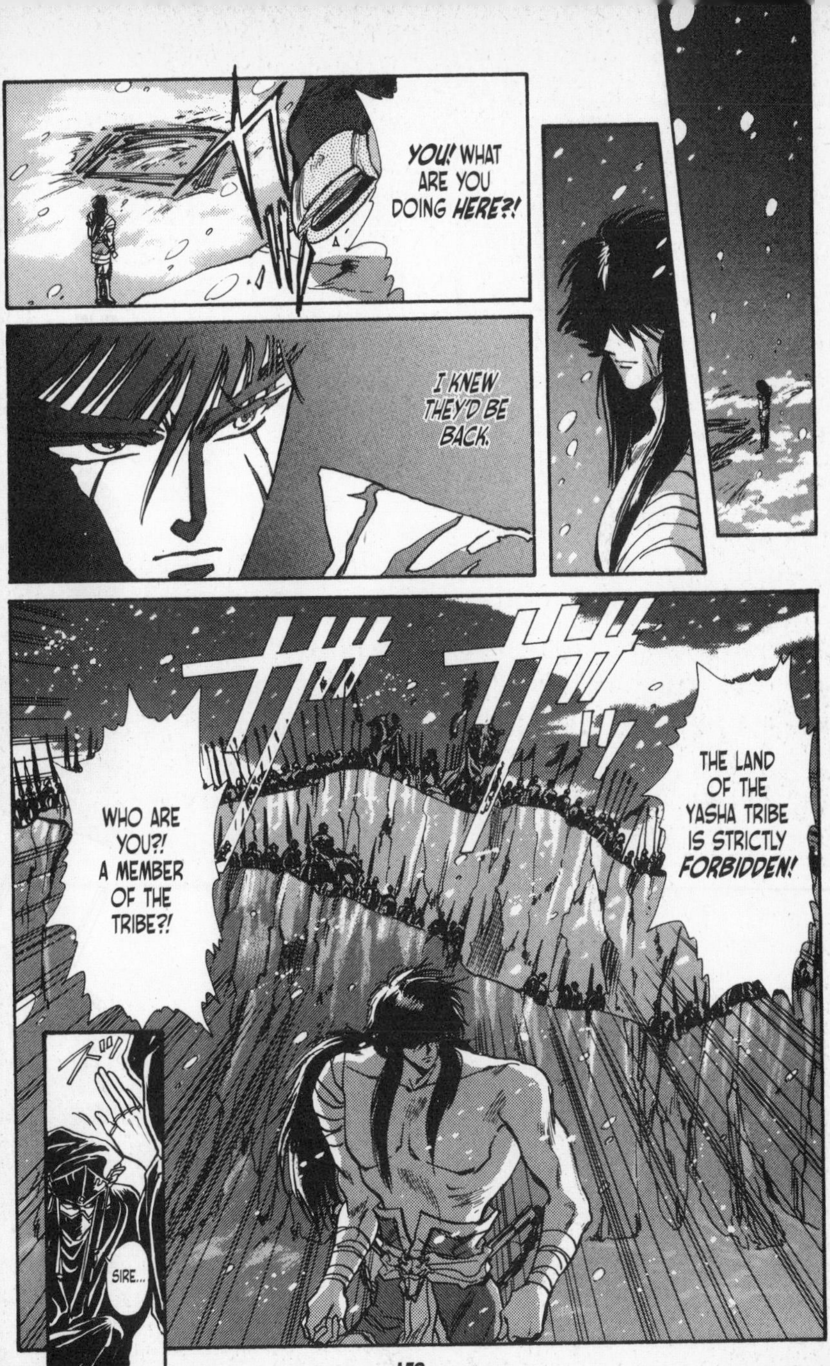
YOU! WHAT ARE YOU DOING HERE?!
I KNEW THEY'D BE BACK.
ザザ
ザザッ
THE LAND OF THE YASHA TRIBE IS STRICTLY FORBIDDEN!
WHO ARE YOU?! A MEMBER OF THE TRIBE?!
SIRE...

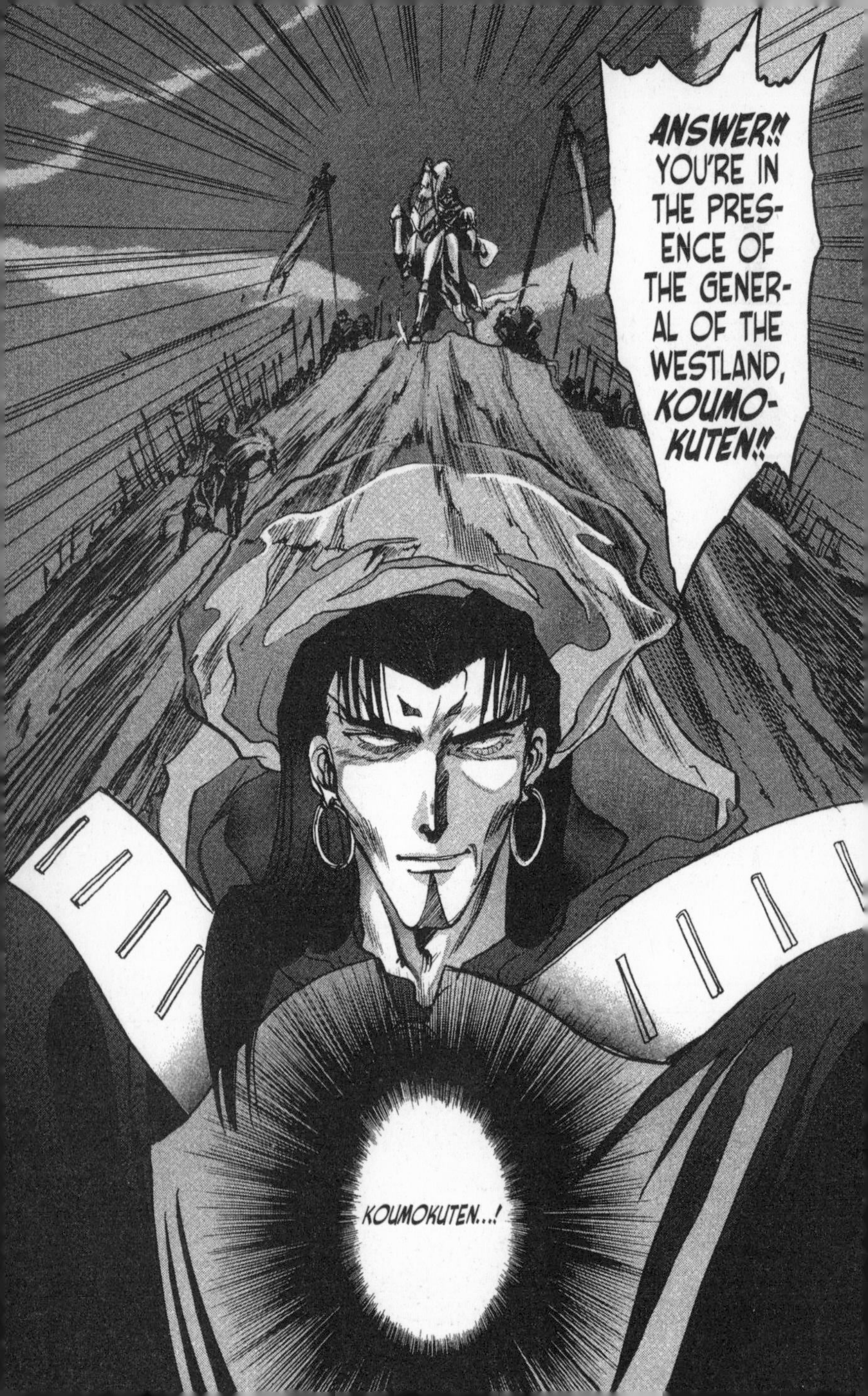
ANSWER!! YOU'RE IN THE PRES-ENCE OF THE GENER-AL OF THE WESTLAND, KOUMO-KUTEN!!
KOUMOKUTEN...!

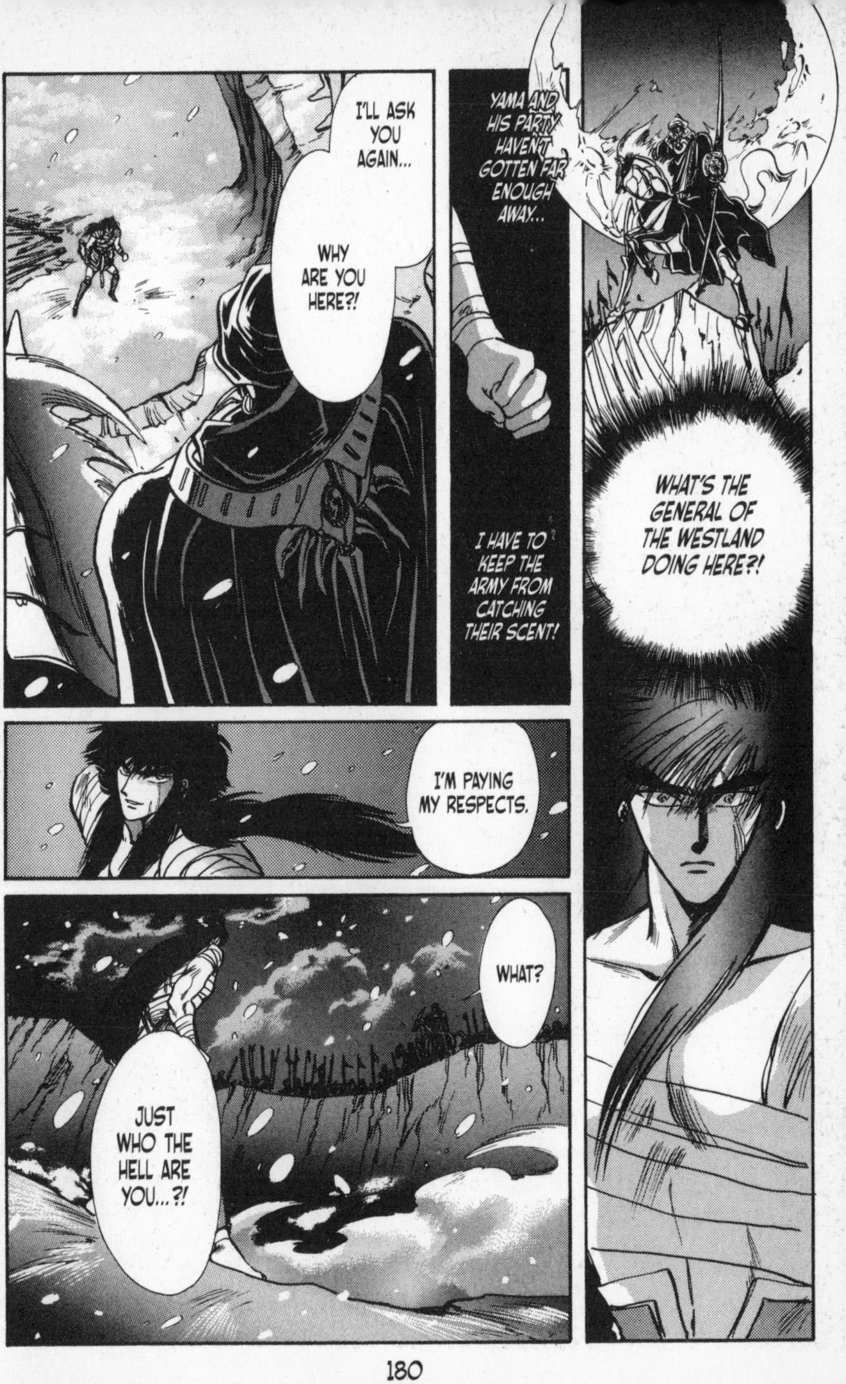
WHAT'S THE GENERAL OF THE WESTLAND DOING HERE?!
YAMA AND HIS PARTY HAVEN'T GOTTEN FAR ENOUGH AWAY...
I HAVE TO KEEP THE ARMY FROM CATCHING THEIR SCENT!
I'LL ASK YOU AGAIN...
WHY ARE YOU HERE?!
I'M PAYING MY RESPECTS.
WHAT?
JUST WHO THE HELL ARE YOU...?!

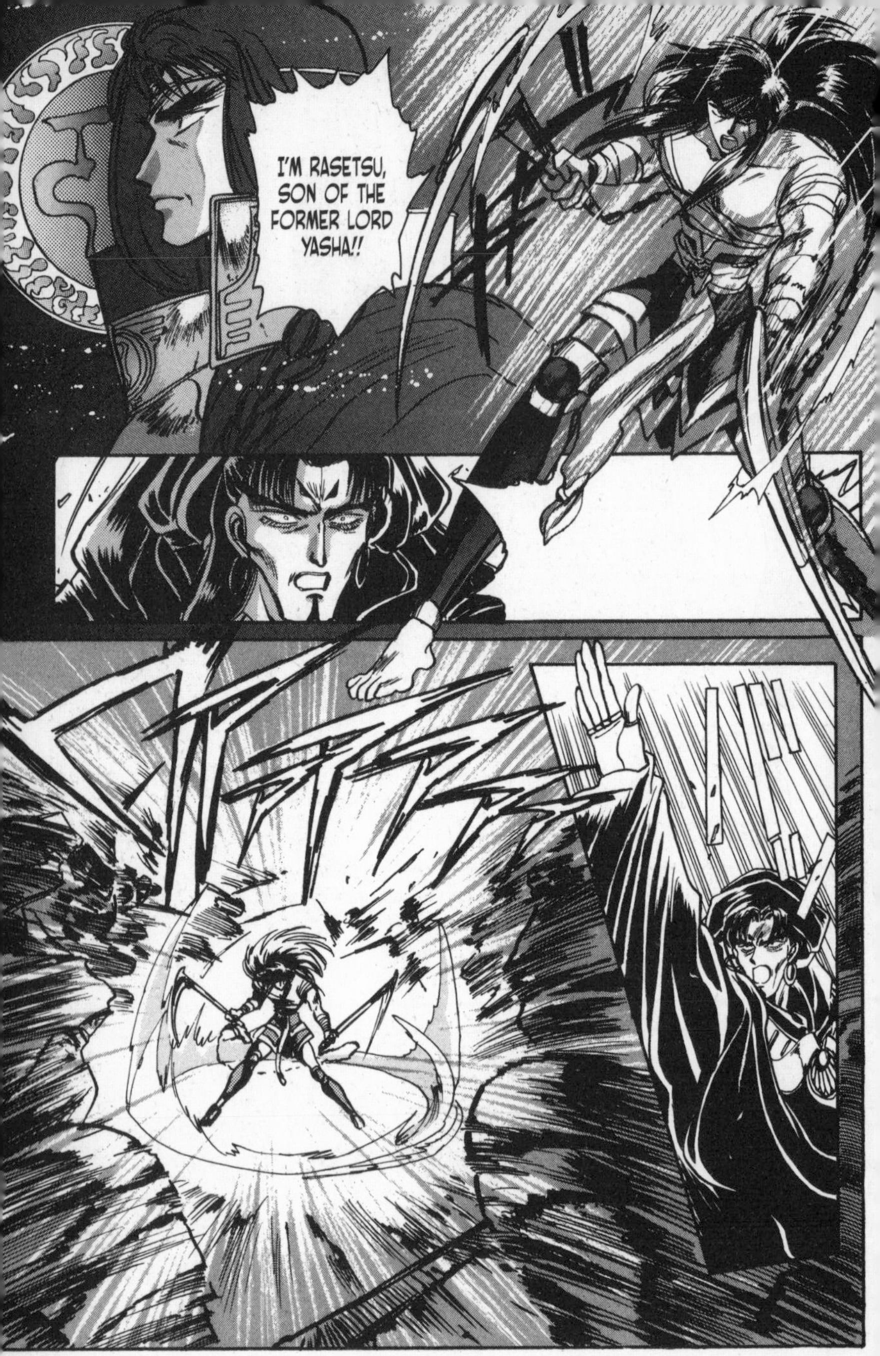
I'M RASETSU, SON OF THE FORMER LORD YASHA!!

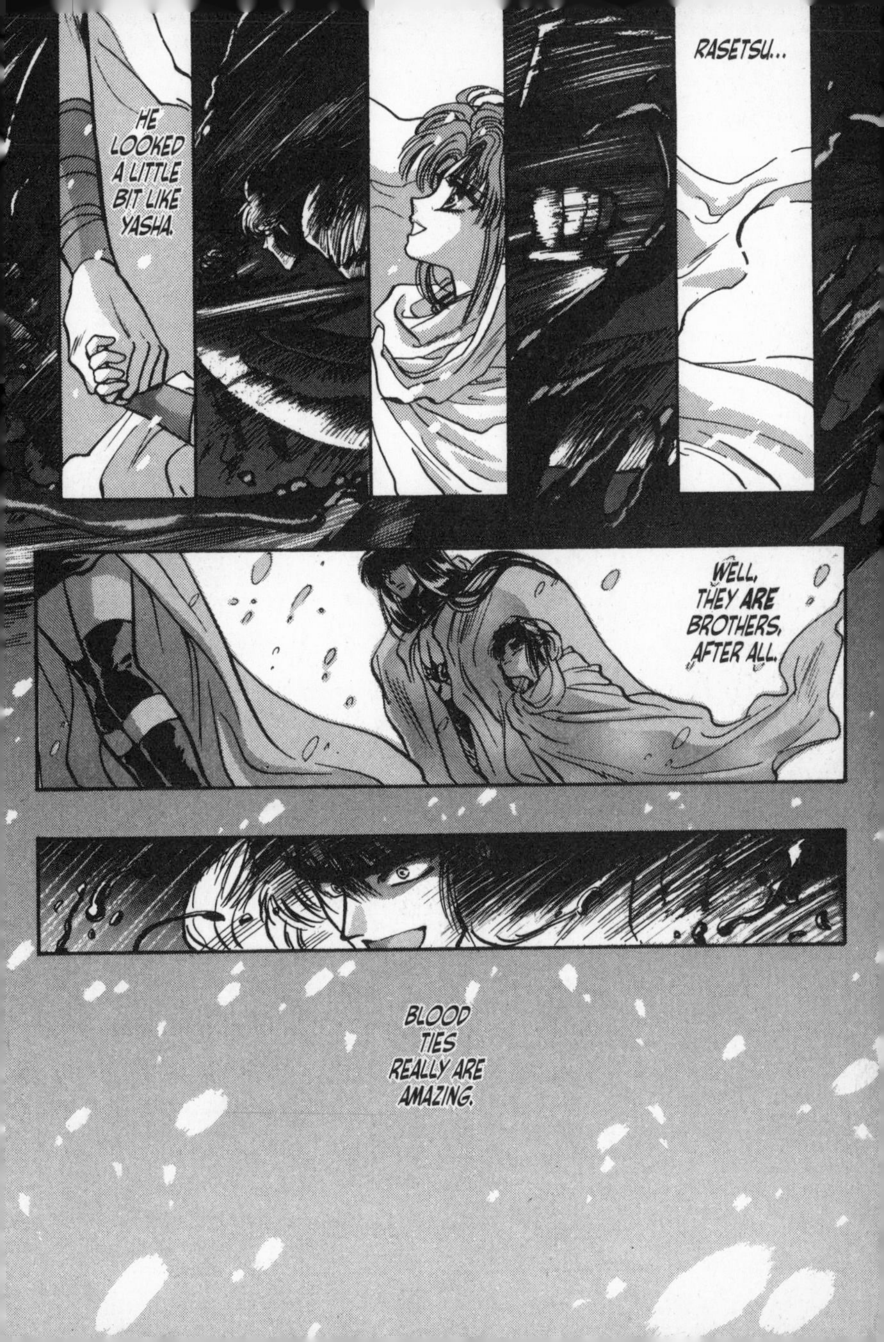
RASETSU...
HE LOOKED A LITTLE BIT LIKE YASHA.
WELL, THEY ARE BROTHERS, AFTER ALL.
BLOOD TIES REALLY ARE AMAZING.

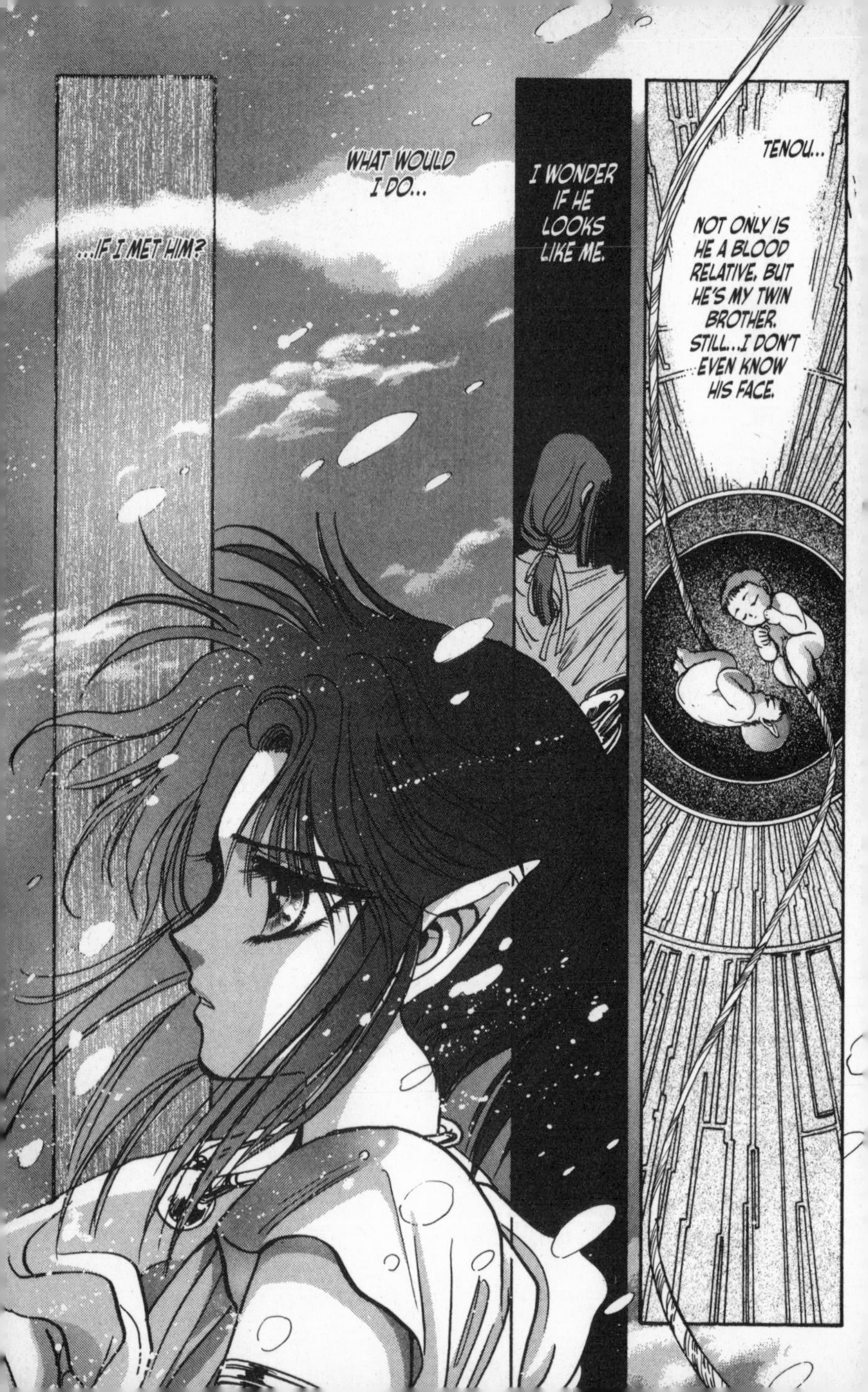
TENOU...
NOT ONLY IS HE A BLOOD RELATIVE, BUT HE'S MY TWIN BROTHER. STILL...I DON'T EVEN KNOW HIS FACE.
I WONDER IF HE LOOKS LIKE ME.
WHAT WOULD I DO...
...IF I MET HIM?

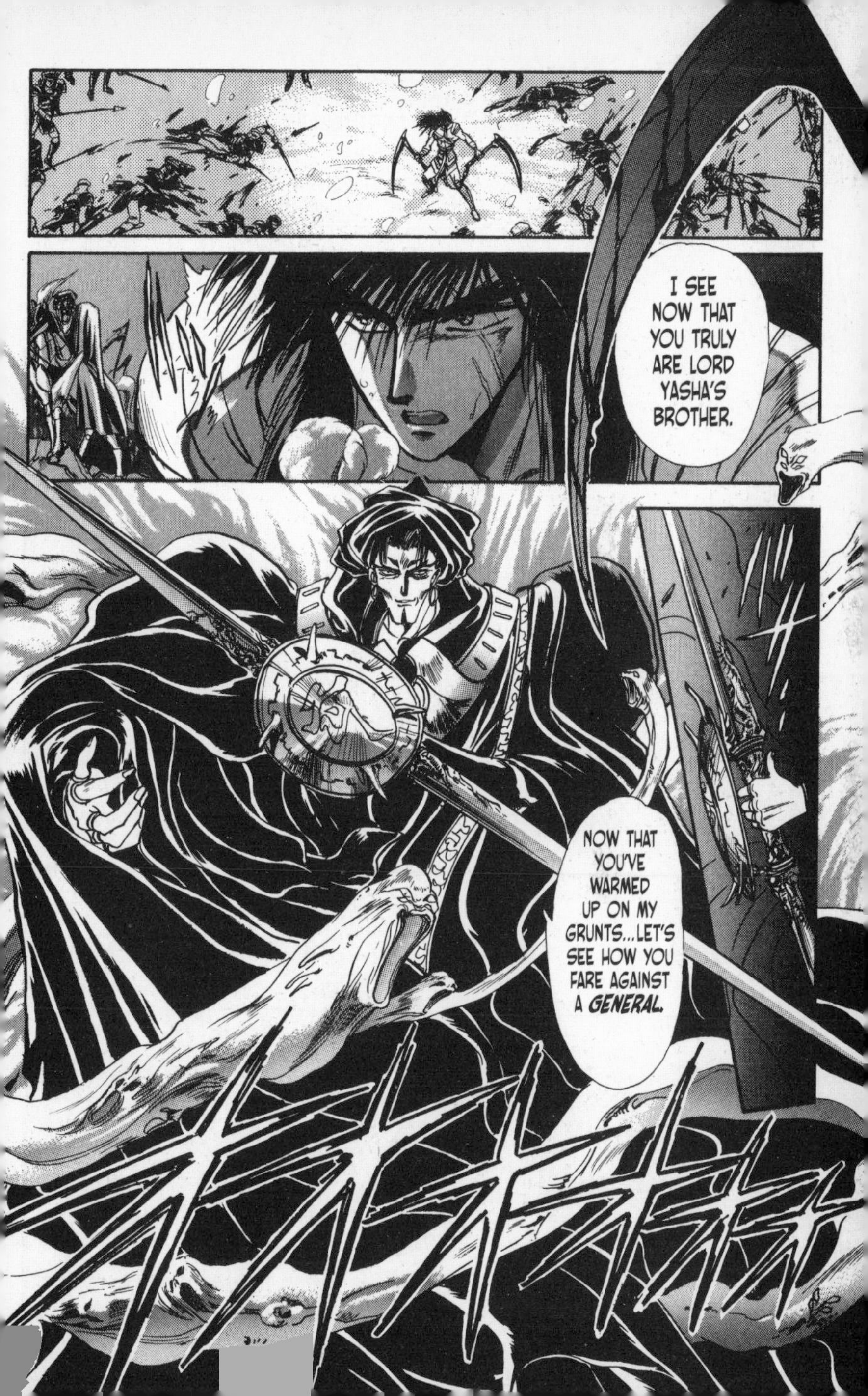
I SEE NOW THAT YOU TRULY ARE LORD YASHA'S BROTHER.
NOW THAT YOU'VE WARMED UP ON MY GRUNTS...LET'S SEE HOW YOU FARE AGAINST A *GENERAL.*

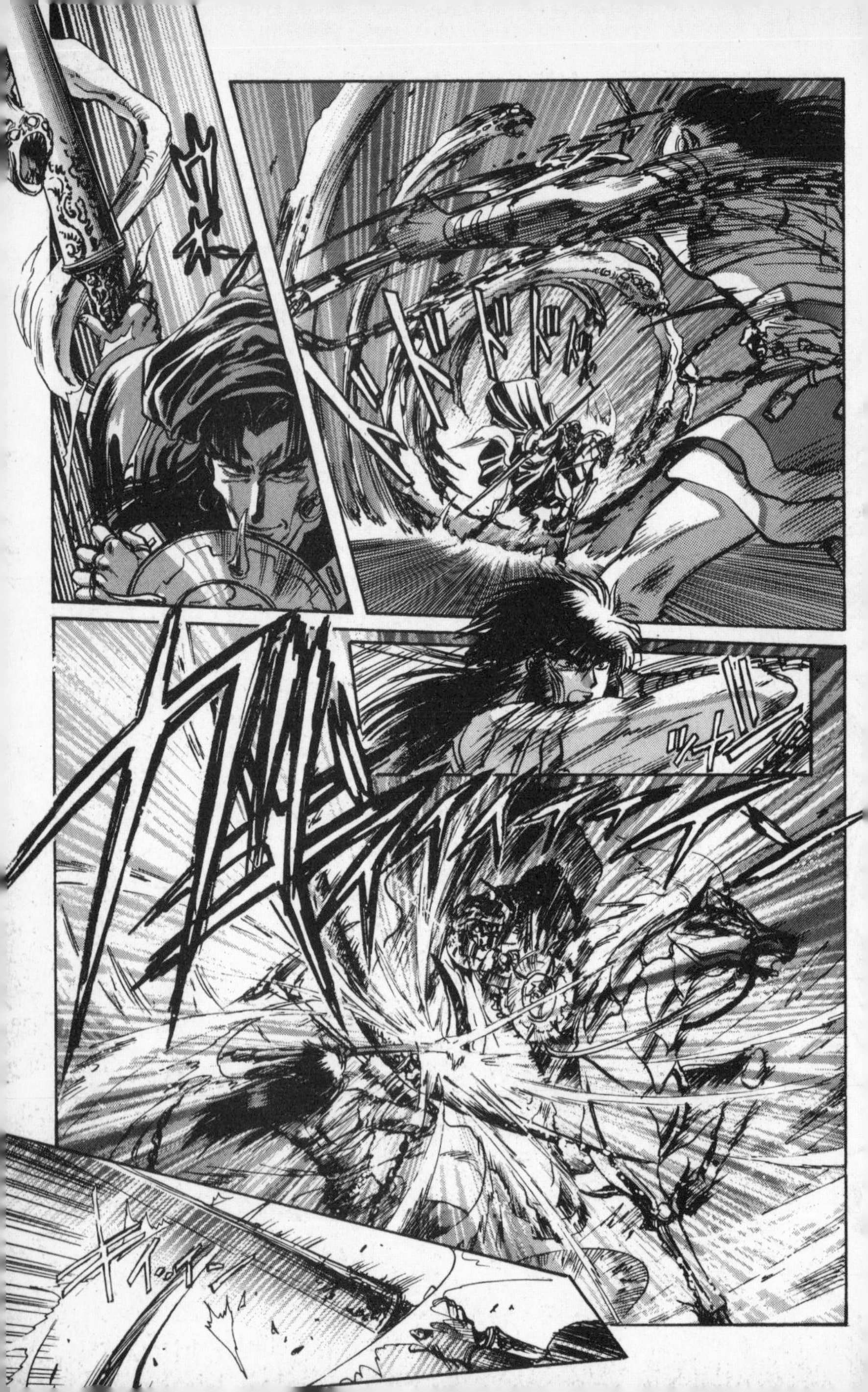

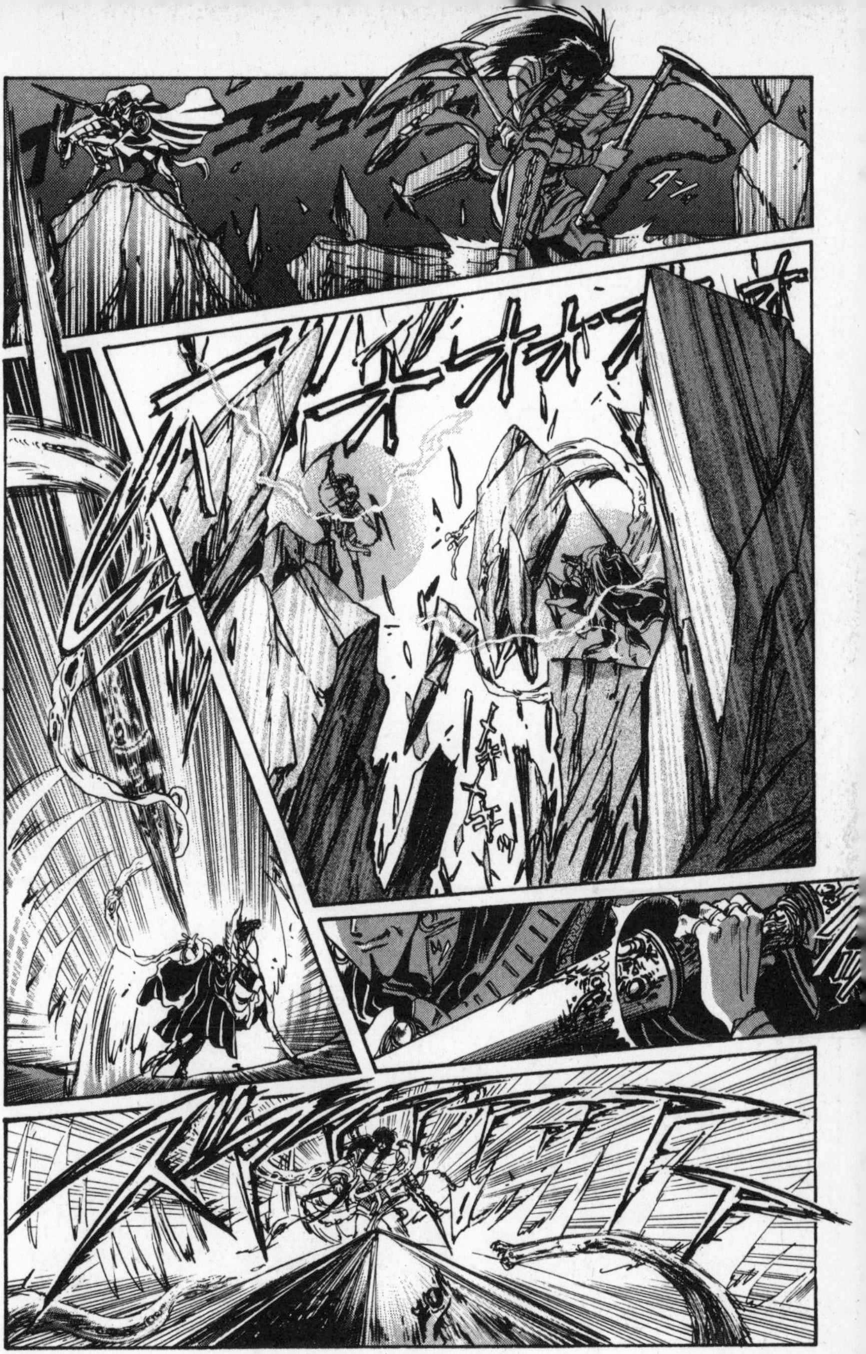

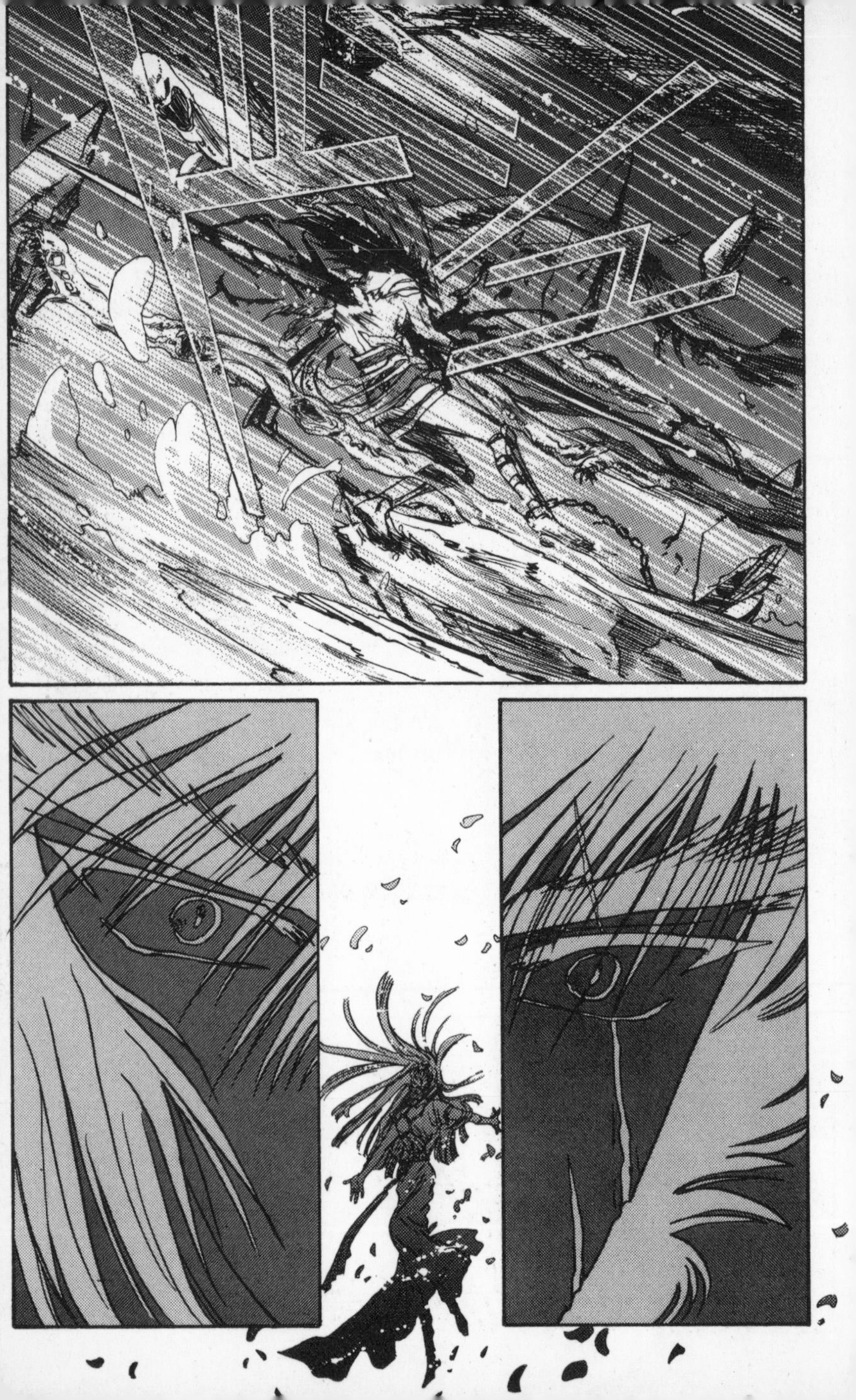

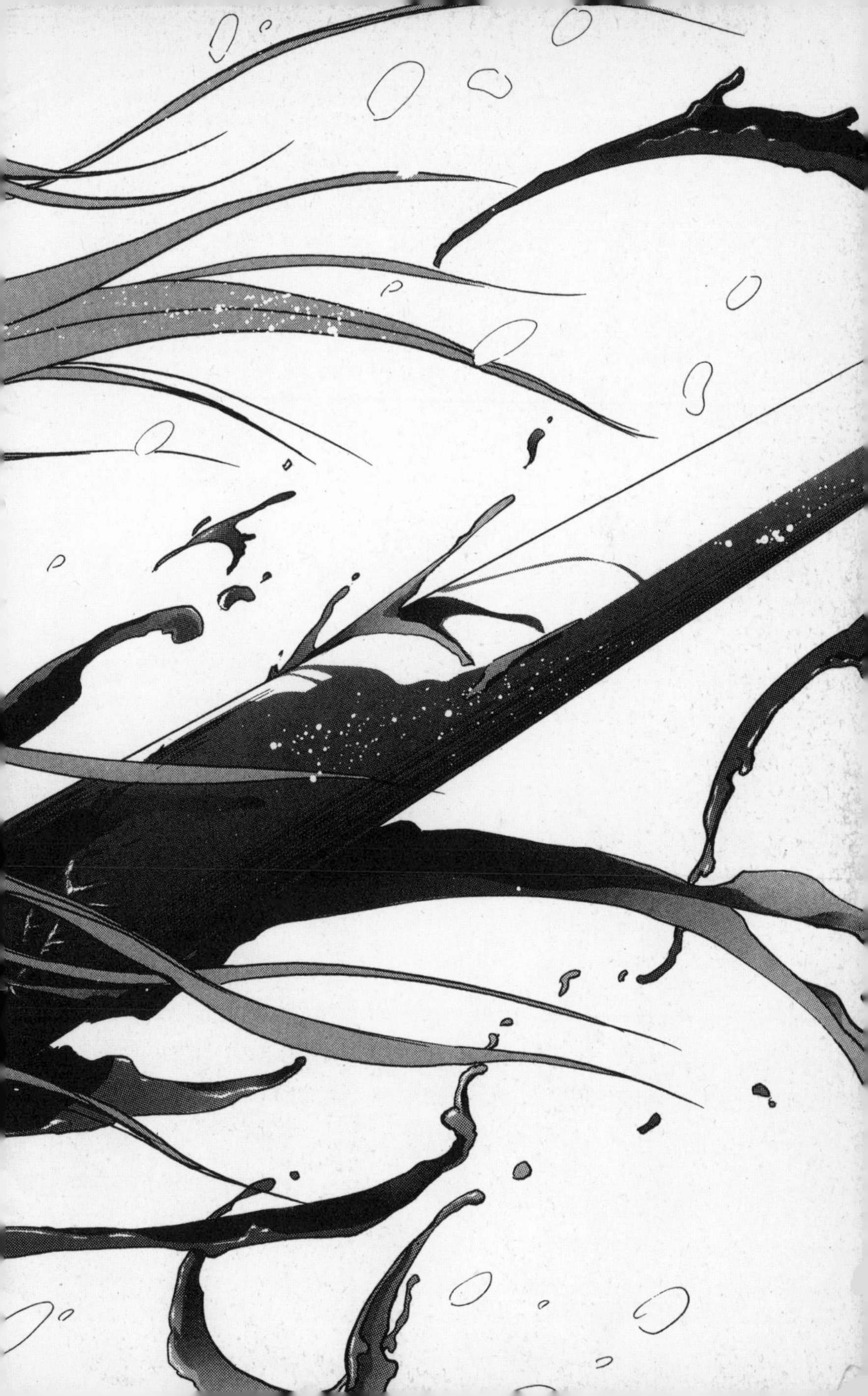

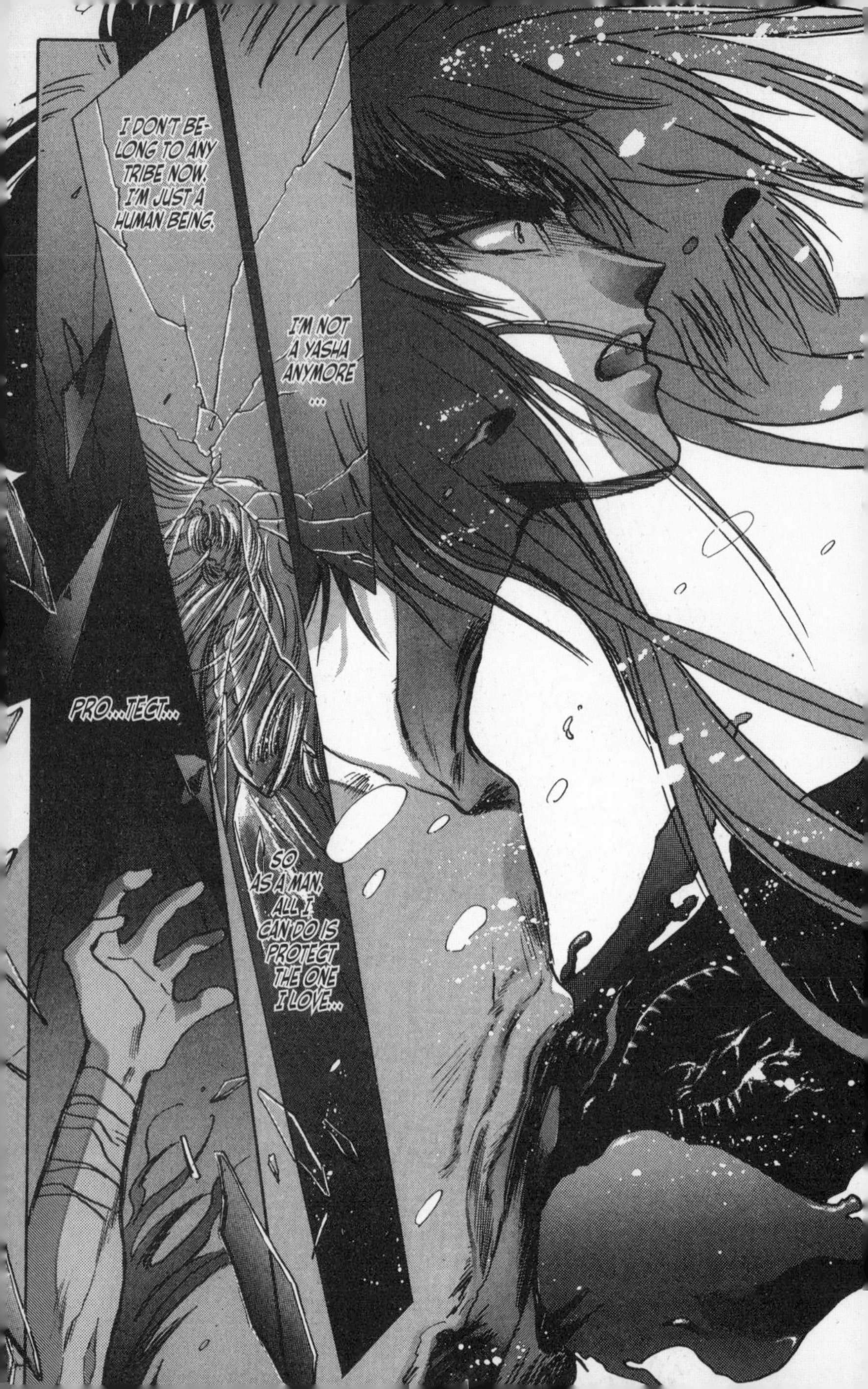
I DON'T BE-LONG TO ANY TRIBE NOW. I'M JUST A HUMAN BEING.
I'M NOT A YASHA ANYMORE ...
PRO...TECT...
SO AS A MAN, ALL I CAN DO IS PROTECT THE ONE I LOVE...

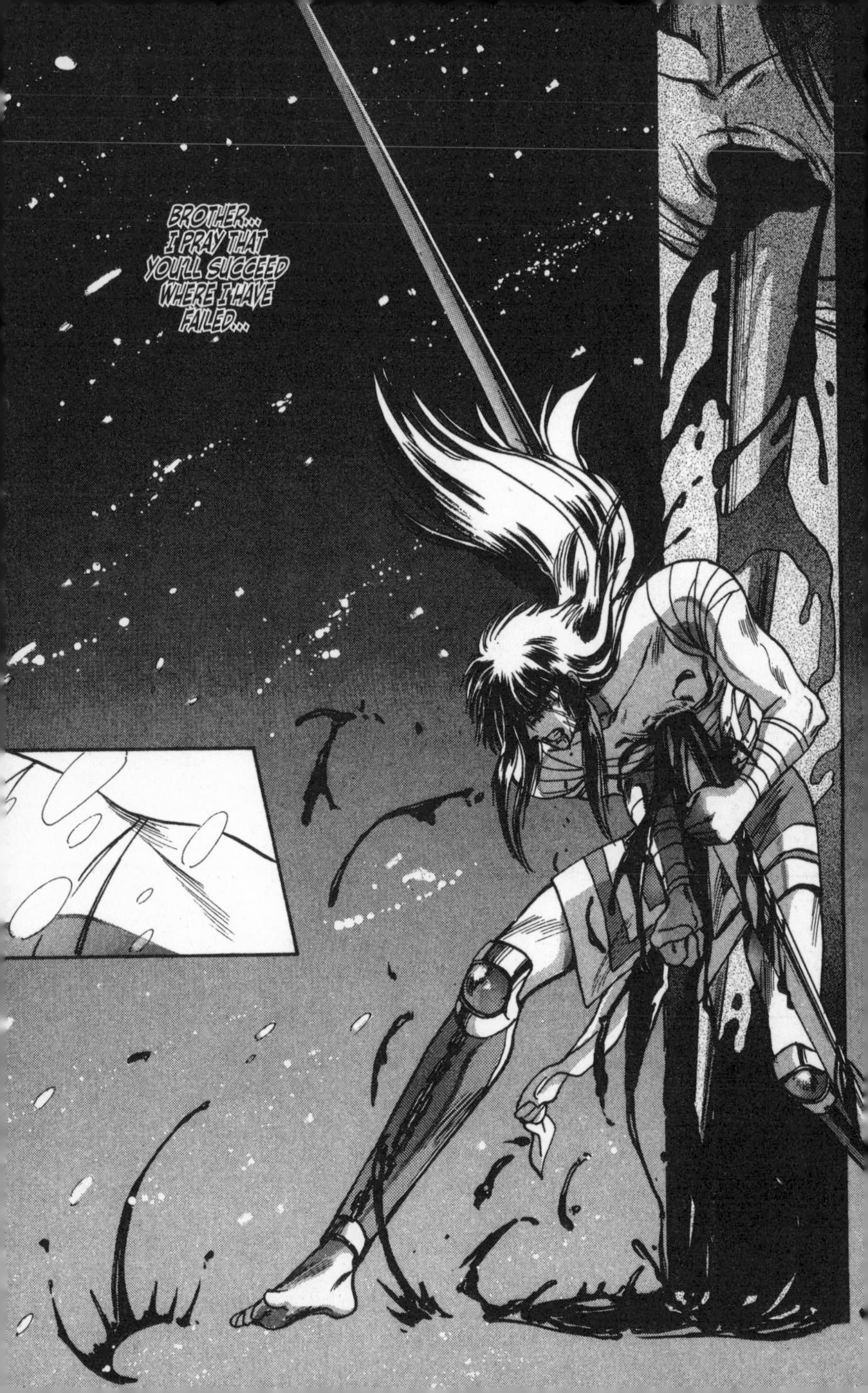
BROTHER... I PRAY THAT YOU'LL SUCCEED WHERE I HAVE FAILED...

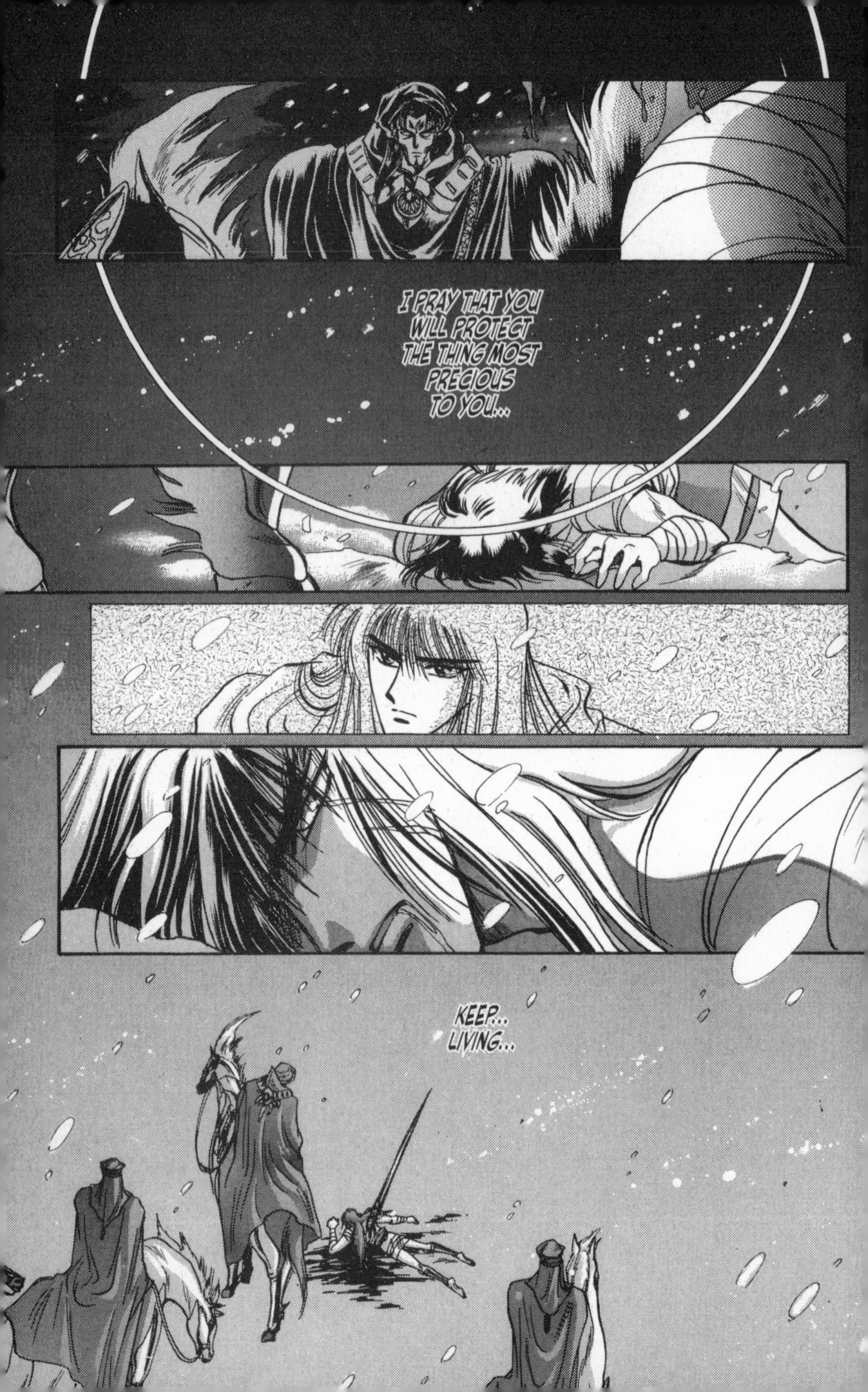
I PRAY THAT YOU WILL PROTECT THE THING MOST PRECIOUS TO YOU...
KEEP... LIVING...

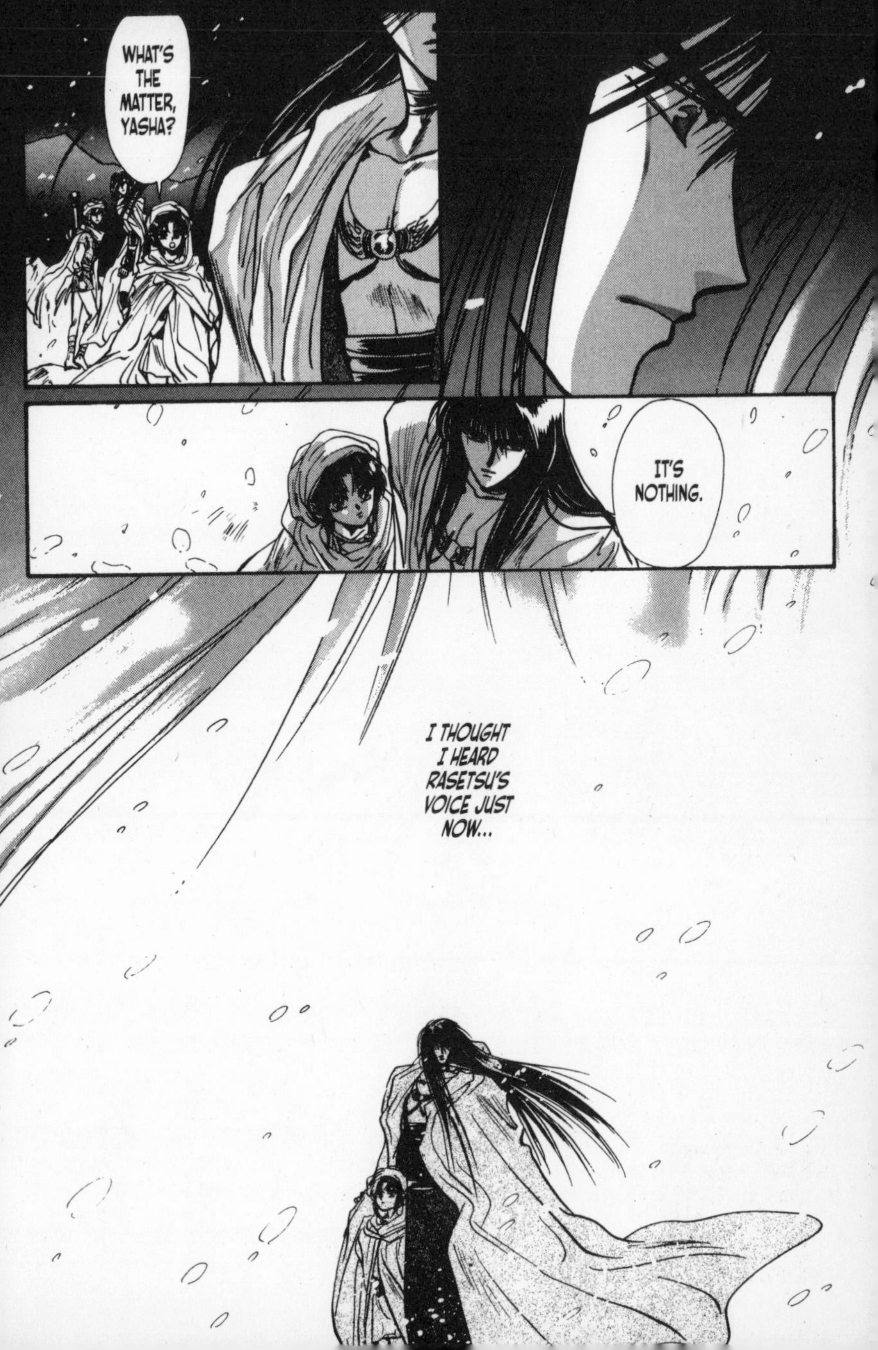
WHAT'S THE MATTER, YASHA?
IT'S NOTHING.
I THOUGHT I HEARD RASETSU'S VOICE JUST NOW...

RG VEDA 聖伝

BATTLE OF WOLVES / END

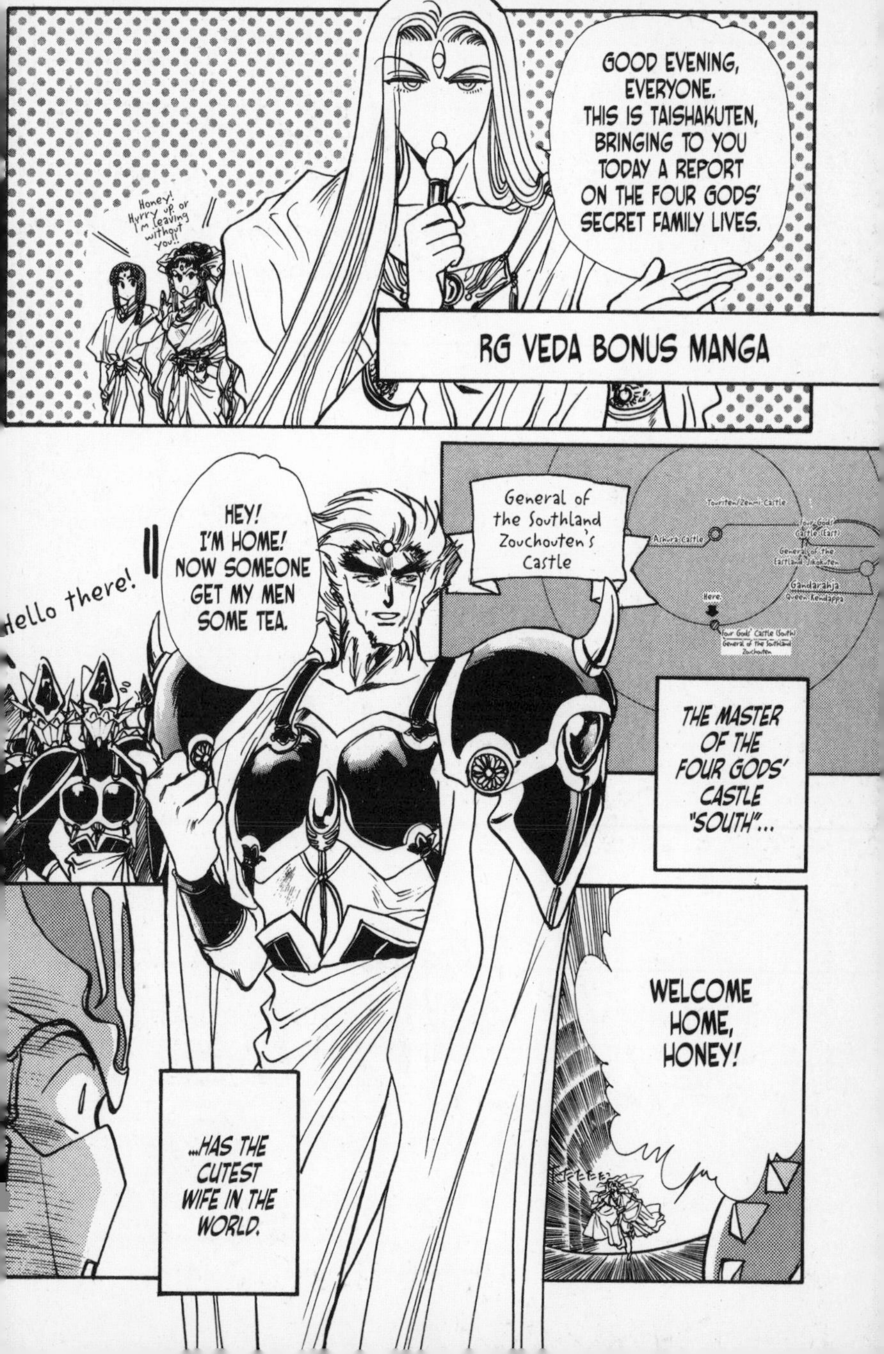
GOOD EVENING, EVERYONE. THIS IS TAISHAKUTEN, BRINGING TO YOU TODAY A REPORT ON THE FOUR GODS' SECRET FAMILY LIVES.
RG VEDA BONUS MANGA
Honey! Hurry up or I'm leaving without you!!
General of the Southland Zouchouten's Castle
Touriten/Zenmi Castle
Ashura Castle
Four Gods' Castle (East)
General of the Eastland Jikokuten
Gandarahja
Queen Kendappa
Here
Four Gods' Castle (South)
General of the Southland Zouchouten
THE MASTER OF THE FOUR GODS' CASTLE "SOUTH"...
HEY! I'M HOME! NOW SOMEONE GET MY MEN SOME TEA.
Hello there!
WELCOME HOME, HONEY!
...HAS THE CUTEST WIFE IN THE WORLD.

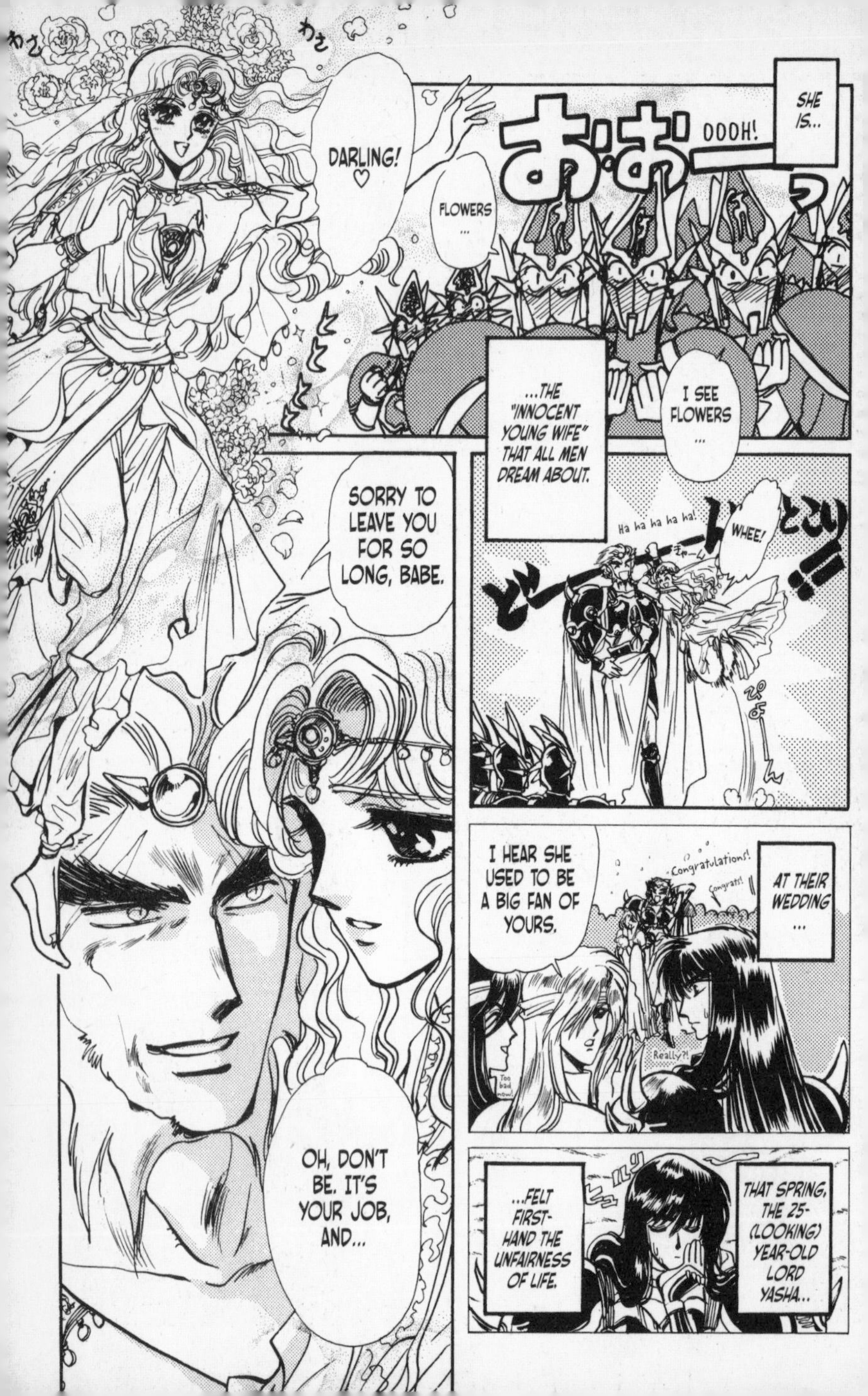
SHE IS...
おおーっ
OOOH!
...THE "INNOCENT YOUNG WIFE" THAT ALL MEN DREAM ABOUT.
I SEE FLOWERS...
WHEE!
Ha ha ha ha ha!
AT THEIR WEDDING...
Congratulations!
Congrats!
I HEAR SHE USED TO BE A BIG FAN OF YOURS.
Really?!
Too bad now!
THAT SPRING, THE 25-(LOOKING) YEAR-OLD LORD YASHA...
...FELT FIRST-HAND THE UNFAIRNESS OF LIFE.
DARLING! ♡
FLOWERS...
SORRY TO LEAVE YOU FOR SO LONG, BABE.
OH, DON'T BE. IT'S YOUR JOB, AND...

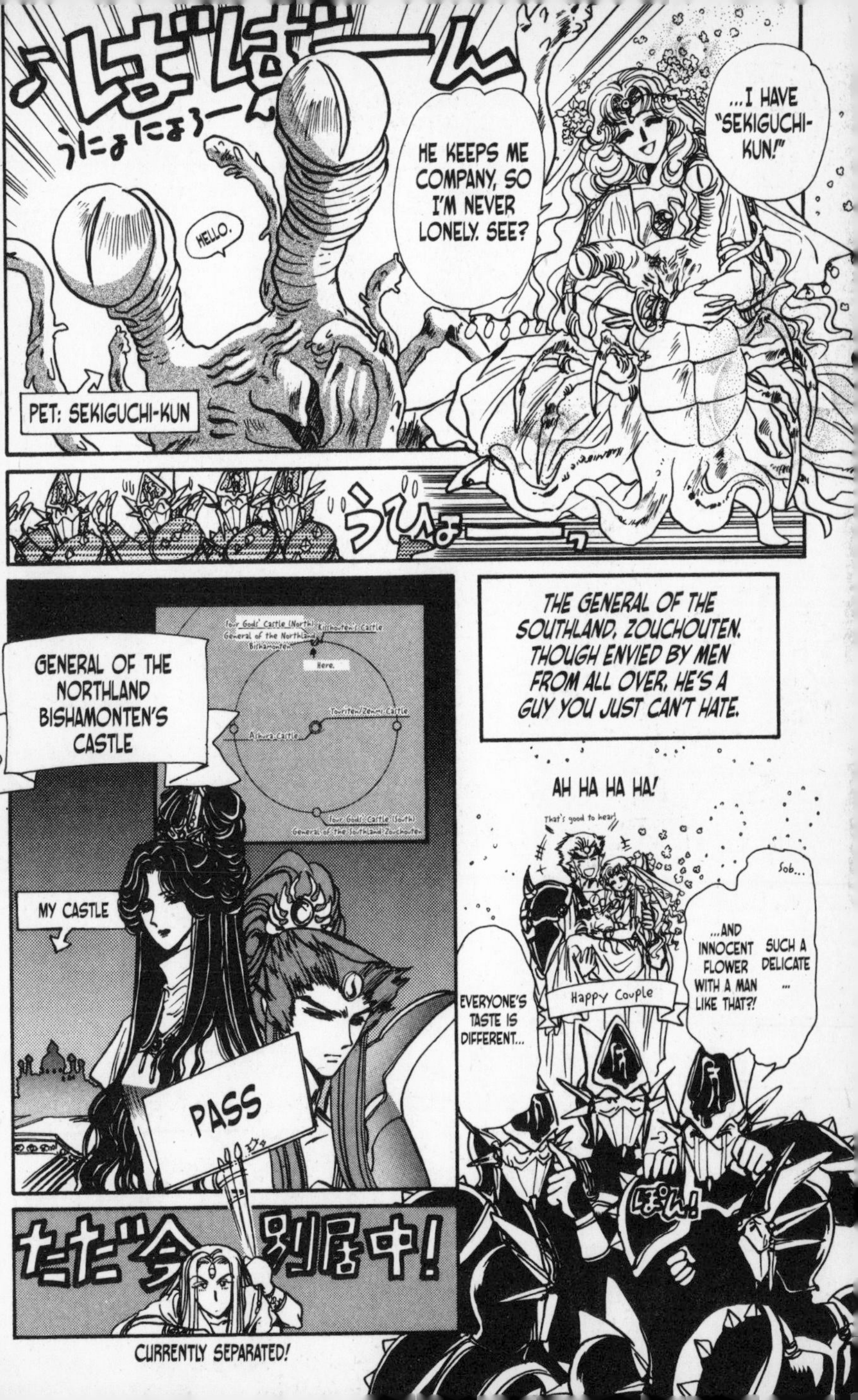
...I HAVE "SEKIGUCHI-KUN!"
HE KEEPS ME COMPANY, SO I'M NEVER LONELY. SEE?
HELLO.
♪しぼしぽーん
うにょにょろーん
PET: SEKIGUCHI-KUN
うひょーーっ
THE GENERAL OF THE SOUTHLAND, ZOUCHOUTEN. THOUGH ENVIED BY MEN FROM ALL OVER, HE'S A GUY YOU JUST CAN'T HATE.
AH HA HA HA!
That's good to hear!
Sob...
SUCH A DELICATE ...
...AND INNOCENT FLOWER WITH A MAN LIKE THAT?!
Happy Couple
EVERYONE'S TASTE IS DIFFERENT...
ぽん!
Four Gods' Castle (North)
General of the Northland Bishamonten
Kisshouten's Castle
Here.
Touriten/Zenmi Castle
Ashura Castle
Four Gods' Castle (South)
General of the Southland Zouchouten
GENERAL OF THE NORTHLAND BISHAMONTEN'S CASTLE
MY CASTLE
PASS
ただ今別居中!
CURRENTLY SEPARATED!

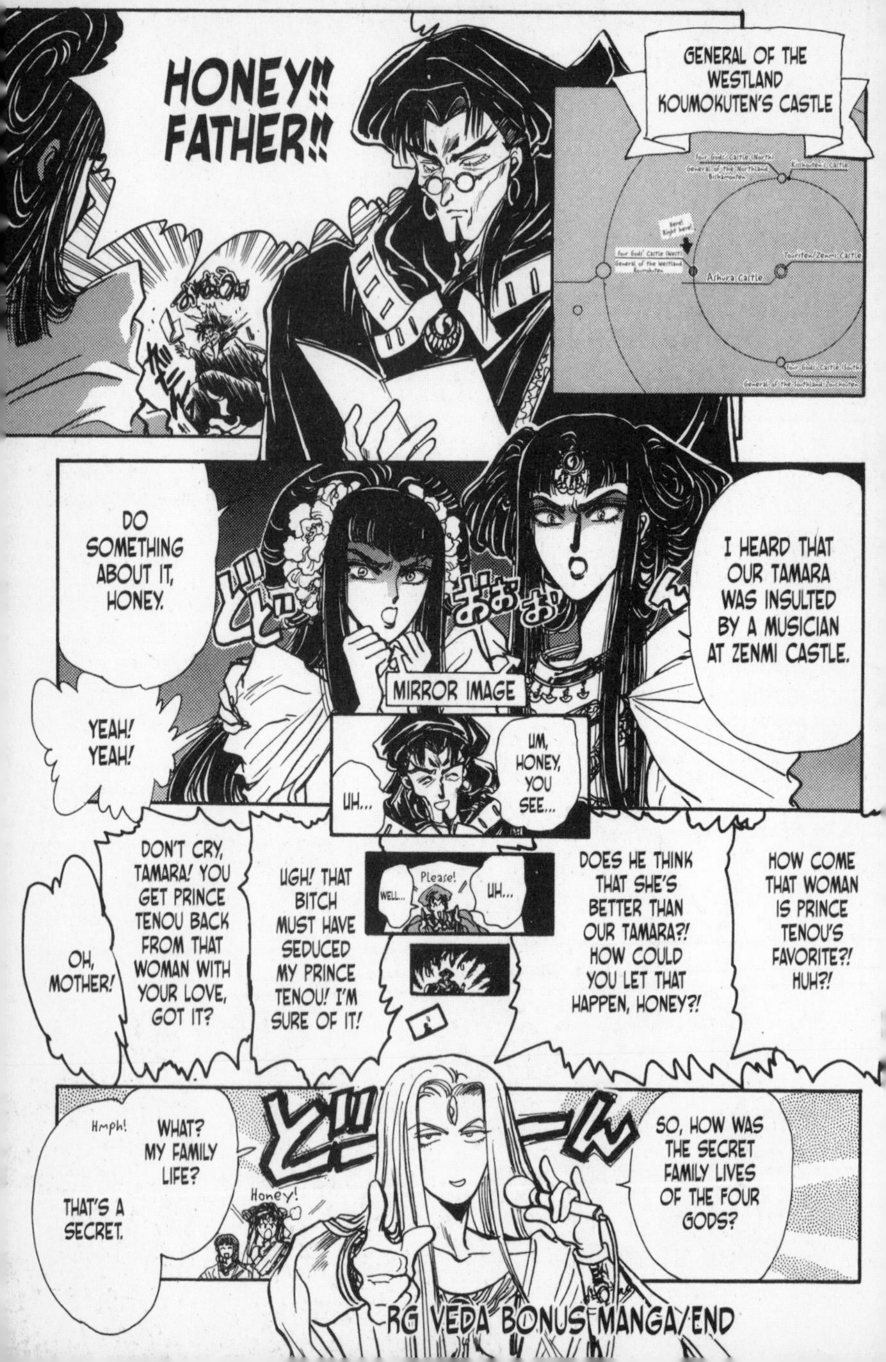
GENERAL OF THE WESTLAND KOUMOKUTEN'S CASTLE
Four Gods' Castle (North)
General of the Northland Bishamonten
Kisshouten's Castle
Here! Right here!
Four Gods' Castle (West)
General of the Westland Koumokuten
Touriten/Zenmi Castle
Ashura Castle
Four Gods' Castle (South)
General of the Southland Zouchouten
HONEY!! FATHER!!
I HEARD THAT OUR TAMARA WAS INSULTED BY A MUSICIAN AT ZENMI CASTLE.
DO SOMETHING ABOUT IT, HONEY.
MIRROR IMAGE
UM, HONEY, YOU SEE...
UH...
YEAH! YEAH!
HOW COME THAT WOMAN IS PRINCE TENOU'S FAVORITE?! HUH?!
DOES HE THINK THAT SHE'S BETTER THAN OUR TAMARA?! HOW COULD YOU LET THAT HAPPEN, HONEY?!
UH...
Please!
WELL...
UGH! THAT BITCH MUST HAVE SEDUCED MY PRINCE TENOU! I'M SURE OF IT!
DON'T CRY, TAMARA! YOU GET PRINCE TENOU BACK FROM THAT WOMAN WITH YOUR LOVE, GOT IT?
OH, MOTHER!
SO, HOW WAS THE SECRET FAMILY LIVES OF THE FOUR GODS?
Honey!
WHAT? MY FAMILY LIFE?
Hmph!
THAT'S A SECRET.
RG VEDA BONUS MANGA/END

## NEXT TIME IN RG VEDA

YASHA AND HIS PARTY SEEK SHELTER WITH A HUMAN WOMAN NAMED SHARA...UNAWARE THAT SHE IS RASETSU'S WIFE. THINGS ARE PEACEFUL FOR A WHILE...UNTIL KOUMOKUTEN'S ARMY ARRIVES. BUT JUST WHEN THINGS ARE AT THEIR BLEAKEST, YASHA AND THE OTHERS RECEIVE HELP FROM AN UNEXPECTED COMRADE...

**COMING SOON!**

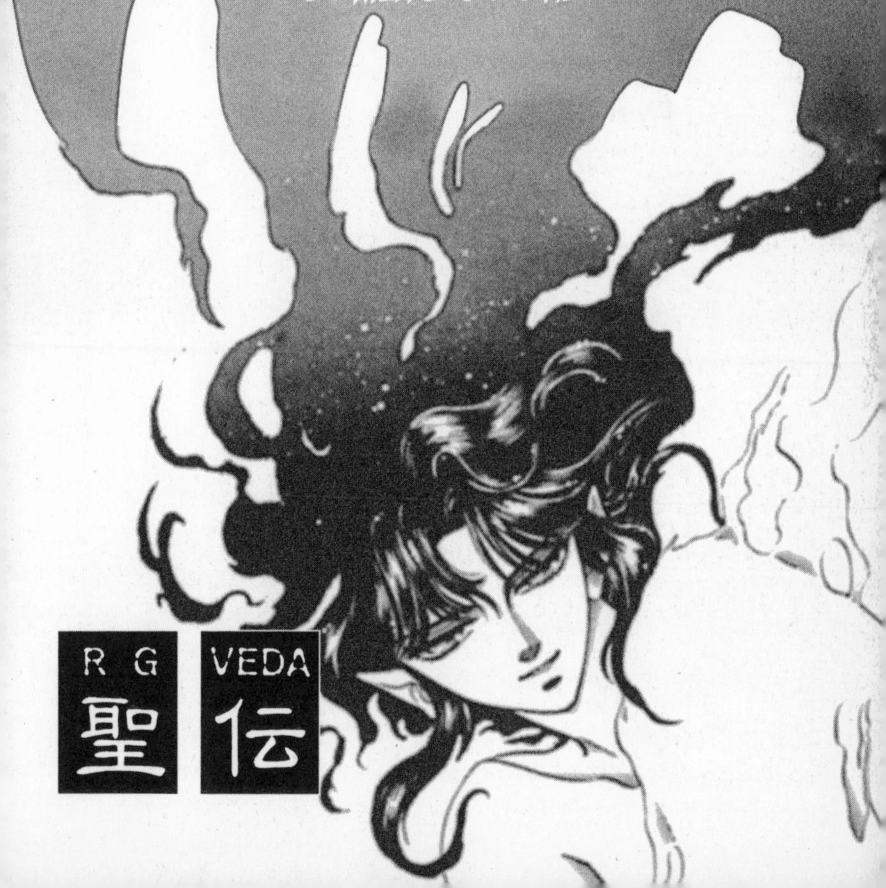
R G VEDA
聖伝

# BECK: MONGOLIAN CHOP SQUAD

OT
OLDER TEEN
AGE 16+

## ROCK IN MANGA!

BECK
MONGOLIAN CHOP SQUAD
TOKYOPOP
Harold Sakuishi
1

Yukio Tanaka is one boring guy with no hobbies, a weak taste in music and only a small vestige of a personality. But his life is forever changed when he meets Ryusuke Minami, an unpredictable rocker with a cool dog named Beck. Recently returned to Japan from America, Ryusuke inspires Yukio to get into music, and the two begin a journey through the world of rock 'n' roll dreams! With cameos of music's greatest stars—from John Lennon to David Bowie—and homages to supergroups such as Led Zeppelin and Nirvana, anyone who's anyone can make an appearance in *Beck*...even Beck himself! With action, music and gobs of comedy, *Beck* puts the rock in manga!

**HAROLD SAKUISHI'S HIGHLY ADDICTIVE MANGA SERIES THAT SPAWNED A HIT ANIME HAS FINALLY REACHED THE STATES!**



FOR MORE INFORMATION VISIT: WWW.TOKYOPOP.COM

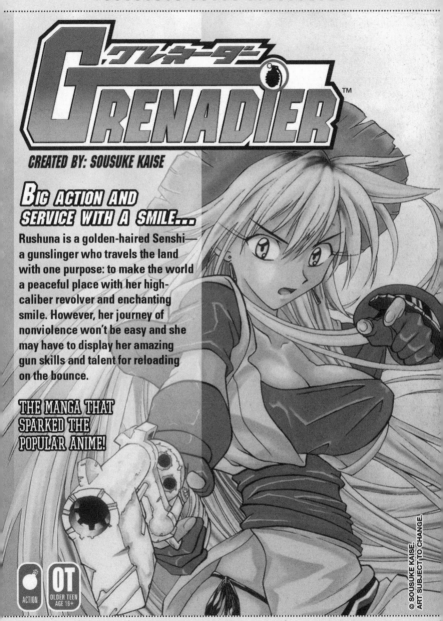

# クレネーダー GRENADIER™

**CREATED BY: SOUSUKE KAISE**

## BIG ACTION AND SERVICE WITH A SMILE...

Rushuna is a golden-haired Senshi—a gunslinger who travels the land with one purpose: to make the world a peaceful place with her high-caliber revolver and enchanting smile. However, her journey of nonviolence won't be easy and she may have to display her amazing gun skills and talent for reloading on the bounce.

### THE MANGA THAT SPARKED THE POPULAR ANIME!

ACTION

**OT** OLDER TEEN AGE 16+

© SOUSUKE KAISE.
ART SUBJECT TO CHANGE.

FOR MORE INFORMATION VISIT: WWW.TOKYOPOP.COM

## TOKYOPOP MANGA SUPPLEMENT

# ARE YOU TRULY ALIVE?

In the collapsing world of the afterlife, two guardians face the ultimate question: Thaddeus yearns for answers, while Mercutio seeks his true love. Will they be able to find it all before it's too late?

## ART BY ROB STEEN AND STORY BY STORMCROW HAYES

A MEDITATIVE AND BROODING EXPLORATION INTO THE ENDLESS POSSIBILITIES OF THE AFTERLIFE.

© Sam Hayes, Rob Steen and TOKYOPOP Inc.

## READ AN ENTIRE CHAPTER FOR FREE: WWW.TOKYOPOP.COM/MANGAONLINE

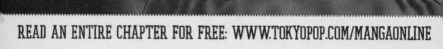

## · hoshi no koe
# voices of a distant star™

### to what distance would you go for your one true love?

As Mikako travels deeper into space to fight against hostile aliens, her only connection with her boyfriend is through cell-phone text messages. But as the years go by, and Mikako barely ages in the timelessness of space while her boyfriend grows old. How can the love of two people, torn apart by war, survive?

### Based on Makoto Shinkai's stellar anime!

### by Mizu Sahara

© M.Shinkai / CW, Mizu Sahara
ART SUBJECT TO CHANGE.

## FOR MORE INFORMATION VISIT: WWW.TOKYOPOP.COM

TOKYOPOP MANGA SUPPLEMENT

The best of humanity in the worst of wars.

# SEIKAI
## CREST OF THE STARS™
### PRINCESS OF THE EMPIRE

THE NEW MANGA NOVEL SERIES FROM TOKYOPOP

AVAILABLE SEPTEMBER 2006

© 1996 · Hiroyuki Morioka All Rights Reserved · First published in Japan by HAYAKAWA PUBLISHING CORPORATION

SCI-FI

CHECK OUT TOKYOPOP'S MANGA NOVELS AT WWW.TOKYOPOP.COM/BOOKS/NOVELS

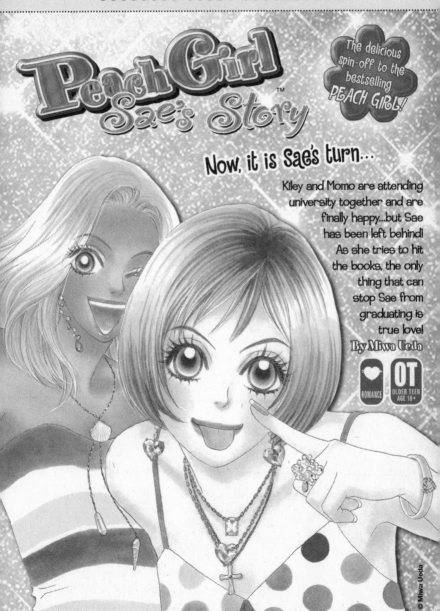

TOKYOPOP MANGA SUPPLEMENT

# Peach Girl
## Sae's Story

The delicious spin-off to the bestselling PEACH GIRL!

### Now, it is Sae's turn...

Kiley and Momo are attending university together and are finally happy...but Sae has been left behind! As she tries to hit the books, the only thing that can stop Sae from graduating is true love!

By Miwa Ueda

ROMANCE

OT OLDER TEEN AGE 16+

© Miwa Ueda

FOR MORE INFORMATION VISIT: WWW.TOKYOPOP.COM

TOKYOPOP MANGA SUPPLEMENT

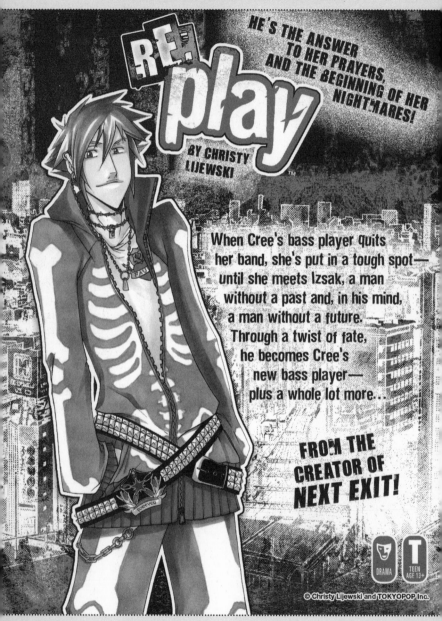

RE: play

BY CHRISTY LIJEWSKI

HE'S THE ANSWER TO HER PRAYERS, AND THE BEGINNING OF HER NIGHTMARES!

When Cree's bass player quits her band, she's put in a tough spot—until she meets Izsak, a man without a past and, in his mind, a man without a future. Through a twist of fate, he becomes Cree's new bass player—plus a whole lot more...

FROM THE CREATOR OF NEXT EXIT!

DRAMA

T
TEEN
AGE 13+

© Christy Lijewski and TOKYOPOP Inc.

READ AN ENTIRE CHAPTER FOR FREE: WWW.TOKYOPOP.COM/MANGAONLINE

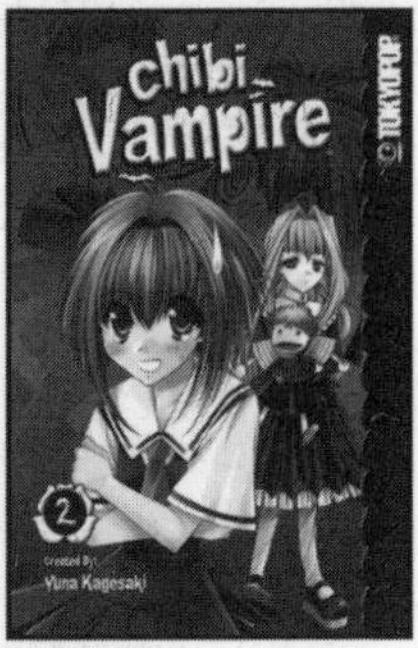
chibi Vampire
TOKYOPOP
2
Created By:
Yuna Kagesaki



# CHIBI VAMPIRE VOLUME 2

## BY YUNA KAGESAKI

This bloody-good vampire has a big crush on her prey!

COMEDY — OT OLDER TEEN AGE 16+

**Inspired the hit anime!**

# DEVIL MAY CRY 3 VOLUME 2

## BY SUGURO CHAYAMACHI

The secret of the seven seals will release the demon world unto the earth!

**It's good against evil... and brother against brother!**

ACTION — OT OLDER TEEN AGE 16+

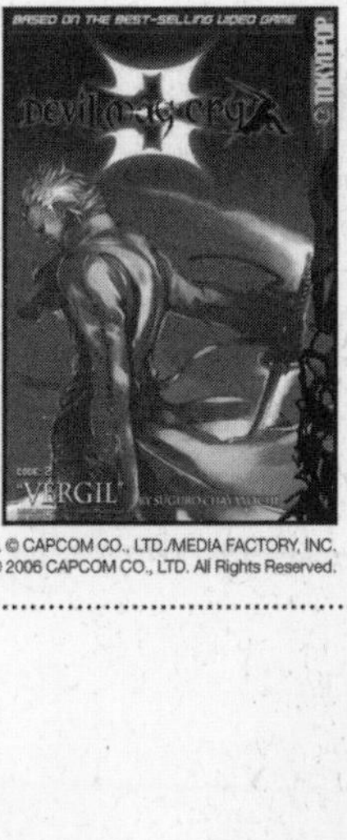
BASED ON THE BEST-SELLING VIDEO GAME
Devil May Cry 3
TOKYOPOP
"VERGIL"



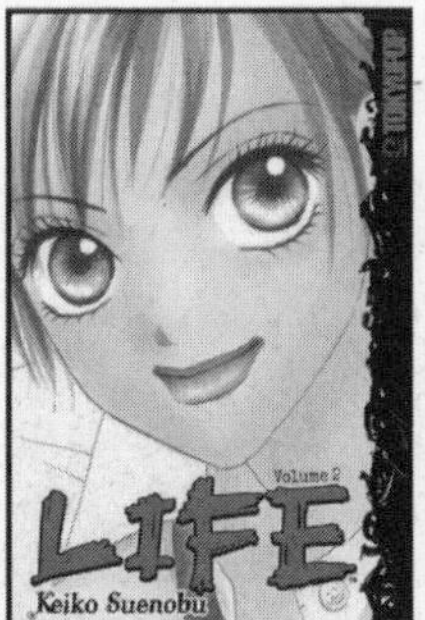
TOKYOPOP
Volume 2
LIFE
Keiko Suenobu



# LIFE VOLUME 2

## BY KEIKO SUENOBU

It's about real teenagers...
real high school...
real life!

DRAMA — OT OLDER TEEN AGE 16+

**Every life has a story...
Every story has a life of its own.**

TOKYOPOP MANGA SUPPLEMENT

# RIDING SHOTGUN™

**Killers for hire with one small problem: They need some cash!**

Doyle and Abby must take on a big hit for an even bigger payback!

**From the creators of the underground comic hit *Nate and Steve*!**
By Nate Bowden and Tracy Yardley

COMEDY

OT
OLDER TEEN
AGE 16+

© Nate Bowden, Tracy Yardley and TOKYOPOP Inc.

READ A CHAPTER ONLINE FOR FREE: WWW.TOKYOPOP.COM/MANGAONLINE

S0-BMV-585

# STOP!

## This is the back of the book.
## You wouldn't want to spoil a great ending!

This book is printed "manga-style," in the authentic Japanese right-to-left format. Since none of the artwork has been flipped or altered, readers get to experience the story just as the creator intended. You've been asking for it, so TOKYOPOP® delivered: authentic, hot-off-the-press, and far more fun!

# DIRECTIONS

If this is your first time reading manga-style, here's a quick guide to help you understand how it works.

It's easy... just start in the top right panel and follow the numbers. Have fun, and look for more 100% authentic manga from TOKYOPOP®!